CLYMER®

YAMAHA

WARRIOR • 1987-2004

CLYMER®

P.O. Box 12901, Overland Park, Kansas 66282-2901

Copyright ©2004 Prism Business Media Inc.

FIRST EDITION
First Printing April, 1995
Second Printing August, 1997
Third Printing November, 1998
Fourth Printing November, 1999

SECOND EDITION
First Printing October, 2000
Second Printing August, 2001

THIRD EDITION
First Printing July, 2002

FOURTH EDITION
First Printing July, 2003

FIFTH EDITION
First Printing October, 2004
Second Printing June, 2006

Printed in U.S.A.

CLYMER and colophon are registered trademarks of Prism Business Media Inc.

ISBN: 0-89287-923-8

Library of Congress: 2004113151

AUTHOR: Ron Wright.

TECHNICAL PHOTOGRAPHY: Ron Wright. Yamaha Warrior for research and photography provided by Richard Nelson. Also, we would like to thank Clawson Motorsports in Fresno, California, for additional research and photography.

TECHNICAL ILLUSTRATIONS: Steve Amos.

PRODUCTION: Veronica Bollin.

TOOLS AND EQUIPMENT: K & L Supply Co. at www.klsupply.com.

COVER: 2003 Warrior photographed by Mark Clifford Photography at www.markclifford.com. Cover designed by Tony Barmann.

CLYMER®

Publisher Shawn Etheridge

EDITORIAL

Managing Editor
James Grooms

Associate Editors
Richard Arens
Steven Thomas

Technical Writers
Jay Bogart
Jon Engleman
Michael Morlan
George Parise
Mark Rolling
Ed Scott
Ron Wright

Group Production Manager
Dylan Goodwin

Senior Production Editors
Greg Araujo
Darin Watson

Production Editors
Julie Jantzer-Ward
Justin Marciniak
Holly Messinger

Associate Production Editor
Susan Hartington

Technical Illustrators
Steve Amos
Errol McCarthy
Mitzi McCarthy
Bob Meyer

MARKETING/SALES AND ADMINISTRATION

Sales Channel & Brand Marketing Coordinator
Melissa Abbott Mudd

Art Director
Chris Paxton

Sales Managers
Justin Henton
Dutch Sadler
Matt Tusken

Business Manager
Ron Rogers

Customer Service Manager
Terri Cannon

Customer Service Representatives
Felicia Dickerson
Courtney Hollars
April LeBlond

Warehouse & Inventory Manager
Leah Hicks

PRISM
BUSINESS MEDIA™

P.O. Box 12901, Overland Park, KS 66282-2901 • 800-262-1954 • 913-967-1719

The following books and guides are published by Prism Business Media

More information available at *clymer.com*

CONTENTS

QUICK REFERENCE DATA

ATV INFORMATION

MODEL:_____ YEAR:_____

VIN NUMBER:_____

ENGINE SERIAL NUMBER:_____

CARBURETOR SERIAL NUMBER OR I.D. MARK:_____

TIRE INFLATION PRESSURE

	Standard psi (kPa)	Minimum psi (kPa)
Front		
1987-1989	4.3 (29)	3.8 (26.5)
1990-on	4.4 (30)	3.6 (25)
Rear		
1987-1989	3.6 (25)	3.1 (21.6)
1990-on	3.6 (25)	3.2 (22)

RECOMMENDED LUBRICANTS AND FUEL

Engine oil	SAE 10W-40 type SE motor oil
Air filter	Foam air filter oil
Drive chain*	Non-tacky O-ring chain lubricant or SAE 30-50 weight engine motor oil
Brake fluid	DOT 4
Steering and suspension lubricant	Lithium base grease
Fuel	Regular gasoline
Control cables	Cable lube**

* Use kerosene to clean drive chain.
** Do not use drive chain lubricant to lubricate control cables.

ENGINE OIL CAPACITY

	Liters	U.S. qt.	Imp. qt.
Oil drain	2.4	2.53	2.11
Oil drain and filter change	2.5	2.64	2.20
Total amount	3.2	3.38	2.82

DRIVE CHAIN FREE PLAY MEASUREMENT

	mm	in.
Free play	30-40	1.18-1.57

TUNE-UP SPECIFICATIONS

Engine compression (at sea level)	
Standard	121 psi (850 kPa)
Minimum	114 psi (800 kPa)
Maximum	128 psi (900 kPa)
Valve clearance	
Intake	0.06-0.10 mm (0.0023-0.0039 in.)
Exhaust	0.16-0.20 mm (0.0063-0.0078 in.)
Ignition timing specifications	
BTDC	10° at 1,000 rpm
Advanced	33° at 5,000 rpm
Checking with timing light	See text

SPARK PLUG TYPE AND GAP

	Type	Gap
Standard	NGK D8EA/ND X24ES-U	0.6-0.7 mm (0.024-0.028 in.)

CARBURETOR SPECIFICATIONS

Engine idle speed	1,450-1,550 rpm
Pilot air screw adjustment	
1987-1989	1 1/4 turns out
1990-on	2 turns out

REPLACEMENT BULBS

Item	Voltage/wattage
Headlight	12V 25W/25W
Taillight	12V 3.8W
Neutral light	12V 3.4W
Reverse light	12V 3.4W

DRIVE CHAIN SPECIFICATIONS

Size	520
Number of links	
1987-1989	100
1990-on	98
Chain free play	30-40 mm (1.18-1.57 in.)

REAR SHOCK REBOUND DAMPING ADJUSTMENT

	Clicks
1987-1989	
Standard	15 clicks out
Minimum	20 clicks out
Maximum	0 clicks out
1990-on	
Standard	12 clicks out
Minimum	20 clicks out
Maximum	0 clicks out

CLYMER®

YAMAHA

WARRIOR • 1987-2004

INTRODUCTION

The venerable Yamaha Warrior, first introduced in 1987, has remained basically unchanged through an amazing 15+ year production run. The Warrior powerplant, unlike its smaller sport ATV brothers the Blaster and Banshee, which use two-stroke engines, is a four-stroke. This provides a linear power band that is well matched to the six-speed transmission. With a reverse gear and electric starter the Warrior provides features that a pure sport machine like the Banshee does not provide, while only being 11 pounds heavier.

The engine's predictable torque, combined with an equally stable suspension featuring a rear shock with adjustable rebound dampening, and overall light weight makes the Warrior an ideal trail machine. With the addition of a pair of racks, many Warriors have also proven to be adequate utility mounts (the Wolverine uses the same engine). Little wonder that with such versatility, simple design features and quality construction, the Warrior has been a long running part of Yamaha's ATV lineup.

CHAPTER ONE

GENERAL INFORMATION

This detailed, comprehensive manual covers the 1987-2003 Yamaha YFM350X Warrior.

Troubleshooting, tune-up, maintenance and repair are not difficult, if you know what tools and equipment to use and what to do. Step-by-step instructions guide you through jobs ranging from simple maintenance to complete engine and suspension overhaul.

This manual can be used by anyone from a first time do-it-yourselfer to a professional mechanic. Detailed drawings and clear photographs give you all the information you need to do the work right.

Some of the procedures in this manual require the use of special tools. The resourceful mechanic can, in many cases, think of acceptable substitutes for special tools—there is always another way. This can be as simple as using a few pieces of threaded rod, washers and nuts to remove or install a bearing or fabricating a tool from scrap material. However, using a substitute for a special tool is not recommended as it can be dangerous to and may damage the part. If you find that a tool can be designed and safely made, but will require some type of machine work, you may want to search out a local community college or high school that has a machine shop curriculum. Shop teachers sometimes welcome outside work that can be used as practical shop applications for advanced students.

Table 1 lists model coverage with engine serial numbers.

Table 2 lists general vehicle dimensions.

Table 3 lists weight specifications.

Table 4 lists decimal and metric equivalents.

Table 5 lists conversion tables.

Table 6 lists general torque specifications.

Table 7 lists technical abbreviations.

Table 8 lists metric tap drill sizes.

Table 9 lists windchill factors.

Tables 1-9 are at the end of the chapter.

MANUAL ORGANIZATION

This chapter provides general information and discusses equipment and tools useful both for preventive maintenance and troubleshooting.

Chapter Two provides methods and suggestions for quick and accurate diagnosis and repair of problems. Troubleshooting procedures discuss typical symptoms and logical methods to pinpoint the trouble.

Chapter Three explains all periodic lubrication and routine maintenance necessary to keep your Yamaha operating well. Chapter Three also includes recommended tune-up procedures, eliminating the need to consult other chapters constantly on the various assemblies.

Subsequent chapters describe specific systems such as the engine top end, engine bottom end, clutch, transmission, fuel, exhaust, electrical, suspension, drive train, steering and brakes. Each chapter provides disassembly, repair, and assembly procedures in simple step-by-step form. If a repair is impractical for a home mechanic, it is so indicated. It is usually faster and less expensive to take such repairs to a Yamaha dealer or competent repair shop. Specifications concerning a particular system are included at the end of the appropriate chapter.

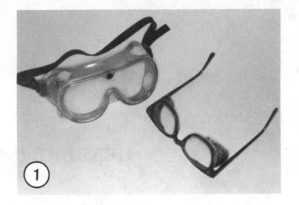

NOTES, CAUTIONS AND WARNINGS

The terms NOTE, CAUTION and WARNING have specific meanings in this manual. A NOTE provides additional information to make a step or procedure easier or clearer. Disregarding a NOTE could cause inconvenience, but would not cause damage or personal injury.

A CAUTION emphasizes an area where equipment damage could occur. Disregarding a CAUTION could cause permanent mechanical damage; however, personal injury is unlikely.

A WARNING emphasizes an area where personal injury or even death could result from negligence. Mechanical damage may also occur. WARNINGS *are to be taken seriously*. In some cases, serious injury and death has resulted from disregarding similar warnings.

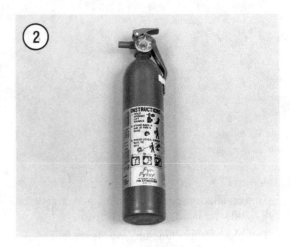

SAFETY FIRST

Professional mechanics can work for years and never sustain a serious injury. If you observe a few rules of common sense and safety, you can enjoy many safe hours servicing your own machine. If you ignore these rules you can hurt yourself or damage the equipment.

1. *Never* use gasoline as a cleaning solvent.
2. *Never* smoke or use a torch in the vicinity of flammable liquids, such as cleaning solvent, in open containers.

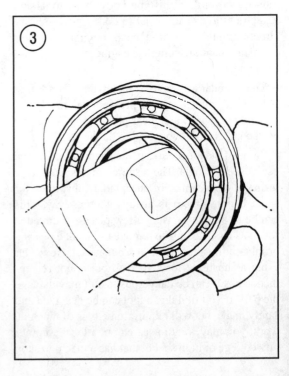

3. If welding or brazing is required on the machine, remove the fuel tank and shock absorbers to a safe distance, at least 50 feet (15 m) away.

4. Use the proper sized wrenches to avoid damage to fasteners and injury to yourself.

5. When loosening a tight or stuck nut, be guided by what would happen if the wrench should slip. Be careful; protect yourself accordingly.

6. When replacing a fastener, make sure to use one with the same measurements and strength as the old one. Incorrect or mismatched fasteners can result in damage to the vehicle and possible personal injury. Beware of fastener kits that are filled with cheap and poorly made nuts, bolts, washers and cotter pins. Refer to *Fasteners* in this chapter for additional information.

7. Keep all hand and power tools in good condition. Wipe greasy and oily tools after using them. They are difficult to hold and can cause injury. Replace or repair worn or damaged tools.

8. Keep your work area clean and uncluttered.

9. Wear safety goggles (**Figure 1**) during all operations involving drilling, grinding, the use of a cold chisel or *anytime* you feel unsure about the safety of your eyes. Safety goggles should also be worn anytime solvent and compressed air is used to clean parts.

10. Keep an approved fire extinguisher (**Figure 2**) nearby. Be sure it is rated for gasoline (Class B) and electrical (Class C) fires.

11. When drying bearings or other rotating parts with compressed air, never allow the air jet to rotate the bearing or part. The air jet is capable of rotating them at speeds far in excess of those for which they were designed. The bearing or rotating part is very likely to disintegrate and cause serious injury and damage. To prevent bearing damage when using

compressed air, hold the inner bearing race by hand (**Figure 3**).

SERVICE HINTS

Most of the service procedures covered are straightforward and can be performed by anyone reasonably handy with tools. It is suggested, however, that you consider your own capabilities carefully before attempting any operation involving major disassembly of the engine assembly.

Take your time and do the job right. Do not forget that a newly rebuilt engine must be broken-in the same way as a new one. Keep the rpm within the limits given in your Yamaha Warrior owner's manual when you get back out in the dirt.

1. "Front," as used in this manual, refers to the front of the vehicle; the front of any component is the end closest to the front of the vehicle. The "left-" and "right-hand" sides refer to the position of the parts as viewed by a rider sitting on the seat facing forward. For example, the throttle control is on the right-hand side. These rules are simple, but confusion can cause a major inconvenience during service.

2. Whenever servicing the engine or clutch, or when removing a suspension component, the vehicle should be secured in a safe manner and the parking brake applied.

> *WARNING*
> *Never disconnect the positive (+) battery cable unless the negative (–) cable has first been disconnected. Disconnecting the positive cable while the negative cable is still connected may cause a spark. This could ignite hydrogen gas given off by the battery, causing an explosion.*

3. Disconnect the negative battery cable (**Figure 4**) when working on or near the electrical, clutch, or starter systems and before disconnecting any electrical wires. On batteries used in your Yamaha, the negative terminal will be marked with a minus (–) sign and the positive terminal with a plus (+) sign.

4. Tag all similar internal parts for location and mark all mating parts for position (A, **Figure 5**). Record number and thickness of any shims as they are removed. Small parts such as bolts can be iden-

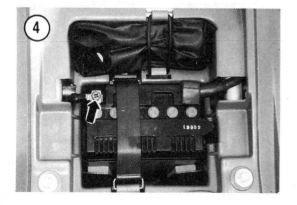

tified by placing them in plastic sandwich bags (B, **Figure 5**). Seal and label them with masking tape.

5. Place parts from a specific area of the engine (e.g. cylinder head, cylinder, clutch, shift mechanism, etc.) into plastic boxes (C, **Figure 5**) to keep them separated.

6. When disassembling transmission shaft assemblies, use an egg flat (the type that restaurants get their eggs in) (D, **Figure 5**) and set the parts from the shaft in one of the depressions in the same order in which it was removed.

7. Wiring should be tagged with masking tape and marked as each wire is removed. Again, do not rely on memory alone.

8. Finished surfaces should be protected from physical damage or corrosion. Keep gasoline and brake fluid off painted surfaces.

9. Use penetrating oil on frozen or tight bolts, then strike the bolt head a few times with a hammer and punch (use a screwdriver on screws). Avoid the use of heat where possible, as it can warp, melt or affect the temper of parts. Heat also ruins finishes, especially paint and plastics.

10. No parts removed or installed (other than bushings and bearings) in the procedures given in this manual should require unusual force during disassembly or assembly. If a part is difficult to remove or install, find out why before proceeding.

11. Cover all openings after removing parts or components to prevent dirt, small tools, etc. from falling in.

12. Read each procedure *completely* while looking at the actual parts before starting a job. Make sure you *thoroughly* understand what is to be done and then carefully follow the procedure, step by step.

13. Recommendations are occasionally made to refer service or maintenance to a Yamaha dealer or a specialist in a particular field. In these cases, the work will be done more quickly and economically than if you performed the job yourself.

14. In procedural steps, the term "replace" means to discard a defective part and replace it with a new or exchange unit. "Overhaul" means to remove, disassemble, inspect, measure, repair or replace defective parts, reassemble and install major systems or parts.

15. Some operations require the use of a hydraulic press. It would be wiser to have these operations performed by a shop equipped for such work, rather than to try to do the job yourself with makeshift equipment that may damage your machine.

16. Repairs go much faster and easier if your machine is clean before you begin work. There are many special cleaners on the market, like Bel-Ray Degreaser, for washing the engine and related parts. Follow the manufacturer's directions on the container for the best results. Clean all oily or greasy parts with cleaning solvent as you remove them. See *Washing the Vehicle* in this chapter.

> **CAUTION**
> *Prior to using a degreaser or other chemical to clean your Warrior, first remove the O-ring drive chain. These and other chemicals may cause the O-rings in the chain to swell, permanently damaging the chain.*

> **WARNING**
> *Never use gasoline as a cleaning agent. It presents an extreme fire hazard. Be sure to work in a well-ventilated area when using cleaning solvent. Keep a fire extinguisher, rated for gasoline fires, handy in any case.*

> **CAUTION**
> *If you use a car wash to clean your vehicle, do not direct the high pressure water hose at steering bearings, carburetor hoses, suspension linkage components, wheel bearings, electrical components or the O-ring drive chain. The water will flush grease out of the bearings or damage the seals.*

17. Much of the labor charges for repairs made by dealers are for the time involved during the removal, disassembly, assembly, and reinstallation of other parts in order to reach the defective part. It is frequently possible to perform the preliminary opera-

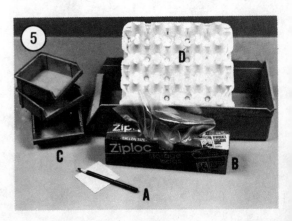

tions yourself and then take the defective unit to the dealer for repair at considerable savings.

18. If special tools are required, make arrangements to get them before you start. It is frustrating and time-consuming to get partly into a job and then be unable to complete it.

19. Make diagrams (take a Polaroid picture or video) wherever similar-appearing parts are found. For instance, crankcase bolts are often not the same length. You may think you can remember where everything came from—but mistakes are costly. There is also the possibility that you may be side-tracked and not return to work for days or even weeks—in which the time carefully laid out parts may have become disturbed.

20. When assembling parts, be sure all shims and washers are replaced exactly as they came out.

21. Whenever a rotating part butts against a stationary part, look for a shim or washer. Use new gaskets if there is any doubt about the condition of the old ones. A thin coat of oil on non-pressure type gaskets may help them seal more effectively.

22. High spots may be sanded off a piston with sandpaper, but fine emery cloth and oil will do a much more professional job.

23. Carbon can be removed from the head, the piston crown and the exhaust port with a dull screwdriver. Do *not* scratch machined surfaces. Wipe off the surface with a clean cloth when finished.

24. Heavy grease can be used to hold small parts in place if they tend to fall out during assembly. However, keep grease and oil away from electrical and brake components.

WASHING THE VEHICLE

Since the Warrior is an off-road vehicle, if you are using it often and maintaining it properly, you will spend a lot of time cleaning it. After riding it in extremely dirty areas, wash it down thoroughly. Doing this will make maintenance and service procedures quick and easy. More important, proper cleaning will prevent dirt from falling into critical areas undetected. Failing to clean the vehicle or cleaning it incorrectly will add to your maintenance costs and shop time because dirty parts wear out prematurely. It's unthinkable that your vehicle could break because of improper cleaning, but it can happen.

When cleaning your Yamaha, you will need a few tools, shop rags, scrub brush, bucket, liquid cleaner and access to water. Many riders use a coin-operated car wash. Coin-operated car washes are convenient and quick, but with improper use, the high water pressures can do more damage than good to your vehicle.

NOTE
A safe biodegradable, non-toxic and non-flammable liquid cleaner that works well for washing your vehicle as well as for removing grease and oil from engine and suspension parts is Simple Green. Simple Green can be purchased through some supermarkets, hardware, garden and discount supply houses. Follow the directions on the container for recommended dilution ratios.

When cleaning your vehicle, and especially when using a spray type degreaser, remember that what goes on the vehicle will rinse off and drip onto your driveway or into your yard. If you can, use a degreaser at a coin-operated car wash. If you are cleaning your vehicle at home, place thick cardboard or newspapers underneath the vehicle to catch the oil and grease deposits that are rinsed off.

1. Place the vehicle on level ground and set the parking brake.

2. Check the following before washing the vehicle:
   a. Make sure the gas filler cap is screwed on tightly.
   b. Make sure the engine oil cap is on tight.
   c. Plug the muffler opening with a large cork or rag.
   d. Remove the seat and cover the air box with plastic.
   e. If you are going to use some type of chemical degreaser to clean your Yamaha, first remove the O-ring drive chain.

3. Wash the vehicle from top to bottom with soapy water. Use the scrub brush to get excess dirt out of the wheel rims and engine crannies. Concentrate on the upper controls, engine, side panels and gas tank during this wash cycle. Do not forget to wash dirt and mud from underneath the fenders, suspension and engine crankcase.

4. Concentrate the second wash cycle on the frame tube members, outer airbox areas, suspension linkage, shock absorbers and swing arm.

5. Direct the hose underneath the engine and swing arm. Wash this area thoroughly.

6. The final wash is the rinse. Use cold water without soap and spray the entire vehicle again. Use as much time and care when rinsing the vehicle as when washing it. Built up soap deposits will quickly corrode electrical connections and remove the natural oils from tires, causing premature cracks and wear. Make sure you thoroughly rinse the vehicle off.

7. Tip the vehicle from side to side to allow any water that has collected on horizontal surfaces to drain off.

8. Remove the seat and the plastic cover from around the air box.

9. If you are washing the vehicle at home, start the engine. Idle the engine to burn off any internal moisture.

10. Before taking the vehicle into the garage, wipe it dry with a soft cloth or chamois. Inspect the machine as you dry it for further signs of dirt and grime. Make a quick visual inspection of the frame and other painted pieces. Spray any worn-down spots with WD-40 or Bel-Ray 6-in-1 to prevent rust from building on the bare metal. When the vehicle is back at your work area you can repaint the bare areas with touch-up paint after cleaning off the WD-40. A quick shot from a touch-up paint can each time you work on the vehicle will keep it looking sharp and stop rust from building and weakening parts.

TORQUE SPECIFICATIONS

The materials used in the manufacture of your Yamaha may be subjected to uneven stresses if the fasteners used to hold the sub-assemblies are not installed and torqued correctly. Improper bolt tightening can cause cylinder head warpage, crankcase leaks, premature bearing and seal failure and suspension failure from loose or missing fasteners. An accurate torque wrench (described in this chapter) should be used together with the torque specifications listed at the end of most chapters.

Torque specifications throughout this manual are given in Newton-meters (N•m) and foot-pounds (ft.-lb.).

Existing torque wrenches calibrated in meter kilograms can be used by performing a simple conversion. All you have to do is move the decimal point one place to the right; for example, 3.5 mkg = 35 N•m. This conversion is accurate enough for me-

chanical work even though the exact mathematical conversion is 3.5 mkg = 34.3 N•m.

Refer to **Table 6** for standard torque specifications for various size screws, bolts and nuts that may not be listed in the respective chapters. To use the table, first determine the size of the bolt or nut. Use a vernier caliper and measure the inside dimension of the threads of the nut (**Figure 6**) and across the threads for a bolt (**Figure 7**).

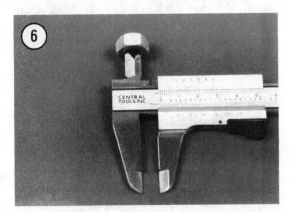

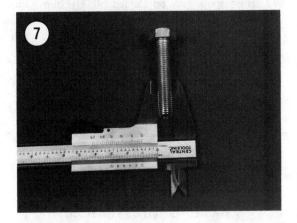

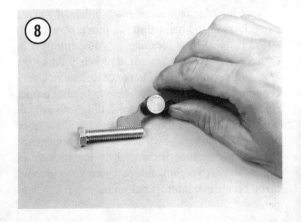

FASTENERS

The materials and designs of the various fasteners used on your Yamaha are not arrived at by chance or accident. Fastener design determines the type of tool required to work the fastener. Fastener material is carefully selected to decrease the possibility of physical failure.

Nuts, bolts and screws are manufactured in a wide range of thread patterns. To join a nut and bolt, the diameter of the bolt and the diameter of the hole in the nut must be the same. It is just as important that the threads on both be properly matched.

The best way to tell if the threads on 2 fasteners are matched is to turn the nut on the bolt (or the bolt into the threaded hole in a piece of equipment) with fingers only. Be sure both pieces are clean. If much force is required, check the thread condition on each fastener. If the thread condition is good but the fasteners jam, the threads are not compatible. A thread pitch gauge (**Figure 8**) can also be used to determine pitch. Yamaha ATV's and motorcycles are manufactured with ISO (International Organization for Standardization) metric fasteners. The

threads are cut differently than those of American fasteners (**Figure 9**).

Most threads are cut so that the fastener must be turned clockwise to tighten it. These are called right-hand threads. Some fasteners have left-hand threads; they must be turned counterclockwise to be tightened. Left-hand threads are used in locations where normal rotation of the equipment would tend to loosen a right-hand threaded fastener.

ISO Metric Screw Threads (Bolts, Nuts and Screws)

ISO (International Organization for Standardization) metric threads come in 3 standard thread sizes: coarse, fine and constant pitch. The ISO coarse pitch is used for almost all common fastener applications. The fine pitch thread is used on certain precision tools and instruments. The constant pitch thread is used mainly on machine parts and not for fasteners. The constant pitch thread, however, is used on all metric thread spark plugs.

Metric screws and bolts are classified by length (L, **Figure 10**), nominal diameter (D) and distance between thread crests (T). A typical bolt might be identified by the numbers $8–1.25 \times 130$, which would indicate that the bolt has a nominal diameter of 8 mm, the distance between thread crests is 1.25 mm and bolt length is 130 mm.

The strength of metric screws and bolts is indicated by numbers located on the top of the screw or bolt as shown in **Figure 10**. The higher the number the stronger the screw or bolt. Unnumbered screws or bolts are the weakest.

> *CAUTION*
> *Do not install screws or bolts with a lower strength grade classification than installed originally by the manufacturer. Doing so may cause engine or equipment failure and possible injury.*

The measurement across 2 flats on the head of the bolt indicates the proper wrench size to be used. **Figure 7** shows how to determine bolt diameter.

When purchasing a bolt from a dealer or parts store, it is important to know how to specify bolt length. The correct way to measure bolt length is by measuring the length starting from underneath the bolt head to the end of the bolt (**Figure 11**). Always

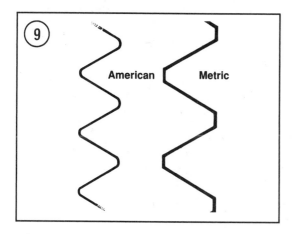

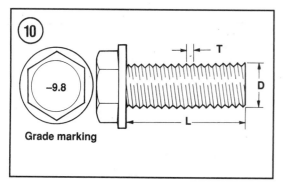

measure bolt length in this manner to avoid purchasing bolts that are too long.

Machine Screws

There are many different types of machine screws. **Figure 12** shows a number of screw heads requiring different types of turning tools. Heads are also designed to protrude above the metal (round) or to be slightly recessed in the metal (flat). See **Figure 13**.

Nuts

Nuts are manufactured in a variety of types and sizes. Most are hexagonal (6-sided) and fit on bolts, screws and studs with the same diameter and pitch.

Figure 14 shows several types of nuts. The common nut is generally used with a lockwasher. Self-locking nuts have a nylon insert which prevents the nut from loosening; no lockwasher is required. Wing nuts are designed for fast removal by hand. Wing nuts are used for convenience in non-critical locations.

To indicate the size of a metric nut, manufacturers specify the diameter of the opening and the thread pitch. This is similar to bolt specifications, but without the length dimension. The measurement across 2 flats on the nut indicates the proper wrench size to be used (**Figure 15**).

Self-Locking Fasteners

Several types of bolts, screws and nuts incorporate a system that develops an interference between the bolt, screw, nut or tapped hole threads. Interference is achieved in various ways: by distorting threads, coating threads with dry adhesive or nylon,

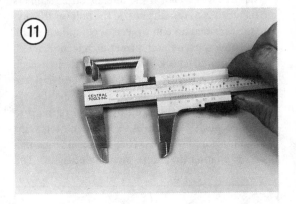

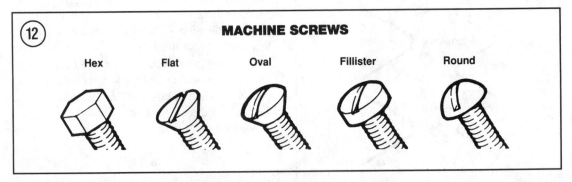

MACHINE SCREWS

Hex   Flat   Oval   Fillister   Round

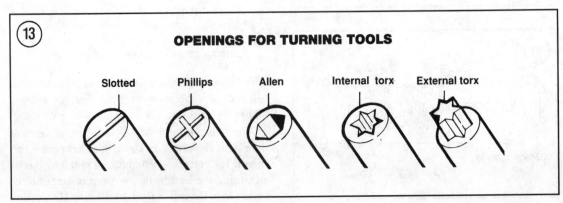

OPENINGS FOR TURNING TOOLS

Slotted   Phillips   Allen   Internal torx   External torx distorting the top of an all-metal nut, using a nylon insert in the center or at the top of a nut, etc.

Self-locking fasteners offer greater holding strength and better vibration resistance. Some self-locking fasteners can be reused if in good condition. Others, like the nylon insert nut, form an initial locking condition when the nut is first installed; the nylon forms closely to the bolt thread pattern, thus reducing any tendency for the nut to loosen. When the nut is removed, the locking efficiency is greatly reduced. For greatest safety, self-locking fasteners should be discarded and new ones installed whenever components are removed or disassembled.

Common nut **Self-locking nut**

Wing nut

Washers

There are 2 basic types of washers: flat washers and lockwashers. Flat washers are simple discs with a hole to fit a screw or bolt. Lockwashers are designed to prevent a fastener from working loose due to vibration, expansion and contraction. **Figure 16** shows several types of washers. Washers are also used in the following functions:

a. As spacers.
b. To prevent galling or damage of the equipment by the fastener.
c. To help distribute fastener load during torquing.
d. As seals.

Note that flat washers are often used between a lockwasher and a fastener to provide a smooth bearing surface. This allows the fastener to be turned easily with a tool.

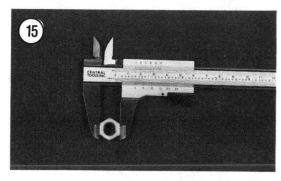

Cotter Pins

Cotter pins (**Figure 17**) are used to secure special kinds of fasteners. The threaded stud must have a hole in it; the nut or nut lock piece has castellations around which the cotter pin ends wrap. Cotter pins should *not* be reused after removal.

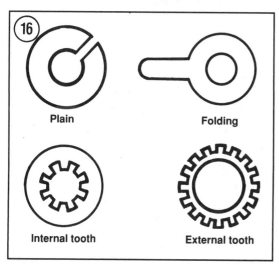

Plain **Folding**

Internal tooth **External tooth**

Circlips

Circlips (snap rings) can be internal or external design. They are used to retain items on shafts (external type); within tubes or housing bores (internal type). In some applications, circlips of varying thicknesses are used to control the end play of parts assemblies. These are often called selective circlips. Circlips should be replaced during installation, as removal weakens and deforms them.

Two basic styles of circlips are available: machined and stamped circlips. Machined circlips (**Fig-**

-gure 18) can be installed in either direction (shaft or housing) because both faces are machined, thus creating two sharp edges. Stamped circlips (**Figure 19**) are manufactured with one sharp edge and one rounded edge. When installing stamped circlips in a thrust situation (transmission shafts, fork tubes, etc.), the sharp edge must face away from the part producing the thrust unless the text specifies otherwise. When installing circlips, observe the following:

a. Compress or expand circlips only enough to install them.

b. After the circlip is installed, make sure it is completely seated in its groove.

c. Transmission circlips become worn with use and increase side play. For this reason, always use new circlips whenever a transmission is be reassembled.

LUBRICANTS

Periodic lubrication assures long life for any type of equipment. The type of lubricant used is just as important as the lubrication service itself, although in an emergency the wrong type of lubricant is better than none at all. The following paragraphs describe the types of lubricants most often used on ATV and motorcycle equipment. Be sure to follow the manufacturer's recommendations for lubricant types.

Generally, all liquid lubricants are called "oil." They may be mineral-based (including petroleum bases), natural-based (vegetable and animal bases), synthetic-based or emulsions (mixtures). "Grease" is an oil to which a thickening base has been added so that the end product is semi-solid. Grease is often classified by the type of thickener added; lithium soap is commonly used.

Engine Oil

Four-cycle oil for motorcycle and automotive engines is classified by the American Petroleum Institute (API) and the Society of Automotive Engineers (SAE) in several categories. Oil containers display these ratings on the top or label.

API oil classification is indicated by letters; oils for gasoline engines are identified by an "S". Yamaha models described in this manual require SG oil.

Viscosity is an indication of the oil's thickness. The SAE uses numbers to indicate viscosity; thin oils have low numbers while thick oils have high numbers. A "W" after the number indicates that the viscosity testing was done at low temperature to simulate cold-weather operation. Engine oils fall into the 5 to 50 range.

Multi-grade oils (for example 10W-40) are less viscous (thinner) at low temperatures and more viscous (thicker) at high temperatures. This allows the

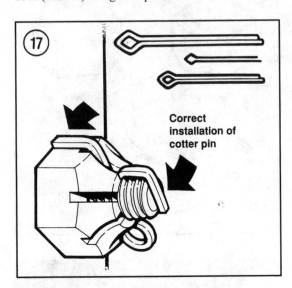

(17) Correct installation of cotter pin

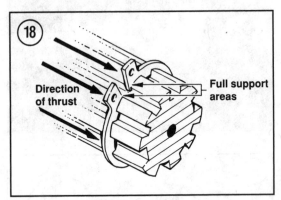

(18) Direction of thrust   Full support areas

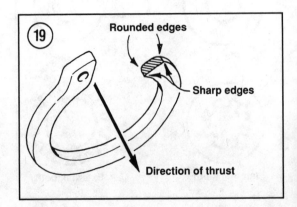

(19) Rounded edges   Sharp edges   Direction of thrust

oil to perform efficiently across a wide range of engine operating conditions. The lower the number, the better the engine will start in cold climates. Higher numbers are usually recommended for engine running in hot weather conditions.

Grease

Greases are graded by the National Lubricating Grease Institute (NLGI). Greases are graded by number according to the consistency of the grease; these range from No. 000 to No. 6, with No. 6 being the most solid. A typical multipurpose grease is NLGI No. 2. For specific applications, equipment manufacturers may require grease with an additive such as molybdenum disulfide (MOS2) (**Figure 20**).

THREADLOCK

A threadlock should be used to help secure many of the fasteners used on your Yamaha. A threadlock will lock fasteners against vibration loosening and seal against leaks. Loctite 242 (blue) and 271 (red) are recommended for many threadlock requirements described in this manual (**Figure 21**). There are other quality threadlock brands on the market.

EXPENDABLE SUPPLIES

Certain expendable supplies are required during maintenance and repair work. These include grease, oil, gasket cement, wiping rags and cleaning solvent. Ask your dealer for the special locking compounds, silicone lubricants and other products which make vehicle maintenance simpler and easier. Cleaning solvent or kerosene is available at some service stations, paint or hardware stores.

WARNING
Having a stack of clean shop rags on hand is important when performing engine and suspension service work. However, to prevent the possibility of fire damage from spontaneous combustion from a pile of solvent soaked rags, store them in a lid sealed metal container until they can be washed or discarded.

NOTE
Wear a pair of petroleum-resistant rubber gloves to prevent solvent and other chemicals from absorbing into your skin while cleaning parts. These can be purchased through industrial supply houses or well-equipped hardware stores.

PARTS REPLACEMENT

Yamaha makes frequent changes during a model year, some minor, some relatively major. When you order parts from the dealer or other parts distributor, always order by frame and engine numbers. The frame serial number is stamped on the left-hand lower frame member (**Figure 22**). The engine num-

ber is stamped on a raised pad on the right-hand side of the crankcase (**Figure 23**).

The first 3 digits are for model identification. The remaining digits are production numbers.

Record these numbers in the *Quick Reference Data* section at the front of this manual. Compare new parts to old before purchasing them. If they are not alike, have the parts manager explain the difference to you. **Table 1** lists engine and frame serial numbers for the models covered in this manual.

When purchasing electrical components, make sure all other possibilities that could cause a malfunction have been eliminated. Check electrical connections, wires and ground points before assuming an electrical component is defective. Most parts suppliers will not accept returns on electrical components. This caution is especially true when considering electrical component replacement because the part may have failed a resistance test by a small amount. Resistance tests fail to check the component under actual operating conditions and variables such as temperature and a particular meter's design can influence a resistance test.

BASIC HAND TOOLS

Many of the procedures in this manual can be carried out with simple hand tools and test equipment familiar to the average home mechanic. Keep your tools clean and in a tool box. Keep them organized with the sockets and related drives together, the open-end combination wrenches together, etc. After using a tool, wipe off dirt and grease with a clean cloth and return the tool to its correct place.

Top quality tools are essential; they are also more economical in the long run. If you are now starting to build your tool collection, stay away from the "advertised specials" featured at some parts houses, discount stores and chain drug stores. These are usually a poor grade tool that can be sold cheaply and that is exactly what they are—cheap. They are usually made of inferior material, and are thick, heavy and clumsy. Their rough finish makes them difficult to clean and they usually do not last very long. If it is ever your misfortune to use such tools, you will probably find out that the wrenches do not fit the heads of bolts and nuts correctly and will damage the fastener.

Quality tools are made of alloy steel and are heat treated for greater strength. They are lighter and better balanced than cheap ones. Their surface is smooth, making them a pleasure to work with and easy to clean. The initial cost of good quality tools may be more but they are cheaper in the long run. Do not try to buy everything in all sizes in the beginning; buy a few at a time until you have the necessary tools.

Screwdrivers

The screwdriver is a very basic tool, but if used improperly it will do more damage than good. The slot on a screw has a definite dimension and shape.

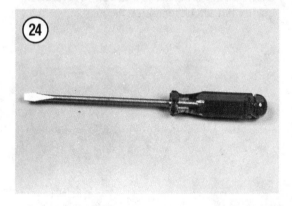

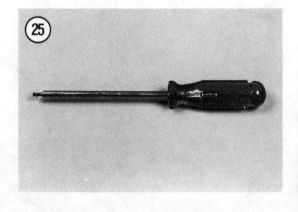

A screwdriver must be selected to conform with that shape. Use a small screwdriver for small screws and a large one for large screws or the screw head will be damaged.

Two basic types of screwdrivers are required: common (flat-blade) screwdrivers (**Figure 24**) and Phillips screwdrivers (**Figure 25**).

Screwdrivers are available in sets which often include an assortment of common and Phillips blades. If you buy them individually, buy at least the following:

    a. Common screwdriver—5/16 × 6 in. blade.

    b. Common screwdriver—3/8 × 12 in. blade.

    c. Phillips screwdriver—size 2 tip, 6 in. blade.

    d. Phillips screwdriver—size 3 tip, 6 and 10 in. blade.

Use screwdrivers only for driving screws. Never use a screwdriver for prying or chiseling metal. Do not try to remove a Phillips or Allen head screw with a common screwdriver (unless the screw has a combination head that will accept either type); you can damage the head so that the proper tool will be unable to remove it.

Keep screwdrivers in the proper condition and they will last longer and perform better. Always keep the tip of a common screwdriver in good condition. **Figure 26** shows how to grind the tip to the proper shape if it becomes damaged. Note the symmetrical sides of the tip.

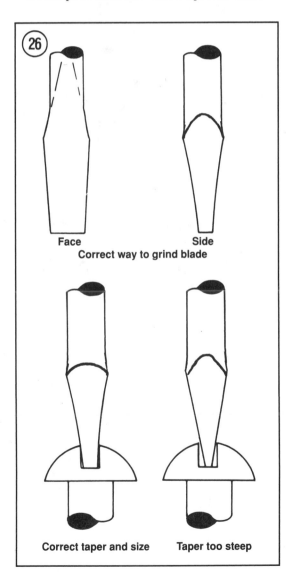

Face   **Side**
Correct way to grind blade

Correct taper and size   **Taper too steep**

Pliers

Pliers come in a wide range of types and sizes. Pliers are useful for cutting, bending and crimping. They should never be used to cut hardened objects or to turn bolts or nuts. **Figure 27** shows several pliers useful in ATV and motorcycle repair.

Each type of pliers has a specialized function. Slip-joint pliers are general purpose pliers and are used mainly for holding things and for bending.

Needlenose pliers are used to hold or bend small objects. Groove joint pliers can be adjusted to hold various sizes of objects; the jaws remain parallel to grip around objects such as pipe or tubing. There are many more types of pliers. The ones described here are most suitable for vehicle repairs.

Vise-grip Pliers

Vise-grip pliers (**Figure 28**) are used to hold objects very tightly like a vise. But avoid using them

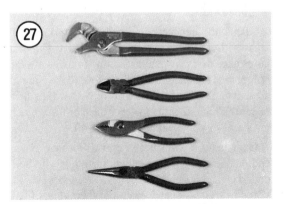

unless absolutely necessary since their sharp jaws will permanently scar any objects which are held. Vise-grip pliers are available in many types for more specific tasks.

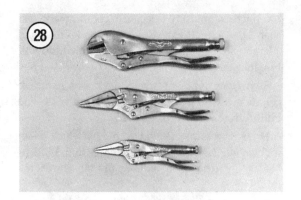

Circlip (Snap ring) Pliers

Circlip (snap ring) pliers (**Figure 29**) are made for removing and installing circlips and should not be used for any other purpose. External pliers (spreading) are used to remove circlips that fit on the outside of a shaft. Internal pliers (squeezing) are used to remove circlips which fit inside a gear or housing.

> *WARNING*
> *Because circlips can slip and "fly off" when removing and installing them, always wear safety glasses.*

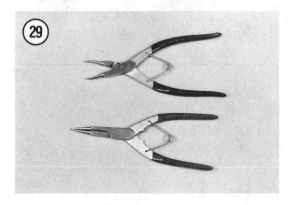

Box, Open-end and Combination Wrenches

Box-end, open-end and combination wrenches are available in sets or separately in a variety of sizes. On open and box end wrenches, the number stamped near the end refers to the distance between 2 parallel flats on the hex head bolt or nut. On combination wrenches, the number is stamped near the center.

Box-end wrenches require clear overhead access to the fastener but can work well in situations where the fastener head is close to another part. They grip on all six edges of a fastener for a very secure grip. They are available in either 6-point or 12-point. The 6-point gives superior holding power and durability but requires a greater swinging radius. The 12-point works better in situations where the swinging radius is limited.

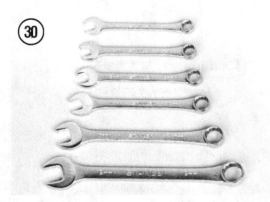

Open-end wrenches are speedy and work best in areas with limited overhead access. Their wide flat jaws make them unsuitable for situations where the bolt or nut is sunken in a well or close to the edge of a casting. These wrenches grip only two flats of a fastener so, if either the fastener head or the wrench jaws are worn, the wrench may slip off.

Combination wrenches (**Figure 30**) have open-end on one side and box-end on the other with both ends being the same size. These wrenches are favored by professionals because of their versatility.

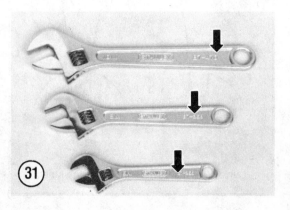

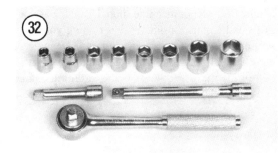

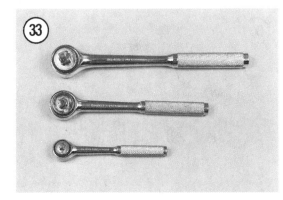

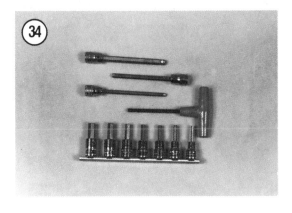

Adjustable (Crescent) Wrenches

An adjustable wrench (sometimes called crescent wrench) can be adjusted to fit nearly any nut or bolt head which has clear access around its entire perimeter. Adjustable wrenches (**Figure 31**) are best used as a backup wrench to keep a large nut or bolt from turning while the other end is being loosened or tightened with a proper wrench.

Adjustable wrenches have only two gripping surfaces which make them more subject to slipping off the fastener and damaging the part and possibly injuring your hand. The fact that one jaw is adjustable only aggravates this shortcoming.

These wrenches are directional; the solid jaw must be the one transmitting the force. Apply force in direction indicated in **Figure 31**. If you use the adjustable jaw to transmit the force, it may loosen and the wrench may slip off.

Adjustable wrenches come in all sizes but something in the 6 to 8 in. range is recommended as an all-purpose wrench.

Socket Wrenches

This type is undoubtedly the fastest, safest and most convenient to use. Sockets which attach to a ratchet handle (**Figure 32**) are available with 6-point or 12-point openings and 1/4, 3/8, 1/2 and 3/4 in. drives. The drive size indicates the size of the square hole which mates with the ratchet handle (**Figure 33**).

Allen Wrenches

Allen wrenches are available in sets or separately in a variety of sizes. These sets come in SAE and metric size, so be sure to buy a metric set. Allen bolts are sometimes called socket bolts. Sometimes the bolts are difficult to reach and it is suggested that a variety of Allen wrenches be purchased (e.g. socket driven, T-handle and extension type) as shown in **Figure 34**.

Torque Wrench

A torque wrench is used with a socket to measure how tightly a nut or bolt is installed. They come in a wide price range and with either 1/4, 3/8 or 1/2 in. square drive (**Figure 35**). The drive size indicates the size of the square drive which mates with the socket.

Impact Driver

This tool might have been designed with the ATV and motorcycle rider in mind. This tool makes removal of fasteners easy and eliminates damage to bolts and screw slots. Impact drivers and interchangeable bits (**Figure 36**) are available at most large hardware, motorcycle or auto parts stores. Do not purchase a cheap one as it will not work as well and require more force (the "use a larger hammer" syndrome) than a moderately priced one. Sockets can also be used with a hand impact driver; however, make sure that the socket is designed for use with an impact driver or air tool. Do not use regular hand sockets, as they may shatter during use.

Hammers

The correct hammer (**Figure 37**) is necessary for repairs. A hammer with a face (or head) of rubber or plastic or the soft-faced type that is filled with buckshot is sometimes necessary in engine teardowns. *Never* use a metal-faced hammer on engine or suspension parts, as severe damage will result in most cases. You can produce the same amount of force with a soft-faced hammer. The shock of a metal-faced hammer, however, is required for using an hand impact driver.

PRECISION MEASURING TOOLS

Measurement is an important part of engine and suspension service. When performing many of the service procedures in this manual, you will be required to make a number of measurements. These include basic checks such as valve clearance, engine compression and spark plug gap. As you get deeper into engine disassembly and service, measurements will be required to determine the size and condition of the piston and cylinder bore, valve and guide wear, camshaft wear, crankshaft runout and so on. When making these measurements, the degree of accuracy will dictate which tool is required. Precision measuring tools are expensive. If this is your first experience at engine or suspension service, it may be more worthwhile to have the checks made at

a Yamaha dealer or machine shop. However, as your skills and enthusiasm increase for doing your own service work, you may want to purchase some of these specialized tools. The following is a description of the measuring tools required during engine and suspension overhaul.

Feeler Gauge

Feeler gauges come in assorted sets and types (**Figure 38**). The feeler gauge is made of either a

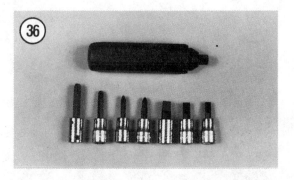

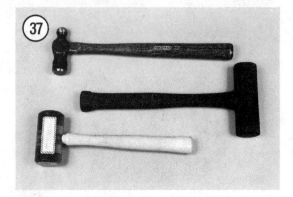

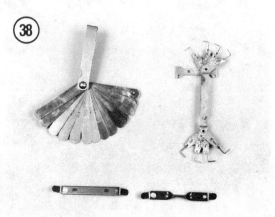

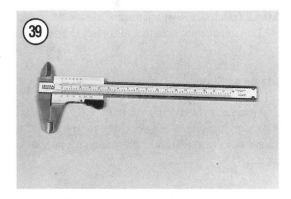

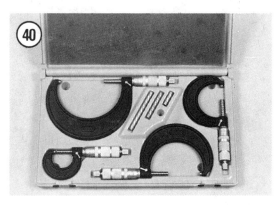

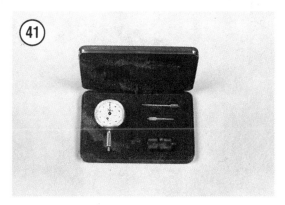

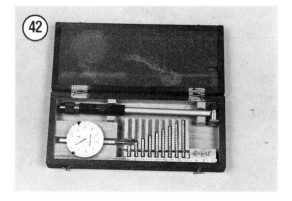

piece of a flat or round hardened steel of a specified thickness. Wire gauges are used to measure spark plug gap. Flat gauges are used for other measurements. Feeler gauges are also designed for specialized uses. For example, the end of a gauge is usually small and angled to facilitate checking valve clearances.

Vernier Caliper

This tool (**Figure 39**) is invaluable when reading inside, outside and depth measurements with close precision. Common uses of a vernier caliper are measuring the length of the clutch springs and the thickness of clutch plates, shims and thrust washers.

Outside Micrometers

One of the most reliable tools used for precision measurement is the outside micrometer (**Figure 40**). Outside micrometers will be required to measure valve shim thickness, piston diameter and valve stem diameter. Outside micrometers are also used with other tools to measure the cylinder bore and the valve guide inside diameters. Micrometers can be purchased individually or as a set.

Dial Indicator

Dial indicators (**Figure 41**) are precision tools used to check dimension variations on machined parts such as transmission shafts and axles and to check crankshaft and axle shaft end play. Dial indicators are available with various dial types and mountings for different measuring requirements.

Cylinder Bore Gauge

The cylinder bore gauge is a very specialized precision tool. The gauge set shown in **Figure 42** is comprised of a dial indicator, handle and a number of length adapters to adapt the gauge to different bore sizes. The bore gauge can be used to make cylinder bore measurements such as bore size, taper and out-of-round. Depending on the bore gauge, it can sometimes be used to measure brake caliper and master cylinder bore sizes. An outside micrometer must be used together with the bore gauge to determine bore dimensions.

Small Hole Gauges

A set of small hole gauges allows you to measure a hole, groove or slot ranging in size up to 13 mm (0.500 in.). A small hole gauge will be required to measure valve guide, brake caliper and brake master cylinder bore diameters. An outside micrometer must be used together with the small hole gauge to determine bore dimensions.

Compression Gauge

An engine with low compression cannot be properly tuned and will not develop full power. A compression gauge (**Figure 43**) measures engine compression. The one shown has a flexible stem with an extension that allows you to hold it while kicking the engine over. Open the throttle all the way when checking engine compression. See Chapter Three.

Strobe Timing Light

This instrument is useful for checking ignition timing. By flashing a light at the precise instant the spark plug fires, the position of the timing mark can be seen. The flashing light makes a moving mark appear to stand still.

Suitable lights range from inexpensive neon bulb types to powerful xenon strobe lights (**Figure 44**). A light with an inductive pickup is recommended to eliminate any possible damage to ignition wiring. Connect and use the timing light according to manufacturer's instructions.

Multimeter or VOM

This instrument (**Figure 45**) is invaluable for electrical system troubleshooting. See *Electrical Troubleshooting* in Chapter Nine for its use.

Screw Pitch Gauge

A screw pitch gauge (**Figure 46**) determines the thread pitch of bolts, screws, studs, etc. The gauge is made up of a number of thin plates. Each plate has a thread shape cut on one edge to match one thread pitch. When using a screw pitch gauge to determine

a thread pitch size, try to fit different blade sizes onto the bolt thread until both threads match (**Figure 47**).

Magnetic Stand

A magnetic stand (**Figure 48**) is used to hold a dial indicator securely when checking the runout of a round object or when checking the end play of a shaft.

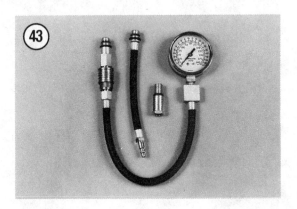

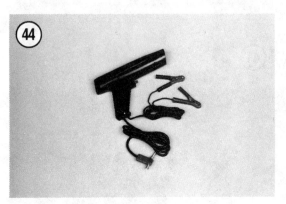

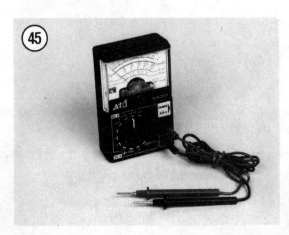

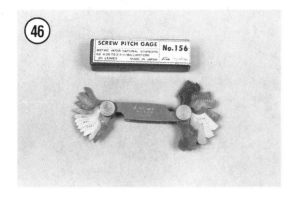

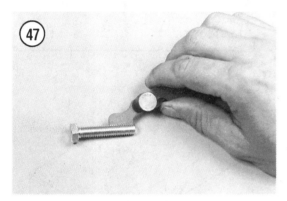

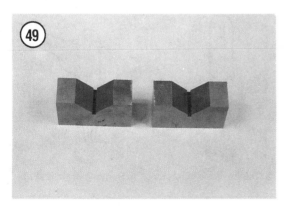

V-Blocks

V-blocks (**Figure 49**) are precision ground blocks used to hold a round object when checking its runout or condition. In ATV and motorcycle repair, V-blocks can be used when checking the runout of such items as valve stems, camshaft, balancer shaft, crankshaft, wheel axles and other shafts and collars.

SPECIAL TOOLS

A few special tools may be required for major service. These are described in the appropriate chapters and are available either from a Yamaha dealer or other manufacturers as indicated.

This section describes special tools unique to this type of vehicle's service and repair.

The Grabbit

The Grabbit (**Figure 50**) is a special tool used to hold the clutch boss when removing the clutch nut and to secure the drive sprocket when removing the sprocket nut.

Alternator Rotor Puller

A rotor puller (**Figure 51**) will be required whenever it is necessary to remove the rotor. In addition,

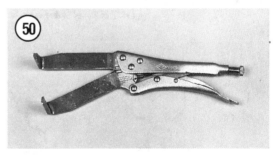

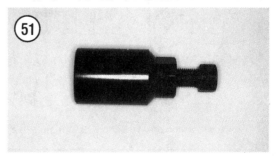

when disassembling the engine, the rotor must be
removed before the crankcases can be split. There
is no satisfactory substitute for this tool. Because
the rotor is a taper fit on the crankshaft, makeshift
removal often results in crankshaft and rotor damage. Don't think about removing the rotor without
this tool. This tool can be ordered through Yamaha
dealers (part No. YM-01404).

Engine Disassembly Tools

A crankcase separator will be required to separate
the crankcases and to remove the crankshaft. This
tool is shown in Chapter Five.

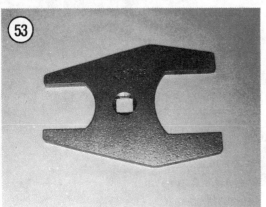

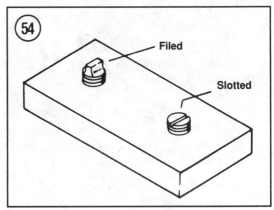

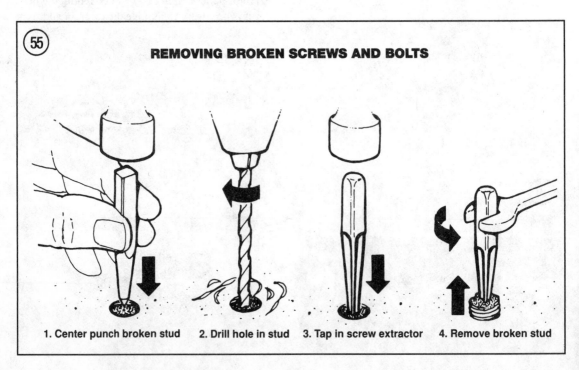

REMOVING BROKEN SCREWS AND BOLTS

1. Center punch broken stud   2. Drill hole in stud   3. Tap in screw extractor   4. Remove broken stud

Crankshaft Installer Tool

A crankshaft installer tool assembly will be required to install the crankshaft prior to assembling the crankcases. This tool is shown in Chapter Five.

Ball-Joint Wrench

A ball-joint wrench (**Figure 52**) will be required to loosen and tighten the suspension ball joints (1987 models). This tool can be ordered through Yamaha dealers (part No. YM-01405).

Rear Axle Nut Wrench

The 50 mm rear axle nuts require a rear axle nut wrench (**Figure 53**) for their removal and installation. This tool can be ordered through Yamaha dealers (part No. YM-37132).

MECHANIC'S TIPS

Removing Frozen Nuts and Screws

When a fastener rusts and cannot be removed, several methods may be used to loosen it. First, apply penetrating oil such as Liquid Wrench or WD-40 (available at hardware or auto supply stores). Apply it liberally and let it penetrate for 10-15 minutes. Rap the fastener several times with a small hammer; do not hit it hard enough to cause damage. Reapply the penetrating oil if necessary.

For frozen screws, apply penetrating oil as described, then insert a screwdriver in the slot and rap the top of the screwdriver with a hammer. This loosens the rust so the screw can be removed in the normal way. If the screw head is too chewed up to use this method, grip the head with vise-grip pliers and twist the screw out.

Avoid applying heat unless specifically instructed, as it may melt, warp or remove the temper from parts.

Removing Broken Screws or Bolts

When the head breaks off a screw or bolt, several methods are available for removing the remaining portion.

If a large portion of the remainder projects out, try gripping it with vise-grip pliers. If the projecting portion is too small, file it to fit a wrench or cut a slot in it to fit a screwdriver. See **Figure 54**.

If the head breaks off flush, use a screw extractor. To do this, centerpunch the exact center of the remaining portion of the screw or bolt. Drill a small hole in the screw and tap the extractor into the hole. Back the screw out with a wrench on the extractor. See **Figure 55**.

Remedying Stripped Threads

Occasionally, threads are stripped through carelessness or impact damage. Often the threads can be cleaned up by running a tap (for internal threads on nuts) or die (for external threads on bolts) through the threads. See **Figure 56**. To clean or repair spark plug threads, a spark plug tap can be used (**Figure 57**).

NOTE
*Tap and dies can be purchased individually or in a set as shown in **Figure 58**.*

If an internal thread is damaged, it may be necessary to install a thread insert; see **Figure 59**, typical. Follow the manufacturer's instructions when installing their insert.

If it is necessary to drill and tap a hole, refer to **Table 8** for metric tap drill sizes.

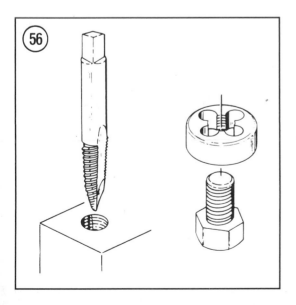
56

BALL BEARING REPLACEMENT

Ball bearings (**Figure 60**) are used throughout the engine and chassis to reduce power loss, heat and noise resulting from friction. Because ball bearings are precision made parts, they must be maintained by proper lubrication and maintenance. When a bearing is found to be damaged, it should be replaced immediately. However, when installing a new bearing, care should be taken to prevent damage to the new bearing. While bearing replacement is described in the individual chapters where applicable, the following should be used as a guideline.

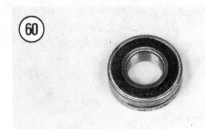

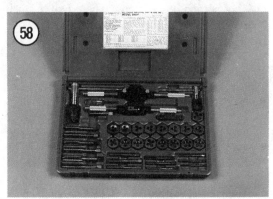

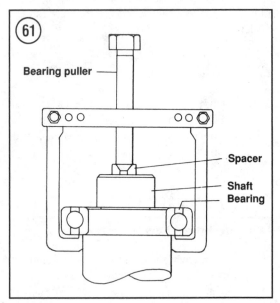

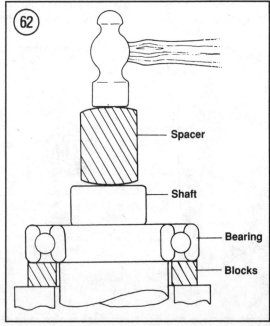

NOTE
Unless otherwise specified, install bearings with the manufacturer's mark or number facing outward.

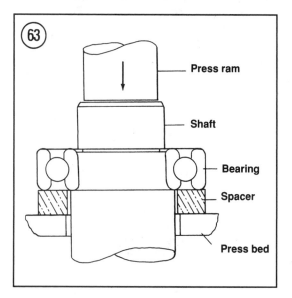

Bearing Removal

While bearings are normally removed only when damaged, there may be times when it is necessary to remove a bearing that is in good condition. However, improper bearing removal will damage the bearing and maybe the shaft or case half. Note the following when removing bearings.

1. When using a puller to remove a bearing from a shaft, take care that shaft is not damaged. Always place a piece of metal between the end of the shaft and the puller screw. In addition, place the puller arms next to the inner bearing race. See **Figure 61**.

2. When using a hammer to remove a bearing from a shaft, do not strike the hammer directly against the shaft. Instead, use a brass or aluminum rod between the hammer and shaft (**Figure 62**) and make sure to support both bearing races with wood blocks as shown.

3. The most ideal method of bearing removal is with a hydraulic press. However, certain procedures must be followed or damage may occur to the bearing, shaft or bearing housing. Note the following when using a press:

   a. Always support the inner and outer bearing races with a suitable size wood or aluminum ring (**Figure 63**). If you only support the outer race, pressure applied against the balls and/or the inner race will damage them.

   b. Always make sure the press ram (**Figure 63**) aligns with the center of the shaft. If the ram is not centered, it may damage the bearing and/or shaft.

   c. The moment the shaft is free of the bearing, it will drop to the floor. Secure or hold the shaft to prevent it from falling.

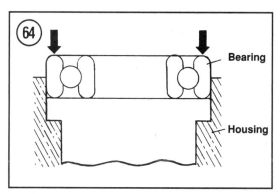

Bearing Installation

1. When installing a bearing in a housing, pressure must be applied to the *outer* bearing race (**Figure 64**). When installing a bearing on a shaft, pressure must be applied to the *inner* bearing race (**Figure 65**).

2. When installing a bearing as described in Step 1, some type of driver will be required. Never strike the bearing directly with a hammer or the bearing will be damaged. When installing a bearing, a piece of pipe or a socket with a diameter that matches the bearing race will be required. **Figure 66** shows the

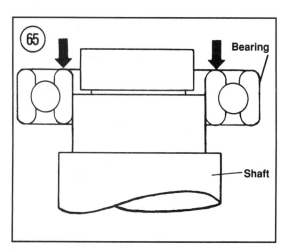

correct way to use a socket and hammer when installing a bearing.

3. Step 1 describes how to install a bearing in a case half or over a shaft. However, when installing a bearing over a shaft and into a housing at the same time, a snug fit will be required for both outer and inner bearing races. In this situation, a spacer must be installed underneath the driver tool so that pressure is applied evenly across *both* races. See **Figure 67**. If the outer race is not supported as shown in **Figure 67**, the balls will push against the outer bearing track and damage it.

Shrink Fit

1. *Installing a bearing over a shaft*: When a tight fit is required, the bearing inside diameter will be smaller than the shaft. In this case, driving the bearing on the shaft using normal methods may cause bearing damage. Instead, the bearing should be heated before installation. Note the following:

    a. Secure the shaft so that it is ready for bearing installation.

    b. Clean all residue from the bearing surface of the shaft. Remove burrs with a file or sandpaper.

    c. Fill a suitable pot or beaker with clean mineral oil. Place a thermometer (rated higher than 120° C [248° F]) in the oil. Support the thermometer so that it does not rest on the bottom or side of the pot.

    d. Remove the bearing from its wrapper and secure it with a piece of heavy wire bent to hold it in the pot. Hang the bearing in the pot so that it does not touch the bottom or sides of the pot.

    e. Turn the heat on and monitor the thermometer. When the oil temperature rises to approximately 120° C (248° F), remove the bearing from the pot and quickly install it. If necessary, place a socket on the inner bearing race and tap the bearing into place. As the bearing chills, it will tighten on the shaft so you must work quickly when installing it. Make sure the bearing is installed all the way.

2. *Installing a bearing in a housing*: Bearings are generally installed in a housing with a slight interference fit. Driving the bearing into the housing using normal methods may damage the housing or cause bearing damage. Instead, the housing should be heated before the bearing is installed. Note the following:

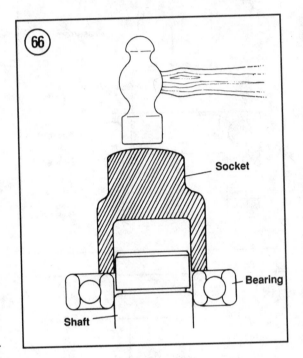

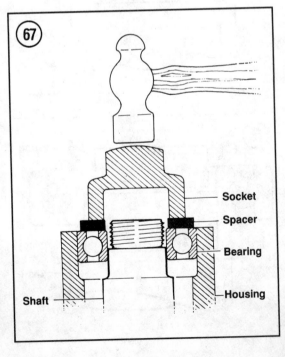

a. The housing must be heated to a temperature of about 212° F (100° C) in an oven or on a hot plate. An easy way to check that it is at the proper temperature is to drop tiny drops of water on the case; if they sizzle and evaporate immediately, the temperature is correct. Heat only one housing at a time.

CAUTION
Do not heat the housing with a torch (propane or acetylene)—never bring a flame into contact with the bearing or housing. The direct heat will destroy the case hardening of the bearing and will likely warp the housing.

b. Remove the housing from the oven or hot plate and hold onto the housing with a kitchen pot holder, heavy gloves, or heavy shop cloths—*it is hot.*

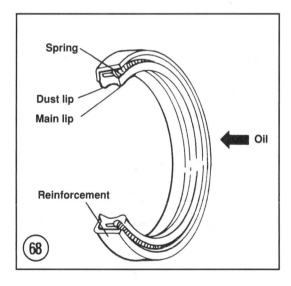

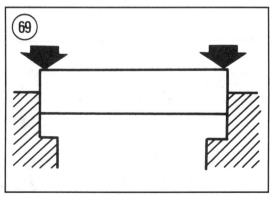

NOTE
A suitable size socket and extension works well for removing and installing bearings.

c. Hold the housing with the bearing side down and tap the bearing out. Repeat for all bearings in the housing.

d. Prior to heating the bearing housing, place the new bearing in a freezer, if possible. Chilling a bearing will slightly reduce its outside diameter while the heated bearing housing assembly is slightly larger due to heat expansion. This will make bearing installation much easier.

NOTE
Always install bearings with the manufacturer's mark or number facing outward.

e. While the housing is still hot, install the new bearing(s) into the housing. Install the bearings by hand, if possible. If necessary, lightly tap the bearing(s) into the housing with a socket placed on the outer bearing race. *Do not* install new bearings by driving on the inner bearing race. Install the bearing(s) until it seats completely.

OIL SEALS

Oil seals (**Figure 68**) are used to prevent leakage of oil, water, grease or combustion gasses from between a housing and a shaft. Improper removal of a seal can damage the housing or shaft. Improper installation of the seal can damage the seal. Note the following:

a. Prying is generally the easiest and most effective method of removing a seal from a housing. However, always place a rag underneath the pry tool to prevent damage to the housing.

b. Waterproof grease should be packed in the seal lips before the seal is installed.

c. Oil seals should always be installed so that the manufacturer's numbers or marks face out.

d. Oil seals should be installed with a socket placed on the outside of the seal as shown in **Figure 69**. Make sure the seal is driven squarely into the housing. Never install a seal by hitting against the top of the seal with a hammer.

RIDING SAFETY

General Tips

1. Read your owner's manual and know your machine.

2. Check the throttle and brake controls before starting the engine.

3. Know how to make an emergency stop.

4. Never add fuel while anyone is smoking in the area or when the engine is running.

5. Never wear loose scarves, belts or boot laces that could catch on moving parts.

6. Always wear eye protection, head protection and protective clothing to protect your *entire* body (**Figure 70**).

7. Riding in the winter months requires a good set of clothes to keep your body dry and warm, otherwise your entire trip may be miserable. If you dress properly, moisture will evaporate from your body. If you become too hot and if your clothes trap the moisture, you will become cold. **Figure 71** shows some recommended inner and outer layers of cold weather clothing. Even mild temperatures can be very uncomfortable and dangerous when combined with a strong wind or traveling at high speed. See **Table 9** for wind chill factors. Always dress according to what the wind chill factor is, not the ambient temperature.

WINTER PROTECTIVE CLOTHING

Inner layers — Outer layers

Safety helmet
Goggles
Face mask
Wool shirt — Insulated suit
Glove liners — Leather gloves
Thermal underwear
Heavy pants
Wool socks — Motorcycle or snowmobile boots

⑦⑪ 71

70

Safety helmet
Goggles
Chest, collarbone and shoulder protector
Jersey
Off-road type gloves
Riding pants
Motorcycle boots

72

8. Never allow anyone to operate the vehicle without proper instruction. This is for their bodily protection and to keep your machine from damage or destruction.

9. Use the "buddy system" for long trips, just in case you have a problem or run out of gas.

10. Never attempt to repair your machine with the engine running except when necessary for certain tune-up procedures.

11. Check all of the machine components and hardware frequently, especially the wheels and the steering.

Operating Tips

1. Never operate the machine in crowded areas or steer toward persons.

2. Avoid dangerous terrain.

3. Cross highways (where permitted) at a 90° angle after looking in both directions. Post traffic guards if crossing in groups.

4. Do not ride the vehicle on or near railroad tracks. Engine and exhaust noise can drown out the sound of an approaching train.

5. Keep the headlight and taillight free of dirt and never ride at night without the headlight and taillight ON.

6. Do not ride your Yamaha without the seat and fenders in place.

7. Always steer with both hands.

8. Be aware of the terrain and avoid operating the Yamaha at excessive speed.

9. Do not panic if the throttle sticks. Turn the engine stop switch (Figure 72) to the OFF position.

10. Do not speed through wooded areas. Hidden obstructions, hanging tree limbs, unseen ditches and even wild animals and hikers can cause injury and damage to you and your Yamaha.

11. Do not tailgate. Rear end collisions can cause injury and machine damage.

12. Do not mix alcoholic beverages or drugs with riding—ride straight.

13. Keep both feet on the foot pegs. Do not permit your feet to hang out to stabilize the machine when making turns or in near spill situations; broken limbs could result.

14. Check your fuel supply regularly. Do not travel farther than your fuel supply will permit you to return.

15. Check to make sure that the parking brake is *completely released* while riding. If left on, the rear brake pads will be damaged.

Table 1 STARTING ENGINE AND FRAME SERIAL NUMBERS

Year and model number	Engine/frame serial no. starting number
1987 YFM350XT	1UY-000101
1988 YFM350XU	2XK-000101
1989 YFM350XW	3GD-000101
1990 YFM350XA	3GD-051101-on
1991 YFM350XB	3GD-063101-on
1992 YFM350XD	3GD-080101-on
1993 YFM350XE	3GD-095101-on
1994 YFM350XF	3GD-108101-on
1995 YFM350XG	3GD-124101
1996 YFM350XH	NA
1997 YFM350XJ	NA
1998 YFM350XK	NA
1999 YFM350XL	NA
2000 YFM350XM	NA
2001 (49-state) YFM350XN	NA
2001 (California) YFM350XNC	NA
2002 (49-state) YFM350XP	NA
2002 (California) YFM350XPC	NA
2003	NA

TABLE 2 GENERAL DIMENSIONS

	mm	in.
Overall height	1,080	42.5
Seat height	765	30.1
Overall length	1,840	72.4
Overall width	1,080	42.5
Wheelbase	1,200	47.2
Minimum ground clearance		
1987-1989	135	5.31
1990-on	125	4.92
Minimum turning radius	3,500	138

Table 3 DRY WEIGHT SPECIFICATIONS*

	kg	lbs.
1987-1989	188	414
1990-on	191	421

* With oil and fuel tank full.

Table 4 DECIMAL AND METRIC EQUIVALENTS

Fractions	Decimal in.	Metric mm	Fractions	Decimal in.	Metric mm
1/64	0.015625	0.39688	33/64	0.515625	13.09687
1/32	0.03125	0.79375	17/32	0.53125	13.49375
3/64	0.046875	1.19062	35/64	0.546875	13.89062
1/16	0.0625	1.58750	9/16	0.5625	14.28750
5/64	0.078125	1.98437	37/64	0.578125	14.68437
3/32	0.09375	2.38125	19/32	0.59375	15.08125
7/64	0.109375	2.77812	39/64	0.609375	15.47812
1/8	0.125	3.1750	5/8	0.625	15.87500
9/64	0.140625	3.57187	41/64	0.640625	16.27187
5/32	0.15625	3.96875	21/32	0.65625	16.66875
11/64	0.171875	4.36562	43/64	0.671875	17.06562
3/16	0.1875	4.76250	11/16	0.6875	17.46250
13/64	0.203125	5.15937	45/64	0.703125	17.85937
7/32	0.21875	5.55625	23/32	0.71875	18.25625
15/64	0.234375	5.95312	47/64	0.734375	18.65312
1/4	0.250	6.35000	3/4	0.750	19.05000
17/64	0.265625	6.74687	49/64	0.765625	19.44687
9/32	0.28125	7.14375	25/32	0.78125	19.84375
19/64	0.296875	7.54062	51/64	0.796875	20.24062
5/16	0.3125	7.93750	13/16	0.8125	20.63750
21/64	0.328125	8.33437	53/64	0.828125	21.03437
11/32	0.34375	8.73125	27/32	0.84375	21.43125
23/64	0.359375	9.12812	55/64	0.859375	22.82812
3/8	0.375	9.52500	7/8	0.875	22.22500
25/64	0.390625	9.92187	57/64	0.890625	22.62187
13/32	0.40625	10.31875	29/32	0.90625	23.01875
27/64	0.421875	10.71562	59/64	0.921875	23.41562
7/16	0.4375	11.11250	15/16	0.9375	23.81250
29/64	0.453125	11.50937	61/64	0.953125	24.20937
15/32	0.46875	11.90625	31/32	0.96875	24.60625
31/64	0.484375	12.30312	63/64	0.984375	25.00312
1/2	0.500	12.70000	1	1.00	25.40000

Table 5 CONVERSION TABLES

Multiply	By	To get equivalent of
Length		
Inches	25.4	Millimeter
Inches	2.54	Centimeter
Miles	1.609	Kilometer
Feet	0.3048	Meter
Millimeter	0.03937	Inches
Centimeter	0.3937	Inches
Kilometer	0.6214	Mile
Meter	0.006214	Mile
Fluid volume		
U.S. quarts	0.9463	Liters
U.S. gallons	3.785	Liters
U.S. ounces	29.573529	Milliliters
Imperial gallons	4.54609	Liters
Imperial quarts	1.1365	Liters
Liters	0.2641721	U.S. gallons
Liters	1.0566882	U.S. quarts
Liters	33.814023	U.S. ounces
Liters	0.22	Imperial gallons
Liters	0.8799	Imperial quarts
Milliliters	0.033814	U.S. ounces
Milliliters	1.0	Cubic centimeters
Milliliters	0.001	Liters
Torque		
Foot-pounds	1.3558	Newton-meters
Foot-pounds	0.138255	Meters-kilograms
Inch-pounds	0.11299	Newton-meters
Newton-meters	0.7375622	Foot-pounds
Newton-meters	8.8507	Inch-pounds
Meters-kilograms	7.2330139	Foot-pounds
Volume		
Cubic inches	16.387064	Cubic centimeters
Cubic centimeters	0.0610237	Cubic inches
Temperature		
Fahrenheit	$(F - 32°) \times 0.556$	Centigrade
Centigrade	$(C \times 1.8) + 32$	Fahrenheit
Weight		
Ounces	28.3495	Grams
Pounds	0.4535924	Kilograms
Grams	0.035274	Ounces
Kilograms	2.2046224	Pounds
Pressure		
Pounds per square inch	0.070307	Kilograms per square centimeter
Kilograms per square centimeter	14.223343	Pounds per square inch
Speed		
Miles per hour	1.609344	Kilometers per hour
Kilometers per hour	0.6213712	Miles per hour

Table 6 GENERAL TORQUE SPECIFICATIONS (ft.-lb.)*

Type**	Body Size or Outside Diameter									
	1/4	5/16	3/8	7/16	1/2	9/16	5/8	3/4	7/8	1
SAE 2	6	12	20	32	47	69	96	155	206	310
SAE 5	10	19	33	54	78	114	154	257	382	587
SAE 7	13	25	44	71	110	154	215	360	570	840
SAE 8	14	29	47	78	119	169	230	380	600	700

* Convert ft.-lb. specification to N•m by multiplying by 1.3558.
** Fastener strength of SAE bolts can be determined by the bolt head grade markings. Unmarked bolt heads and cap screws are usually mild steel. More grade markings indicate higher fastener quality.

SAE 2   SAE 5   SAE 7   SAE 8

Table 7 TECHNICAL ABBREVIATIONS

ABDC	After bottom dead center
ATDC	After top dead center
BBDC	Before bottom dead center
BDC	Bottom dead center
BTDC	Before top dead center
C	Celsius (Centigrade)
cc	Cubic centimeters
CDI	Capacitor disharge ignition
cu. in.	Cubic inches
F	Fahrenheit
ft.-lb.	Foot-pounds
gal.	Gallons
hp	Horsepower
in.	Inches
kg	Kilogram
kg/cm^2	Kilograms per square centimeter
kgm	Kilogram meters
km	Kilometer
l	Liter
m	Meter
ml	Milliliter
mm	Millimeter
N•m	Newton-meters
oz.	Ounce
psi	Pounds per square inch
pts.	Pints
qt.	Quarts
rpm	Revolutions per minute

Table 8 METRIC TAP DRILL SIZES

Metric tap (mm)	Drill size	Decimal equivalent	Nearest fraction
3 × 0.50	No. 39	0.0995	3/32
3 × 0.60	3/32	0.0937	3/32
4 × 0.70	No. 30	0.1285	1/8
4 × 0.75	1/8	0.125	1/8
5 × 0.80	No. 19	0.166	11/64
5 × 0.90	No. 20	0.161	5/32
6 × 1.00	No. 9	0.196	13/64
7 × 1.00	16/64	0.234	15/64
8 × 1.00	J	0.277	9/32
8 × 1.25	17/64	0.265	17/64
9 × 1.00	5/16	0.3125	5/16
9 × 1.25	5/16	0.3125	5/16
10 × 1.25	11/32	0.3437	11/32
10 × 1.50	R	0.339	11/32
11 × 1.50	3/8	0.375	3/8
12 × 1.50	13/32	0.406	13/32
12 × 1.75	13/32	0.406	13/32

Table 9 WINDCHILL FACTORS

Estimated wind speed in mph	Actual thermometer reading (°F)											
	50	40	30	20	10	0	−10	−20	−30	−40	−50	−60
	Equivalent temperature (°F)											
Calm	50	40	30	20	10	0	−10	−20	−30	−40	−50	−60
5	48	37	27	16	6	−5	−15	−26	−36	−47	−57	−68
10	40	28	16	4	−9	−21	−33	−46	−58	−70	−83	−95
15	36	22	9	−5	−18	−36	−45	−58	−72	−85	−99	−112
20	32	18	4	−10	−25	−39	−53	−67	−82	−96	−110	−124
25	30	16	0	−15	−29	−44	−59	−74	−88	−104	−118	−133
30	28	13	−2	−18	−33	−48	−63	−79	−94	−109	−125	−140
35	27	11	−4	−20	−35	−49	−67	−82	−98	−113	−129	−145
40 *	26	10	−6	−21	−37	−53	−69	−85	−100	−116	−132	−148
	Little danger (for properly clothed person)			Increasing danger				Great danger				
				• Danger from freezing of exposed flesh •								

*Wind speeds greater than 40 mph have little additional effect.

CHAPTER TWO

TROUBLESHOOTING

Diagnosing mechanical problems is relatively simple if you use orderly procedures and keep a few basic principles in mind. The first step in any troubleshooting procedure is to define the symptoms as closely as possible and then localize the problem. Subsequent steps involve testing and analyzing those areas which could cause the symptoms. A haphazard approach may eventually solve the problem, but it can be very costly in terms of wasted time and unnecessary parts replacement.

Proper lubrication, maintenance and periodic tune-ups as described in Chapter Three will reduce the necessity for troubleshooting. Even with the best of care, however, all vehicles are prone to problems which will require troubleshooting.

Never assume anything. Do not overlook the obvious. If the engine won't start, is the kill switch shorted out? Is the engine flooded with fuel?

If the engine suddenly quits, what sound did it make? Consider this and check the easiest, most accessible problem first. If the engine sounded like it ran out of fuel, check to see if there is fuel in the tank. If there is fuel in the tank, is it reaching the carburetor? If not, the fuel tank vent hose may be plugged, preventing fuel from flowing from the fuel tank to carburetor.

If nothing obvious turns up in a quick check, look a little further. Learning to recognize and describe symptoms will make repairs easier for you or a mechanic at the shop. Describe problems accurately and fully.

Gather as many symptoms as possible to aid in diagnosis. Note whether the engine lost power gradually or all at once, what color smoke came from the exhaust and so on. Remember that the more complicated a machine is, the easier it is to troubleshoot because symptoms point to specific problems.

After the symptoms are defined, areas which could cause problems are tested and analyzed. Guessing at the cause of a problem may provide the solution, but it can easily lead to frustration, wasted time and a series of expensive, unnecessary parts replacements.

You do not need fancy equipment or complicated test gear to determine whether repairs can be attempted at home. A few simple checks could save a large repair bill and lost time while the ATV sits in a dealer's service department. On the other hand, be realistic and do not attempt repairs beyond your abilities. Service departments tend to charge heavily for putting together a disassembled engine that may have been abused. Some won't even take on such a job—so use common sense, don't get in over your head.

OPERATING REQUIREMENTS

An engine needs 3 basics to run properly: correct fuel/air mixture, compression and a spark at the right time (**Figure 1**). If one basic requirement is missing, the engine will not run. Two-stroke engine operating principles are described in Chapter Four under *Engine Principles*.

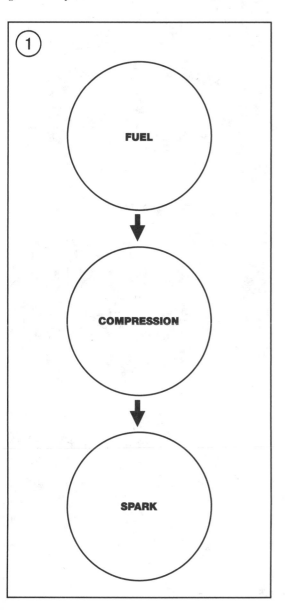

If the ATV has been sitting for any length of time and refuses to start, check and clean the spark plug. If the plug is not fouled, look to the fuel delivery system. This includes the fuel tank, fuel shutoff valve, in-line fuel filter (if used) and fuel line. If the ATV sat for a while with fuel in the carburetor, fuel deposits may have gummed up the fuel inlet valve, carburetor jets and air passages. Gasoline tends to lose its potency after standing for long periods. Condensation may contaminate it with water. Drain the old gas and try starting with a fresh tankful.

TROUBLESHOOTING INSTRUMENTS

Chapter One lists the instruments needed and instruction on their use.

STARTING THE ENGINE

When your engine refuses to start, frustration can cause you to forget basic starting principles and procedures. The following outline will guide you through basic starting procedures. In all cases, make sure that there is an adequate supply of fuel in the tank.

Starting a Cold Engine

1. Shift the transmission into NEUTRAL.
2. Turn the fuel valve on (**Figure 2**).
3. Pull the choke knob out (**Figure 3**).
4. With the throttle completely *closed*, operate the starter button or pull on the starter rope.
5. When the engine starts, work the throttle slightly to keep it running.

6. Idle the engine approximately for a minute or until the throttle responds cleanly and the choke can be closed. The engine should be sufficiently warmed to prevent cold seizure.

Starting a Warm or Hot Engine

1. Shift the transmission into NEUTRAL.
2. Turn the fuel valve on (**Figure 2**).
3. Make sure the choke knob (**Figure 3**) is pushed in.
4. Open the throttle slightly and operate the starter button or pull on the starter rope.

Starting a Flooded Engine

If the engine will not start and there is a strong gasoline smell, the engine may be flooded. If so, open the throttle all the way and operate the starter button or pull on the starter rope. Make sure that choke knob (**Figure 3**) is pushed in. Do *not* pull the choke knob out.

> *NOTE*
> *If the engine refuses to start, check the carburetor overflow hose attached to the fitting at the bottom of the float bowl (**Figure 4**). If fuel is running out of the hose, the float is stuck open, allowing the carburetor to overfill.*

STARTING DIFFICULTIES

When the engine turns over but is difficult to start, or won't start at all, it doesn't help to drain the battery. Check for obvious problems even before getting out your tools. Go down the following list step-by-step. Do each one while remembering the 3 engine operating requirements that were described under *Operating Requirements* earlier in this chapter.

If the engine still will not start, refer to the appropriate troubleshooting procedures which follow in this chapter.

1. Is the choke in the right position? The choke knob should be pulled *out* for a cold engine and pushed *in* for a warm or hot engine (**Figure 3**).
2. Is there fuel in the tank? Fill the tank if necessary. Has it been a while since the engine was run? If in doubt, drain the fuel and fill with a fresh tank full. Check that the fuel tank vent tube (**Figure 5**) is not

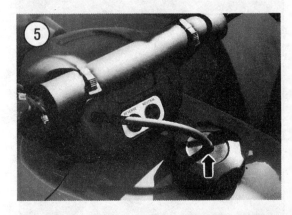

clogged. Remove the tube from the filler cap, wipe off one end and blow through it. Remove the filler cap and check that its hose nozzle is not plugged.

WARNING
Do not use an open flame to check in the tank. A serious explosion is certain to result.

3. Pull off the fuel line at the carburetor and insert the end of the hose into a clear, glass container. Turn the fuel valve on (**Figure 2**) and see if fuel flows freely. If fuel does not flow out and there is a fuel filter installed in the fuel line, remove the filter and turn the fuel valve on again. If fuel flows, the filter is clogged and should be replaced. If no fuel comes out, the fuel valve may be shut off, blocked by foreign matter, or the fuel cap vent may be plugged.

4. If you suspect that the cylinder is flooded, or there is a strong smell of gasoline, open the throttle all the way and operate the starter button or pull the starter rope. If the cylinder is severely flooded (fouled or wet spark plug), remove the plug and dry the base

and electrode thoroughly with a soft cloth. Reinstall the plug and attempt to start the engine.

5. Check the carburetor overflow hose on the bottom of the float bowl (**Figure 4**). If fuel is running out of the hose, the float is stuck open. Turn the fuel valve off and tap the carburetor a few times. Then turn the fuel valve back on. If fuel continues to run out of the hose, remove and service the carburetor as described in Chapter Eight. Check the carburetor vent hoses to make sure they are clear. Check the end of the hoses for contamination.

NOTE
Now that you have determined that fuel is reaching the carburetor, the fuel system could still be the problem. The jets (pilot and main) could be clogged or the air filter could be severely restricted. However, before removing the carburetor, continue with Step 6 to make sure that the ignition provides an adequate spark.

6. Make sure the engine stop switch (**Figure 6**) is not stuck or working improperly or that the wire is broken and shorting out. If necessary, test the engine stop switch as described in Chapter Nine.

NOTE
*If you have installed an aftermarket kill switch like the one shown in **Figure 7**, check the switch for proper operation. This switch may be faulty.*

7. Make sure the spark plug wire is on tight (**Figure 8**) Push it on and slightly rotate it to clean the electrical connection between the plug and the connector. Also check that the high-tension lead ends at the coil and plug cap are pushed in all the way.

NOTE
If the engine will still not start, proceed with the following.

8. Perform a spark test as described under *Engine Fails to Start (Spark Test)* in this chapter. If there is a strong spark, perform Step 9. If there is no spark or if the spark is very weak, test the ignition system as described in this chapter.

NOTE
Now that you have established that the fuel and ignition system are working properly, the one remaining area to check is the mechanical system. Unless

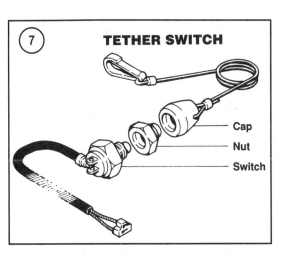

⑦ **TETHER SWITCH**

— Cap
— Nut
— Switch

⑧

the engine seized or there was some other type of mechanical problem, mechanical problems affecting the top end generally occur over a period of time. What you want to do is to isolate the mechanical problem to one of these areas: top end, bottom end, clutch or transmission. The top and bottom end (as they relate to engine compression) will be covered in Step 9. Clutch and transmission problems are covered elsewhere in this chapter.

9. Check cylinder compression as follows:
   a. Turn the fuel valve off.
   b. Remove and ground the spark plug shell against the cylinder head.

CAUTION
The spark plug must be grounded when performing the following steps or the ignition system may be permanently damaged.

   c. Put your finger tightly over the spark plug hole.
   d. If equipped with a manual (rope) starter, have an assistant pull the starter rope. If not equipped with a manual starter, operate the electric starter. When the piston comes up on the compression stroke, pressure in the cylinder should force your finger from the spark plug hole. This indicates that the cylinder probably has sufficient compression to start the engine.

NOTE
You may still have a compression problem even though it seems okay with the previous test. Engine compression can be checked more accurately with a compression gauge as described under **Tune-up** *in Chapter Three.*

ENGINE STARTING TROUBLES

An engine that refuses to start or is difficult to start is very frustrating. More often than not, the problem is very minor and can be found with a simple and logical troubleshooting approach.

The following items show a beginning point from which to isolate engine starting problems.

Engine Fails to Start (Spark Test)

Perform the following spark test to determine if the ignition system is operating properly.

CAUTION
Before removing the spark plug in Step 1, clean all dirt and debris away from the plug base. Dirt that falls into the cylinder will cause rapid piston, piston ring and cylinder wear.

1. Disconnect the plug wire and remove the spark plug (**Figure 8**).
2. Insert the spark plug into its cap and touch the spark plug base against the cylinder head to ground it (**Figure 9**). Position the spark plug so you can see the electrode.

NOTE
If the spark plug appears fouled, use a new spark plug.

3. Turn the engine over with the starter button or pull on the starter rope. A fat blue spark should be evident across the spark plug electrode. If there is strong sunlight on the plug, shade the plug with your hand so that you can see the plug better.

WARNING
Do not hold the spark plug, wire or connector or a serious electrical shock may result.

4. If the spark is good, check for one or more of the following possible malfunctions:

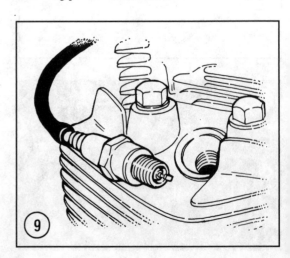
9

a. Obstructed fuel line or fuel filter.

b. Low compression or engine damage.

c. Flooded engine.

5. If the spark is weak or if there is no spark, refer to *Engine is Difficult to Start*.

NOTE
If the engine backfires when you are attempting to start it, the ignition timing may be incorrect. Incorrect ignition timing can be caused by a loose alternator rotor, loose stator coil mounting screws or a faulty ignition component.

ENGINE IS DIFFICULT TO START

The following section groups the 3 main engine operating systems (**Figure 1**) with probable causes.

Electrical System

On off-road vehicles, the electrical system is a common source of engine starting problems. Troubles usually occurs at the wiring harness and connectors.

1. Spark plug—check for:
   a. Incorrect spark plug gap.
   b. Incorrect heat range; see Chapter Three.
   c. Worn or damaged spark plug electrodes.
   d. Damaged spark plug.
   e. Damaged spark plug cap or secondary wire.
2. Ignition coil—check for:
   a. Loose or damaged secondary or primary wire leads.
   b. Cracked ignition coil body (**Figure 10**).
   c. Loose or corroded ground wire.
3. Switches and wiring—check for:

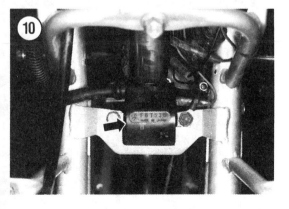

a. Dirty or loose-fitting terminals.

b. Damaged wires or connectors.

c. Damaged start switch.

d. Damaged engine stop switch.

e. Damaged main switch.

f. Damaged neutral switch.

4. Starter motor—check for:
   a. Damaged starter motor.
   b. Damaged starter relay.
   c. Damaged starter circuit cut-off relay.
5. CDI unit—check for:
   a. Damaged source coil.
   b. Damaged pick-up coil.
   c. Damaged crankshaft Woodruff key.
   d. Damaged CDI unit.
6. Discharged or damaged battery.

Fuel System

A fuel system that is contaminated with dirt will cause engine starting and performance related problems. It only takes a small amount of dirt in the fuel valve, fuel line or carburetor to cause problems.

1. Air filter—check for:
   a. Clogged air filter.
   b. Clogged air filter housing.
   c. Damaged air filter housing to carburetor air boot.
2. Fuel valve—check for:
   a. Clogged fuel hose.
   b. Clogged fuel valve.
   c. Damaged fuel valve pickup tubes (installed in fuel tank).
3. Fuel tank—check for:
   a. No fuel.
   b. Clogged fuel filter.
   c. Clogged fuel tank breather hose.
   d. Contaminated fuel.
4. Carburetor—check for:
   a. Clogged or damaged choke.
   b. Clogged starter jet.
   c. Clogged pilot jet.
   d. Loosely installed pilot jet or main jet.
   e. Clogged pilot air passage.
   f. Incorrect float level.
   g. Leaking or otherwise damaged float.
   h. Damaged fuel valve needle and seat.
   i. Severely worn or damaged needle valve.

Engine Compression

Engine compression can be checked with a compression gauge as described in Chapter Three. For a more accurate method of gauging engine wear, an engine leak down test should be performed. Refer to *Engine Leak Down Test* in this chapter.

1. Cylinder and cylinder head—check for:
   a. Loose spark plug.
   b. Missing spark plug gasket.
   c. Leaking cylinder head gasket.
   d. Leaking cylinder base gasket.
   e. Severely worn or seized cylinder.
   f. Incorrectly sealed valve(s).
   g. Worn or damaged valve and valve seat surfaces.
   h. Broken valve spring(s).
   i. Incorrect valve timing.
2. Valve train—check for:
   a. Incorrect valve clearance.
   b. Incorrect valve timing.
   c. Broken valve spring(s).
3. Piston and piston rings—check for:
   a. Worn piston rings.
   b. Damaged piston rings.
   c. Piston seizure or piston damage.
4. Crankcase and crankshaft—check for:
   a. Seized crankshaft.
   b. Damaged crankcases.

POOR IDLE SPEED PERFORMANCE

If the engine starts but off-idle performance is poor (engine hesitation, cutting out, etc.), check the following:

1. Parking brake on, activating engine speed limiter (1992-2002).
2. Clogged or damaged air filter.
3. Carburetor—check for:
   a. Clogged pilot jet.
   b. Loose pilot jet.
   c. Faulty choke plunger.
   d. Incorrect throttle cable adjustment.
   e. Incorrect carburetor adjustment.
   f. Flooded carburetor (visually check carburetor overflow hose for fuel).
4. Incorrectly adjusted valve clearance.
5. Electrical system—check for:
   a. Damaged battery.
   b. Damaged spark plug.
   c. Damaged ignition coil.
   d. Damaged pickup coil.
   e. Damaged CDI unit.

POOR MEDIUM AND HIGH SPEED PERFORMANCE

1. Carburetor—check for:
   a. Incorrect fuel level.
   b. Incorrect jet needle clip position (if adjustable).
   c. Clogged or loose main jet.
2. Clogged air filter.

ENGINE STARTING SYSTEM

This section describes troubleshooting procedures for the electric starting system. A fully charged battery, ohmmeter and jumper cables will be re-

quired to perform many of the troubleshooting procedures.

Description

An electric starter motor (**Figure 11**) is used on all YFM350X models. The starter motor is mounted horizontally to the front of the engine.

The electric starting system requires a fully charged battery to provide the large amount of current required to operate the starter motor. A charge coil (mounted on the stator plate) and a voltage regulator, connected in circuit with the battery, keeps the battery charged while the engine is running. The battery can also be charged externally.

The starting circuit consists of the battery, a stop-start switch, starter solenoid, the starter motor and connecting wiring.

The starter relay carries the heavy electrical current to the motor (**Figure 11**). Depressing the starter switch (**Figure 12**, typical) allows current to flow through the relay coil. The relay contacts close and allow current to flow from the battery through the relay to the starter motor.

> *CAUTION*
> *Do not operate an electric starter motor continuously for more than 5 seconds. Allow the motor to cool for at least 15 seconds between attempts to start the engine.*

Troubleshooting

Before troubleshooting the starting circuit, make sure that:
  a. The battery is fully charged.
  b. Battery cables are the proper size and length. Replace cables that are undersize or damaged.
  c. All electrical connections are clean and tight.
  d. The wiring harness is in good condition, with no worn or frayed insulation or loose harness sockets.
  e. The fuel system is filled with an adequate supply of fresh gasoline.

Starter Troubleshooting (1987)

During this test procedure, after each step is completed, reconnect the electrical connector to the component that was just tested, providing it tested okay. When operating the starter switch, turn the engine stop switch to RUN and the main switch to ON.

If the starter does not operate, perform the following.

1. First check the main fuse. Locate the fuse holder adjacent to the battery (**Figure 13**). Open the fuse holder and pull the fuse out and visually inspect it. If the fuse is blown, refer to *Fuses* in Chapter Nine. If the main fuse is okay, reinstall it, or install a new one, then proceed to the next step.

2. Test the battery specific gravity as described under *Battery* in Chapter Three. Note the following:
  a. If the specific gravity reading is correct, perform Step 3.
  b. If the specific gravity reading is not within the prescribed range, clean and recharge the battery as required. If the battery is damaged, replace it.

> *WARNING*
> *The jumper cable installed in Step 3 must be the same gauge as that of the battery leads or the jumper cable may burn.*

3. Momentarily touch a jumper wire across the starter relay terminals as shown in **Figure 14**. The

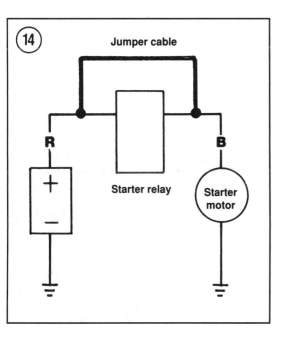
(14) Jumper cable
R
B
Starter relay
Starter motor

starter relay is shown in A, **Figure 15**. Note the following:

    a. If the starter operates by touching the jumper wire, the relay may need to be replaced.

    b. If the starter does not operate by touching the jumper wire, the starter is bad and should be repaired or replaced.

NOTE
*When it is required to operate the starter in the following procedures, turn the main switch to ON and the engine stop switch to RUN (**Figure 6**). Shift the transmission into NEUTRAL and push the starter button. Turn the main switch OFF after performing each test.*

4. After checking operation with jumper wire, note the following:

    a. Starter does not turn: If the battery is fully charged (see Step 3), remove the starter and bench test it as described under *Electric Starter* in Chapter Nine.

    b. Starter turns: Perform Step 5.

5. Disconnect the starter relay red/white and black connector. Then connect 2 jumper wires to the starter relay as shown in **Figure 16**. Operate the starter by momentarily connecting the 2 jumper wires as shown. Note the following:

    a. Starter does not turn: Replace the starter relay as described in Chapter Nine.

    b. Starter turns: Perform Step 6.

6. Locate the CDI unit underneath the rear fender (**Figure 17**). Then disconnect the CDI unit electrical connector. Connect a jumper from the CDI unit electrical connector (wiring harness side) yellow/black terminal and ground (**Figure 18**). Operate the starter. Note the following:

    a. Starter does not turn: Check the starter switch and main switch as described in Chapter Nine. If both switches are okay, replace the starting circuit cut-off relay and retest.

    b. Starter turns: Perform Step 7.

    c. Disconnect the jumper wire.

7. Disconnect the CDI unit electrical connector. Turn the main switch to ON and shift the transmission into NEUTRAL; the NEUTRAL light should come on. Shift the transmission into any gear; the NEUTRAL light should turn off. Note the following:

    a. If the neutral light did not operate properly, check the neutral light indicator bulb and test the neutral and reverse switches as described in Chapter Nine. If these parts are okay, replace the neutral switch relay as described in Chapter Nine.

    b. If the neutral light operated properly, perform Step 8.

8. Disconnect the CDI unit electrical connector. Then connect a jumper wire between the yellow/black CDI unit connector pins and another jumper wire between the black/yellow connector

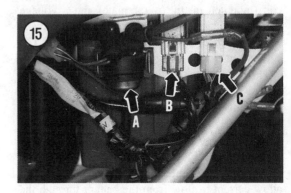

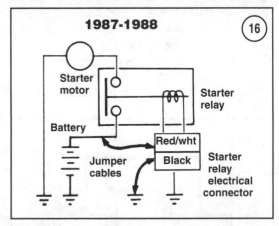

pins. Connect a jumper wire from the white/black connector pin (on the CDI unit side) to ground. See **Figure 19**. Operate the starter. Note the following:

   a. Starter does not turn: Check the engine stop switch as described in Chapter Nine. If the switch is okay, replace the CDI unit and retest.

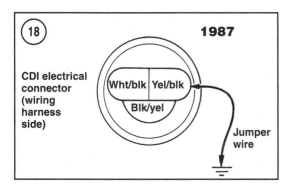

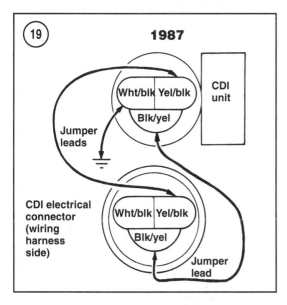

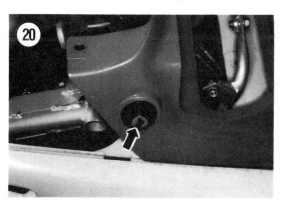

   b. Starter turns: Disconnect the ground jumper lead, pull in the clutch lever and operate the starter. The starter should turn. If not, check the engine stop switch and clutch switch as described in Chapter Nine. If both switches are okay, replace the CDI unit and retest.

9. If you have not located the problem, check the wiring system for dirty or loose-fitting terminals or damaged wires; clean and repair as required. If all of the connectors and wires are in good condition, the CDI unit is probably faulty. Replace the CDI unit and retest.

10. Make sure all connectors disassembled during this procedure are free of corrosion and are reconnected properly.

Starter Troubleshooting (1988-on)

   If the starter does not operate, perform the following.

   During this test procedure, after each step is completed, reconnect the electrical connector to the component that was just tested, providing it tested okay. When operating the starter switch, turn the engine stop switch to RUN and the main switch to ON.

1. First check the main fuse. Locate the fuse holder adjacent to the battery (). Open the fuse holder and pull the fuse out and visually inspect it. If the fuse is blown, refer to *Fuse* in Chapter Nine. If the main fuse is okay, reinstall it, or install a new one, then proceed to the next step.

2. Test the battery specific gravity as described under Battery in Chapter Three. Note the following:

   a. If the specific gravity reading is correct, perform Step 3.

   b. If the specific gravity reading is not within the prescribed range, clean and recharge the battery as required. If the battery is damaged, replace it.

3. Disconnect the main switch (**Figure 20**) electrical connector. Test the main switch as described under *Switches* in Chapter Nine. Note the following:

   a. If the main switch tested correctly, perform Step 4.

   b. If the main switch did not test correctly, the switch is faulty and should be replaced.

4. Disconnect the start switch (**Figure 12**) electrical connectors from the wiring harness. Test the start

switch as described under *Switches* in Chapter Nine. Note the following:

  a. If the start switch tested correctly, perform Step 5.

  b. If the start switch did not test correctly, the switch is faulty and should be replaced.

5. Disconnect the engine stop switch (**Figure 6**) electrical connectors from the wiring harness. Test the engine stop switch as described under *Switches* in Chapter Nine. Note the following:

  a. If the engine stop switch tested correctly, perform Step 6.

  b. If the engine stop switch did not test correctly, the switch is faulty and should be replaced.

6. Disconnect the clutch switch (**Figure 21**) electrical connectors from the wiring harness. Test the clutch switch as described under *Switches* in Chapter Nine. Note the following:

  a. If the clutch switch tested correctly, perform Step 7.

  b. If the clutch switch did not test correctly, the switch is faulty and should be replaced.

WARNING
The jumper cable installed in Step 7 must be the same gauge as that of the battery leads or the jumper cable may burn.

WARNING
Because the test results in Step 7 may cause sparks, perform this test with the vehicle placed away from all flammable fluids, etc.

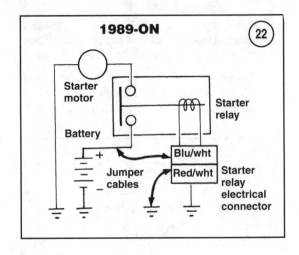

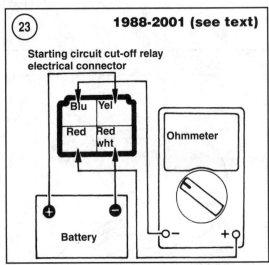

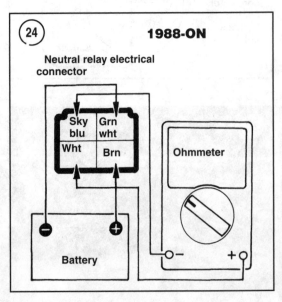

7. Connect a jumper cable between the battery positive cable (+) and the starter motor as shown in **Figure 14**. The starter motor should run when the jumper cable is connected as described. Disconnect the jumper cable. Note the following:

   a. Starter turns: Perform Step 8.

   b. Starter does not turn: Remove and bench test the starter motor as described under *Electric Starter* in Chapter Nine.

8. Disconnect the coupler leading to the starter relay (A, **Figure 15**). Connect jumper wires to the coupler as shown in **Figure 16** (1988 model) or **Figure 22** (1989-on) models. When the second wire is connected, the relay should make an audible click. Disconnect the wires.

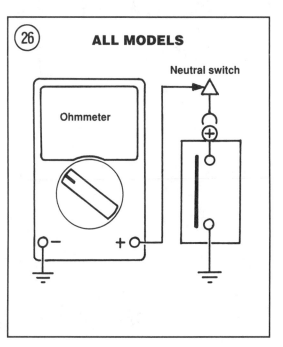

ALL MODELS

Neutral switch

Ohmmeter

a. Starter relay clicks: Perform Step 9.

b. Starter relay does not click: Replace the starter relay as described in Chapter Nine.

c. Reconnect the starter relay connector.

9. For 1988-2001 models only, disconnect the coupler leading to the starting circuit cut-off relay (B, **Figure 15**). Make the connections as shown in **Figure 23**. For 1997-2001 models, brown wires are used in place of the red/white wires shown. The ohmmeter should read continuity (0 ohms). Disconnect the battery and ohmmeter from the coupler. Note the following:

   a. If there is continuity, perform Step 10.

   b. If there is no continuity, starting circuit cut-off relay is faulty and should be replaced as described in Chapter Nine.

   c. Reconnect the starting circuit cut-off relay coupler.

10. Disconnect the neutral relay coupler green/white, brown, white/black and sky blue coupler from the wiring harness. The neutral relay is shown at C, **Figure 15**. Connect a 12-volt battery and ohmmeter to the neutral relay coupler as shown in **Figure 24**. With the battery connected as shown in **Figure 24**, the ohmmeter should read continuity (0 ohms). Disconnect the battery and ohmmeter from the coupler. Note the following:

   a. If there is continuity, perform Step 11.

   b. If there is no continuity, neutral relay is faulty and should be replaced as described in Chapter Nine.

   c. Reconnect the neutral relay coupler.

11. Disconnect the neutral switch electrical connector at the switch (**Figure 25**). Connect an ohmmeter (set on R x 1) between the neutral switch lead and ground as shown in **Figure 26**. With the transmission in NEUTRAL, the ohmmeter should show continuity (0 ohms). With the transmission in gear, the ohmmeter should show infinity. Note the following:

   a. If the meter reading is correct for both tests, perform Step 12.

   b. If the meter reading is incorrect for one or both tests, neutral switch is faulty and should be replaced.

   c. Reconnect the neutral switch wire.

12. Disconnect the lever switch green/white wire from the wiring harness. The lever switch is shown

in **Figure 27**. Connect an ohmmeter (set on R x 1) between the lever switch lead and ground as shown in **Figure 28**. With the lever (**Figure 29**) in the forward position, the ohmmeter should show continuity (to ohms). Note the following:

    a. If the meter reading is correct for both tests, perform Step 13.

    b. If the meter reading is incorrect for one or both tests, reverse lever switch is faulty and should be replaced.

    c. Reconnect the lever switch wire.

13. If you have not found the starting system problem, recheck the wiring system for dirty or loose fitting terminals or damaged wires; clean and repair as required. If all of the connectors and wires are in good condition, the CDI unit (**Figure 17**) is probably faulty. Replace the CDI unit and retest.

14. Make sure all connectors disassembled during this procedure are free of corrosion and are reconnected properly.

CHARGING SYSTEM

A malfunction in the charging system generally causes the battery to remain undercharged.

Troubleshooting

Before testing the charging system, visually check the following.

1. Make sure the battery cables are properly connected. If polarity is reversed, check for a damaged rectifier/regulator.

2. Carefully inspect all working between the battery and stator charge coils for worn or cracked insulation or loose connections. Replace wiring or clean and tighten connections as required.

3. Check battery condition (**Figure 30**). Clean and recharge as required. See Chapter Three.

4. Perform the output test listed under *Charging System* in Chapter Nine.

IGNITION SYSTEM

All models are equipped with a capacitor discharge ignition (CDI) system. This solid state system uses no contact breaker points or other moving parts. Because of the solid state design, problems

within the capacitor discharge system are relatively few. However, when problems arise they stem from one of the following:

    a. Weak spark.

    b. No spark.

    b. No spark.

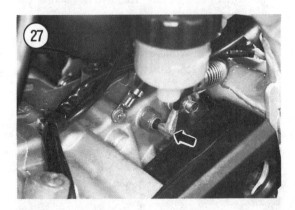

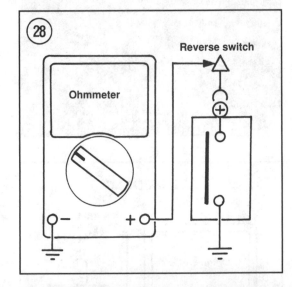

It is possible to check CDI systems that:

a. Do not spark.

b. Have broken or damaged wires.

c. Have a weak spark.

It is difficult to check CDI systems that malfunction due to:

a. Vibration problems.

b. Components that malfunction only when the engine is hot or under a load.

The troubleshooting procedures in **Figure 31** will help you isolate the ignition problem fast.

FUEL SYSTEM

Many riders automatically assume that the carburetor is at fault when the engine does not run properly. While fuel system problems are not uncommon, carburetor adjustment is seldom the answer. In many cases, adjusting the carburetor only compounds the problem by making the engine run worse.

Fuel system troubleshooting should start at the gas tank and work through the system, reserving the carburetor as the final point. Most fuel system problems result from an empty fuel tank, a plugged fuel filter or fuel valve, or sour fuel. Fuel system troubleshooting is covered thoroughly under *Engine Is*

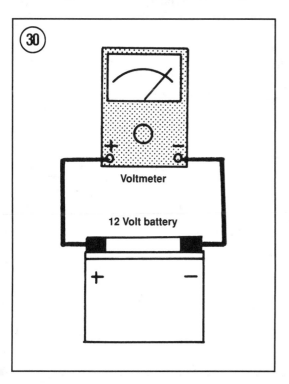

(30)

Voltmeter

12 Volt battery

Difficult To Start, Poor Idle Speed Performance and Poor Medium and *High Speed Performance* in this chapter.

Carburetor chokes can also present problems. A choke that is stuck will show up as a hard starting problem or as a flooding condition. Check the choke operation; push and pull the carburetor choke knob (**Figure 3**). The choke should move freely without binding or sticking in one position. If necessary, disassemble the choke (Chapter Eight) and inspect its plunger and spring for severe wear or damage.

ENGINE OVERHEATING

Engine overheating is a serious problem in that it can quickly cause engine seizure and damage. The following section groups 5 main systems with probable causes that can lead to engine overheating.

1. Ignition system—check for:

   a. Incorrect spark plug gap.

   b. Incorrect heat range; see Chapter Three.

   c. Faulty CDI unit/incorrect ignition timing.

2. Engine compression system—check for:

   a. Cylinder head gasket leakage.

   b. Heavy carbon build-up in combustion chamber.

3. Engine lubrication system—check for:

   a. Incorrect oil level.

   b. Incorrect oil viscosity.

   c. Faulty oil pump.

   d. Plugged oil line.

4. Fuel system—check for:

   a. Clogged air filter element.

   b. Incorrect float level.

   c. Incorrect carburetor adjustment or jetting.

5. Brake and rear axle—check for:

   a. Dragging brake.

   b. Damaged or partially seized rear axle bearings.

ENGINE

Engine troubles generally indicate something wrong in a support system, such as ignition, fuel or starting.

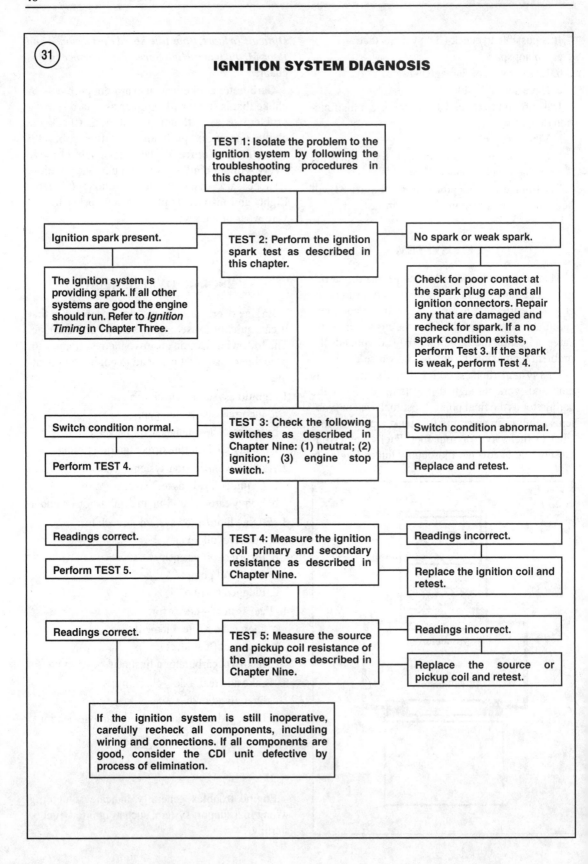

(31)

IGNITION SYSTEM DIAGNOSIS

TEST 1: Isolate the problem to the ignition system by following the troubleshooting procedures in this chapter.

Ignition spark present.

TEST 2: Perform the ignition spark test as described in this chapter.

No spark or weak spark.

The ignition system is providing spark. If all other systems are good the engine should run. Refer to *Ignition Timing* in Chapter Three.

Check for poor contact at the spark plug cap and all ignition connectors. Repair any that are damaged and recheck for spark. If a no spark condition exists, perform Test 3. If the spark is weak, perform Test 4.

Switch condition normal.

TEST 3: Check the following switches as described in Chapter Nine: (1) neutral; (2) ignition; (3) engine stop switch.

Switch condition abnormal.

Perform TEST 4.

Replace and retest.

Readings correct.

TEST 4: Measure the ignition coil primary and secondary resistance as described in Chapter Nine.

Readings incorrect.

Perform TEST 5.

Replace the ignition coil and retest.

Readings correct.

TEST 5: Measure the source and pickup coil resistance of the magneto as described in Chapter Nine.

Readings incorrect.

Replace the source or pickup coil and retest.

If the ignition system is still inoperative, carefully recheck all components, including wiring and connections. If all components are good, consider the CDI unit defective by process of elimination.

Preignition

Preignition is the premature burning of fuel and is caused by hot spots in the combustion chamber. The fuel actually ignites before it is supposed to. Glowing deposits in the combustion chamber, inadequate cooling or an overheated spark plug can all cause preignition. This is first noticed in the form of a power loss but will eventually result in extended damage to the internal parts of the engine because of higher combustion chamber temperatures.

Detonation

Commonly called "spark knock" or "fuel knock," detonation is the violent explosion of fuel in the combustion chamber prior to the proper time of combustion. Severe damage can result. Use of low octane gasoline is a common cause of detonation.

Even when high octane gasoline is used, detonation can still occur if the engine is improperly timed. Other causes are over-advanced ignition timing, lean fuel mixture at or near full throttle, inadequate engine cooling, or the excessive accumulation of deposits on piston and combustion chamber.

Power Loss

Several factors can cause a lack of power and speed. Look for a clogged air filter or a fouled or damaged spark plug. A piston or cylinder that is galled, incorrect piston clearance or worn or sticky piston rings may be responsible. Look for loose bolts, defective gaskets or leaking machined mating surfaces on the cylinder head, cylinder or crankcase.

Piston Seizure

This is caused by incorrect bore clearance, piston rings with an improper end gap, compression leak, incorrect engine oil, spark plug of the wrong heat range, incorrect ignition timing or lubrication system failure. Overheating from any cause may result in piston seizure.

Piston Slap

Piston slap is an audible slapping or rattling noise resulting from excessive piston-to-cylinder clear-ance. When allowed to continue, piston slap will eventually cause the piston skirt to shatter. In some cases, a shattered piston skirt will cause some form of secondary engine damage.

This type of damage can be prevented by measuring the cylinder bore and piston diameter at specified intervals by close visual inspection of all top end components, checking each part for scuff marks, scoring, cracks and other signs of abnormal wear. Replace parts that exceed wear limits or show damage.

ENGINE NOISES

1. *Knocking or pinging during acceleration*—May be caused by using a lower octane fuel than recommended or a poor grade of fuel. Pinging can also be caused by a spark plug of the wrong heat range and incorrect carburetor jetting. Refer to *Correct Spark Plug Heat Range* in Chapter Three. Check also for excessive carbon buildup in the combustion chamber or a faulty CDI unit.

2. *Slapping or rattling noises at low speed or during acceleration*—May be caused by piston slap, i.e., excessive piston-cylinder wall clearance. Check also for a bent connecting rod or worn piston pin and/or piston pin holes in the piston.

3. *Knocking or rapping while decelerating*—Usually caused by excessive rod bearing clearance.

4. *Persistent knocking and vibration or other noise*—Usually caused by worn main bearings. If the main bearings are okay, consider the following:
   a. Loose engine mounts.
   b. Cracked frame.
   c. Leaking cylinder head gasket.
   d. Exhaust pipe leakage at cylinder head.
   e. Stuck piston ring.
   f. Broken piston ring.
   g. Partial engine seizure.
   h. Excessive small end connecting rod bearing clearance.
   i. Excessive big end connecting rod bearing clearance.
   j. Excessive crankshaft runout.
   k. Worn or damaged primary drive gear.

5. *Rapid on-off squeal*—Compression leak around cylinder head gasket or spark plug.

ENGINE LEAK DOWN TEST

An engine leak down test can determine engine problems from leaking valves, blown head gasket or broken, worn or stuck piston rings. A cylinder leakage test is performed by applying compressed air to the cylinder and then measuring the percent of leakage. A cylinder leakage tester and an air compressor are required to perform this test (**Figure 32**).

Follow the manufacturer's directions along with the following information when performing a cylinder leakage test.

1. Start and run the engine until it reaches normal operating temperature. Then turn engine off.
2. Remove the air filter assembly. Open and secure the throttle so that it is at its wide open position.
3. Set the piston for the cylinder being tested to TDC on its compression stroke.
4. Remove the spark plug.

NOTE
The engine may want to turn over when air pressure is applied to the cylinder. To prevent this from happening, shift the transmission into fifth gear and set the parking brake.

5. Make a cylinder leakage test following the manufacturer's instructions. Listen for air leaking while noting the following:

a. Air leaking through the exhaust pipe points to a leaking exhaust valve.
b. Air leaking through the carburetor points to a leaking intake valve.
c. Air leaking through the crankcase breather tube indicates worn piston rings.
6. Any cylinder with 10% cylinder leakdown requires further service.

CLUTCH

The 2 basic clutch troubles are:
a. Clutch slipping.
b. Clutch dragging.

All clutch troubles, except adjustments, require partial engine disassembly to identify and cure the problem. Refer to Chapter Six for procedures.

Clutch Slipping

1. Clutch wear or damage—check the following:
a. Weak or damaged clutch springs.
b. Worn friction plates.
c. Warped steel plates.
d. Loose clutch springs.
e. Incorrectly assembled clutch.
f. Incorrect clutch adjustment.
2. Engine oil—check for the following:

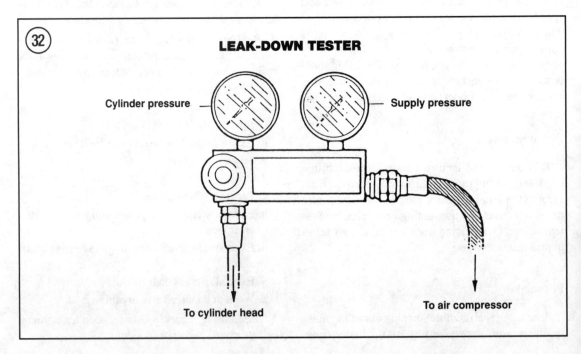

LEAK-DOWN TESTER

Cylinder pressure — Supply pressure

To cylinder head   To air compressor

a. Low oil level.
b. Oil additives.
c. Low viscosity oil.

Clutch Dragging

1. Clutch wear or damage—check the following:
   a. Warped steel plates.
   b. Swollen friction plates.
   c. Warped pressure plate.
   d. Incorrect clutch spring tension.
   e. Incorrectly assembled clutch.
   f. Loose clutch nut.
   g. Burned primary driven gear bushing.
   h. Damaged clutch boss.
   i. Incorrect clutch adjustment.
2. Engine oil—check for the following:
   a. Oil level too high.
   b. High viscosity oil.

TRANSMISSION

The basic transmission troubles are:
   a. Difficult shifting.
   b. Gears pop out of mesh.
Transmission symptoms are sometimes hard to distinguish from clutch symptoms. Be sure that the clutch is not causing the trouble before working on the transmission.

Difficult Shifting

If the shift shaft does not move smoothly from one gear to the next, check the following.
1. Shift shaft—check the following:
   a. Incorrectly installed shift lever.
   b. Stripped shift lever-to-shift shaft splines.
   c. Bent shift shaft.
   d. Damaged shift shaft return spring.
   e. Damaged shift shaft where it engages the shift drum.
2. Stopper lever—check the following:
   a. Seized or damaged stopper lever roller.
   b. Broken stopper lever mounting bolt.
3. Shift drum and shift forks—check the following:
   a. Bent shift fork(s).
   b. Damaged shift fork guide pin(s).
   c. Seized shift fork (on shaft)
   d. Broken shift fork or shift fork shaft.
   e. Damaged shift drum groove(s).

f. Damaged shift drum bearing.

Gears Slip out of Mesh

If the transmission shifts into gear but then slips out, check the following.
1. Shift shaft—check the following:
   a. Incorrect shift lever position/adjustment.
   b. Stopper lever fails to move or set properly.
2. Shift drum—check the following:
   a. Incorrect thrust play.
   b. Severely worn or damaged shift drum groove(s).
3. Shift forks may be bent.
4. Transmission—check the following:
   a. Worn or damaged gear dogs.
   b. Excessive gear thrust play.
   c. Worn or damaged shaft circlips or thrust washers.

Inoperative Reverse

If the transmission fails to go into or operate in reverse properly, check the following:
1. Reverse lever—check the following:
   a. Incorrect reverse lever adjustment.
   b. Stripped reverse lever-to-reverse shift drum splines.
2. Reverse axle—check the following:
   a. Damaged reverse axle pinion gear thrust play.
   b. Excessive reverse axle pinion gear play.
3. Counter axle—check for damaged counter axle gear bearings or shaft.
   4. Reverse shift drum and fork—check the following:
   a. Damaged reverse shift drum groove.
   b. Bent reverse shift fork.

DRIVE TRAIN NOISE

This section deals with noises that are restricted to the drive train assembly—drive chain, clutch and transmission. While some drive train noises are normal, abnormal noises are a good indicator of a developing problem. The problem is recognizing the difference between normal and abnormal noises. One thing that is in your favor, however, is that by maintaining and riding your Yamaha, you become accustomed to the normal noises that occur during engine starting and when riding. A new noise, no matter how minor, should be investigated.

1. *Drive chain noise*—Normal drive chain noise can be considered a low-pitched, continuous whining sound. The noise will vary, depending on the speed of the vehicle and the terrain you are riding on, as well as proper lubrication, wear (both chain and sprocket) and alignment. When checking abnormal drive chain noise, consider the following:

    a. Inadequate lubrication—A dry chain will give off a loud whining sound. Clean and lubricate the drive chain at regular intervals; see Chapter Eleven.

    b. Incorrect chain adjustment—Check and adjust the drive chain as described in Chapter Three.

    c. Worn chain—Chain wear should be checked at regular intervals, and replaced when its overall length exceeds the wear limit specified in Chapter Three.

    d. Worn or damaged sprockets—Worn or damaged sprockets will accelerate chain wear. Inspect the sprockets carefully as described in Chapter Three.

    e. Worn, damaged or missing drive chain rollers—Chain rollers are in constant contact with the chain. They should be checked often for loose, damaged or missing parts. A missing chain roller will increase chain slack and may cause rapid wear against the frame or swing arm.

    f. Worn swing arm/chain protector—A damaged or worn through protector will allow the chain to act much like a chain saw and grind away at the swing arm or frame. Chain wear will also increase rapidly. A new, regular clicking or grinding noise may point to a worn through protector. Inspect the protector(s) regularly. Replace worn protectors before the chain wears through and causes expensive secondary damage.

2. *Clutch noise*—Any noise that develops in the clutch should be investigated. First, drain the clutch/transmission oil, checking for bits of metal or clutch plate material. If the oil looks and smells okay, remove the clutch cover and clutch (Chapter Six) and check for the following:

    a. Worn or damaged clutch housing gear teeth.

    b. Excessive clutch housing axial play.

    c. Excessive clutch housing-to-friction plate clearance.

    d. Excessive clutch housing gear-to-primary drive gear backlash.

3. *Transmission noise*—The transmission will exhibit more normal noises than the clutch, but like the clutch, a new noise in the transmission should be investigated. Drain the clutch/transmission oil into a clean container. Wipe a small amount of oil on a finger and rub the finger and thumb together. Check for the presence of metallic particles. Inspect the drain container for signs of water separation from the oil. Some transmission-associated noises are caused by:

    a. Insufficient transmission oil level.

    b. Contaminated transmission oil.

    c. Transmission oil viscosity too thin. A too thin "oil viscosity" will raise the transmission operating temperature.

    d. Worn transmission gear(s).

    e. Chipped or broken transmission gear(s).

    f. Excessive gear side play.

    g. Worn or damaged crankshaft-to-transmission bearing(s).

NOTE
If metallic particles are found in Step 2 or Step 3, remove and inspect the clutch, then, if necessary, remove and inspect the transmission.

HANDLING

Poor handling will reduce overall performance and may cause you to crash. If you are experiencing poor handling, check the following items:

1. *Handlebars*—check the following:

    a. Loose or damaged handlebar clamps.

    b. Incorrect handlebar clamp installation.

    c. Bent or cracked handlebar.

2. *Tires*—check the following:

    a. Incorrect tire pressure.

    b. Uneven tire pressure (both sides).

    c. Worn or damaged tires.

3. *Wheels*—check the following:

    a. Loose or damaged hub bearings.

    b. Loose or bent wheel axle.

    c. Damaged wheel.

    d. Loose wheel nuts.

    e. Excessive wheel runout.

4. *Steering*—check the following:
   a. Incorrect toe-in adjustment.
   b. Damaged steering shaft.
   c. Damaged steering shaft bushing or bearing(s).
   d. Incorrectly installed steering shaft.
   e. Bent tie-rods.
   f. Damaged steering knuckles.
   g. Bent upper and/or lower arm(s).
5. *Swing arm*—check the following:
   a. Damaged swing arm.
   b. Severely worn or damaged swing arm bearings.
   c. Improperly tightened swing arm pivot shaft.
   d. Damaged axle bearing housing.
   e. Damaged relay arm and/or connecting rod.
   f. Severely worn or damaged relay arm and/or connecting rod.
6. *Rear axle*—check the following:
   a. Loose rear axle mounting bolts.
   b. Seized or otherwise damaged rear axle bearings.
   c. Bent rear axle.
   d. Loose or damaged rear axle bearing housing.
7. *Shock absorber(s)*—check the following:
   a. Damaged damper rod.
   b. Leaking damper housing.
   c. Sagged shock spring(s).
   d. Incorrect shock adjustment.
   e. Loose or damaged shock mount bolts.
8. *Frame*—check the following:
   a. Damaged frame.
   b. Cracked or broken engine mount brackets.

FRAME NOISE

Noises that can be traced to the frame or suspension are usually caused by loose, worn or damaged parts. Various noises that are related to the frame are listed below:

1. *Disc brake noise*—A screeching sound during braking is the most common disc brake noise. Some other disc brake associated noises can be caused by:
   a. Glazed brake pad surface.
   b. Severely worn brake pads.
   c. Warped brake disc.
   d. Loose brake disc mounting bolts.
   e. Loose or missing caliper mounting bolts.
   f. Damaged caliper.
2. *Rear shock absorber noise*—Check for the following:
   a. Loose shock absorber mounting bolts.
   b. Cracked or broken shock spring.
   c. Damaged shock absorber.
3. Some other frame associated noises are caused by:
   a. Broken frame.
   b. Broken swing arm.
   c. Loose engine mounting bolts.
   d. Damaged steering bearing.
   e. Loose mounting bracket(s).

BRAKES

The front and rear disc brake units are critical to riding performance and safety. The brakes should be inspected frequently and any problems located and repaired immediately. When replacing or refilling the brake fluid, use only DOT 4 brake fluid from a closed and sealed container. See Chapter Twelve for additional information on brake fluid and disc brake service. The troubleshooting procedures in **Figure 33** will help you isolate the majority of disc brake troubles.

When checking brake pad wear, check that the brake pads in each caliper contact the disc squarely. If one of the brake pads is wearing unevenly, suspect a warped or bent brake disc or damaged caliper.

Figure 33 is on page 52.

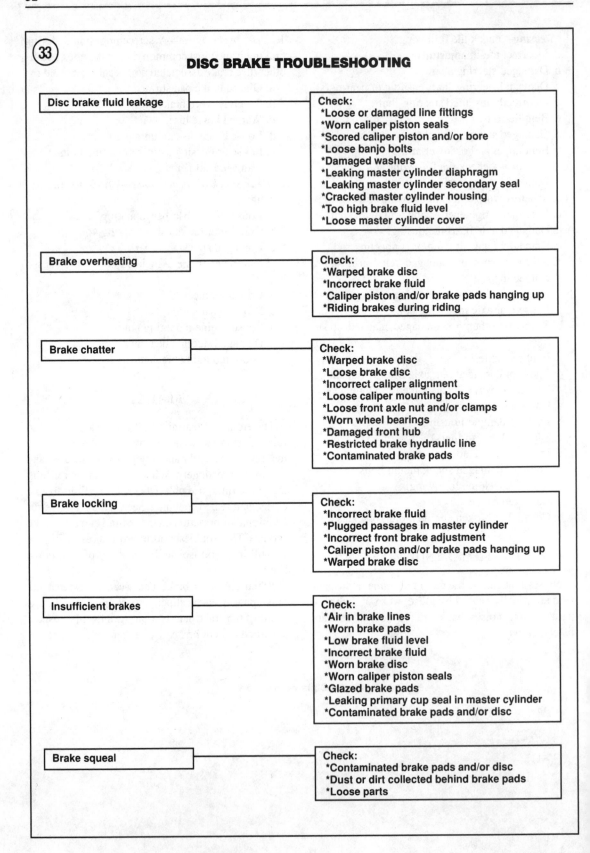

33 **DISC BRAKE TROUBLESHOOTING**

Disc brake fluid leakage

Check:
*Loose or damaged line fittings
*Worn caliper piston seals
*Scored caliper piston and/or bore
*Loose banjo bolts
*Damaged washers
*Leaking master cylinder diaphragm
*Leaking master cylinder secondary seal
*Cracked master cylinder housing
*Too high brake fluid level
*Loose master cylinder cover

Brake overheating

Check:
*Warped brake disc
*Incorrect brake fluid
*Caliper piston and/or brake pads hanging up
*Riding brakes during riding

Brake chatter

Check:
*Warped brake disc
*Loose brake disc
*Incorrect caliper alignment
*Loose caliper mounting bolts
*Loose front axle nut and/or clamps
*Worn wheel bearings
*Damaged front hub
*Restricted brake hydraulic line
*Contaminated brake pads

Brake locking

Check:
*Incorrect brake fluid
*Plugged passages in master cylinder
*Incorrect front brake adjustment
*Caliper piston and/or brake pads hanging up
*Warped brake disc

Insufficient brakes

Check:
*Air in brake lines
*Worn brake pads
*Low brake fluid level
*Incorrect brake fluid
*Worn brake disc
*Worn caliper piston seals
*Glazed brake pads
*Leaking primary cup seal in master cylinder
*Contaminated brake pads and/or disc

Brake squeal

Check:
*Contaminated brake pads and/or disc
*Dust or dirt collected behind brake pads
*Loose parts

3

LUBRICATION, MAINTENANCE
AND TUNE-UP

Your Yamaha requires periodic maintenance so that it can operate efficiently without breaking down. This chapter covers all of the regular maintenance required to keep your Yamaha in top shape. Regular maintenance is something you can not afford to ignore. Neglecting regular maintenance will reduce the engine life and performance of your Yamaha.

This chapter explains lubrication, maintenance and tune-up procedures required for the models described in this manual. **Table 1** is a suggested maintenance schedule. **Tables 1-11** are at the end of the chapter.

NOTE
Due to the number of models and years covered in this book, be sure to follow the correct procedure and specifications for your specific model and year. Also use the correct quantity and type of fluid as indicated in the tables.

PRE-RIDE CHECKLIST

The following checks should be performed prior to the first ride of the day.

1. Inspect all fuel lines and fittings for wetness.

2. Make sure the fuel tank is full of fresh gasoline.
3. Make sure the engine oil level is correct; add oil if necessary.
4. Make sure the air filter is clean.
5. Check the operation of the clutch and adjust if necessary.
6. Check the throttle and the brake levers. Make sure they operate properly with no binding.
7. Check the brake fluid level in the front and rear master cylinder reservoirs; add fluid if necessary.
8. Inspect the front and rear suspension; make sure it has a good solid feel with no looseness.
9. Check chain adjustment and adjust if necessary.
10. Check tire pressure, refer to **Table 2**.
11. Check the exhaust system for damage.
12. Check the tightness of all fasteners, especially engine mounting hardware.
13. Make sure the headlights and taillight work.

SERVICE INTERVALS

The services and intervals shown in **Table 1** are recommended by the factory. Strict adherence to these recommendations will insure long service from your Yamaha. However, if the vehicle is run in an area of high humidity the lubrication and services must be done more frequently to prevent possible rust damage. This is especially true if you have run the Yamaha through water (especially salt water) and sand.

For convenience when maintaining your vehicle, most of the services shown in **Table 1** are described in this chapter. However, some procedures which require more than minor disassembly or adjustment are covered elsewhere in the appropriate chapter.

TIRES AND WHEELS

Tire Pressure

Tire pressure should be checked and adjusted to maintain the smoothness of the tire, good traction and handling and to get the maximum life out of the tire. An accurate low pressure gauge (**Figure 1**) can be purchased for a few dollars and should be carried in your tool box. The appropriate tire pressures are listed in **Table 2**.

NOTE
The tire pressure specifications listed in ***Table 2*** *are for the stock tires that originally come equipped on your Yamaha. If you have installed different tires, follow the tire pressure recommendations specified by the tire manufacturer.*

WARNING
Always inflate both rear tires to the same pressure. If the vehicle is run with unequal air pressures, it will cause the vehicle to always run toward one side and cause poor handling.

CAUTION
Do not overinflate the stock tires as they will be permanently distorted and damaged. If overinflated, they will bulge out similar to inflating an inner tube that is not within the constraints of a tire. If this happens, the tire ***will not*** *return to its original contour.*

Tire Inspection

The tires take a lot of punishment due to the variety of terrain they are subject to. Inspect them periodically for excessive wear, cuts, abrasions, etc. If you find a nail or other object in the tire, mark its

location with a light crayon prior to removing it. This will help locate the hole for repair. Refer to Chapter Ten for tire changing and repair information.

Measure tire wear with a ruler as shown in **Figure 2**. To obtain an accurate measurement of tire wear, measure a number of different knobs around the tire. The maximum tire wear limit for stock front and rear tires is 3.0 mm (0.12 in.). If your measurements determine that a tire is worn out, replace it as described in Chapter Ten.

WARNING
Do not ride your vehicle with worn out tires. Worn out tires can cause you to lose control. Replace worn out tires immediately.

Rim Inspection

Frequently inspect the condition of the wheel rims, especially the outer side (**Figure 3**). If the wheel has hit a tree or large rock, rim damage may be sufficient to cause an air leak or knock it out of alignment. Improper wheel alignment can cause se-

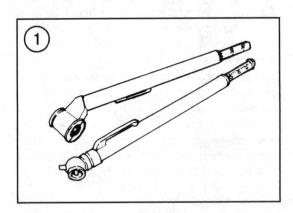

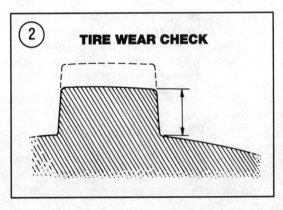

TIRE WEAR CHECK

vere vibration and result in an unsafe riding condition.

Make sure the 4 lug nuts (**Figure 3**) are securely in place on all wheels. If they are loose or lost—it's good-bye wheel. Tighten lug nuts to the torque specification listed in **Table 3**.

BATTERY

The battery is an important component in the ATV electrical system, yet most electrical system troubles can be traced to battery neglect. In addition to checking and correcting the battery electrolyte level on a weekly basis, the battery should be cleaned and inspected at periodic intervals. Battery capacity is listed in **Table 4**.

NOTE
*Recycle your old battery. When you replace the old battery, be sure to turn in the old battery at that time. The lead plates and the plastic case can be recycled. Most ATV dealers will accept your old battery in trade when you purchase a new one. **Never** place an old battery in your household trash since it is illegal, in most states, to place any acid or lead (heavy metal) contents in landfills. There is also the danger of the battery being crushed in the trash truck and spraying acid on the truck or landfill operator.*

Safety Precautions

When working with batteries, use extreme care to avoid spilling or splashing the electrolyte. This solution contains sulfuric acid, which can ruin clothing

and cause serious chemical burns. If any electrolyte is spilled or splashed on clothing or skin, immediately neutralize with a solution of baking soda and water, then flush with an abundance of clean water.

WARNING
Electrolyte splashed into the eyes is extremely harmful. Safety glasses should always be worn while working with batteries. If you get electrolyte in your eyes, call a physician immediately and force your eyes open and flood them with cool, clean water for approximately 15 minutes or until medical help arrives.

If electrolyte is spilled or splashed onto any surface, it should be immediately neutralized with baking soda and water solution and then rinsed with clean water.

While batteries are being charged, highly explosive hydrogen gas forms in each cell. Some of this gas escapes through filler cap openings and may form an explosive atmosphere in and around the battery. This condition can persist for several hours. Sparks, an open flame or a lighted cigarette can ignite the gas, causing an explosion and possible serious personal injury.

Take the following precautions to prevent an explosion:

1. Do not smoke or permit any open flame near any battery being charged or which has been recently charged.

2. Do not disconnect live circuits at battery terminals since a spark usually occurs when a live circuit is broken.

3. Take care when connecting or disconnecting any battery charger. Be sure its power switch is off before making or breaking connections. Poor connections are a common cause of electrical arcs which cause explosions.

4. Keep children and pets away from charging equipment and batteries.

For maximum battery life, it should be checked periodically for electrolyte level, state of charge and corrosion. During hot weather periods, frequent checks are recommended. If the electrolyte level is below the bottom of the vent well in one or more cells, add distilled water as required. To assure proper mixing of the water and acid, operate the engine immediately after adding water. *Never* add battery acid instead of water—this will shorten the battery's life.

On all models covered in this manual, the negative side is grounded. When removing the battery, disconnect the negative (–) cable first, then the positive (+) cable. This minimizes the chance of a tool shorting to ground when disconnecting the "hot" positive cable.

> *WARNING*
> *When performing the following procedures, protect your eyes, skin and clothing. If electrolyte gets into your eyes, flush your eyes thoroughly with clean water and get prompt medical attention.*

Battery Removal

The battery is mounted underneath the seat. A hold-down strap, placed across the battery, and rubber pads mounted inside the battery box, hold the battery in place.

1. Remove the seat.

2. Disconnect the negative battery cable from the battery (A, **Figure 4**).

3. Disconnect the positive battery cable from the battery (B, **Figure 4**).

4. Disconnect the battery hold down strap (C, **Figure 4**). Then lift the battery slightly and disconnect the battery vent tube at the battery (**Figure 5**) and remove the battery.

> *CAUTION*
> *Be careful not to spill battery electrolyte on painted or polished surfaces. The liquid is highly corrosive and will damage the finish. If it is spilled, wash it off immediately with soapy water and thoroughly rinse with clean water.*

Cleaning and Inspection

1. Inspect the battery pads in the battery box (**Figure 6**) for contamination or damage. Clean with a solution of baking soda and water.

2. Check the entire battery case (**Figure 7**) for cracks or other damage. If the battery case is warped, discolored or has a raised top, the battery has been suffering from overcharging or overheating.

3. Check the battery hold-down strap for acid damage, cracks or other damage. Replace strap if required.

4. Check the battery terminal parts—bolts, spacers and nuts—for corrosion or damage. Clean parts thoroughly with a solution of baking soda and water. Replace severely corroded or damaged parts.

> *NOTE*
> *Keep cleaning solution out of the battery cells or the electrolyte level will be seriously weakened.*

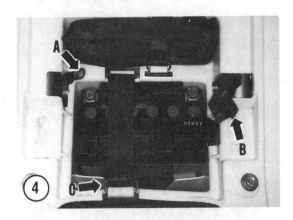

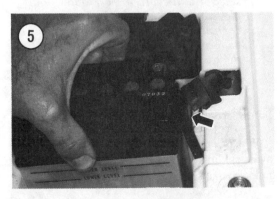

5. Clean the top of the battery with a stiff bristle brush using the baking soda and water solution.

6. Check the battery cable clamps for corrosion and damage. If corrosion is minor, clean the battery cable clamps with a stiff wire brush. Replace severely worn or damaged cables.

NOTE
Do not overfill the battery cells in Step 7. The electrolyte expands due to heat from charging and will overflow if the level is above the upper level line.

7. Remove the caps (**Figure 8**) from the battery cells and check the electrolyte level. Add distilled water, if necessary, to bring the level within the upper and lower level lines on the battery case (**Figure 7**).

Battery Installation

1. Reinstall the battery into the battery compartment with the terminals facing as shown in **Figure 4**. Make sure the rubber pads are installed in the battery box prior to installing the battery.
2. Reconnect the battery vent tube to the battery (**Figure 5**) while sliding the battery into position.

NOTE
*If the battery vent tube was removed from the ATV, refer to **Battery Vent Tube Routing** in this chapter.*

WARNING
After installing the battery, make sure the vent tube is not pinched. A pinched or kinked tube would allow high pressure to accumulate in the battery and cause the battery to explode. If the vent tube is damaged, replace it.

3. Install and tighten the positive battery cable (B, **Figure 4**).
4. Install and tighten the negative battery cable (A, **Figure 4**).

CAUTION
Be sure the battery cables are connected to their proper terminals. Connecting the battery backwards will reverse the polarity and damage the rectifier.

5. Coat the battery connections with dielectric grease or petroleum jelly.
6. Install the battery hold-down strap across the top of the battery (C, **Figure 4**).
7. Install the seat.

Battery Vent Tube Routing

The battery vent tube must be routed properly and not touch any moving parts. Proper routing will ensure that vent hose outlet is positioned away from all metal components. Replace the vent tube if it becomes kinked or plugged.

Testing

Hydrometer testing is the best way to check battery condition. Use a hydrometer with numbered graduations from 1.100 to 1.300 rather than one with just color-coded bands. To use the hydrometer, squeeze the rubber ball, insert the tip into the cell and release the ball (**Figure 9**).

> *NOTE*
> *Do not attempt to test a battery with a hydrometer immediately after adding water to the cells. Charge the battery for 15-20 minutes at a rate high enough to cause vigorous gassing and allow the water and electrolyte to mix thoroughly.*

Draw enough electrolyte to float the weighted float inside the hydrometer. When using a temperature-compensated hydrometer, release the electrolyte and repeat this process several times to make sure the thermometer has adjusted to the electrolyte temperature before taking the reading.

Hold the hydrometer vertically and note the number in line with the surface of the electrolyte (**Figure 10**). This is the specific gravity for this cell. Return the electrolyte to the cell from which it came.

The specific gravity of the electrolyte in each battery cell is an excellent indication of that cell's condition (**Table 5**). A fully charged cell will read 1.260-1.280 while a cell in good condition reads from 1.230-1.250 and anything below 1.140 is dead. Charging is also necessary if the specific gravity varies more than 0.050 from cell to cell.

> *NOTE*
> *If a temperature-compensated hydrometer is not used, add 0.004 to the specific gravity reading for every 10° above 80° F (25° C). For every 10° below 80° F (25° C), subtract 0.004.*

Charging

A good state of charge should be maintained in batteries used for starting. When charging the battery, note the following:

a. During charging, the cells will show signs of gas bubbling. If one cell has no gas bubbles or if its specific gravity is low, the cell is probably shorted.

b. If a battery not in use loses its charge within a week after charging or if the specific gravity drops quickly, the battery is defective. A good battery should only self-discharge approximately 1% each day.

> *CAUTION*
> *Always remove the battery from the vehicle before connecting charging equipment.*

> *WARNING*
> *During charging, highly explosive hydrogen gas is released from the battery. The battery should be charged only in a well-ventilated area, and open flames*

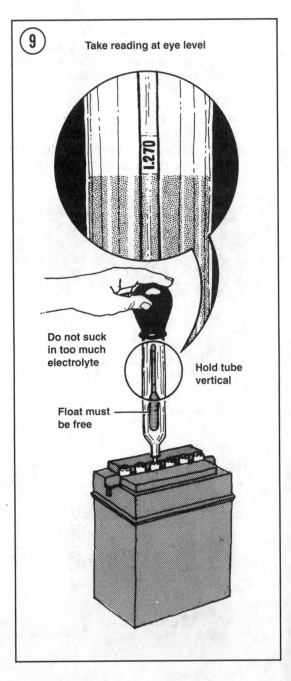

9

Take reading at eye level

1.270

Do not suck in too much electrolyte

Hold tube vertical

Float must be free

and cigarettes should be kept away. Never check the charge of the battery by arcing across the terminals; the resulting spark can ignite the hydrogen gas.

1. Remove the battery from the vehicle as described in this chapter.

2. Connect the positive (+) charger lead to the positive battery terminal and the negative (–) charger lead to the negati e battery terminal.

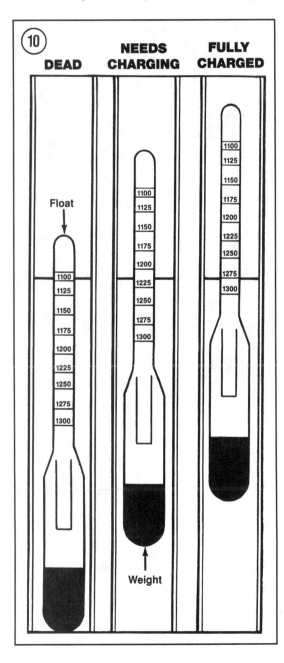

3. Remove all vent caps (**Figure 8**) from the battery, set the charger at 12 volts, and switch it on. Normally, a battery should be charged at a slow charge rate of 1/10 its given capacity. The standard charging time is 1.2 amps at 10 hours.

CAUTION
The electrolyte level must be maintained at the upper level during the charging cycle; check and refill with distilled water as necessary.

4. The charging time depends on the discharged condition of the battery. The chart in **Figure 11** can be used to determine approximate charging times at different specific gravity readings. For example, if the specific gravity of your battery is 1.180, the approximate charging time would be 6 hours.

5. After the battery has been charged for the pre-determined time, turn the charger off, disconnect the leads and check the specific gravity. It should be within the limits specified in **Table 5**. If it is, and remains stable for one hour, the battery is charged.

New Battery Installation

When replacing the old battery with a new one, be sure to charge it completely (specific gravity, 1.260-1.280) before installing it. Failure to do so, or using the battery with a low electrolyte level will permanently damage the battery.

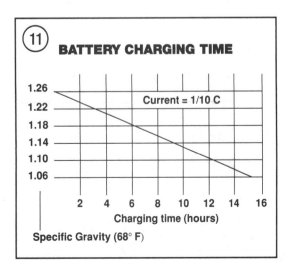

LUBRICANTS

Engine Oil

Oil is graded according to its viscosity, which is an indication of how thick it is. The Society of Automotive Engineers (SAE) system distinguishes oil viscosity by numbers, called "weights." Thick (heavy) oils have higher viscosity numbers than thin (light) oils. For example, a 5 weight (SAE 5) oil is a light oil while a 90 weight (SAE 90) oil is relatively heavy. The viscosity of the oil has nothing to do with its lubricating properties.

Grease

A good quality grease—preferably waterproof—should be used when grease is called for. Water does not wash grease off parts as easily as it washes off oil. In addition, grease maintains its lubricating qualities better than oil on long and strenuous events.

CLEANING SOLVENT

A number of solvents can be used to remove old dirt, grease, and oil. See your dealer or an auto parts store.

> *WARNING*
> *Never use gasoline as a cleaning solvent. Gasoline is extremely volatile and contains tremendously destructive potential energy. The slightest spark from metal parts hitting each other, or a tool slipping, could cause a fatal explosion.*

PERIODIC LUBRICATION

Engine Oil Level Check

Engine oil level is checked with the dipstick/oil fill cap, located on the front of the clutch cover.

1. Start the engine and let it warm up approximately 2-3 minutes.
2. Place the vehicle on level ground and apply the parking brake.

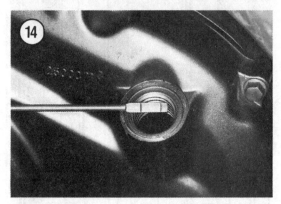

3. Shut off the engine and let the oil settle.

4. Unscrew the dipstick/oil fill cap (**Figure 12**) and wipe it clean. Reinsert it onto the hole; do not screw it in (**Figure 13**). Remove it and check the oil level. The vehicle must be level for a correct reading.

5. The level should be between the 2 lines and not above the upper one (**Figure 14**). If necessary, add the recommended type oil to correct te level. Install the dipstick/oil fill cap and tighten it securely.

Engine Oil and Filter Change

Regular oil changes will contribute more to engine longevity than any other maintenance performed. The factory recommended oil and filter change is listed in **Table 1**. This assumes that the vehicle is operated in moderate climates. If it is operated under dusty conditions, the oil will get dirty more quickly and should be changed more frequently than recommended.

Use only a high quality detergent motor oil with an API classification of SG. The API classification is on the container label (**Figure 15**). Try to use the same brand of oil at each oil change. Refer to Figure 16 for correct oil weight to use under anticipated ambient temperatures (not engine oil temperature).

To change the engine oil and filter you will need the following:

    a. Drain pan.
    b. Funnel.
    c. Can opener or pour spout.
    d. Wrench and sockets.
    e. 3 quarts of oil.
    f. New oil filter.

There are a number of ways to discard the old oil safely. Some service stations and oil retailers will accept your used oil for recycling; some may even give you money for it. Never drain the oil onto the ground.

> *NOTE*
> *Never dispose of motor oil in the trash or pour it on the ground, or down a storm drain. Many service stations accept used motor oil. Many waste haulers provide curbside used motor oil collection. Do not combine other fluids with motor oil to be recycled. To find a recycling location contact the American Petroleum Institute (API) at* ***www. recycleoil.org.***

> *NOTE*
> *Warming the engine allows the oil to heat up; thus it flows freely and carries contamination and any sludge buildup out with it.*

1. Start the engine and let it warm up approximately 2-3 minutes.

2. Place the vehicle on level ground and apply the parking brake.

3. Shut it off and place a drain pan under the engine.

4. Remove the skid plate.

5. Loosen the drain plug (**Figure 17**) mounted in the bottom of the engine. Then remove the drain plug, oil strainer, spring and O-ring (**Figure 17**).

6. Remove the dipstick/oil fill cap, this will speed up the flow of oil.

7. Allow the oil to drain for at least 15-20 minutes.

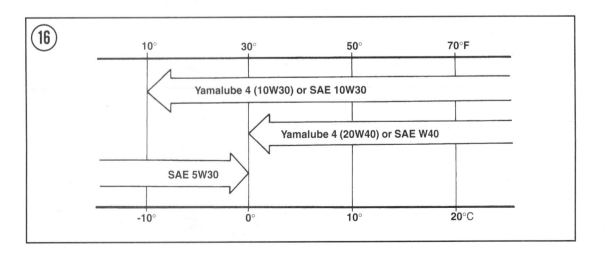

8. To replace the oil filter, perform the following:

a. Remove the bolts securing the filter cover on the left-hand crankcase cover and remove the filter cover (**Figure 18**). Do not lose the O-ring (**Figure 19**) installed in the filter cover.

b. Remove the oil filter (**Figure 20**) from the filter receptacle in the left-hand crankcase.

c. Thoroughly clean out the filter receptacle (A, **Figure 21**) in the left-hand crankcase. If necessary, scrape out any oil sludge.

d. Inspect the O-ring seal (**Figure 19**) on the filter cover. Replace if it has become hard or is starting to deteriorate.

Prior to installation, apply a lithium soap base grease to the O-ring.

CAUTION
If the oil filter is installed backwards, oil flow will be restricted, leading to costly engine damage.

e. Install the new oil filter with its hole opening (A, **Figure 22**) facing against the crankcase. The oil filter's closed side should face out as shown in **Figure 20**.

f. Align the oil filter cover with the crankcase and place it in position. The 3 oil filter cover holes

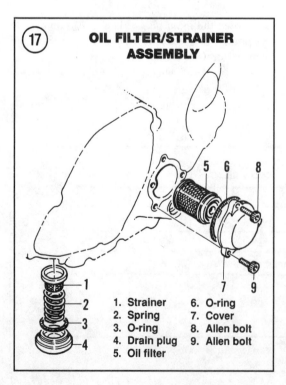

OIL FILTER/STRAINER ASSEMBLY

1. Strainer
2. Spring
3. O-ring
4. Drain plug
5. Oil filter
6. O-ring
7. Cover
8. Allen bolt
9. Allen bolt

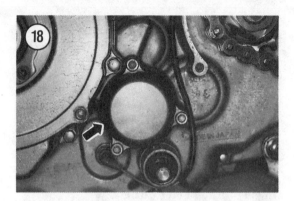

will only align one way. This ensures that the notch in the cover (B, **Figure 22**) will align correctly with the oil hole in the crankcase when the cover is installed; see B, **Figure 21**.

g. Hold the oil filter cover in place and install the mounting bolts finger tight. Then snug up the bolts in a crisscross pattern and tighten to the torque specification in **Table 3**.

> *CAUTION*
> *Overtightening the oil filter cover mounting bolts may damage the oil filter. Do not exceed the tightening torque in* **Table 3**.

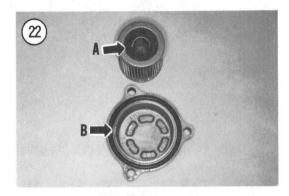

9. Clean the oil strainer, compression spring and drain plug in solvent and dry thoroughly. Inspect the oil strainer for damage; replace if necessary.

10. Inspect the drain plug O-ring for severe wear, hardness, cracks or other damage. Replace if necessary.

11. Install the O-ring into the drain plug groove. Then install the compression spring and oil strainer as shown in **Figure 17**. Install the oil drain plug assembly and torque to the specification in **Table 3**.

12. Insert a funnel into the oil fill hole and fill the engine with the correct weight (**Figure 16** and **Table 6**) and quantity oil. Refer to **Table 7** for refill capacities.

13. Screw in the dipstick/oil fill cap securely.

14. Loosen, but do not remove, the oil pressure check bolt (**Figure 23**) mounted in the cylinder head.

15. Start the engine and allow it to idle. Oil should start to seep out of the oil check bolt within one minute of starting the engine. When oil begins to seep out of the check bolt, stop the engine and tighten the bolt to the torque specification in **Table 3**. If there is no oil visible at the check bolt within one minute, stop the engine immediately and check the lubrication system.

16. Check the drain plug and oil filter cover for leaks.

17. Turn the engine off and check for correct oil level; adjust as necessary.

> *WARNING*
> *Avoid prolonged contact with used oil. It is advisable to wash your hands thoroughly with soap and water as soon as possible after handling or coming in contact with motor oil.*

Control Cable Lubrication

The clutch, throttle and parking brake cables should be cleaned and lubricated at the intervals indicated in **Table 1**. In addition, the cables should be checked for kinks and signs of wear and damage or fraying that could cause the cables to fail or stick. Cables are expendable items and will not last forever under the best of conditions.

The most positive method of control cable lubrication involves the use of a cable lubricator like the one shown in **Figure 24**. A can of cable lube or a general lubricant will also be required. Do *not* use chain lube as a cable lubricant.

1. Loosen the clutch cable adjuster at the handlebar and disconnect the clutch cable (A, **Figure 25**).

2. Disconnect the parking brake cable (B, **Figure 25**) at the handlebar.

3. Disconnect the throttle cable from the handlebar to the junction box (if used) and then from the junction box to carburetor. See Chapter Eight.

4. Attach a cable lubricator to the end of the cable following the manufacturer's instructions (**Figure 26**).

5. Insert the lubricant can nozzle into the lubricator, press the button on the can and hold down until the lubricant begins to flow out of the other end of the cable. If you cannot get the cable lube to flow through the cable from one end, remove the lubricator and try at the opposite cable end.

> *NOTE*
> *Place a shop cloth at the end of the cable to catch the oil as it runs out.*

6. Disconnect the lubricator.

7. Apply a light coat of grease to the cable ends before reconnecting them.

8. Reconnect the cables and adjust the cables as described in this chapter. Attach the throttle cable(s) as described in Chapter Eight.

9. Operate the throttle, checking that it opens and closes smoothly with no binding.

Clutch and Brake Lever Pivot Bolt Lubrication

Periodically remove the clutch and brake lever pivot bolts and lubricate the bolts with 10W/30 motor oil.

Drive Chain Lubrication

All models were originally equipped with an O-ring drive chain (**Figure 27**). A properly maintained chain will provide maximum service life and reliability.

> *NOTE*
> *If you previously installed a tacky chain lubricant to the O-ring chain, the chain (and sprockets) should be cleaned in*

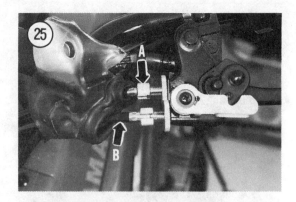

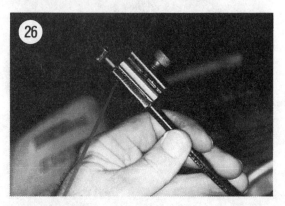

kerosene to remove all residue, dirt and grit. Clean the chain as described under **Drive Chain** *in Chapter Eleven.*

1. Support the vehicle with both rear wheels off the ground.
2. Shift the transmission into NEUTRAL.

3. Externally lubricate the chain with an SAE 30-50 weight motor oil or a good grade of chain lubricant (non-tacky) specifically formulated for O-ring chains, following the manufacturer's instructions.

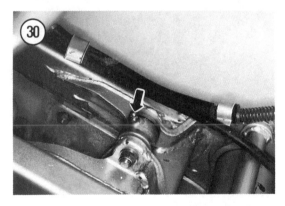

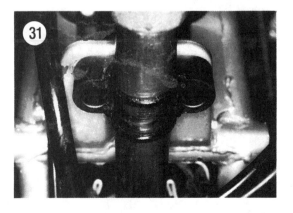

CAUTION
Do not use a tacky chain lubricant on O-ring chains. Dirt and other abrasive materials that stick to the lubricant will grind away at the O-rings and damage them. An O-ring chain is pre-lubricated during its assembly at the factory. External oiling is only required to prevent chain rust and to keep the O-rings pliable.

4. Wipe off all excess oil from the rear hub and axle.
5. Check that the master link is properly installed and secured.

Steering and Suspension Lubrication (Grease Fitting)

The following components should be lubricated with a grease gun equipped with lithium base grease:

NOTE
Prior to and then after lubricating the following components, wipe off the grease fitting with a clean rag.

a. Lower steering shaft bushings (1987 models).
b. Upper arm pivot bolts (**Figure 28**).
c. Lower arm pivot bolts (**Figure 29**).
d. Both connecting rod pivot bolts (**Figure 30**).
e. Relay arm pivot bolt.

Upper Steering Bearing Block and Dust Seals

While not a part of the periodic maintenance schedule, the upper steering bearing block and dust seals (**Figure 31**) should be removed, cleaned and lubricated during the riding season. Refer to Chapter Ten for service procedures.

Lower Steering Bearing (1988-on)

A double-sealed bearing (**Figure 32**) is used on all 1988-on models. The bearing boss on the frame is not equipped with a grease fitting. Periodic lubrication is not required. When inspecting the steering shaft for excessive play, inspect the upper and lower bearing oil seals for damage. Replace damaged oil seals as described in Chapter Ten.

Front Hub Wheel Bearings

The front hub wheel bearings (**Figure 33**) should be lubricated with a lithium base grease. New oil seals should be installed after lubricating the bearings. Refer to Chapter Ten for service.

Rear Axle Bearings and Oil Seals

Double sealed rear axle bearings are installed in the axle housing. Periodic lubrication of the bearings is not required. Periodically, inspect the outer oil seals (**Figure 34**). Severely worn or damaged oil seals should be replaced immediately; leaking oil seals (**Figure 35**) allow dirt, water and sand to enter the axle housing, damaging the bearing and causing rust and corrosion to build on the axle and center hub spacer. If dirt has entered the axle housing, the housing should be removed and disassembled; refer to Chapter Eleven.

Whenever the rear axle has been removed, pack the oil seal lips with grease before reinstalling the axle.

Swing Arm Bearing Assembly Lubrication

The swing arm bearing assembly (**Figure 36**, typical) should be lubricated at the intervals specified in **Table 1**. The swing arm must be removed and partially disassembled to lubricate the bearings—do not remove the needle bearings (**Figure 37**) for periodic lubrication. Refer to Chapter Eleven for service procedures.

Rear Shock Absorber Bearing and Pivot Bolt Lubrication

The shock absorber bearings and pivot bolts (**Figure 38**) should be lubricated at the intervals indicated in **Table 1**. The shock absorber must be removed to lubricate these parts. Do not remove the bearings (**Figure 39**) for periodic lubrication. Refer to Chapter Eleven.

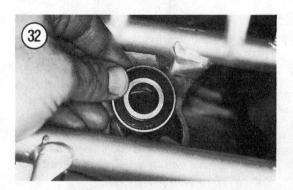

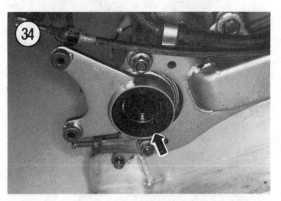

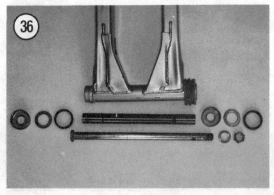

Rear Brake Pedal Pivot Shaft Lubrication

Remove the rear brake pedal and lubricate the pivot shaft (**Figure 40**) with waterproof grease. Reverse to install. Inspect the pedal return spring for weakness or damage.

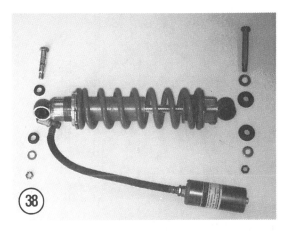

Shift Lever Lubrication

Remove the shift lever pedal and lubricate the pivot shaft (**Figure 41**) with waterproof grease. Reverse to install.

PERIODIC MAINTENANCE

Periodic maintenance intervals are listed in **Table 1**.

Drive Chain Cleaning

Refer to *Drive Chain* in Chapter Eleven.

Drive Chain/Sprocket Wear Inspection

The drive chain should be checked frequently and replaced when excessively worn or damaged.

A quick check will give you an indication of when to actually measure chain wear. At the rear sprocket,

pull one of the links away from the sprocket. If the link pulls away more than 1/2 the height of a sprocket tooth, the chain is excessively worn (**Figure 42**).

To measure chain wear, perform the following:

1. Support the vehicle with both rear wheels off the ground.

2. Loosen the upper and lower axle housing mounting bolts.

3. Loosen the chain adjuster locknuts.

4. Tighten the chain adjusters to move the rear axle rearward until the drive chain is tight (no slack).

5. Lay a scale along the top chain run, and measure the length of any 21 pins in the chain as shown in **Figure 43**. The nominal 21-pin length for a 520 chain is 318 mm (12.5 in.). If the 21-pin length is 327 mm (12.75 in.) or longer, the drive chain is excessively worn and should be replaced.

6. Check the inner plate chain faces. They should be lightly polished on both sides. If they show considerable uneven wear on one side, the sprockets are not aligned. Severe wear requires chain and sprocket replacement.

7. If the drive chain is worn, inspect the drive and driven sprockets for the following defects:

   a. Undercutting or sharp teeth.

   b. Broken teeth.

8. If wear is evident, replace the chain and sprockets as a set, or you'll soon wear out a new drive chain.

9. Adjust the drive chain as described in this chapter.

Drive Chain Adjustment

The drive chain must have adequate play so that the chain is not strung tight when the swing arm is horizontal. On the other hand, too much play may cause the chain to jump off the sprockets with potentially disastrous results.

When riding in mud and sand, the dirt buildup will make the chain tighter. Recheck chain play and readjust as required.

The drive chain should be checked and adjusted prior to each ride. Drive chain free play is listed in **Table 8**.

1. Support the vehicle with both rear wheels off the ground.

2. Turn the rear axle and check the chain tightness at several spots in the middle of the lower chain run

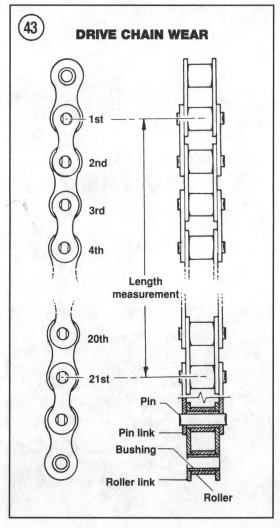

DRIVE CHAIN WEAR

1st

2nd

3rd

4th

Length measurement

20th

21st

Pin

Pin link

Bushing

Roller link

Roller

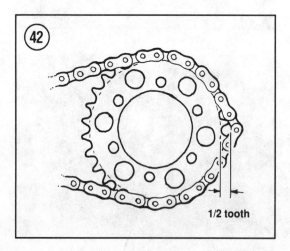

1/2 tooth

(**Figure 44**). Because the chain wears unevenly, you will find that the chain's tightness varies. Check and adjust the chain at its *tightest* point.

3. Compare the drive chain free play with the specifications listed in **Table 8**. If necessary, adjust the drive chain as follows.

> *NOTE*
> *When adjusting the drive chain, you must also maintain rear wheel alignment. A misaligned rear wheel can cause poor handling and pulling to one side or the other, as well as increased chain and sprocket wear. All models have wheel alignment marks on the axle housing and chain adjusters.*

4. Loosen the upper and lower axle housing bolts (and nuts). See **Figure 45**, typical.

> *NOTE*
> *The axle housing on 1987-1988 models uses 4 mounting bolts. The axle housings on 1989-on models use 2 long through bolts and nuts.*

5. Loosen the chain adjuster locknuts and turn the adjuster bolts so that the same mark on each adjuster aligns with the axle housing marks. See **Figure 46**. Recheck chain free play.

6. When chain free play is correct, check wheel alignment by sighting along the chain from the rear sprocket. It should leave the sprocket in a straight line. If it is cocked to one side or the other, adjust wheel alignment by turning one adjuster or the other. Recheck chain play.

7. Tighten the upper and lower axle housing bolts (and nuts) to the torque specification in **Table 3**.

8. Check and adjust the rear brake as described in this chapter.

Drive Chain Guard and Rollers Replacement

Inspect the chain guide, rollers and swing arm cover to make sure that none are missing or severely

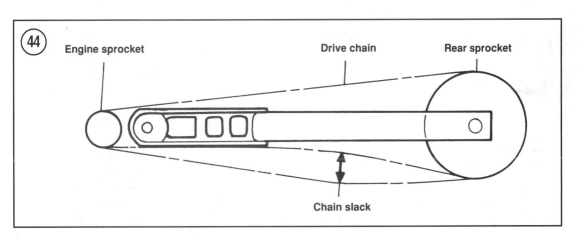
44 Engine sprocket / Drive chain / Rear sprocket / Chain slack

damaged. Running the vehicle with damaged parts
can cause frame and swing arm damage.

To replace the swing arm cover, remove the swing
arm as described in Chapter Eleven.

Front Brake Lever Adjustment

Brake pad wear in the caliper is automatically
adjusted as the pistons moves forward in the calipers. However, the brake lever should be checked for
adequate clearance (free play) between the adjuster
bolt and piston. Reduced clearance can cause brake
drag and premature brake pad wear.

1. Measure the front brake lever free play at the *end*
of the brake lever (**Figure 47**). Correct free play is
4-8 mm (5/32-5/16 in.). If free play is incorrect,
perform Step 2.

2. Loosen the locknut and turn the adjuster bolt
(**Figure 48**) in or out to set free play within prescribed range listed in Step 1. Tighten locknut and
remeasure free play.

Rear Brake Pedal Height Adjustment

Brake pedal height is the only adjustment provided on the rear disc brake system. The brake pedal
height adjustment maintains the proper amount of
brake pedal free play. Free play is the distance the
pedal travels from the at-rest position to the applied
position when the pedal is lightly depressed.

1. Park the vehicle on level ground.

2. Measure the distance from the top of the footpeg
to the top of the brake pedal (**Figure 49**). This
measurement is brake pedal height. The correct
brake pedal height measurement is 10 mm (0.4 in.).
If adjustment is necessary, perform Step 3.

3. Loosen the master cylinder locknut (A, **Figure
50**) and turn the adjust bolt (B, **Figure 50**) in or out
to achieve the correct brake pedal height position.
Tighten the locknut and recheck the height adjustment.

> *WARNING*
> *If the length of the adjust bolt is not
> maintained within the specifications
> shown in **Figure 51**, rear brake failure
> may occur. This could cause you to lose
> control.*

4. Support the vehicle with both rear wheels off the
ground.

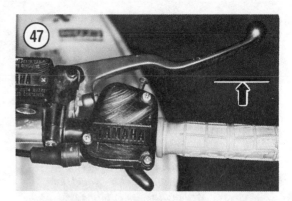

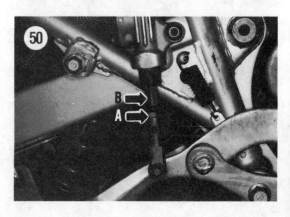

5. Rotate the rear axle and check for brake drag. Also operate the pedal several times to make sure it returns to the at-rest position immediately after release.

6. Lower the rear wheels back onto the ground.

Brake Fluid Level Check

The brake fluid level in the reservoirs should always be kept at its maximum level. See **Figure 52** (front) and **Figure 53** (rear). If the brake fluid drops below half-full, correct by adding fresh DOT 4 brake fluid.

NOTE
If the brake fluid level lowers rapidly, check the brake hose and fittings.

1. Place the ATV on level ground.

2. Clean any dirt from the cover prior to removing the cover.

3A. *Front*: Perform the following:

   a. Turn the handlebar so that the master cylinder reservoir is level.

   b. Remove the 2 top cover screws and remove the cover (**Figure 52**) and diaphragm.

3B. *Rear*: Perform the following:

   a. Remove the reservoir cover, if equipped.

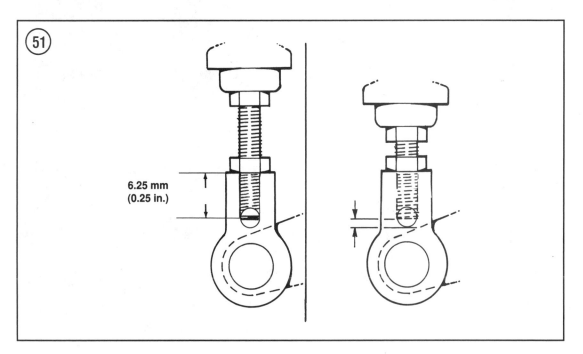

6.25 mm
(0.25 in.)

b. Unscrew the cover (**Figure 53**) and remove it
and the diaphragm.

4. Add fresh DOT 4 brake fluid from a sealed container.

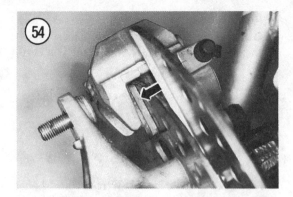

> *WARNING*
> *Use brake fluid clearly marked DOT 4*
> *and specified for disc brakes. Others*
> *may vaporize and cause brake failure.*
> *Do not intermix different brands or*
> *types of brake fluid as they may not be*
> *compatible. Do not intermix a silicone*
> *based (DOT 5) brake fluid as it can*
> *cause brake component damage lead-*
> *ing to brake system failure.*

> *CAUTION*
> *Be careful when handling brake*
> *fluid. Do not spill it on painted or*
> *plastic surfaces as it will destroy the*
> *surface. Wash the area immediately*
> *with soap and water and thoroughly*
> *rinse it off.*

5. Reinstall the diaphragm and top cover. On front
master cylinders, install the screws and tighten securely.

Disc Brake Hoses

Check the brake hoses between the master cylinder and the brake caliper. If there is any leakage,
tighten the bolt or hose and then bleed the brake as
described in Chapter Thirteen. If this does not stop
the leak or if a brake line is obviously damaged,
cracked or chafed, replace the brake hose and bleed
the system (Chapter Twelve).

Disc Brake Pad Wear

Replace the brake pads when the lining thickness
is worn to the wear limit specified in Chapter
Twelve, when a pad shows uneven wear and scoring,
or if there is grease or oil on the friction surface; see
Figure 54 (front) and **Figure 55** (rear). Check the
disc for scoring and warpage. Refer to Chapter
Twelve.

Disc Brake Fluid Change

Every time the reservoir cap is removed, a small
amount of dirt and moisture enters the brake fluid.

The same thing happens if a leak occurs or any part of the hydraulic system is loosened or disconnected. Dirt can clog the system and cause unnecessary wear. Water in the brake fluid vaporizes at high temperature, impairing the hydraulic action and reducing the brake's stopping ability.

To maintain peak performance, change the brake fluid every year and when rebuilding a caliper or master cylinder. To change brake fluid, follow the brake bleeding procedure in Chapter Twelve.

> *WARNING*
> *Use brake fluid clearly marked DOT 4 only. Others may vaporize and cause brake failure. Dispose of any unused fluid according to local EPA regulations—never reuse brake fluid. Contaminated brake fluid can cause brake failure.*

Brake Master Cylinder
(Front and Rear)

The master cylinder piston assembly should be replaced whenever the master cylinder is leaking or

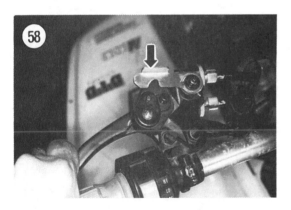

disassembled. Refer to Chapter Twelve for service procedure.

Brake Caliper
(Front and Rear)

The brake caliper piston seals (dust and piston) should be replaced whenever the caliper is leaking or disassembled. Refer to Chapter Twelve for service procedures.

Parking Brake
Check and Adjustment

The parking brake lever (A, **Figure 56**) is an integral part of the clutch lever assembly. The cable operated parking brake locks the rear wheels only.

1. To set and check the parking brake:
   a. Depress the parking brake button (**Figure 57**) and pull in the clutch lever.
   b. Hold the clutch lever in and move the parking brake lever (**Figure 58**) over so that the notch in the lever contacts the locking pin mounted on the clutch lever assembly. Then release the clutch lever, making sure that the parking brake lever engages the pin as shown in **Figure 59**. The parking brake is now set.
   c. With the parking brake set and with the transmission in NEUTRAL, you should not be able to roll the vehicle forwards or backwards. If you can roll the machine, adjust the parking brake, starting with Step 2.

2. Release the parking brake.

3. Loosen the parking brake adjuster locknut (B, **Figure 56**) and turn the adjuster in to provide as much cable slack as possible.

4. Loosen the parking brake cable adjuster locknut on the rear brake caliper (A, **Figure 60**) and back the adjuster bolt (B, **Figure 60**) out.

5. Slowly screw the adjuster bolt (B, **Figure 60**) into the caliper until it feels tight, then back it out 1/4 turn. Hold the adjuster bolt and tighten the locknut (A, **Figure 60**) securely.

6. Adjust the parking brake cable length as follows:
   a. At the handlebar, turn the parking brake cable adjuster out (C, **Figure 56**) to obtain a parking brake cable length (at the rear caliper) of 46-50 mm (1.81-1.97 in.); see **Figure 61**.
   b. Tighten the adjuster locknut (B, **Figure 56**).

7. Support the vehicle with both rear wheels off the ground.

8. With the parking brake off, make sure the rear axle rotates freely. There should be no brake drag. Then set the parking brake and check that the rear axle is locked.

9. If there is brake drag or if the rear axle is not locked, readjust the parking brake.

10. Lower the vehicle so that both rear wheels are on the ground.

Clutch Adjustment

Clutch adjustment takes up slack caused by cable stretch and clutch wear. Insufficient free play will cause clutch slippage and rapid clutch disc wear.

1. Measure the clutch lever free play at the *end* of the clutch lever; see **Figure 62**. Correct free play is 5-10 mm (0.2-0.4 in.). If free play is incorrect, perform Step 2.

2. See **Figure 63**. At the hand lever loosen the locknut (A) and turn the adjuster (B) in or out to obtain the correct amount of free play. Tighten the locknut.

3. If the proper amount of free play cannot be achieved at the clutch lever adjuster, perform the following:

   a. At the clutch lever, loosen the locknut (A, **Figure 63**) and turn the adjuster (B, **Figure 63**) in all the way to obtain as much cable slack as possible. Tighten the locknut.

   b. Loosen the mid-cable adjuster locknuts (A, **Figure 64**) and move the cable (B, **Figure 64**) forwards or backwards to increase or decrease clutch cable slack. Then tighten both locknuts (A, **Figure 64**).

   c. Turn the cable adjuster (B, **Figure 63**) out to obtain the correct clutch lever free play. When the free play measurement is correct, tighten the locknut (A, **Figure 63**).

4. If the proper amount of free play cannot be achieved by using this adjustment procedure, either the clutch cable has stretched to the point that it needs to be replaced or the friction discs are worn and need replacing. Refer to Chapter Six for cable and clutch plate replacement.

Throttle Cable Adjustment and Operation

Some throttle cable play is necessary to prevent changes in the idle speed when you turn the handle-

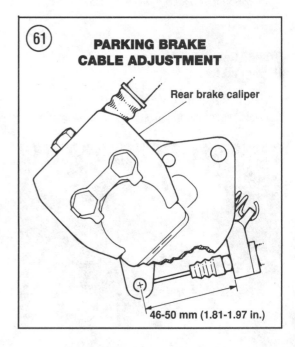
61 **PARKING BRAKE CABLE ADJUSTMENT**
Rear brake caliper
46-50 mm (1.81-1.97 in.)

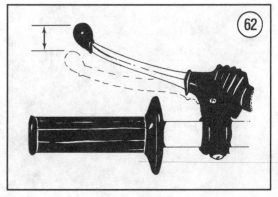
62

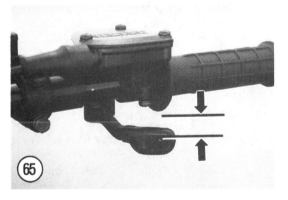

bars. Yamaha specifies a throttle cable free play of 3-5 mm (1/8-3/16 in.), measured at the end of the throttle lever; see **Figure 65**.

In time, the throttle cable free play will become excessive from cable stretch. This will delay throttle response and affect low speed operation. On the other hand, if there is no throttle cable free play, an excessively high idle can result.

Minor adjustments can be made at the throttle grip adjuster. Major adjustments can be made at the throttle cable adjuster that attaches to the carburetor cap.

1. Set the engine idle speed as described under *Idle Speed Adjustment* in this chapter.

2. Start the engine and allow it to idle in NEUTRAL.

3. With the engine running at idle speed, push the throttle lever to increase engine speed.

4. Measure the amount of movement (free play) required to raise the engine speed from idle. If the free play measurement (**Figure 65**) is incorrect, perform the following.

5. At the throttle housing, loosen the throttle cable adjuster locknut (A, **Figure 66**) and turn the adjuster (B, **Figure 66**) in or out to achieve proper free play rotation. Tighten the locknut.

6. If the adjustment cannot be corrected at the throttle housing adjuster, turn the throttle cable adjuster (B, **Figure 66**) all the way in. Then slide back the rubber boot and loosen the locknut(s) (A, **Figure 67**) at the carburetor. Turn the adjuster(s) (B, **Figure 67**) out as required, making sure the adjuster(s) does not thread out. Complete adjustment by turning the adjuster at the throttle grip. Tighten the locknuts.

7. Slide the rubber boot(s) back over the cable adjuster(s).

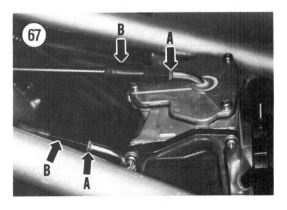

8. If the throttle cable cannot be adjusted properly, the cable has stretched excessively and must be replaced.

9. Make sure the throttle lever rotates freely from a fully closed to fully open position.

10. Start the engine and allow it to idle in NEUTRAL. Turn the handlebar from side to side. If the idle increases, the throttle cable is routed incorrectly or there is not enough cable free play.

NOTE
A damaged throttle cable will prevent the engine from idling properly.

Speed Limiter
Adjustment

The throttle housing is equipped with a speed limiter (A, **Figure 68**) that can be set to prevent the rider from opening the throttle all the way. The speed limiter can be set for beginning riders or to control engine rpm when breaking in a new engine.

The speed limiter adjustment is set by varying the length of the speed limiter screw, measured from the throttle housing to the bottom of the screw head; see **Figure 68**. The standard speed limiter setting is 12 mm (0.47 in.).

1. Check throttle cable free play as described in this chapter. If necessary, adjust throttle cable free play, then continue with Step 2.

2. Loosen the locknut (B, **Figure 68**).

3. Turn the speed limiter screw (A, **Figure 68**) in or out as required. Do not exceed the 12 mm (0.47 in.) adjustment limit. Tighten the locknut (B, **Figure 68**).

WARNING
Do not operate the vehicle with the speed limiter screw removed from the housing. Do not exceed the 12 mm (0.47 in.) adjustment limit. If you are adjusting the speed limiter for a beginning rider, start and ride the vehicle yourself, making sure it is positioned where you want it.

Air Filter

A clogged air filter will decrease the efficiency and life of the engine. Never run the ATV without an air filter properly installed. Even minute particles

of dust can cause severe internal engine wear and may clog carburetor passages.

Figure 69 is an exploded view of the air filter assembly.

1. Remove the seat to access the air filter.

2. Disconnect the crankcase breather hose at the air box cover (**Figure 70**).

3. Remove the screws holding the air box cover (**Figure 71**) to the air box. Lift the cover off the air box and remove it.

4. Lift the rear of the air filter (**Figure 72**) and remove it from the air box.

5. Use a flashlight and check the air box-to-carburetor boot inside diameter for dirt or other contamination that may have passed through the air filter.

6. Wipe the inside of the air box with a clean rag. If you cannot clean the air box with it bolted to the ATv, remove and clean the air box thoroughly with solvent. Then clean with hot soapy water and rinse with water from a garden hose. Remove and install the air box as described in Chapter Eight.

7. Cover the air box opening with a clean shop rag.

8. Inspect all fittings, hoses and connections from the air box to the carburetor. Check each hose clamp for tightness.

9. Turn the end plate (**Figure 73**) 90° and remove it from the air filter (**Figure 74**).

10. Pull the foam element off the filter guide (**Figure 75**).

WARNING
Do not clean the air filter element with gasoline.

11. Clean the filter element with a filter solvent to remove oil and dirt, then allow to dry. If you are using an accessory air filter, the manufacturer may sell or recommend an air filter cleaning solvent.

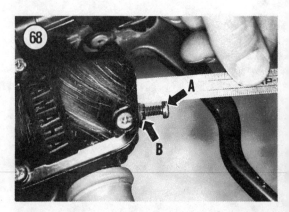

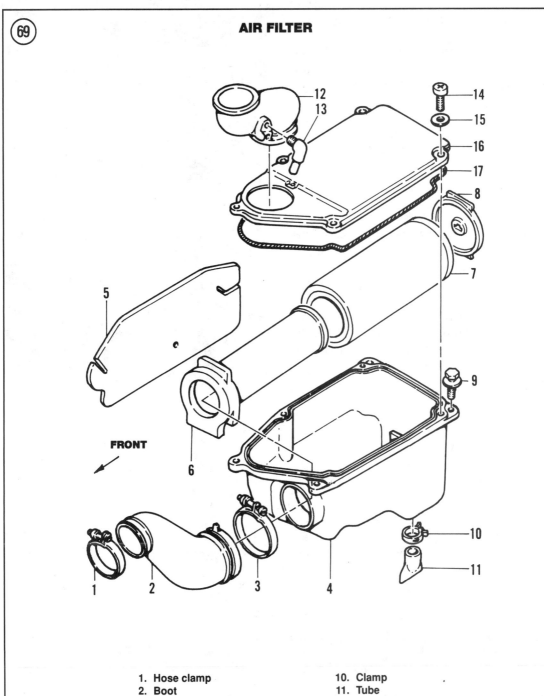

AIR FILTER

1. Hose clamp
2. Boot
3. Hose clamp
4. Air box
5. Cover
6. Filter guide
7. Air filter element
8. End cover
9. Bolt
10. Clamp
11. Tube
12. Air intake nozzle
13. Hose nozzle
14. Screw
15. Washer
16. Cover
17. O-ring

12. Fill a clean pan with liquid cleaner and warm water.

13. Submerge the filter into the cleaning solution and gently work the cleaner into the filter pores. Soak and squeeze (gently) the filter to clean it.

> *CAUTION*
> *Do not wring or twist the filter when cleaning it. This harsh action could damage a filter pore or tear the filter loose at a seam. This would allow unfiltered air to enter the engine and cause severe and rapid wear.*

14. Rinse the filter under warm water while soaking and gently squeezing it.

15. Repeat Step 13 and Step 14 two or three times or until there are no signs of dirt being rinsed from the filter.

16. After cleaning the element, inspect it carefully. If it is torn or broken in any area it should be replaced. Do not run with a damaged element as it may allow dirt to enter the engine and cause severe engine wear.

17. Set the filter aside and allow it to dry thoroughly.

18. Clean the end plate and filter guide in solvent and dry thoroughly.

> *CAUTION*
> *Make sure the filter is completely dry before oiling it.*

19. Properly oiling an air filter element is a messy job. You may want to wear a pair of disposable rubber gloves when performing this procedure. Oil the filter as follows:

    a. Purchase a box of gallon size storage bags. The bags can be used when cleaning the filter as well

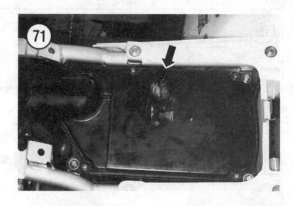

as for storing engine and carburetor parts during disassembly.

b. Place the air filter into a storage bag (**Figure 76**).

c. Pour foam air filter oil onto the filter to soak it.

d. Gently squeeze and release the filter to soak filter oil into the filter's pores. Repeat until all of the filter's pores are discolored with the oil.

e. Remove the filter from the bag and check the pores for uneven oiling. This is indicated by light or dark areas. If necessary, soak the filter and squeeze it again.

f. When the filter oiling is even, squeeze the filter a final time.

20. Apply some wheel bearing grease to the filter guide where it will seat against the filter; see arrow in **Figure 75**.

21. Remove the filter from the bag and slide it onto the filter guide. Position the end of the filter so that the hook on the end of the filter guide is pushed through the slot in the filter.

22. Align the slot in the end plate with the hook on the filter guide and install the end plate onto the filter (**Figure 74**). Then turn the end plate 90° to lock it (**Figure 73**).

23. Apply a coat of wheel bearing grease to the filter's sealing surface as shown in A, **Figure 77**.

24. Insert the filter guide (B, **Figure 77**) into the receptacle (A, **Figure 78**) in the air box and install the air filter. See **Figure 72**.

NOTE
*The rear portion of the air filter will rest on the molded tab (B, **Figure 78**) in the air box.*

25. Install the air filter cover. Position the circular guide on the air filter cover (A, **Figure 79**) so that it is located behind the air filter guide shown in B, **Figure 79**. This will apply pressure against the air filter and hold it in place.

26. Install the screws that secure the air filter cover to the air box and tighten them securely. See **Figure 71**.

27. Reconnect the crankcase breather hose (**Figure 70**).

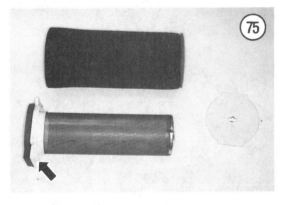

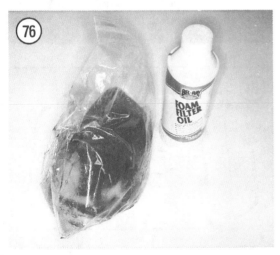

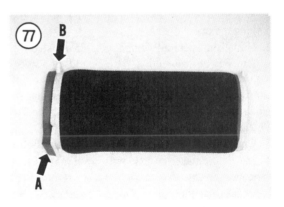

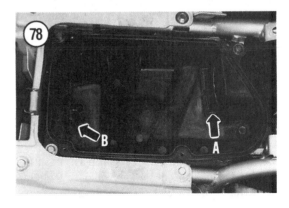

28. Install the seat.

29. Pour the leftover filter oil from the bag back into the bottle for reuse.

30. Dispose of the plastic bag.

Fuel Line Inspection

Inspect the fuel line (**Figure 80**) from the fuel tank to the carburetor. Replace the fuel line if it is cracked or starting to deteriorate. Make sure the small hose clamps are in place and holding securely. Check that the overflow and vent tubes are in place.

> *WARNING*
> *A damaged or deteriorated fuel line presents a very dangerous fire hazard to both the rider and the machine if fuel should spill onto a hot engine or exhaust pipe.*

**Steering System and
Front Suspension Inspection**

The steering system and front suspension should be checked at the interval indicated in **Table 1**.

1. Park the vehicle on level ground and set the parking brake.

2. Visually inspect all components of the steering system. Pay close attention to the tie rods and steering shaft, especially after a hard spill or collision. If damage is apparent the steering components must be repaired. Refer to service procedures described in Chapter Ten.

3. Check the tightness of the handlebar holder bolts.

4. Make sure the front axle nuts are tight and that the cotter pins are in place.

5. Check that the cotter pins are in place on all steering components. If any cotter pin is missing, check the nut(s) for looseness. Torque the nut(s) and install new cotter pins.

> *CAUTION*
> *If any of the previously mentioned bolts and nuts are loose, refer to Chapter Ten for correct procedures and torque specifications.*

6. Check steering shaft play as follows:

   a. To check steering shaft radial play, move the handlebar from side to side (without attempting to move the wheels). If radial play is excessive,

the upper steering bearings are probably worn and should be replaced.

   b. To check steering shaft thrust play, lift up and then push down on the handlebar. If excessive thrust play is noted, check the lower steering shaft nut for looseness. If the nut is torqued properly, then the lower steering shaft bushing (1987) or bearing (1988-on) is worn and should be replaced.

   c. Replace worn or damaged steering shaft parts as described in Chapter Ten.

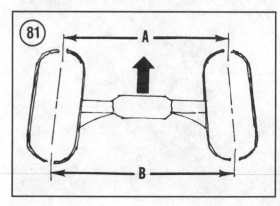

7. Check steering knuckle and tie rod ball joints as follows:

    a. Turn the handlebar quickly from side to side. If there is appreciable looseness between the handlebar and tires, check the ball joints for severe wear or damage.

    b. Replace worn or damaged steering knuckle and tie rod components as described in Chapter Ten.

NOTE
When removing cotter pins to check fastener tightness, new cotter pins must be installed.

Toe-in Adjustment

Toe-in is a condition where the front of the tires are closer together than the back; see **Figure 81**. The front wheel toe-in alignment should be checked at the interval specified in **Table 1**. Toe-in is adjusted by changing the length of the tie rods.

1. Inflate all 4 tires to the recommended tire pressure specified in **Table 2**.

2. Park the vehicle on level ground and set the parking brake. Raise and support the front end so that both front tires just clear the ground.

3. Turn the handlebar so that the wheels are at the straight-ahead position.

4. Using a ruler, carefully measure the distance between the center of both front tires as shown in A, **Figure 81**. Mark the tires with a piece of chalk at these points. Write down the measurement.

5. Turn each tire exactly 180° and measure the distance between the center of both front tires at the points marked in Step 4. Write down the measurement.

6. Subtract the measurement in Step 4 from Step 5 as shown in **Figure 81**. Toe-in is correct if the difference is 17-27 mm (0.67-1.06 in.). If the toe-in is incorrect, proceed to Step 7.

7. Loosen the locknuts securing each tie rod. See **Figure 82** and **Figure 83**.

8. Use a wrench on the flat portion of the tie rods and slowly turn both tie rods the *same* amount until the tie rod measurement is correct.

NOTE
It is important to turn both tie rods the same number of turns. This ensures that both tie rods will be the same length.

WARNING
If the tie rod lengths are different, the vehicle will tend to drift to the left or right, even though the handlebar is pointed straight ahead. This may cause you to lose control and crash. If you cannot adjust the toe-in properly, have a dealer inspect the front end and then adjust the toe-in for you.

9. When the tie rod adjustment is correct, hold each tie rod in place and tighten the locknuts to the torque specification in **Table 3**.

Front Hub Bearings

The front hub bearings should be inspected for excessive wear or damage at the intervals specified in **Table 1**. Refer to *Front Hub Wheel Bearings* under *Periodic Lubrication* in this chapter for bearing and oil seal lubrication.

1. Support the vehicle with both front wheels off the ground.

2. Turn both front wheels by hand. The wheels should turn smoothly with no roughness, excessive noise, excessive play or other abnormal conditions.

3. If necessary, service the front hub bearings as described in Chapter Ten.

Nuts, Bolts, and Other Fasteners

Constant vibration can loosen many of the fasteners on the Warrior. Check the tightness of all fasteners, especially those on:

    a. Engine mounting hardware.

    b. Cylinder head bracket bolts.

    c. Engine crankcase covers.

    d. Handlebar.

    e. Gearshift lever.

    f. Brake pedal and lever.

    g. Exhaust system.

NON-SCHEDULED MAINTENANCE

Rear Axle Housing Bearings

Inspect the rear axle housing bearings for excessive wear or damage. Refer to *Rear Axle Bearings and Oil Seals* under *Periodic Lubrication* in this chapter for bearing and oil seal lubrication.

1. Support the vehicle with both rear wheels off the ground.

2. Turn the rear axle by hand. The axle should turn smoothly with no roughness, excessive noise, excessive play or other abnormal conditions.

3. If necessary, service the axle housing bearings as described in Chapter Ten.

Fuel Valve
Cleaning

Periodically remove and clean the fuel valve (**Figure 80**) as described in Chapter Eight.

Carburetor Cleaning

Remove, disassemble and clean the carburetor as described in Chapter Eight.

Sprocket Bolt Tightness

Check the driven sprocket bolts and nuts for looseness. Tighten the nuts to the torque specification listed in **Table 3**.

Exhaust System

Frequently inspect the exhaust system. Refer to Chapter Eight for service and repair procedures.

1. Inspect the exhaust pipe for cracks or dents which could alter performance.

2. Check all of the exhaust pipe fasteners and mounting points for loose or damaged parts.

Handlebar

Inspect the handlebar weekly for any sign of damage. A bent or damaged handlebar should be replaced. The knurled section of the bar should be very rough. Keep the clamps clean with a wire brush. Any time that the bars slip in the clamps they should be removed and wire brushed clean to prevent small

balls of aluminum from gathering in the clamps and reducing gripping abilities.

NOTE
If you have installed aluminum bars, make sure you follow the manufacturer's directions for installing the bars and clamps.

Handlebar Grips

Inspect the handlebar grips (**Figure 84**) for tearing, looseness or severe wear. Install new grips when required, safety wiring the grips to prevent them from slipping. Follow manufacturer's instructions when installing grips.

Frame Inspection

Routinely inspect the frame for cracks or other damage.

ENGINE TUNE-UP

The number of definitions of the term "tune-up" is probably equal to the number of people defining it. For the purposes of this book, a tune-up is general adjustment and maintenance to insure peak engine performance.

The following paragraphs discuss each facet of a proper tune-up which should be performed in the order given. Unless otherwise specified, the engine should be thoroughly cool before starting any tune-up procedure.

Have the new parts on hand before you begin.

To perform a tune-up on your Yamaha, you will need the following tools and equipment:

a. 14 mm spark plug wrench.
b. Socket wrench and assorted sockets.
c. Phillips head screwdriver.
d. Spark plug wire feeler gauge and gapper tool.
e. Feeler gauge set.

Cam Chain Adjustment

An automatic cam chain tensioner assembly is used. No adjustment is required.

Valve Clearance
Check and Adjustment

Valve clearance should be checked and adjusted with the engine cold. The exhaust valve is located at the front of the engine and the intake valve is at the rear of the engine.

1. Park the vehicle on level ground and set the parking brake.
2. Remove the fuel tank as described in Chapter Eight.
3. Remove the front fender as described in Chapter Thirteen.
4A. If so equipped, remove the pull-starter assembly as described in Chapter Five.
4B. Remove the left-hand crankcase cover (**Figure 85**) and O-ring.
5. Remove the ignition timing window plug and O-ring (**Figure 86**).
6. Remove the cylinder head side cover and O-rings (A, **Figure 87**).
7. Remove the exhaust (B, **Figure 87**) and intake (C, **Figure 87**) valve covers.

NOTE
Early models are equipped with a decompression cam assembly mounted in the exhaust valve cover.

8. Remove the spark plug. This will make it easier to turn the engine by hand.
9. The engine must be set to top dead center (TDC) on its compression stroke before checking and adjusting the valve clearance. Perform the following:
   a. With a wrench on the crankshaft starter pulley (**Figure 88**), turn the crankshaft counterclockwise and align the camshaft sprocket index mark (A, **Figure 89**) with the cylinder head mark (B, **Figure 89**).

b. Now check that the "T" mark on the rotor is aligned with the crankcase index mark; see **Figure 90** and **Figure 91**. If these marks are not aligned, turn the crankshaft one revolution counterclockwise and align the rotor "T" mark with the crankcase index mark.

c. When the camshaft sprocket and rotor marks are properly aligned, both rocker arms will have a valve clearance, indicating that both the intake and exhaust valves are closed. Check by moving each rocker arm by hand. There should be some side movement.

10. Check the clearance of both the intake valve and exhaust valve by inserting a flat feeler gauge between the rocker arm pad and the valve stem as shown in **Figure 92**. The correct valve clearances for the intake and exhaust valves are listed in **Table 9**. When the clearance is correct, there will be a slight resistance on the feeler gauge when it is inserted and withdrawn.

11. To correct the clearance, perform the following:

a. Use a 10 mm wrench and back off the valve adjuster locknut.

b. Use a 4 mm wrench and turn the adjuster in or out so there is a slight resistance felt on the feeler gauge (**Figure 93**).

c. Hold the adjuster to prevent it from turning and tighten the locknut to the torque specification listed in **Table 3**.

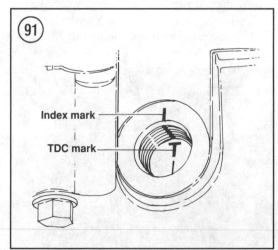

Index mark

TDC mark

d. Then recheck the clearance to make sure the adjuster did not slip when the locknut was tightened. Readjust the valve clearance if necessary.

12. Inspect the rubber O-rings used in the valve covers, cylinder head side cover and timing hole plug. Replace O-rings that are twisted, flattened, cut, cracked or swollen.

NOTE
Apply a lithium soap base grease to the valve cover and cylinder head side cover O-rings prior to installation.

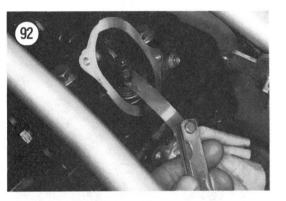

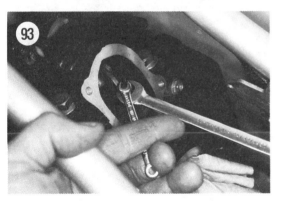

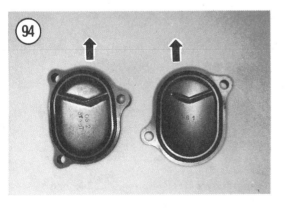

NOTE
Early models are equipped with a decompression cam assembly mounted in the exhaust valve cover.

13. Install the valve covers with their inner ridge (**Figure 94**) facing upward. Install and tighten the valve cover mounting bolts to the torque specification in **Table 3**.

14. Install the cylinder head side cover and O-ring. Tighten mounting bolts to the torque specification in **Table 3**.

15. Install the ignition timing window plug and O-ring. Tighten the plug securely.

16A. If removed, install the pull-starter assembly as described in Chapter Five.

16B. Install the left-hand crankcase cover and O-ring. Tighten the mounting bolts securely.

17. Install the spark plug and reconnect the spark plug cap.

18. Install the front fender as described in Chapter Thirteen.

19. Install the fuel tank as described in Chapter Eight.

Cylinder Compression

A cylinder cranking compression check is one of the quickest ways to check the internal condition of the engine: rings, head gasket, etc. It's a good idea to check compression at each tune-up, write it down, and compare it with the reading you get at the next tune-up. This will help you spot any developing problems.

1. Warm the engine to normal operating temperature.

2. Remove the spark plug. Then insert the plug into the plug cap and ground the plug against the cylinder head (**Figure 95**).

3. Thread or insert the tip of a compression gauge into the cylinder head spark plug hole. Make sure the gauge is seated properly.

NOTE
*Make sure the engine stop switch (A, **Figure 96**) is in the OFF position when performing Step 4.*

4. Hold the throttle wide open and turn the engine over with the starter motor (B, **Figure 96**) for several revolutions until the gauge gives its highest reading.

Record the pressure reading and compare to the compression specifications listed in Table 9.

5. If the reading is higher than normal, there may be a buildup of carbon deposits in the combustion chamber or on the piston crown.

6. If a low reading is obtained, it indicates a leaking cylinder head gasket, valve(s) or piston ring trouble. To determine which, pour about a teaspoon of engine oil through the spark plug hole onto the top of the piston. Turn the engine over once to distribute the oil, then make another compression test and record the reading. If the compression increases significantly, the valves are good but the rings are worn or damaged. If compression does not increase, the valves require servicing. A valve could be hanging open but not burned or a piece of carbon could be on the valve seat.

> *NOTE*
> *If the compression is low, the engine cannot be tuned to maximum performance. The worn parts must be replaced and the engine rebuilt.*

Correct Spark Plug Heat Range

Spark plugs are available in various heat ranges, both hotter and colder than the plugs originally installed at the factory.

Select plugs of the heat range designed for the loads and conditions under which your Yamaha will operating. Use of incorrect heat ranges can cause the plug to foul or engine to overheat, resulting in piston damage.

In general, use a hot plug for low speeds and low temperatures. Use a cold plug for high speeds, high engine loads and high temperatures. The plug should operate hot enough to burn off unwanted deposits, but not so hot that they burn themselves or cause preignition. A spark plug of the correct heat range will show a light tan color on the portion of the insulator within the cylinder after the plug has been in service.

The reach (length) of a plug is also important. A spark plug that is too short will cause excessive carbon build-up, hard starting and plug fouling. A too long plug will cause overheating or may contact the top of the piston. Both conditions will cause engine damage. See **Figure 97**. If the spark plug is too ling, the exposed threads will be coated with carbon and

removal of the spark plug will probably damage the threads in the cylinder head.

The standard heat range spark plug for the various models is listed in Table 10.

Spark Plug Removal

> *CAUTION*
> *Whenever the spark plug is removed, dirt around it can fall into the plug hole. This can cause expensive engine damage.*

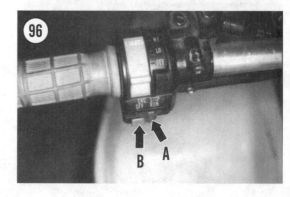

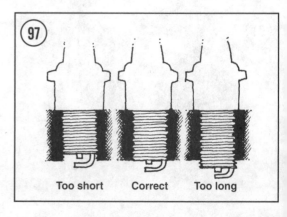

Too short   Correct   Too long

1. Grasp the spark plug lead (**Figure 98**) as near the plug as possible and pull it off the plug. If it is stuck to the plug, twist it slightly to break it loose.

2. Blow away any dirt that has collected around the spark plug.

3. Remove the spark plug with a spark plug socket.

NOTE
If the plug is difficult to remove, apply penetrating oil, like WD-40 or Liquid Wrench, around the base of the plug and let it soak in about 10-20 minutes.

4. Inspect the plug carefully. Look for a broken center porcelain, excessively eroded electrodes, and excessive carbon or oil fouling.

Gapping and Installing the Plug

A new spark plug should be carefully gapped to ensure a reliable, consistent spark. You must use a special spark plug gapping tool and a wire feeler gauge.

1. Remove the new spark plug from the box. If necessary, screw the small adapter onto the end of the plug (**Figure 99**).

2. Insert a wire feeler gauge between the center and side electrode (**Figure 100**). The correct gap is listed in **Table 10**. If the gap is correct, you will feel a slight drag as you pull the wire through. If there is no drag, or the gauge won't pass through, bend the side electrode with a gapping tool (**Figure 101**) to set the proper gap.

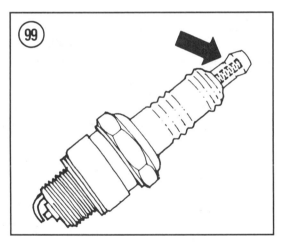

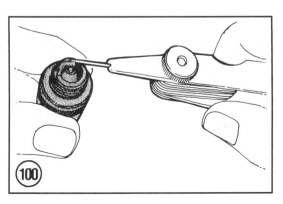

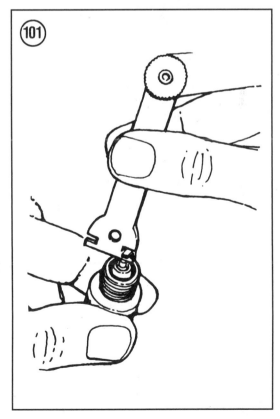

3. Apply anti-seize to the plug threads before installing the spark plug. Do not use engine oil on the plug threads.

> *NOTE*
> *Anti-seize can be purchased at most automotive parts stores.*

4. Screw the spark plug in by hand until it seats. Very little effort should be required. If force is necessary, you have the plug cross-threaded. Unscrew it and try again.
5. Use a spark plug wrench and tighten the spark plug to the torque specification in **Table 3**. If you do not have a torque wrench, tighten the plug an additional 1/4 to 1/2 turn after the gasket has made contact with the head. If you are installing an old, regapped plug and reusing the old gasket, only tighten an additional 1/4 turn.

> *NOTE*
> *Do not overtighten. This will only squash the gasket and destroy its sealing ability.*

6. Attach the spark plug wire. Make sure it is on tight.

> *CAUTION*
> *Make sure the spark plug wire is located away from the exhaust pipe.*

Reading Spark Plugs

Much information about engine and spark plug performance can be determined by careful examination of the spark plug. This information is more valid after performing the following steps.
1. Ride the ATV a short distance at full throttle in any gear.
2. Push the engine stop switch to OFF before closing the throttle and simultaneously pull in the clutch or shift to neutral; coast and brake to a stop.
3. Remove the spark plug and examine it. Compare it to **Figure 102** and note the following:

Normal condition

If the plug has a light tan- or gray-colored deposit and no abnormal gap wear or erosion, good engine, carburetion and ignition condition are indicated.

The plug in use is of the proper heat range and may be serviced and returned to use.

Carbon fouled

Soft, dry, sooty deposits covering the entire firing end of the plug are evidence of incomplete combustion. Even though the firing end of the plug is dry, the plug's insulation decreases. An electrical path is formed that lowers the voltage from the ignition system. Engine misfiring is a sign of carbon fouling. Carbon fouling can be caused by one or more of the following:
a. Too rich fuel mixture.
b. Spark plug heat range too cold.
c. Clogged air filter.
d. Over-retarded ignition timing.
e. Ignition component failure.
f. Low engine compression.
g. Prolonged idling.

Oil fouled

The tip of an oil fouled plug has a black insulator tip, a damp oily film over the firing end and a carbon layer over the entire nose. The electrodes will not be worn. Common causes for this condition are:
a. Incorrect carburetor jetting.
b. Low idle speed or prolonged idling.
c. Ignition component failure.
d. Spark plug heat range too cold.
e. Engine still being broken in.
f. Valve guides worn.
g. Piston rings worn or broken.
Oil fouled spark plugs may be cleaned in an emergency, but it is better to replace them. It is important to correct the cause of fouling before the engine is returned to service.

Gap bridging

Plugs with this condition exhibit gaps shorted out by combustion deposits between the electrodes. If this condition is encountered, check for an improper oil type or excessive carbon in the combustion chamber. Be sure to locate and correct the cause of this condition.

SPARK PLUG CONDITION

NORMAL

GAP BRIDGED

CARBON FOULED

OVERHEATED

OIL FOULED

SUSTAINED PREGNITION

Overheating

Badly worn electrodes and premature gap wear are signs of overheating, along with a gray or white "blistered" porcelain insulator surface. The most common cause for this condition is using a spark plug of the wrong heat range (too hot). If you have not changed to a hotter spark plug and the plug is overheated, consider the following causes:

  a. Lean fuel mixture.
  b. Ignition timing too advanced.
  c. Engine lubrication system malfunction.
  d. Engine air leak.
  e. Improper spark plug installation (overtightening).
  f. No spark plug gasket.

Worn out

Corrosive gases formed by combustion and high voltage sparks have eroded the electrodes. Spark plugs in this condition require more voltage to fire under hard acceleration. Replace with a new spark plug.

Preignition

If the electrodes are melted, preignition is almost certainly the cause. Check for carburetor mounting or intake manifold leaks and overadvanced ignition timing. It is also possible that a plug of the wrong heat range (too hot) is being used. Find the cause of the preignition before returning the engine into service.

Ignition Timing

All models are equipped with a capacitor discharge ignition system (CDI). This system uses no breaker points, but timing does have to be checked to make sure all components of the ignition system are functioning properly.

Incorrect ignition timing can cause a drastic loss of engine performance and efficiency. It may also cause overheating.

Before starting on this procedure, check all electrical connections related to the ignition system. Make sure all connections are tight and free from corrosion and that all ground connections are clean and tight.

1. Start the engine and let it warm up approximately 2-3 minutes.

2. Place the vehicle on level ground and apply the parking brake, shut off the engine.

3. Remove the ignition timing window plug and O-ring (**Figure 103**).

4. Connect a portable tachometer following the manufacturer's instructions.

5. Connect a timing light following the manufacturer's instructions.

6. Restart the engine and let it run at the idle speed indicated in **Table 11**.

7. Adjust the idle speed if necessary as described in this chapter.

8. Aim the timing light at the timing window and pull the trigger. The timing is correct if the "F" mark aligns with the fixed index mark (**Figure 104**) on the crankcase.

9. If timing is incorrect, test the ignition system electrical components as described in Chapter Nine.

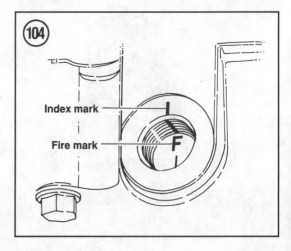

Index mark

Fire mark

10. Disconnect the timing light and portable tachometer.

11. Install the ignition timing window plug and O-ring (**Figure 103**).

Pilot Air Screw Adjustment

Carefully turn the pilot air screw (A, **Figure 105**) in until it *lightly* seats, then back it out the number of turns listed in **Table 11**.

> *NOTE*
> *Figure 106 shows the pilot air screw with the carburetor removed for clarity.*

Idle Speed Adjustment

Before making this adjustment, the air filter must be clean and the engine must have adequate compression; see *Compression Test* in this chapter.

1. Start the engine and let it warm up approximately 2-3 minutes.

2. Place the vehicle on level ground, apply the parking brake and shut off the engine.

3. Connect a portable tachometer following the manufacturer's instructions.

4. Restart the engine and set the idle speed by turning the idle speed adjust screw (B, **Figure 105**).

5. The correct idle speed is listed in **Table 11**.

6. Open and close the throttle a couple of times; check for variation in idle speed. Readjust if necessary.

> *WARNING*
> *With the engine idling, move the handlebar from side to side. If idle speed increases during this movement, the throttle cable needs adjusting or may be incorrectly routed through the frame. Correct this problem immediately. Do not ride the vehicle in this unsafe condition.*

7. Turn the engine off and disconnect the portable tachometer.

STORAGE

Several months of inactivity can cause serious problems and a general deterioration of the ATV's condition. This is especially true in areas of weather extremes. During the winter months it is advisable to prepare the ATV specially for lay-up.

Selecting a Storage Area

Most riders store their ATV's in their home garages. If you do not have a home garage, facilities suitable for long-term ATV storage are readily available for rent or lease in most areas. In selecting a building, consider the following points.

1. The storage area must be dry, free from dampness and excessive humidity. Heating is not necessary, but the building should be well insulated to minimize extreme temperature variations.

2. Buildings with large window areas should be avoided, or such windows should be masked (also a good security measure) if direct sunlight can fall on the ATV.

Preparing Vehicle for Storage

Careful preparation will minimize deterioration and make it easier to restore the ATV to service later. Use the following procedure.

1. Wash the vehicle completely. Make certain to remove all dirt from all the hard to reach parts like the cooling fins on the head and cylinder (early models). Completely dry all parts of the ATV to remove all moisture.

2. Run the engine for about 20-30 minutes to warm up the oil in the clutch and transmission. Drain the oil, regardless of the time since the last oil change. Refill with the normal quantity and type of oil.

3. Drain all gasoline from the fuel tank, interconnecting hose, and the carburetor.

4. Clean and lubricate the drive chain and control cables; refer to specific procedures in this chapter and in Chapter Eleven (chain).

5. Remove the spark plug and add about one teaspoon of engine oil into the cylinder. Reinstall the spark plug and turn the engine over to distribute the oil to the cylinder walls and piston.

6. Tape or tie a plastic bag over the end of the silencer to prevent the entry of moisture.

7. Check the tire pressure, inflate to the correct pressure and move the vehicle to the storage area. Place it securely on a stand with all 4 wheels off the ground.

8. Cover the ATV with a tarp, blanket or heavy plastic drop cloth. Place this cover over the ATV mainly as a dust cover—do not wrap it tightly, especially any plastic material, as it may trap moisture, causing condensation. Leave room for air to circulate around the ATV.

Inspection During Storage

Try to inspect the vehicle weekly while in storage. Any deterioration should be corrected as soon as possible. For example, if corrosion is observed, cover it with a light coat of grease or silicone spray.

Turn the engine over a couple of times. Do not start it.

Restoring Vehicle to Service

A vehicle that has been properly prepared and stored in a suitable area requires only light maintenance to restore to service. It is advisable, however, to perform a spring tune-up.

1. Before removing the vehicle from the storage area, reinflate the tires to the correct pressures. Air loss during storage may have nearly flattened the tires.

2. When the vehicle is brought to the work area, refill the fuel tank with fresh gasoline.

3. Install a fresh spark plug and start up the engine.

4. Perform the standard tune-up as described earlier in this chapter.

5. Check the operation of the engine stop switch. Oxidation of the switch contacts during storage may make it inoperative.

6. Clean and test ride the vehicle.

Table 1 MAINTENANCE AND LUBRICATION SCHEDULE*

Pre-ride checklist	Inspect all fuel lines and fittings for leakage.
	Make sure the fuel tank is full of fresh gasoline.
	Make sure the engine oil level is correct; add oil
	   if necessary.
	Make sure the air filter is clean.
	Check the operation of the clutch and adjust
	   if necessary.
	Check the throttle and the brake levers.
	   Make sure they operate properly with no binding.
	Check the brake fluid level in the front and rear
	   master cylinder reservoirs; add fluid if necessary.
	Inspect the front and rear suspension; make sure it
	   has a good solid feel with no looseness.
	Check chain adjustment and adjust if necessary.
	Check tire pressure, refer to Table 2.
	Check the exhaust system for damage.
	Check the tightness of all fasteners, especially
	   engine mounting hardware.
	Make sure the headlights and taillight work.

**Initial 1st month or after engine
or suspension break-in**
	Check valve clearance, adjust if necessary
	Inspect and clean spark plug, regap if necessary
	Clean air filter
	Change engine oil and filter
	Clean engine oil strainer
	Check drive chain tension and alignment,
	   adjust if necessary
	Clean and lubricate drive chain
	Check and adjust brakes
	Check and adjust clutch
	Check tire and wheel condition
	Check for damaged wheel bearings,
	   replace if necessary
	Check steering system
	Check toe-in, adjust if necessary
	Check engine mounting bolts for tightness
	Check chassis bolts for tightness
	Check battery charge and condition

Initial 3rd month interval	Inspect and clean spark plug, regap if necessary Clean air filter Check and adjust the carburetor Check drive chain tension and alignment, adjust if necessary Clean and lubricate drive chain Check and adjust brakes Check steering system Check toe-in, adjust if necessary Check engine mounting bolts for tightness Check chassis bolts for tightness Check battery charge and condition
Every 6 months	Check valve clearance, adjust if necessary Inspect and clean spark plug, regap if necessary Clean air filter Check and adjust the carburetor Check fuel hose for leaks or other damage, replace if necessary

(continued)

Table 1 MAINTENANCE AND LUBRICATION SCHEDULE* (continued)

Every 6 months (continued)

Change engine oil and filter
Clean engine oil strainer
Check drive chain tension and alignment,
 adjust if necessary
Clean and lubricate drive chain
Check and adjust brakes
Check and adjust clutch
Check tire and wheel condition
Check for damaged wheel bearings,
 replace if necessary
Check steering system
Check toe-in, adjust if necessary
Lubricate steering shaft
Lubricate lower arm pivot assembly
Lubricate rear arm pivot assembly
Check engine mounting bolts for tightness
Check chassis bolts for tightness

* Consider this maintenance schedule a guide to general maintenance and lubrication intervals. Harder than normal use (racing) and exposure to mud, water, sand, high humidity, etc. will dictate more frequent attention to most maintenance items.

Table 2 TIRE INFLATION PRESSURE

	Standard psi (kPa)	Minimum psi (kPa)
Front		
1987-1989	4.3 (29)	3.8 (26.5)
1990-on	4.4 (30)	3.6 (25)
Rear		
1987-1989	3.6 (25)	3.1 (21.6)
1990-on	3.6 (25)	3.2 (22)

Table 3 MAINTENANCE TORQUE SPECIFICATIONS

	N•m	ft.-lb.
Oil drain plug	32	23
Oil filter cover bolt	10	7.2
Oil pressure check bolt	7	5.1
Valve adjuster locknut	20	14
Valve cover bolts	10	7.2
Cylinder head side cover	10	7.2
Spark plug	17.5	12.5
Parking brake locknut	16	11
Rear axle housing		
Lower bolts	50	36
Upper bolts	100	72
Chain adjuster locknuts	16	11
Drive sprocket nuts	15	11
Tie rod locknut	30	22
Wheel lug nuts	45	32

Table 4 BATTERY CAPACITY

Battery capacity	12 volt, 12 amp hour

Table 5 BATTERY STATE OF CHARGE

Specific gravity	State of charge
1.110-1.130	Discharged
1.140-1.160	Almost discharged
1.170-1.190	One-quarter charged
1.200-1.220	One-half charged
1.230-1.250	Three-quarters charged
1.260-1.280	Fully charged

Table 6 RECOMMENDED LUBRICANTS AND FUEL

Engine oil	SAE 10W-40 type SG motor oil
Air filter	Foam air filter oil
Drive chain*	None-tacky O-ring chain lubricant or SAE 30-50 weight engine motor oil
Brake fluid	DOT 4
Steering and suspension lubricant	Lithium base grease
Fuel	Regular gasoline
Control cables	Cable lube**

*Use kerosene to clean drive chain.
**Do not use drive chain lubricant to lubricate control cables.

Table 7 ENGINE OIL CAPACITY

	Liters	U.S. qt.	Imp. qt.
Oil drain	2.4	2.53	2.11
Oil drain and filter change	2.5	2.64	2.20
Total amount	3.2	3.38	2.82

Table 8 DRIVE CHAIN FREE PLAY MEASUREMENT

	mm	in.
Free play	30-40	1.18-1.57

Table 9 TUNE-UP SPECIFICATIONS

Engine compression (at sea level)	
Standard	121 psi (850 kPa)
Minimum	114 psi (800 kPa)
Maximum	128 psi (900 kPa)
Valve clearance	
Intake	0.06-0.10 mm (0.0023-0.0039 in.)
Exhaust	0.16-0.20 mm (0.0063-0.0078 in.)
Ignition timing specifications	
BTDC	10° at 1,000 rpm
Advanced	33° at 5,000 rpm
Checking with timing light	See text

Table 10 SPARK PLUG TYPE AND GAP

	Type	Gap
Standard	NGK D8EA/ND X24ES-U	0.6-0.7 mm (0.024-0.028 in.)

Table 11 CARBURETOR SPECIFICATIONS

Engine idle speed	1,450-1,550 rpm
Pilot air screw adjustment	
1987-1989	1 1/4 turns out
1990-on	2 turns out

CHAPTER FOUR

ENGINE TOP END

The engine is an air-cooled, single cam, two-valve single. Valves are operated by a single chain-driven camshaft.

This chapter provides complete service and overhaul procedures, including information for disassembly, removal, inspection, service and reassembly of the engine top end components. These include the camshaft, valves, cylinder head, piston, piston rings and cylinder block.

Before starting any work, read the service hints in Chapter One. You will do a better job with this information fresh in your mind.

Table 1 lists general engine specifications and **Table 2** lists engine service specifications. **Tables 1-7** are at the end of the chapter.

ENGINE PRINCIPLES

Figure 1 explains basic four-stroke engine operation. This will be helpful when troubleshooting or repairing your engine.

CYLINDER HEAD

The cylinder head can be removed with the engine mounted in the frame. Refer to **Figure 2** when servicing the cylinder head.

Removal

1. Remove the following components as described in Chapter Thirteen:
   a. Seat.
   b. Front panel.
   c. Front fender.
2. Disconnect the negative battery cable (**Figure 3**).
3. Remove the following components as described in Chapter Eight:
   a. Fuel tank.
   b. Carburetor.
   c. Exhaust pipe.
4. Remove the upper front engine mounting brackets.

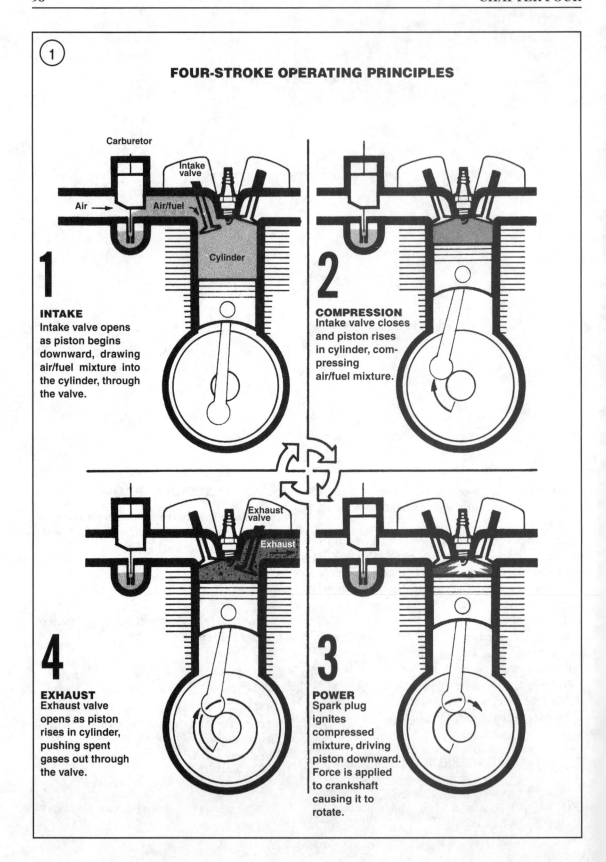

①

FOUR-STROKE OPERATING PRINCIPLES

Carburetor

Intake valve

Air →   Air/fuel

Cylinder

1

INTAKE
Intake valve opens
as piston begins
downward, drawing
air/fuel mixture into
the cylinder, through
the valve.

2

COMPRESSION
Intake valve closes
and piston rises
in cylinder, com-
pressing
air/fuel mixture.

Exhaust valve

Exhaust

4

EXHAUST
Exhaust valve
opens as piston
rises in cylinder,
pushing spent
gases out through
the valve.

3

POWER
Spark plug
ignites
compressed
mixture, driving
piston downward.
Force is applied
to crankshaft
causing it to
rotate.

② **CYLINDER HEAD**

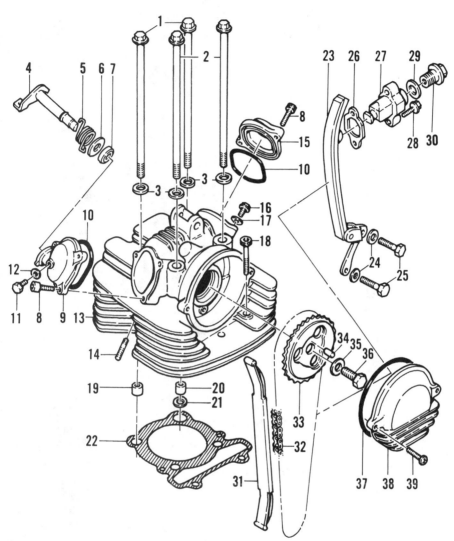

1. Bolt
2. Bolt
3. Washer
4. Decompression lever
   (1987-1988)
5. Spring (1987-1988)
6. Washer (1987-1988)
7. Oil seal (1987-1988)
8. Allen bolt
9. Valve cover (exhaust)
10. O-ring
11. Pin bolt (1987-1988)
12. Washer (1987-1988)
13. Cylinder head

14. Studs
15. Valve cover (intake)
16. Bolt
17. Washer
18. Allen bolt
19. Dowel pin
20. Dowel pin
21. Seal
22. Head gasket
23. Rear chain guide
24. Washer
25. Bolt
26. Gasket

27. Chain tensioner
28. Bolt
29. Washer
30. Tensioner plug
31. Front chain guide
32. Cam chain
33. Sprocket
34. Pin
35. Washer
36. Bolt
37. O-ring
38. Cover
39. Bolt

4

5A. If so equipped, remove the pull-starter assembly as described in Chapter Five.

5B. Remove the left-hand crankcase cover (**Figure 4**) and O-ring.

6. Remove the ignition timing window plug and O-ring (**Figure 5**).

7. Remove the cylinder head side cover and O-rings (A, **Figure 6**).

8. Remove the exhaust (B, **Figure 6**) and intake (C, **Figure 6**) valve covers.

NOTE
Early models are equipped with a decompression cam assembly mounted in the exhaust valve cover.

9. Remove the spark plug. This will make it easier to turn the engine by hand.

10. The engine must be set to top dead center (TDC) on its compression stroke before removing the upper cam sprocket bolt and sprocket in the following procedures. Perform the following:

   a. With a wrench on the crankshaft starter pulley (**Figure 7**), turn the crankshaft counterclockwise and align the camshaft sprocket index mark (A, **Figure 8**) with the cylinder head mark (B, **Figure 8**).

   b. Now check that the "T" mark on the rotor is aligned with the crankcase index mark; see **Figure 9** and **Figure 10**. If these marks are not aligned, turn the crankshaft one revolution counterclockwise and align the rotor "T" mark with the crankcase index mark.

   c. When the camshaft sprocket and rotor marks are properly aligned, both rocker arms will have a valve clearance, indicating that both the intake and exhaust valves are closed. Move each

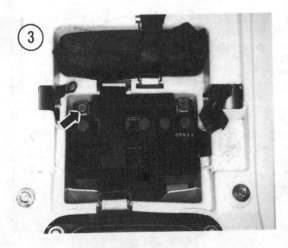

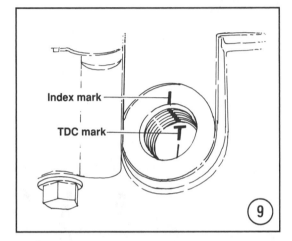

Index mark

TDC mark

rocker arm by hand. There should be some side movement.

11. To remove the cam chain tensioner:

   a. Loosen, but do not remove, the cam chain tensioner end cap bolt (A, **Figure 11**).

   b. Remove the cam chain tensioner mounting bolts (B, **Figure 11**) and remove the tensioner body (C, **Figure 11**) from the cylinder block.

12. Secure the cam chain with safety wire. This will prevent the chain from falling down into the cylinder chain tunnel.

13. Hold the crankshaft starter pulley (**Figure 7**) with a wrench and loosen the camshaft sprocket bolt (A, **Figure 12**).

14. Remove the camshaft sprocket bolt and washer (A, **Figure 12**). Then slide the camshaft sprocket (B, **Figure 12**) from the camshaft and remove it.

NOTE
The camshaft and both rocker arms can be removed with the cylinder head mounted in the frame. To do so, refer to **Camshaft and Rocker Arm Removal** *in this chapter.*

15. Using the crisscross pattern shown in **Figure 13**, loosen the cylinder head mounting bolts in equal amounts until all of the bolts are loose.

16. Remove the 2 cylinder head Allen bolts (**Figure 14**).

17. Remove the 2 rear cylinder head mounting bolts and washers (**Figure 15**).

18. Tap the cylinder head with a rubber mallet to break it free from the head gasket.

19. To remove the cylinder head and the 2 front cylinder head mounting bolts:

NOTE
Because of the cylinder head's mounting position (angle) on the engine, the 2 front cylinder head mounting bolts will contact the upper frame tubes as you try to remove them. These bolts can be removed as follows.

a. Lift the cylinder head slightly and then pivot the rear of the head (intake side) up (**Figure 16**). At the same time, lift the 2 front cylinder head mounting bolts as far as possible (**Figure 17**).

b. Continue to tilt the cylinder head forward until the 2 mounting bolts can be removed by lifting them past the wiring harness and frame tubes as shown in **Figure 18**. Remove both bolts and their washers.

c. Remove the cylinder head.

20. Remove the cylinder head gasket.

21. Remove the exhaust side cam chain guide.

22. Remove the dowel pins and O-ring (**Figure 19**) from the top of the cylinder block.

23. Cover the cylinder block with a clean shop rag or paper towels.

24. If necessary, remove the camshaft and rocker arms as described in this chapter.

Cylinder Head Inspection

1. Remove all traces of gasket residue from the head and cylinder mating surfaces. Do not scratch the gasket surface.

2. Without removing the valves, remove all carbon deposits from the combustion chamber. Use a fine wire brush dipped in solvent or make a scraper from hardwood. Take care not to damage the head, valves or spark plug threads.

CAUTION
If the combustion chamber is cleaned while the valves are removed, you may damage the valve seat surfaces. A damaged or even slightly scratched valve seat will cause poor valve seating.

3. Examine the spark plug threads in the cylinder head for damage. If damage is minor or if the threads are dirty or clogged with carbon, use a spark plug thread tap to clean the threads following the manufacturer's instructions. If thread damage is severe, the threads can be restored by installing a steel thread insert. Thread insert kits can be purchased at auto-

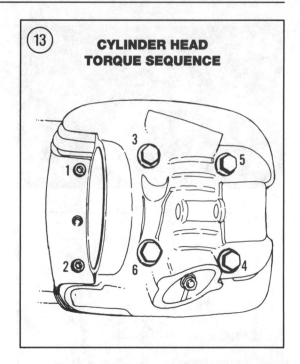

(13) **CYLINDER HEAD TORQUE SEQUENCE**

motive supply stores or you can have the inserts installed by a Yamaha dealer or machine shop.

NOTE
When using a tap to clean spark plug threads, coat the tap with an aluminum tap cutting fluid or kerosene.

NOTE
Aluminum spark plug threads are commonly damaged due to galling, cross-threading and overtightening. To prevent galling, apply an anti-seize compound on the plug threads before installation and do not overtighten.

4. After all carbon is removed from combustion chambers and valve ports, and the spark plug thread holes are repaired, clean the entire head in solvent.

NOTE
If the cylinder head was bead-blasted, make sure to clean the head thoroughly with solvent and then with hot soapy water. Residue grit seats in small crevices and other areas and can be hard to get out. Also chase each exposed thread with a tap to remove grit between the threads or you may damage a thread later. Residue grit left in the engine will contaminate the oil and cause premature piston, ring and bearing wear.

5. Examine the piston crown. The crown should show no signs of wear or damage. If the crown appears pecked or spongy-looking, also check the spark plug, valves and combustion chamber for aluminum deposits. If these deposits are found, the cylinder is suffering from excessive heat caused by a lean fuel mixture or preignition.

6. Inspect the intake manifold for cracks or other damage that would allow unfiltered air to enter the engine.

7. Check for cracks in the combustion chamber and exhaust ports (**Figure 20**). A cracked head must be replaced if it cannot be repaired by welding.

8. After the head has been thoroughly cleaned, place a straightedge across the gasket surface at several points (**Figure 21**). Measure warp by attempting to insert a feeler gauge between the straightedge and cylinder head at each location. Maximum allowable warpage is listed in **Table 2**. Warpage or nicks in the cylinder head surface could

cause an air leak and result in overheating. If warpage exceeds the limit, the cylinder head must be resurfaced or replaced. Consult a Yamaha dealer or machine shop experienced in this type of work.

9. Check the cylinder head bolts for thread damage, cracks and twisting. Check the washers for cracks and other damage.

Cam Chain Tensioner
Inspection

The automatic cam chain tensioner should be checked for damaged parts prior to reassembly.

1. Remove the plug bolt and washer and withdraw the spring (**Figure 22**).

2. Remove all gasket residue from the cam chain tensioner and cylinder block gasket surfaces.

3. Clean all parts in solvent and dry thoroughly.

4. Check plug cap for cracks or damaged threads.

5. Check the spring for bending, unequally spaced coils or other damage.

6. Check the tensioner rack teeth for damage.

7. Replace any component as required.

8. Leave the tensioner disassembled until reassembly.

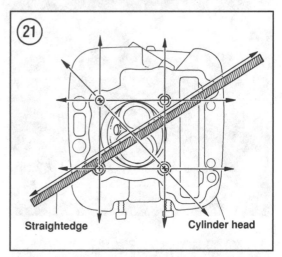

Straightedge   Cylinder head

Installation

1. Clean the cylinder head and cylinder mating surfaces of all gasket residue.

2. If removed, install the following components as described in this chapter:
   a. Valves.
   b. Camshaft.
   c. Rocker arms and shafts.

3. Install the 2 cylinder head dowel pins (**Figure 19**). Install a new O-ring around the rear O-ring (**Figure 19**). Install a new cylinder head gasket.

4. If the crankshaft was rotated away from TDC, perform the following:
   a. Lift the cam chain and make sure it is engaged with the crankshaft cam chain sprocket. Hold the chain in this position when turning the crankshaft.

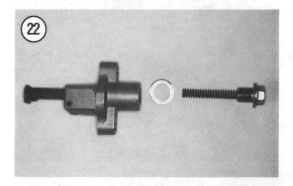

> *CAUTION*
> *The cam chain must be kept tight*
> *against its sprocket when turning the*
> *crankshaft. Otherwise, the chain can*

roll off the sprocket and bind in the lower end, causing chain damage.

b. With a wrench on the crankshaft starter pulley (**Figure 7**), turn the crankshaft counterclockwise and align the "T" mark on the rotor with the crankcase index mark; see **Figure 9** and **Figure 10**.

5. Install the exhaust side cam chain guide into the cylinder head chain guide slot (**Figure 23**). Make sure the chain guide's sliding surface faces toward the cam chain as shown in **Figure 23**.

6. Install a washer on each cylinder head mounting bolt. Then identify the bolts and set them aside, ready for reassembly.

NOTE
Two different length cylinder head mounting bolts are used.

The longer mounting bolts are installed on the left-hand side (**Figure 24**).

7. To install the cylinder head and the 2 front cylinder head mounting bolts:

a. Position the cylinder head between the frame and cylinder block and run the cam chain and its safety wire through the cylinder head chain tunnel (**Figure 25**). Tie the safety wire to the frame.

NOTE
Because of chain slack, the cam chain can easily slip off of the crankshaft sprocket. Pull up on the chain and make sure it is properly engaged with the sprocket before continuing.

b. Tilt the cylinder head forward (**Figure 26**) and hold in this position.

c. Install the 2 front cylinder head mounting bolts and washers (**Figure 27**) through the frame tubes and into the cylinder head. Lower the cylinder head while aligning it with the cylinder block. Continue to feed the bolts (**Figure 28**) through the cylinder head until the head is level with the cylinder block and the bolts can be installed all the way.

d. Lift the cylinder head (slightly) and check that the 2 dowel pins and O-ring (**Figure 19**) are in position.

e. Set the cylinder head onto the cylinder block. Check that the 2 dowel pins, O-ring and head gasket are seated properly.

8. Install the 2 rear cylinder head mounting bolts and washers (**Figure 29**).

9. Tighten the 4 cylinder head mounting bolts finger-tight.

10. Install the 2 cylinder head Allen bolts (**Figure 14**) and tighten finger-tight.

11. Tighten the cylinder mounting bolts and Allen bolts in 2-3 stages in the crisscross pattern shown in **Figure 30**. Tighten to the final torque specification listed in **Table 7**.

12. Install the camshaft and rocker arms, if previously removed, as described in this chapter.

NOTE
Steps 13-19 set camshaft timing. The crankshaft was set at TDC in Step 4.

13. Confirm that the flywheel "T" mark is aligned with the crankcase timing mark as shown in **Figure 31**. If not, repeat Step 4.

14. Turn the camshaft so that its dowel pin (A, **Figure 32**) aligns with the cylinder head index mark (B, **Figure 32**).

15. Remove the safety wire from the top of the cam chain and reconnect at a lower part of the chain so that you can remove it after installing the cam sprocket.

16. Align the cam sprocket so that its timing mark faces out and is positioned at 12 o'clock. Then install the cam chain onto the cam sprocket.

17. Slide the cam sprocket onto the camshaft, engaging the notch in the sprocket with the camshaft pin (A, **Figure 33**).

18. Check that the cam sprocket timing mark (B, **Figure 33**) aligns with the cylinder head timing

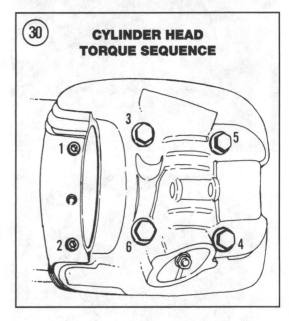

CYLINDER HEAD TORQUE SEQUENCE

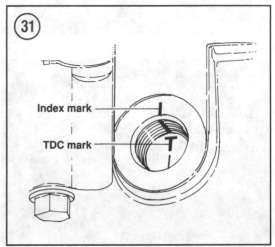

Index mark

TDC mark

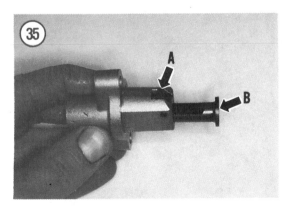

mark (C, **Figure 33**). If not, remove the sprocket and reposition it into the cam chain.

19. When the timing marks are correct, install the cam sprocket mounting bolt and washer and tighten finger-tight (**Figure 34**).

> *CAUTION*
> *Do not rotate the crankshaft more than 1/2 turn (180°) or piston and valve damage may occur.*

20. Turn the crankshaft clockwise and then counterclockwise (less than 1/4 turn both ways) and then realign the timing marks (**Figure 31**). This step removes slack from the front of the cam chain.

21. Insert your finger through the cam chain tensioner hole in the cylinder block and push hard against the cam chain. Now check that the camshaft sprocket timing marks aligns with the cylinder head timing mark (**Figure 33**). If the timing marks align, perform Step 22. If not, remove the cam sprocket and reinstall it so that the timing marks align.

22. Hold the starter pulley with a wrench and torque the cam sprocket bolt to the specification in **Table 7**.

23. Install the cam chain tensioner as follows:

   a. Remove the cam chain tensioner end cap, washer and spring (**Figure 22**), if you have not previously done so.

   b. Release the cam chain tensioner one-way cam (A, **Figure 35**) with your finger and push the tensioner rod (B, **Figure 35**) into the tensioner body until it stops and locks in place. See **Figure 36**.

   c. Install a new gasket onto the cam chain tensioner.

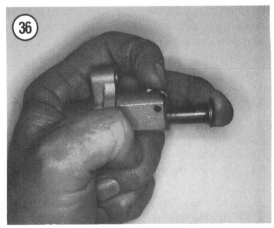

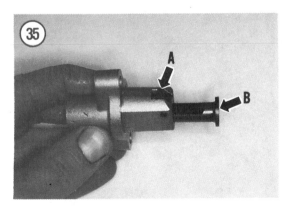

d. Insert the cam chain tensioner into the cylinder with the one-way cam facing down (**Figure 37**).

e. Install the tensioner body 6 mm mounting bolts (**Figure 38**) and tighten to the torque specification in **Table 7**.

f. Install the spring, washer and end cap bolt (**Figure 39**). Push the end cap bolt into position and thread it into the tensioner body. Tighten the tensioner end cap bolt (**Figure 40**) to the torque specification in **Table 7**.

24. Check valve adjustment as described in Chapter Three.

NOTE
Apply a lithium soap base grease to the valve cover and cylinder head side cover O-rings prior to installation.

NOTE
Early models are equipped with a decompression cam assembly mounted in the exhaust valve cover.

25. Install the valve covers with their inner ridge (**Figure 41**) facing upward. Install and tighten the valve cover mounting bolts to the torque specification in **Table 7**.

26. Install the cylinder head side cover and O-ring. Tighten mounting bolts to the torque specification in **Table 7**.

27. Install the ignition timing window plug and O-ring. Tighten the plug securely.

28A. If removed, install the pull-starter assembly as described in Chapter Five.

28B. Install the left-hand crankcase cover and O-ring. Tighten the mounting bolts securely.

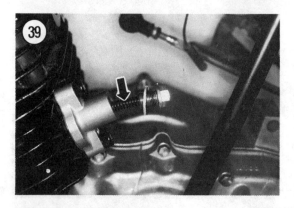

29. Install the spark plug and reconnect the spark plug cap.

30. Install the upper front engine mounting bracket, mounting bolts and nut (**Figure 42**). Tighten to the torque specification in **Table 7**. Reposition the throttle cable(s) and wiring harness through the mounting bracket guides.

31. Install the following components as described in Chapter Eight:

a. Exhaust pipe.

b. Carburetor.

c. Fuel tank.

32. Reconnect the negative battery cable at the battery.

33. Install the following components as described in Chapter Thirteen:

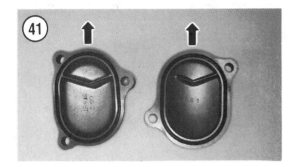

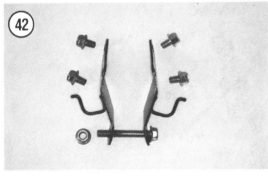

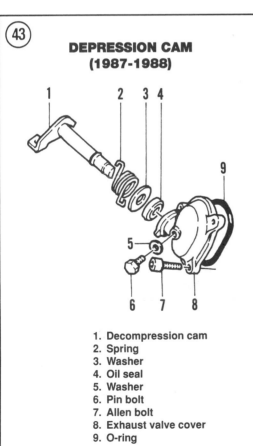

**DEPRESSION CAM
(1987-1988)**

1. Decompression cam
2. Spring
3. Washer
4. Oil seal
5. Washer
6. Pin bolt
7. Allen bolt
8. Exhaust valve cover
9. O-ring

a. Front fender.

b. Front panel.

c. Seat.

34. Start the engine and check for fuel, exhaust and compression leaks.

DECOMPRESSION CAM
(1987-1988)

A hand-operated decompression cam assembly (**Figure 43**) is mounted in the exhaust valve cover on 1987-1988 models.

Removal/Disassembly

1. Remove the following components as described in Chapter Thirteen:

a. Seat.

b. Front panel.

c. Front fender.

2. Remove the exhaust valve cover mounting bolts and remove the exhaust valve cover and O-ring.

3. Remove the pin bolt and washer.

4. Withdraw the decompression cam, spring and washer.

5. Install by reversing these steps, while noting the following.

6. Engage the pin bolt into the pin bolt groove in the decompression cam. Tighten the pin bolt securely.

7. Apply a lithium soap base grease to the valve cover O-ring prior to installation.

Inspection

1. Clean all components in solvent and dry thoroughly.

2. Check decompression cam for:

a. Damaged cam end.

b. Damaged pin bolt groove.

c. Cracks or other damage.

3. Check the spring and washer for damage.

4. Inspect the exhaust valve cover O-ring for damage.

5. Replace damaged parts as required.

6. Replace the oil seal in the valve cover if leaking or damaged. Pack the oil seal lips with grease.

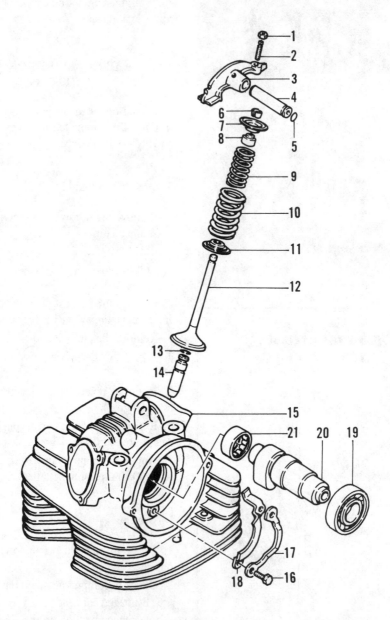

ROCKER ARM, VALVE AND CAMSHAFT

1. Locknut
2. Valve adjuster
3. Rocker arm
4. Rocker arm shaft
5. O-ring
6. Valve keepers
7. Upper valve seat
8. Oil seal
9. Inner valve spring
10. Outer valve spring
11. Lower valve seat
12. Valve
13. Clip
14. Valve guide
15. Cylinder head
16. Bolt
17. Lockwasher
18. Stopper plate
19. Bearing
20. Camshaft
21. Needle bearing

CAMSHAFT AND ROCKER ARMS

A single camshaft is mounted in the cylinder head. The camshaft is held in place with a ball bearing and needle bearing. The camshaft is driven by a chain off of the timing sprocket on the crankshaft. The cam and both rocker arms can be removed with the engine in the frame, or you can remove the cylinder head as previously described.

Refer to **Figure 44** when performing this procedure.

Special Tools

The Yamaha slide hammer set (part No. YU-01083) or equivalent (**Figure 45**) will be required to remove the rocker arms shafts from the cylinder head. If you are going to fabricate or assemble a slide hammer assembly, the threaded shaft requires M6 × 1.00 mm threads.

NOTE
Many of the following steps are shown with the engine removed from the frame. As previously mentioned the camshaft can be removed with the engine either in or out of the frame.

Removal

1. Park the vehicle on level ground and set the parking brake.

2. Remove the camshaft sprocket as described under *Cylinder Head Removal* in this chapter.

NOTE
If the engine is mounted in the frame, it is unnecessary to remove the upper engine mount bracket, carburetor and exhaust pipe when removing the camshaft and rocker arms.

3. Pry back the lockwasher tabs and remove the 2 camshaft retainer bolts.

4. Remove the lockwasher (A, **Figure 46**) and camshaft retainer (B, **Figure 46**).

5. Thread the cam sprocket mounting bolt into the camshaft (**Figure 47**) and carefully pull the camshaft out of the cylinder head. See **Figure 48**.

NOTE
Both rocker arms and shafts are identical (same part numbers). However, because these parts have taken a set wear pattern, the rocker arms and shafts should be labeled to avoid intermixing the parts. When removing the rocker arm assemblies in the following steps, mark them in sets: "E" (exhaust) or "I" (intake).

6. Thread a slide hammer (Yamaha part No. YU-01083) or equivalent into one of the rocker arm shafts (**Figure 49**). Operate the slide hammer and remove the rocker arm shaft and O-ring (**Figure 50**). Remove the rocker arm (**Figure 51**).
7. Repeat Step 7 for the opposite rocker shaft and rocker arm.

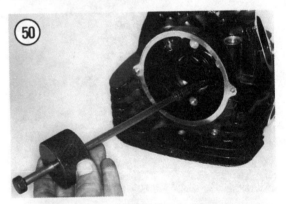

Camshaft Inspection

Camshaft service specifications are listed in **Table 2**.
1. Check cam lobes (A, **Figure 52**) for wear. The lobes should not be scored and the edges should be square.
2. Even though the cam lobe surface appears to be satisfactory, with no visible signs of wear, each lobe must be measured with a micrometer. Measure the lobe height (**Figure 53**) and the base circle diameter (**Figure 54**). Replace the camshaft if worn beyond the service specifications.
3. Check the camshaft right side bearing journal (B, **Figure 52**) for wear and scoring.
4. The left-hand camshaft bearing (C, **Figure 52**) is a press-fit and should not be removed unless you are going to replace it or the camshaft. Refer to *Camshaft Bearings* in this section.

5. Place the camshaft between lathe centers and check its runout with a dial indicator—position the dial indicator stem against the camshaft bearing journal. Replace the camshaft if runout exceeds the service limit in **Table 2**.

Camshaft Bearings Inspection/Replacement

The camshaft bearing assembly (**Figure 44**) consists of the following:
   a. The left-hand bearing is a single row ball bearing, rubber shielded on one side (**Figure 55**).

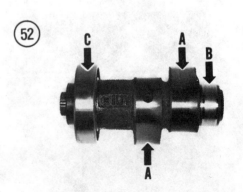

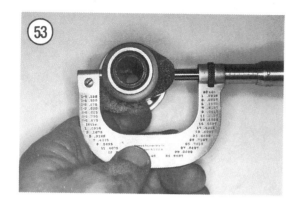

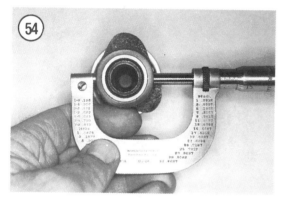

This bearing is installed with a press-fit on the camshaft.

b. A caged needle bearing, which supports the right-hand camshaft journal, is pressed into a recess in the cylinder head (**Figure 56**).

NOTE
Do not remove the bearings unless they require replacement.

1. Clean the camshaft/bearing assembly in solvent. Blow dry with compressed air.

2. Hold the camshaft and rotate the outer bearing race with your hand. The bearing should turn smoothly with no roughness, binding or excessive play. Bearing should show no signs of overheating. Bearing shield should not be dented or otherwise damaged. If the bea᠎ g does not show visual damage but turns roughly, reclean the bearing and re-check. If the condition still persists, replace the bearing as described in Step 3.

3. To replace the ball-bearing, refer to *Ball-Bearing Replacement* in Chapter One while noting the following:

a. Remove the dowel pin from the end of the camshaft.

b. Support the bearing in a press and press the camshaft off of the bearing. Discard the bearing.

c. Reclean the camshaft in solvent. Blow dry.

CAUTION
Align and press the bearing onto the camshaft carefully so that you do not damage the outer shield. A damaged shield will leak oil.

d. Align the new bearing with the camshaft (shielded side facing out) and press the bearing onto the camshaft until it bottoms against the camshaft shoulder.

e. Install the dowel pin.

f. Lubricate the bearing with new engine oil.

NOTE
If the camshaft is not going to be immediately installed in the engine, store the camshaft/bearing assembly in a plastic bag. This is to prevent the bearing from contamination.

4. Inspect the needle bearing (**Figure 56**) for visual damage. Then turn the bearing rollers with a finger, checking for roughness or damaged rollers. If the

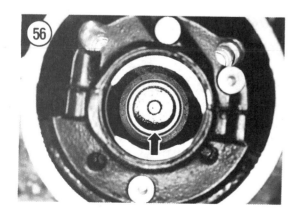

bearing is damaged, replace the bearing as described in Step 5.

5. To replace the needle bearing (**Figure 56**):

   a. Support the cylinder head and remove the needle bearing with a universal internal bearing remover.

   b. Clean the cylinder head in solvent. Blow dry with compressed air.

   c. Support the cylinder head and press the new bearing into the cylinder recess until it bottoms out; the manufacturer's numbers on the bearing should face out.

Camshaft Sprocket Inspection

Inspect the upper camshaft sprocket (**Figure 57**) for broken or chipped teeth. Also check the teeth for cracking or rounding. If the upper sprocket is damaged or severely worn, inspect the lower sprocket mounted on the crankshaft.

> *NOTE*
> *If the camshaft sprockets are worn, check the camshaft chain, chain guides and chain tensioner for damage.*

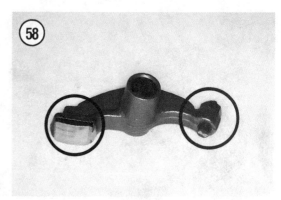

Rocker Arms and Shafts Inspection

1. Clean all parts in solvent. Blow dry with compressed air.

2. Inspect the rocker arm pad where it rides on the cam lobe and where the adjuster rides on the valve stem (**Figure 58**). Check for scratches, flat spots, uneven wear and scoring.

3. Replace the valve adjuster if it has stretched or is damaged in any way.

4. Inspect the rocker arm shaft (A, **Figure 59**) for signs of wear or scoring.

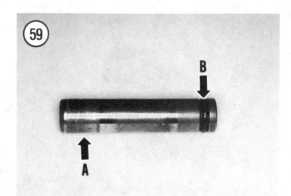

5. Replace the rocker arm shaft O-ring (B, **Figure 59**) prior to installing the rocker arm.

6. Calculate rocker arm shaft clearance as follows:

   a. Measure rocker arm inside bore diameter (**Figure 60**) and record the measurement.

   b. Measure rocker arm shaft outer diameter (**Figure 61**) and record the measurement.

   c. Subtract the measurement in sub-step b from the measurement in sub-step a to determine rocker arm shaft clearance. Replace the rocker arm and

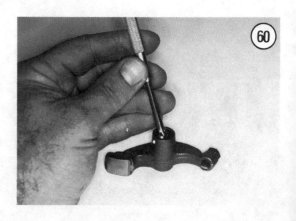

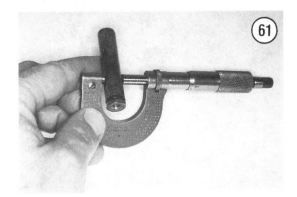

shaft if the clearance meets or exceeds the specification in **Table 2**.

7. Repeat for the other rocker arm assembly.

Installation

1. Install a new O-ring (B, **Figure 59**) on each rocker arm shaft.

2. Coat the rocker arm shaft, O-ring and rocker arm bore with assembly oil.

NOTE
Install the rocker arms and shafts in their original positions.

3. Install the rocker arm shaft (**Figure 62**) with its threaded hole facing out. Partially drive the rocker arm shaft into the cylinder head and position the rocker arm (**Figure 51**) in the cylinder head. The valve adjuster on the rocker arm must be facing out. Continue to drive the rocker arm shaft through the cylinder head until it aligns and enters the rocker arm and then bottoms out.

NOTE
*After installing the rocker arm shaft, check the end of the rocker arm shaft (**Figure 63**) for bits of rubber, indicating that the O-ring was torn during installation. If this material is noted, remove the rocker arm shaft, replace the O-ring and reinstall.*

4. Repeat Step 2 and 3 for the other rocker arm assembly.

5. Coat the camshaft journal, lobes and bearing rollers (open side) with new engine oil.

6. Install the cam through the cylinder head opening and seat it into the needle bearing. The pin on the cam should be facing up when installing the cam. See **Figure 64**.

7. Install the camshaft retainer (**Figure 65**).

8. Install the lockwasher and the 2 camshaft retainer bolts (**Figure 66**). Tighten the camshaft retainer bolts to the torque specification in **Table 7**. Bend the lockwasher tabs over the bolt heads.

9. Install the cylinder head and camshaft sprocket as described in this chapter.

CAM CHAIN

A continuous cam chain is used on all models. Do not cut the chain, as replacement link components are not available.

Removal/Installation

1. Remove the camshaft sprocket as described under *Cylinder Head Removal* in this chapter.
2. Remove the flywheel as described in Chapter Five.
3. Slip the cam chain (A, **Figure 67**) off of the lower sprocket and remove it.
4. Install by reversing these steps.

Inspection

1. Clean cam chain in solvent. Blow dry with compressed air.
2. Check cam chain for:
   a. Worn or damaged pins and rollers.
   b. Cracked or damaged side plates.
3. If the cam chain is damaged, replace it with a new one. If the chain is severely worn, replace the upper and lower sprockets (**Figure 68**) at the same time.

> *CAUTION*
> *Do not attempt to repair the cam chain.*

CHAIN GUIDES

Front and rear chain guides are used.

Removal/Installation

1. To remove the front chain guide, first remove the cylinder head as described in this chapter.
2. To remove the rear chain guide, perform the following:
   a. Remove the cylinder as described in this chapter.
   b. Remove the flywheel as described in Chapter Five.
   c. Remove the rear chain guide mounting bolts and remove the rear chain guide (B, **Figure 67**).
3. Install by reversing these steps. Apply Loctite 242 (blue) to the rear chain guide mounting bolts prior to installation. Tighten the bolts securely.

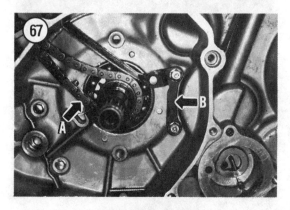

VALVES AND VALVE COMPONENTS

Correct valve service requires a number of special tools. The following procedures describe how to check for valve component wear and to determine what type of service is required. In most cases, valve troubles are caused by poor valve seating, worn valve guides and burned valves. A valve spring compressor will be required to remove and install the valves.

Refer to **Figure 69** for this procedure.

1. Remove the cylinder head as described in this chapter.

2. Install a valve spring compressor squarely over the valve spring seat with the other end of tool placed against valve head (**Figure 70**).

3. Tighten valve spring compressor until the valve keepers separate. Lift valve keepers out through the

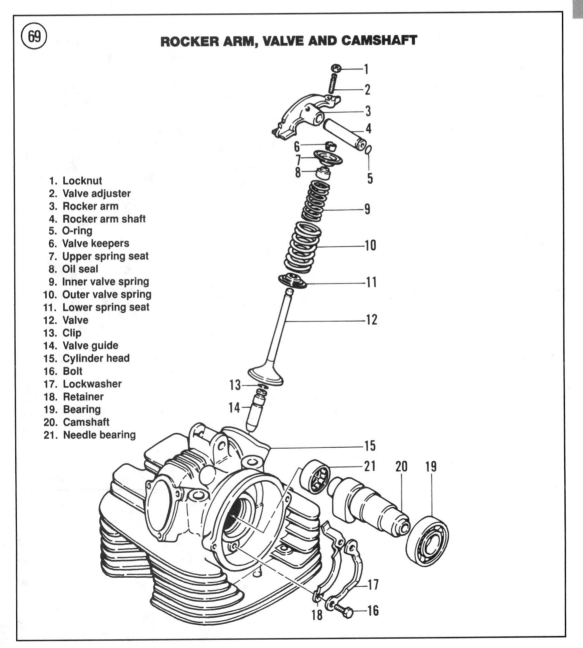

ROCKER ARM, VALVE AND CAMSHAFT

1. Locknut
2. Valve adjuster
3. Rocker arm
4. Rocker arm shaft
5. O-ring
6. Valve keepers
7. Upper spring seat
8. Oil seal
9. Inner valve spring
10. Outer valve spring
11. Lower spring seat
12. Valve
13. Clip
14. Valve guide
15. Cylinder head
16. Bolt
17. Lockwasher
18. Retainer
19. Bearing
20. Camshaft
21. Needle bearing

valve spring compressor (**Figure 71**) with needlenose pliers.

4. Gradually loosen the valve spring compressor
and remove it from the head.

5. Remove the upper spring seat and both valve
springs.

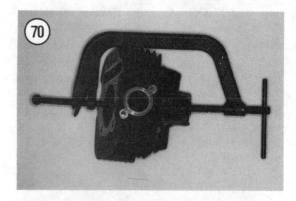

> *CAUTION*
> *Remove any burrs from the valve stem*
> *grooves before removing the valves*
> *(**Figure 72**); otherwise the valve guides*
> *will be damaged as the valve stems are*
> *passed through them.*

6. Remove the valve.

7. Pull the oil seal (**Figure 73**) off of the valve guide.

8. Remove the lower spring seat.

> *CAUTION*
> *All component parts of each valve as-*
> *sembly must be kept together. Do not*
> *intermix components from the different*
> *valves or excessive wear may result.*

9. Repeat Steps 2-8 and remove remaining valve.

Inspection

Refer to the troubleshooting chart in **Figure 74**
when performing valve inspection procedures in this
section. Valve service specifications are listed in
Table 3 and **Table 4**.

1. Clean valves in solvent. Do not gouge or damage
the valve seating surface.

2. Inspect the contact surface (**Figure 75**) of each
valve for burning. Minor roughness and pitting can
be removed by lapping the valve as described in this
chapter. Excessive unevenness to the contact surface
is an indication that the valve is not serviceable.

3. Inspect the valve stems for wear and roughness.
Then measure the valve stem outside diameter for
wear using a micrometer (**Figure 76**). Compare with
specifications in **Table 3**.

4. Remove all carbon and varnish from the valve
guides with a stiff spiral wire brush before measuring wear.

> *NOTE*
> *If you do not have the required measur-*
> *ing tools, proceed to Step 7.*

5. Measure each valve guide at top, center and bottom inside diameter with a small hole gauge. Then

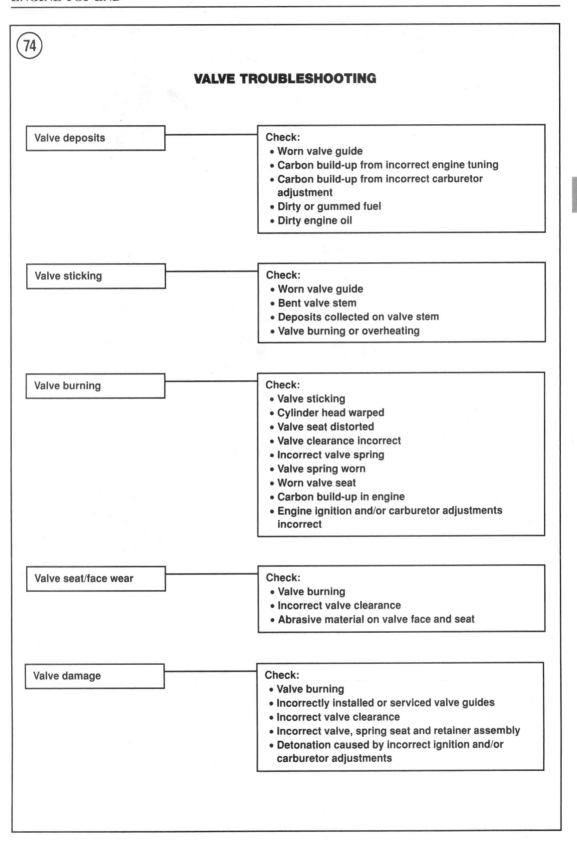

74

VALVE TROUBLESHOOTING

Valve deposits

Check:
- Worn valve guide
- Carbon build-up from incorrect engine tuning
- Carbon build-up from incorrect carburetor adjustment
- Dirty or gummed fuel
- Dirty engine oil

4

Valve sticking

Check:
- Worn valve guide
- Bent valve stem
- Deposits collected on valve stem
- Valve burning or overheating

Valve burning

Check:
- Valve sticking
- Cylinder head warped
- Valve seat distorted
- Valve clearance incorrect
- Incorrect valve spring
- Valve spring worn
- Worn valve seat
- Carbon build-up in engine
- Engine ignition and/or carburetor adjustments incorrect

Valve seat/face wear

Check:
- Valve burning
- Incorrect valve clearance
- Abrasive material on valve face and seat

Valve damage

Check:
- Valve burning
- Incorrectly installed or serviced valve guides
- Incorrect valve clearance
- Incorrect valve, spring seat and retainer assembly
- Detonation caused by incorrect ignition and/or carburetor adjustments

measure the small hole gauge with a micrometer to determine the valve guide inside diameter. Compare measurements with specification in **Table 3**.

6. Subtract the measurement made in Step 3 from the measurement made in Step 5. The difference is the valve stem-to-guide clearance. See **Table 3** for correct clearance. Replace any guide or valve that is not within tolerance. Valve guide replacement is described later in this chapter.

7. If a small hole gauge is not available, insert each valve in its guide. Hold the valve just slightly off its seat and rock it sideways. If the valve rocks more than slightly, the guide is probably worn. However, as a final check, take the cylinder head to a dealer or machine shop and have the valve guides measured.

8. Check the inner and outer valve springs as follows:

    a. Check each of the valve springs for visual damage.

    b. Use a square and check each spring for distortion or tilt (**Figure 77**). Compare to specifications in **Table 4**.

    c. Measure the valve spring length with a vernier caliper (**Figure 78**). All should be of length specified in **Table 4** with no bends or other distortion.

    d. Replace defective springs as a set.

9. Check the valve spring seats and valve keepers.

10. Inspect valve seats (**Figure 79**). If worn or burned, they may be reconditioned as described in this chapter. Seats and valves in near-perfect condition can be reconditioned by lapping with fine carborundum paste. Check as follows:

    a. Clean the valve seat and valve mating areas with contact cleaner.

    b. Coat the valve seat with machinist's blue.

    c. Install the valve into its guide and rotate it against its seat with a valve lapping tool. See *Valve Lapping* in this chapter.

    d. Lift the valve out of the guide and measure the seat width with vernier calipers.

    e. The seat width for intake and exhaust valves should measure within the specifications listed in **Table 3** all the way around the seat. If the seat width exceeds the service limit (**Table 3**), regrind the seats as described in this chapter.

    f. Remove all machinist's blue residue from the seats and valves.

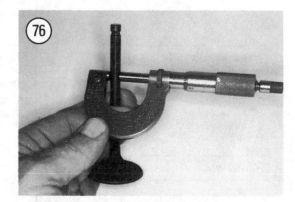

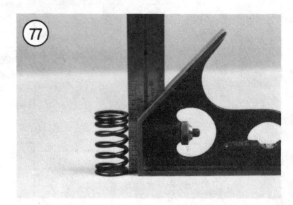

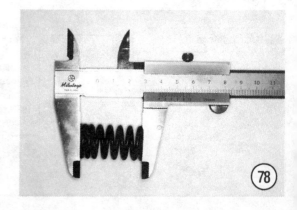

11. Check the valve stem runout with a V-block and dial indicator as shown in **Figure 80**. Compare runout to specifications in **Table 3**.

12. Measure the head diameter of each valve with a vernier caliper or micrometer (**Figure 81**). Compare to specifications in **Table 3**.

Valve Guide Replacement

The valve guides must be removed and installed with special tools that can be ordered from a Yamaha

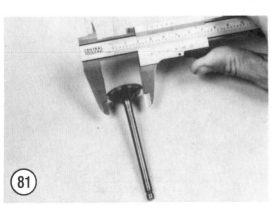

dealer. The required special tools are listed as follows:

    a. Valve guide remover, Yamaha part No. YM-01225.

    b. Valve guide installer, Yamaha part No. YM-04017.

    c. Valve guide reamer, Yamaha part No. YM-01227.

> *NOTE*
> *Before driving the valve guides out of the cylinder head, place the new valve guides in the freezer. The freezing temperature will shrink the new guides slightly and ease installation.*

1. When purchasing new valve guides, purchase valve guide clips also (13, **Figure 69**) and install a clip on each valve guide prior to installing the guides in the following steps.

2. The valve guides are installed with a slight interference fit. The cylinder head must be heated to a temperature of approximately 212-300° F (100-150° C) in a shop oven or hot plate.

> *CAUTION*
> *Do not heat the cylinder head with a torch (propane or acetylene)—never bring a flame into contact with the cylinder head. The direct heat may cause warpage of the cylinder head.*

> *WARNING*
> *Heavy gloves must be worn when performing this procedure—the cylinder head will be very hot.*

3. Remove the cylinder head from the oven or hot plate and place onto wood blocks with the combustion chamber facing *up*.

4. Drive the old valve guide out from the combustion chamber side of the cylinder head with the valve guide remover (**Figure 82**).

5. After the cylinder head cools, check the guide bores for carbon or other contamination. Clean the bores thoroughly.

6. Reheat the cylinder head to approximately 212-300° F (100-150° C).

7. Remove the cylinder head from the oven or hot plate and place it on wood blocks with the combustion chamber facing *down*.

8. Using the valve guide installer, drive the new valve guide into the cylinder head until the clip on the guide bottoms out in the clip recess.

9. After the cylinder head has cooled to room temperature, ream the new valve guides as follows:

   a. Coat the valve guide and valve guide reamer with cutting oil.

> *CAUTION*
> *Always rotate the valve guide reamer in the same direction when installing and removing it from the guide. If the reamer is rotated in the opposite direction, the guide will be damaged and will require replacement.*

   b. Insert the reamer from the top side and rotate the reamer (**Figure 83**). Continue to rotate the reamer and work it down through the entire length of the new valve guide. Apply additional cutting oil during this procedure.

   c. While rotating the reamer *in the same direction*, withdraw the reamer from the valve guide.

   d. Measure the valve guide inside diameter with a small hole gauge. Then measure the small hole gauge with a micrometer to determine the valve guide inside diameter. The valve guide should be within the service specifications listed in **Table 3**.

10. Repeat for the other valve guide.

11. Thoroughly clean the cylinder head and valve guides with solvent to wash out all metal particles. Dry with compressed air.

12. Lightly oil the valve guides to prevent rust.

13. The valve seats must be refaced with a 45° cutter after replacing valve guides. Reface the valve seats as described under *Valve Seat Reconditioning* in this chapter.

Valve Seat Reconditioning

The valve seats must be cut with special tools that are available from a Yamaha dealer. The following tools will be required:

   a. Valve seat cutters (see Yamaha dealer for part numbers).

> *NOTE*
> *The valve seat cutters with angle listed in* ***Figure 84*** *are required for this procedure.*

   b. Vernier caliper.

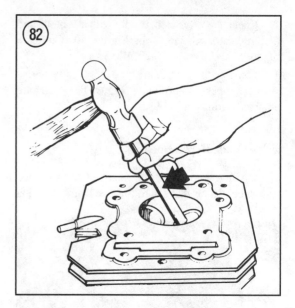

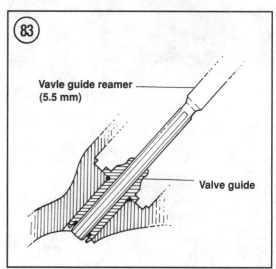

Vavle guide reamer (5.5 mm)

Valve guide

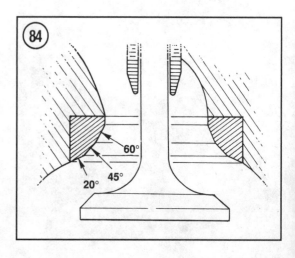

60°
45°
20°

c. Machinist's blue.

d. Valve lapping tool.

NOTE
Follow the manufacturer's instructions
while using valve facing equipment.

1. Inspect valve seats (**Figure 79**). If worn or burned, they should be reconditioned. Seats and valves in near-perfect condition can be recondi-

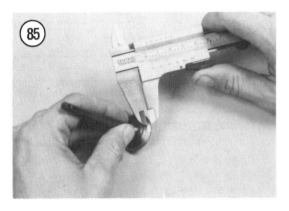

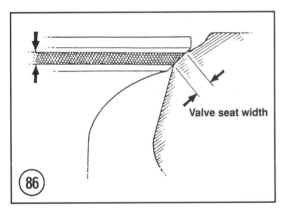

Valve seat width

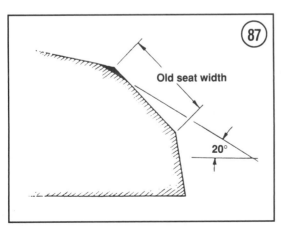

Old seat width

20°

tioned by lapping with fine carborundum paste. Lapping, however, is always inferior to precision grinding. Check as follows:

  a. Clean the valve seat and valve mating areas with contact cleaner.

  b. Coat the valve seat with machinist's blue.

  c. Install the valve into its guide and rotate it against its seat with a valve lapping tool. See *Valve Lapping* in this chapter.

  d. Lift the valve from the guide and measure the seat width with vernier calipers (**Figure 85**). See **Figure 86**.

  e. The seat width for intake and exhaust valves should measure within the specifications listed in **Table 3** all the way around the seat. If the seat width exceeds the service limit (**Table 3**), regrind the seats as follows.

CAUTION
When grinding valve seats, work slowly to avoid overgrinding the seats. Overgrinding the valve seats will sink the valves too far into the cylinder head. Sinking the valves too far may reduce valve clearance and make it impossible to adjust valve clearance. In this condition, the cylinder head would have to be replaced.

2. Install a 45° cutter onto the valve tool and lightly cut the seat to remove roughness.

3. Measure the valve seat with a vernier caliper (**Figure 85**). Record the measurement to use as a reference point when performing the following.

CAUTION
The 20° cutter removes material quickly. Work carefully and check your progress often.

4. Install a 20° cutter onto the valve tool and lightly cut the seat to remove 1/4 of the existing valve seat (**Figure 87**).

5. Install a 60° cutter onto the valve tool and lightly cut the seat to remove the lower 1/4 of the existing valve seat (**Figure 88**).

6. Measure the valve seat with a vernier caliper. Then fit a 45° cutter onto the valve tool and cut the valve seat to the specified seat width listed in **Table 3**. See **Figure 89**.

7. When the valve seat width is correct, check valve seating as follows.

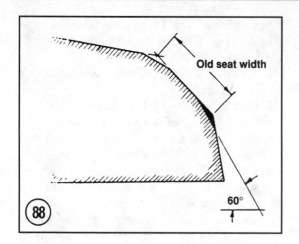

Old seat width

60°

88

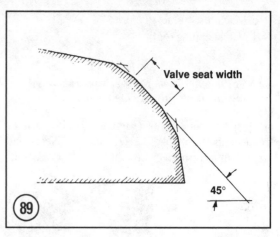

Valve seat width

45°

89

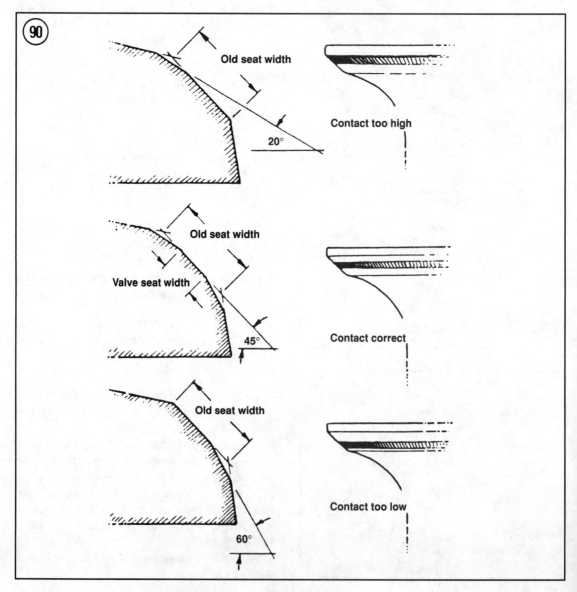

90

Old seat width

20°

Contact too high

Old seat width

Valve seat width

45°

Contact correct

Old seat width

60°

Contact too low

8. Clean the valve seat and valve mating areas with contact cleaner.

9. Coat the valve seat with machinist's blue.

10. Install the valve into its guide and rotate it against its seat with a valve lapping tool. See *Valve Lapping* in this chapter.

11. Remove the valve and check the contact area on the valve (**Figure 90**). Interpret results as follows:

    a. The valve contact area should be approximately in the center of the valve seat area.

    b. If the contact area is too high on the valve, lower the seat with a 20° flat cutter.

    c. If the contact area is too low on the valve, raise the seat with a 60° interior cutter.

    d. Refinish the seat using a 45° cutter.

12. When the contact area is correct, lap the valve as described in this chapter.

Valve Lapping

Valve lapping is a simple operation which can restore the valve seal without machining—if the amount of wear or distortion is not too great.

This procedure should only be performed after determining that valve seat width and outside diameter are within specifications.

1. Smear a light coating of fine grade valve lapping compound on seating surface of valve.

2. Insert the valve into the head.

3. Wet the suction cup of the lapping stick and stick it onto the head of the valve. Lap the valve to the seat by spinning the lapping stick in both directions. Every 5 to 10 seconds, rotate the valve 180° in the valve seat. Continue this action until the mating surfaces on the valve and seat are smooth and equal in size.

4. Closely examine valve seat in cylinder head. It should be smooth and even with a smooth, polished seating "ring."

5. Thoroughly clean the valves and cylinder head in solvent to remove all grinding compound. Any compound left on the valves or the cylinder head will end up in the engine and cause excessive wear and damage.

6. After the lapping has been completed and the valve assemblies have been reinstalled into the head, the valve seal should be tested. Check the seal of each valve by pouring solvent into each of the intake and exhaust ports. There should be no leakage past the seat. If leakage occurs, combustion chamber will appear wet. If fluid leaks past any of the seats, disassemble that valve assembly and repeat the lapping procedure until there is no leakage.

Installation

1. Coat a valve stem with molybdenum disulfide paste and install into its correct guide. Hold the valve in position.

2. Install the lower spring seat (**Figure 91**).

3. Carefully slide a new oil seal (**Figure 92**) over the valve and seat it onto the end of the valve guide. See **Figure 72**.

NOTE
Oil seals should be replaced whenever a valve is removed.

NOTE
*Install valve springs with the narrow pitch end (end with coils closest together) facing the cylinder head. See **Figure 93**.*

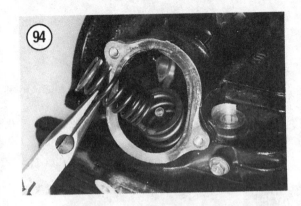

4. Install the inner and outer valve springs (**Figure 94**).

5. Install the upper valve spring seat (**Figure 95**).

6. Push down on the upper valve seat with the valve spring compressor and install the valve keepers (**Figure 96**). After releasing tension from the compressor, examine valve keepers and make sure they are seated correctly (**Figure 97**). Then gently tap the end of the valve stem with a soft-faced hammer. This will ensure that the keepers are properly seated.

7. Repeat Steps 1-6 for opposite valve.

8. After installing the cylinder head onto the engine, check valve clearance and adjust as necessary as described in Chapter Three.

CYLINDER

The alloy cylinder block has a pressed-in cast iron cylinder liner which can be bored to 0.50 mm (0.020 in.) oversize and again to 1.0 mm (0.040 in.) oversize. These oversize piston and ring sizes are available through Yamaha dealers and aftermarket piston suppliers.

The cylinder can be removed with the engine mounted in the frame. Refer to **Figure 98** when servicing the cylinder in the following section.

Removal

1. Remove the cylinder head as described under *Cylinder Head Removal/Installation* in this chapter.

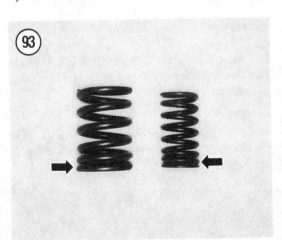

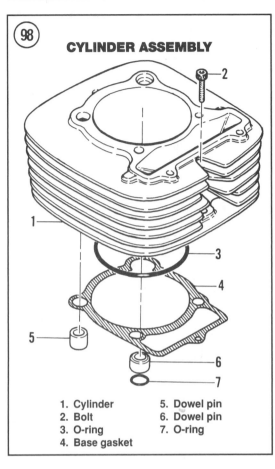

CYLINDER ASSEMBLY

1. Cylinder
2. Bolt
3. O-ring
4. Base gasket
5. Dowel pin
6. Dowel pin
7. O-ring

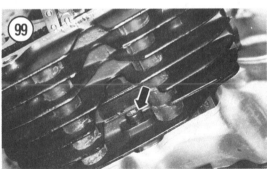

2. Remove the cylinder Allen bolt (**Figure 99**).

3. Loosen the cylinder by tapping around the perimeter with a rubber or plastic mallet.

4. Pull the cylinder straight up and off the crankcase. Remove the base gasket.

5. Remove the 2 dowel pins and O-ring (**Figure 100**).

6. If necessary, remove the piston as described under *Piston Removal/Installation* in this chapter.

7. Cover the crankcase opening to prevent objects and abrasive dust from falling into the crankcase.

Inspection

1. Remove the cylinder O-ring (**Figure 101**) prior to washing the cylinder block in solvent.

2. Remove all gasket residue from the top and bottom cylinder block gasket surfaces.

3. Wash the cylinder block in solvent. Dry with compressed air.

4. Check the dowel pin holes for cracks or other damage.

5. Measure the cylinder bore with a bore gauge or inside micrometer (**Figure 102**). Measure the cylinder bore 40 mm (1.57 in.) from the top of the cylinder as shown in **Figure 103**. Measure in line with the piston pin and 90° to the pin. This measurement determines cylinder bore. Now measure in 3 axes—in line with the piston pin and at 90° to the pin. If the taper or out-of-round is greater than specifications (**Table 2**), the cylinder must be rebored to the next oversize and new piston and rings installed.

NOTE
*The new piston should be obtained first before the cylinder is bored so that the piston can be measured. The cylinder must be bored to match the piston. Piston-to-cylinder clearance is listed in **Table 2**.*

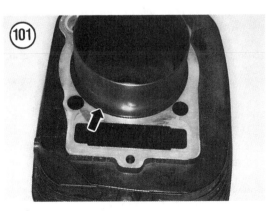

6. If the cylinder is not worn past the service limit, check the bore carefully for scratches or gouges. The bore still may require boring and reconditioning.

7. After the cylinder has been serviced, wash the bore in hot soapy water. This is the only way to clean the cylinder wall of the fine grit material left from the bore or honing job. After washing the cylinder wall, run a clean white cloth through it. The cylinder wall should show no traces of grit or other debris. If the rag is dirty, the cylinder wall is not clean and must be rewashed. After the cylinder is cleaned, lubricate the cylinder wall with clean engine oil to prevent the cylinder liner from rusting.

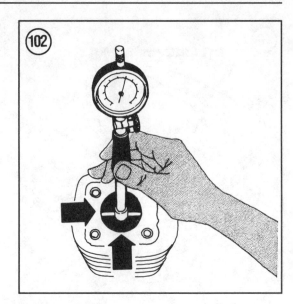

> *CAUTION*
> *A combination of soap and water is the only solution that will completely clean the cylinder wall. Solvent and kerosene cannot wash fine grit out of cylinder crevices. Grit left in the cylinder will act as a grinding compound and cause premature wear to the new rings.*

Installation

1. Check that the top and bottom cylinder surfaces are clean of all gasket residue.

2. Install the O-ring (**Figure 101**) into the groove in the bottom of the cylinder.

3. Install the 2 dowel pins and O-ring into the crankcase (**Figure 100**).

4. Install a new base gasket. Make sure all holes align.

5. If removed, install the piston as described in this chapter.

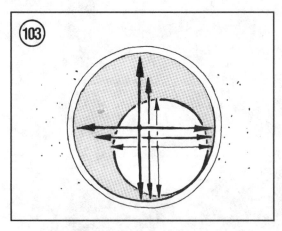

> *CAUTION*
> *Make sure the piston pin circlips are installed and seated correctly.*

6. Install a piston holding fixture under the piston.

> *NOTE*
> *A piston holding fixture can be made out of wood as shown in* ***Figure 104***.

7. Stagger the piston rings around the piston as shown in **Figure 105**.

8. Lubricate the cylinder wall, piston and rings liberally with engine oil prior to installation.

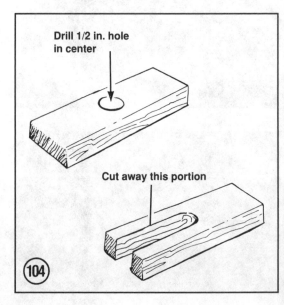

Drill 1/2 in. hole in center

Cut away this portion

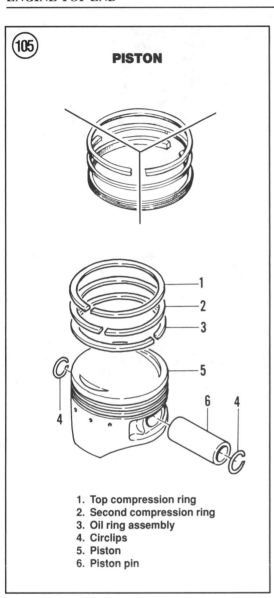

PISTON

1. Top compression ring
2. Second compression ring
3. Oil ring assembly
4. Circlips
5. Piston
6. Piston pin

9. Carefully align the cylinder with the piston and install the cylinder. Compress each ring as it enters the cylinder with your fingers.

NOTE
Once the cylinder is installed, run the chain and wire up through the cylinder.

10. Remove the piston holding fixture and slide the cylinder all the way down (**Figure 106**).
11. While holding the cylinder down with one hand, operate the pull-starter or turn the crankshaft with a wrench. The piston should move smoothly and up and down in the bore.
12. Install the cylinder Allen bolt (**Figure 99**). Tighten the bolt to the torque specification in **Table 7**.
13. Install the cylinder head as described in this chapter.

PISTONS AND PISTON RINGS

The piston is made of an aluminum alloy. The piston pin is made of steel and is a precision fit in the piston. The piston pin is held in place by a clip at each end.

Refer to **Figure 105** when servicing the piston and rings in the following section.

Piston
Removal/Installation

1. Remove the cylinder as described in this chapter.
2. Block off the crankcase below the piston with clean paper towels to prevent the piston pin circlips from falling into the crankcase.
3. Before removing the piston, hold the rod tightly and rock the piston (**Figure 107**). Any rocking motion (do not confuse with the normal sliding motion) indicates wear on the piston pin, rod bushing, pin bore, or more likely, a combination of all three.
4. Remove the circlips from the piston pin bore (**Figure 108**).

NOTE
Discard the piston circlips. New circlips must be installed during reassembly.

5. Push the piston pin (**Figure 109**) out of the piston by hand. If the pin is tight, use a homemade tool (**Figure 110**) to remove it. Do not drive the piston pin out as this action may damage the piston pin, connecting rod or piston.

6. Lift the piston off the connecting rod.

7. Inspect the piston as described in this chapter.

Piston Inspection

1. Remove the piston rings as described in this chapter.

2. Carefully clean the carbon from the piston crown (**Figure 111**) with a soft scraper or wire wheel mounted in a drill. Large carbon accumulations reduce piston cooling and result in detonation and piston damage.

> *CAUTION*
> *Be careful not to gouge or otherwise damage the piston or cylinder when removing carbon. Never use a wire brush to clean the piston skirt. Do not attempt to remove carbon from the sides of the piston above the top ring or from the cylinder bore near the top. Removal of carbon from these two areas may cause increased oil consumption.*

3. After cleaning the piston, examine the crown. The crown should show no signs of wear or damage. If the crown appears pecked or spongy-looking, also check the spark plug, valves and combustion chamber for aluminum deposits. If these deposits are found, the engine is overheating.

4. Examine each ring groove (**Figure 112**) for burrs, dented edges or other damage. Pay particular attention to the top compression ring groove as it usually wears more than the others. Because the oil ring is constantly bathed in oil, this ring and groove wears little compared to the compression rings and their

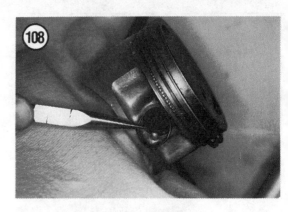

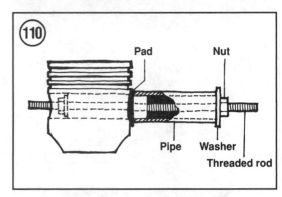

Pad   Nut
Pipe   Washer
Threaded rod

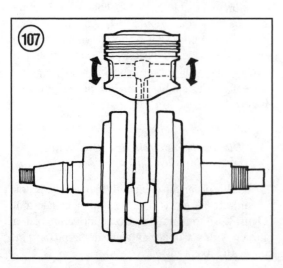

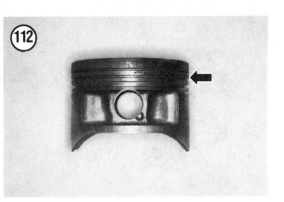

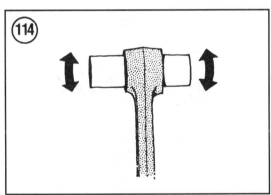

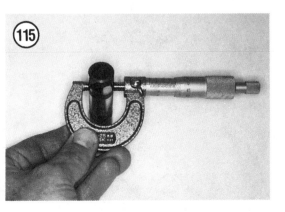

grooves. If there is evidence of oil ring groove wear or if the oil ring assembly is tight and difficult to remove, the piston skirt may have collapsed due to excessive heat and is permanently deformed. Replace the piston.

5. Check the oil control holes in the piston (**Figure 113**) for carbon or oil sludge buildup. Clean the holes with wire.

6. Check the piston skirt for cracks or other damage. If a piston shows signs of partial seizure (bits of aluminum build-up on the piston skirt), the piston should be replaced and the cylinder bored (if necessary) to reduce the possibility of engine noise and further piston seizure.

NOTE
If the piston skirt is worn or scuffed unevenly from side-to-side, the connecting rod may be bent or twisted.

7. Check the piston circlip grooves in the piston for wear, cracks or other damage. Check the circlip fit by installing a new circlip into each groove and then attempt to move the circlip from side-to-side. If the circlip has any side play, the groove is worn and the piston must be replaced.

8. Measure piston-to-cylinder clearance as described under *Piston Clearance* in this chapter.

9. If damage or wear indicate piston replacement, select a new piston as described under *Piston Clearance* in this chapter. If the piston, rings and cylinder are not damaged and are dimensionally correct, they can be reused.

Piston Pin
Inspection

1. Clean the piston pin in solvent and dry thoroughly.

2. Inspect the piston pin for chrome flaking or cracks. Replace if necessary.

3. Oil the piston pin and install it in the connecting rod. Slowly rotate the piston pin and check for radial play (**Figure 114**). If any play exists, the piston pin and/or connecting rod must be replaced. Confirm piston pin clearance by performing the following steps.

4. Measure the piston pin outer diameter (**Figure 115**) with a micrometer. Replace the piston pin if its outer diameter is less than the service limit in **Table 2**. If the piston pin outer diameter is within specifications, perform Step 5.

5. Determine piston pin clearance as follows:

a. Measure piston pin bore inside diameter (**Figure 116**) and record the measurement.

b. Measure piston pin outer diameter (**Figure 115**) and record the measurement.

c. Subtract the measurement in sub-step b from the measurement in sub-step a to determine piston pin clearance. Replace the piston pin and/or piston if the clearance meets or exceeds the service limit in **Table 2**.

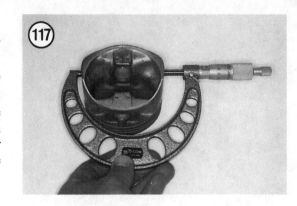

Piston Clearance

1. Make sure the piston and cylinder walls are clean and dry.

2. Measure the cylinder bore with a bore gauge or inside micrometer (**Figure 102**). Measure the cylinder bore 40 mm (1.57 in.) from the top of the cylinder as shown in **Figure 103**. Measure in line with the piston pin and 90° to the pin. Write down the bore diameter measurement.

3. Measure the piston diameter with a micrometer at a right angle to the piston pin bore (**Figure 117**). Measure up from the bottom edge of the piston skirt the distance specified in **Table 5**.

4. Subtract the piston diameter from the largest bore diameter; the difference is piston-to-cylinder clearance. If clearance exceeds specifications in **Table 2**, the piston should be replaced and the cylinder bored oversize and then honed. Purchase the new piston first. Measure its diameter and add the specified clearance to determine the proper cylinder bore diameter.

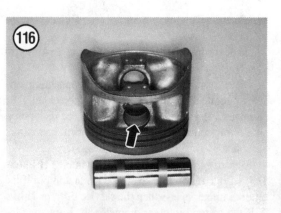

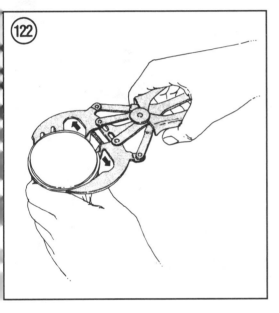

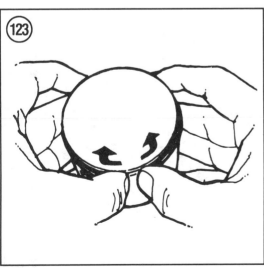

Piston Installation

1. Coat the connecting rod bushing, piston pin and piston with clean engine oil.

2. Slide the piston pin into the piston until its end is flush with the piston pin boss as shown in **Figure 118**.

3. Place the piston over the connecting rod so that the arrow on the piston crown (**Figure 119**) faces forward.

4. Line up the piston pin with the hole in the connecting rod (**Figure 109**). Push the piston pin through the connecting rod and into the other side of the piston until it is centered in the piston.

5. Install new piston pin clips in both ends of the pin boss (**Figure 120**). Make sure both clips are seated in the grooves in the piston. Ends of pin clips should be down toward bottom of piston.

6. Install the piston rings as described in this chapter.

Piston Ring
Inspection and Removal

A 3-ring type piston and ring assembly is used (**Figure 105**). The top and second rings are compression rings. The lower ring is an oil control ring assembly (consisting of 2 ring rails and an expander spacer). **Table 6** identifies piston rings.

1. Measure the side clearance of each ring in its groove with a flat feeler gauge (**Figure 121**) and compare with the specifications in **Table 2**. If the clearance is greater than specified, the rings must be replaced. If the clearance is still excessive with the new rings, the piston must be replaced.

> *WARNING*
> *The edges of all piston rings are very sharp. Be careful when handling them to avoid cutting your fingers.*

> *NOTE*
> *Store the old rings in the order in which they are removed.*

2. Remove the compression rings with a ring expander tool (**Figure 122**) or by spreading the ring ends with your thumbs and lifting the rings up evenly (**Figure 123**).

3. Remove the oil ring assembly (**Figure 124**) by first removing the upper (A, **Figure 125**) and then the lower (B, **Figure 125**) ring rails. Then remove the expander spacer (C, **Figure 125**).

4. Using a broken piston ring, carefully remove carbon and oil residue from the piston ring grooves (**Figure 126**). Do not remove aluminum material from the ring grooves as this will increase ring side clearance.

5. Inspect grooves carefully for burrs, nicks or broken or cracked lands. Replace piston if necessary.

6. Check end gap of each ring. To check, insert the ring into the bottom of the cylinder bore approximately 20 mm (25/32 in.) and square it with the cylinder wall by tapping it with the piston. Measure the end gap with a feeler gauge (**Figure 127**). Compare gap with **Table 2**. Replace rings if gap is too large. If the gap on the new ring is smaller than specified, hold a small file in a vise, grip the ends of the ring with your fingers and enlarge the gap.

> *NOTE*
> *When measuring oil control ring end gap, measure end gap of the upper and lower ring rails only. Do not measure the expander spacer (C, **Figure 125**).*

7. Roll each ring around its piston groove as shown in **Figure 128** to check for binding. Minor binding may be cleaned up with a fine-cut file.

Piston Ring Installation

1. If new rings are installed, the cylinders must be deglazed or honed. This will help to seat the new rings. If necessary, refer honing service to a Yamaha dealer or motorcycle repair shop. After honing, measure the end gap of each ring and compare to dimensions in **Table 2**.

> *NOTE*
> *If the cylinders were deglazed or honed, clean the cylinders as described under* ***Cylinder Block Inspection*** *in this chapter.*

2. Clean the piston and rings in solvent. Dry with compressed air.

> *NOTE*
> *The top and 2nd compression rings are different. Refer to **Table 6** to identify these rings.*

3. Install piston rings as follows:

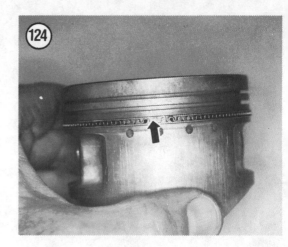

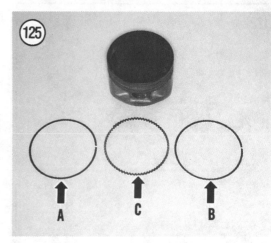

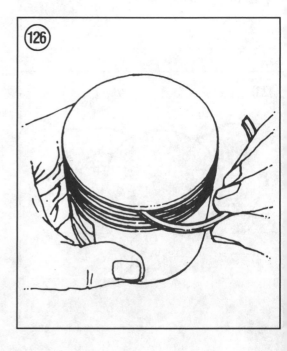

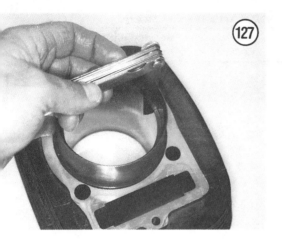

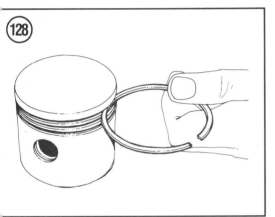

NOTE
Install the piston rings—first the bottom, then the middle, then the top ring—by carefully spreading the ends with your thumbs and slipping the rings over the top of the piston. Remember that the piston rings must be installed with the marks on them facing up toward the top of the piston. If incorrectly installed, there is the possibility of oil pumping past new rings.

a. Install the oil ring assembly into the bottom ring groove. First install the expander spacer, then the bottom and top ring rails (**Figure 124**).

b. Install all rings with the manufacturer's markings facing up.

c. Install the 2nd or middle compression ring.

d. Install the top compression ring.

4. Make sure the rings are seated completely in their grooves all the way around the piston and that the end gaps are distributed around the piston as shown in **Figure 105**. It is important that the ring gaps are not aligned with each other when installed to prevent compression pressures from escaping past them.

5. If installing oversize compression rings, check the number to make sure the correct rings are being installed. The ring numbers should be the same as the piston oversize number.

Table 1 GENERAL ENGINE SPECIFICATIONS

Engine	4-stroke, SOHC
Displacement	348 cc (21.2 cu. in.)
Bore x stroke	83 x 64.5 mm (3.27 x 2.54 in.)
Compression ratio	9.2:1
Lubrication system	Wet sump

Table 2 ENGINE SERVICE SPECIFICATIONS

	New mm (in.)	Service limit mm (in.)
Cylinder head warp limit	—	0.003
	—	(0.00012)
Cylinder bore diameter	82.97-83.02	83.10
	(3.267-3.269)	(3.272)
Taper limit	—	0.05
	—	(0.002)
Piston skirt diameter	82.92-82.97	—
	(3.2646-3.2665)	—
(continued)		

Table 2 ENGINE SERVICE SPECIFICATIONS (continued)

	New mm (in.)	Service limit mm (in.)
Piston-to-cylinder clearance	0.040-0.060 (0.0016-0.0024)	0.15 (0.006)
Oversize pistons		
No. 2 over	83.50 (3.287)	—
No. 3 over	84.00 (3.307)	—
Piston rings		
Sectional measurements	See Table 6	
End gap		
Top	0.20-0.40 (0.008-0.016)	— —
Second	0.20-0.40 (0.008-0.016)	— —
Oil ring	0.30-0.90 (0.012-0.036)	— —
Side clearance		
Top	0.04-0.08 (0.016-0.032)	— —
Second	0.03-0.07 (0.0012-0.0028)	— —
Piston pin		
Outer diameter	18.990-19.000 (0.7476-0.7480)	— —
Bore (in piston)	19.004-19.015 (0.7481-0.7486)	— —
Piston pin clearance	0.014-0.02 (0.0006-0.0008)	0.07 (0.003)
Camshaft		
Intake and exhaust		
Lobe height	40.62-40.72 (1.599-1.603)	— —
Base circle diameter	32.18-32.28 (1.267-1.271)	— —
Runout limit	—	0.03 (0.001)
Rocker arm-to-shaft clearance	0.009-0.037	(0.0004-0.0015)

Table 3 VALVE SERVICE SPECIFICATIONS

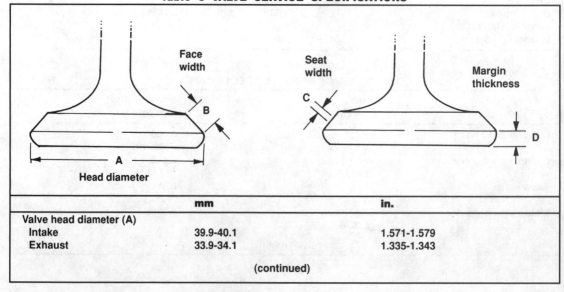

	mm	in.
Valve head diameter (A)		
Intake	39.9-40.1	1.571-1.579
Exhaust	33.9-34.1	1.335-1.343

(continued)

Table 3 VALVE SERVICE SPECIFICATIONS (continued)

	mm	in.
Valve face width (B)		
Intake & exhaust	2.26	0.09
Valve seat width (C)		
1987		
Intake & exhaust	1.0-1.1	0.039-0.043
1988-on		
Intake & exhaust	1.2-1.4	0.047-0.055
Valve margin thickness limit (D)		
Intake	1.0-1.4	0.039-0.055
Exhaust	0.8-1.2	0.0315-0.0472
Valve stem outside diameter		
Intake	6.975-6.990	0.2746-0.2752
Exhaust	6.955-6.970	0.2738-0.2744
Valve guide inside diameter		
Intake & exhaust		
Standard	7.000-7.012	0.2756-0.2761
Limit	7.5	0.295
Valve stem-to-guide clearance		
Intake	0.010-0.037	0.0004-0.0015
Exhaust	0.030-0.057	0.0012-0.0022
Limit (intake & exhaust)	0.1	0.004
Valve stem runout limit	0.01	0.0004
Valve seat width	0.9-1.1	0.035-0.043

Table 4 VALVE SPRING SPECIFICATIONS

	mm	in.
Free length		
Inner spring		
Intake & exhaust	39.9	1.571
Outer spring		
Intake & exhaust	43.27	1.703
Installed length		
(with valve closed)		
Inner spring		
Intake & exhaust	33.6	1.323
Outer spring		
Intake & exhaust	36.6	1.441
Spring tilt limit		
Intake & exhaust	1.6	0.063
Compressed spring force		
(measured with spring gauge)		
Inner spring	10.7-12.3 kg at 33.6 mm (23.59-27.12 lbs. at 1.323 in.)	
Outer spring	24.0-25.6 kg at 36.6 mm (52.91-56.44 lbs. at 1.441 in.)	

Table 5 PISTON MEASURING POINT

Model	mm	in.
All models	5.5	0.217

Table 6 PISTON RING SECTIONAL DIMENSIONS

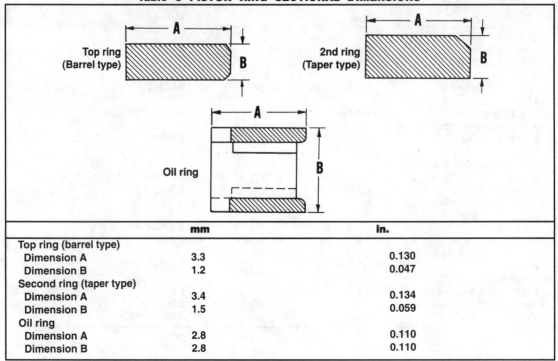

	mm	in.
Top ring (barrel type)		
Dimension A	3.3	0.130
Dimension B	1.2	0.047
Second ring (taper type)		
Dimension A	3.4	0.134
Dimension B	1.5	0.059
Oil ring		
Dimension A	2.8	0.110
Dimension B	2.8	0.110

Table 7 ENGINE TIGHTENING TORQUE

	N·m	ft.-lb.
Cylinder head mounting bolts		
M8 Allen bolts	20	14
M10 flange bolts	40	29
Cylinder Allen bolt	10	7.2
Cylinder head side cover bolts	10	7.2
Valve cover bolts	10	7.2
Cam sprocket bolt	60	43
Camshaft retainer bolts	8	5.8
Valve adjuster locknut	20	14
Oil check bolt	7	5.1
Spark plug	17.5	12.5
Cam chain tensioner		
M6 (body mounting bolts)	10	7.2
M10 (end cap bolt)	38	27
Exhaust system		
Muffler mount flange bolt	27	19
Exhaust pipe 6 mm nut	12	8.7
Exhaust pipe protector screws	8	8.8
Muffler and exhaust pipe hex bolt	20	14
Upper front engine mounting bracket		
At frame	33	24
At engine	33	24

ENGINE LOWER END

This chapter describes service procedures for the following lower end components:

a. Crankcases.

b. Crankshaft.

c. Connecting rod.

d. Transmission and reverse shift assembly (removal and installation).

e. Internal shift mechanism (removal and installation).

f. Recoil starter.

Prior to removing and disassembling the crankcase, clean the entire engine and frame with a good grade commercial degreaser, like Gunk or Bel-Ray engine degreaser or equivalent. It is easier to work on a clean engine and you will do a better job.

CAUTION
Prior to using a commercial degreaser to clean your vehicle, remove or cover the O-ring drive chain; otherwise, the degreaser will cause the O-rings to swell, permanently damaging the chain.

Make certain that you have all the necessary tools available, especially any special tool(s), and purchase replacement parts prior to disassembly. Also make sure you have a clean place to work.

One of the more important aspects of engine overhaul is preparation. Improper preparation before and failing to identify and store parts during removal will make it difficult to reassemble the engine. Before removing the first bolt and to prevent frustration during installation, get a number of boxes, plastic bags and containers and store the parts as they are removed (**Figure 1**). Also have on hand a roll of masking tape and a permanent, waterproof marking pen to label parts as required.

In the text there is frequent mention of the left-hand and right-hand side of the engine. This refers to the engine as it sits in the vehicle's frame, not as it sits on your workbench.

Engine specifications are listed in **Table 1** and **Table 2**. **Tables 1-3** are at the end of the chapter.

SERVICING ENGINE IN FRAME

Some of the components can be serviced while the engine is mounted in the frame (the vehicle's frame is a great holding fixture—especially for breaking loose stubborn bolts and nuts):

a. Cylinder head.

b. Cylinder and piston.

c. Gearshift mechanism.

d. Clutch.

e. Recoil-starter.

f. Oil pump.

g. Carburetor.

h. Magneto.

i. Starter.

ENGINE REMOVAL

This procedure describes engine removal. If service work requires only the removal of a top end component, the engine can be left in the frame and the top end disassembled only as far as required to remove the desired sub-assembly. If the engine requires crankcase disassembly, it will be easier to remove as many sub-assemblies from the engine before removing the engine from the frame. By following this method, the frame can be used as a holding fixture as the engine is disassembled. Attempting to disassemble the complete engine while it is placed on a workbench is more time consuming and will require an assistant to help hold the engine while you loosen many of the larger nuts and bolts.

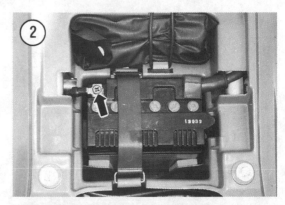

1. Support the vehicle on a level surface. Set the parking brake.

2. Remove the seat and front fender as described in Chapter Thirteen.

3. Remove the fuel tank as described in Chapter Eight.

4. Disconnect the negative battery terminal (**Figure 2**).

5. Remove the exhaust pipe and muffler assembly as described in Chapter Eight.

6. Remove the carburetor as described in Chapter Eight.

7. Loosen the clutch cable locknut (A, **Figure 3**) at the clutch release lever and disconnect the cable from its mounting bracket. Then disconnect the cable (B, **Figure 3**) from the release lever.

NOTE
To obtain additional clutch cable slack,
loosen the clutch cable adjuster at the
handlebar and disconnect the cable.

8. Remove the reverse lever bolt (**Figure 4**) and disconnect the reverse lever from the engine.

9. Remove the shift lever pinch bolt (**Figure 5**) and pull the shift lever off the shaft. Then remove the left-hand footpeg assembly.

10. Disconnect the rear master cylinder pushrod at the brake lever (A, **Figure 6**). Then remove the right-hand footpeg assembly.

11. Remove the drive sprocket as follows:
    a. Remove the sprocket cover.
    b. Pry the lockwasher tab away from the sprocket nut.
    c. Set the parking brake and shift the transmission into gear. Then loosen the sprocket nut (**Figure 7**).
    d. Remove the nut, lockwasher and sprocket.

NOTE
If the drive chain is tight, loosen the
axle housing bolts and loosen the
chain adjusters.

12. Disconnect the following electrical connectors:
    a. Spark plug lead.
    b. Engine ground cable (A, **Figure 8**).
    c. Reverse switch connector (B, **Figure 8**) at switch.
    d. Neutral switch connector (**Figure 9**) at switch.
    e. CDI magneto electrical connectors (on left-hand side).
    f. Starter motor lead at starter motor (**Figure 10**).

13. If the engine requires disassembly, remove the following sub-assemblies:

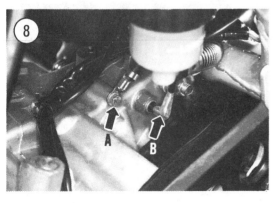

a. Cylinder head (Chapter Four).

b. Cylinder and piston (Chapter Four).

c. Magneto/starter clutch (this chapter).

d. Clutch (Chapter Six).

e. Primary drive gear and balancer driven gear assemblies (this chapter).

f. Oil pump (this chapter).

14. If the engine is being removed with the top end installed, remove the upper front engine mounting brackets.

15. Remove the engine assembly as follows:

a. Place a jack underneath the engine. Raise the jack so that the pad just rests against the bottom of the engine. If necessary, place a block of wood on the jack pad to protect the engine case. If you do not have access to a jack, place wood blocks underneath the engine.

b. Remove the front engine mounting bolts and brackets (A, **Figure 11**).

c. Remove the upper rear mounting bolt (B, **Figure 11**).

d. Remove the lower rear mounting bolt (C, **Figure 11**).

e. Move all cables, wires and harnesses out of the way so they will not get snagged during engine removal.

NOTE
A minimum of 2 people will be required to remove an assembled engine.

NOTE
If the engine has been disassembled down to the crankcase, there will still be approximately 0.5 qt. (0.47 l) of oil in the bottom of the crankcase. Tipping the engine to one side when removing it will allow the oil to pour out of the crankcase.

f. Lift the engine up and remove it from the frame.

16. While the engine is removed, check the engine frame mounts (**Figure 12**) for cracks or other damage.

ENGINE INSTALLATION

1. Clean all engine mount bolts and nuts in solvent. Dry with compressed air. Remove corrosion from bolts with a wire brush.

2. Prior to installation, spray the engine mount bolts with a commercial rust inhibitor.

NOTE
A minimum of 2 people will be required to install an assembled engine.

3. Place the engine in the frame.

4. Install all of the engine mount bolts from the right-hand side; see **Figure 11**.

5. Install the engine mount bolt nuts and tighten to the torque specification in **Table 3**.

6. If the top end is installed on the engine, install the upper front engine mounting brackets, mounting

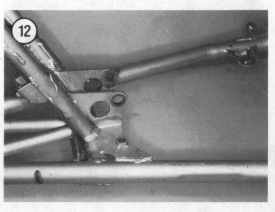

bolts and nut (**Figure 13**). Tighten to the torque specification in **Table 3**. Reposition the throttle cable(s) and wiring harness through the mounting bracket guides.

7. If the engine was partially assembled, install the following sub-assemblies:

  a. Oil pump (this chapter).

  b. Primary drive gear and balancer driven gear assemblies (this chapter).

  c. Clutch (Chapter Six).

  d. Magneto/starter clutch (this chapter).

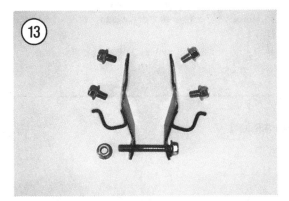

  e. Piston and cylinder (Chapter Four).

  f. Cylinder head (Chapter Four).

8. Clean the electrical connectors with contact cleaner.

9. Reconnect the following electrical connectors:

  a. Starter motor lead (**Figure 10**). Tighten nut securely.

  b. CDI magneto electrical connectors (on left-hand side).

  c. Neutral switch connector (**Figure 9**) at switch.

  d. Reverse switch connector (B, **Figure 8**) at switch.

  e. Engine ground cable (A, **Figure 8**). Remove crankcase bolt and install ground cable. Tighten crankcase bolt to the torque specification in **Table 3**.

  f. Spark plug lead.

10. Install the drive sprocket as follows:

  a. Install the spacer, if removed.

  b. Fit the drive chain over the drive sprocket and slide the sprocket onto the drive axle.

  c. Install the lockwasher and drive sprocket nut. Set the parking brake and shift the transmission into gear. Then tighten the nut to the torque specification in **Table 3**.

11. Install the right-hand footpeg assembly (B, **Figure 6**) and mounting bolts. Tighten bolts to the torque specification in **Table 3**. Reconnect the rear master cylinder pushrod at the brake lever (A, **Figure 6**).

NOTE
Check that the rear brake works properly.

12. Install the left-hand footpeg assembly and mounting bolts. Tighten bolts to the torque specification in **Table 3**. Install the shift lever boss onto the shift shaft (**Figure 5**). Tighten the pinch bolt securely.

13. Install the reverse lever boss (**Figure 14**) onto the reverse drum (**Figure 15**). Install the mounting bolt and washer (**Figure 4**); tighten bolt securely.

14. Reconnect the clutch cable (B, **Figure 3**) at its mounting bracket. Adjust the clutch as described in Chapter Three.

15. Install the carburetor as described in Chapter Eight.

16. Install the exhaust pipe and muffler as described in Chapter Eight.

17. Install the fuel tank as described in Chapter Eight.

18. Install the engine oil filter and refill the engine with new oil (if drained) as described in Chapter Three.

19. Reconnect the negative battery cable at the battery (**Figure 2**).

20. Install the front fender and seat as described in Chapter Thirteen.

PRIMARY DRIVE GEAR, BALANCER GEARS AND OIL PUMP DRIVE GEAR

The primary drive, balancer and oil pump drive gear assemblies (Figure 16) are mounted on the right-hand side of the engine.

Removal

1. Remove the clutch as described in Chapter Six.

NOTE
*Air tools can be used to remove the primary drive gear and balancer driven gear nuts. Otherwise, hold the crankshaft with a wrench on the starter pulley (**Figure 17**).*

2. Bend the lockwasher tabs away from the primary drive gear (A, **Figure 18**) and balancer driven gear (B, **Figure 18**) nuts. Then loosen both nuts.

3. Remove the primary drive gear nut (A, **Figure 18**).

4. Remove the lockwasher and special washer.

5. Remove the primary drive gear.

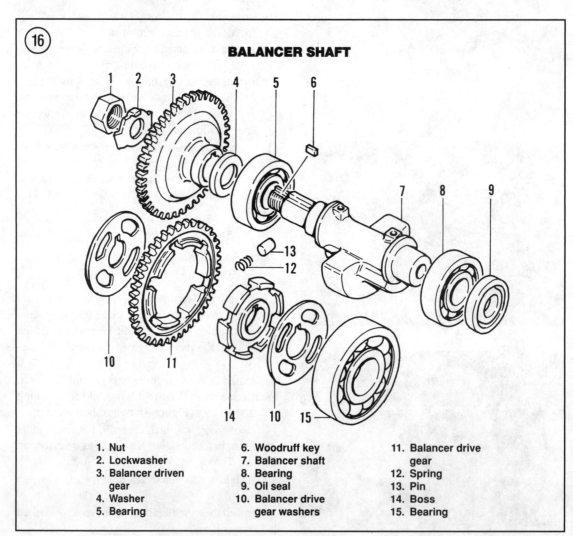

(16)

BALANCER SHAFT

1. Nut	6. Woodruff key
2. Lockwasher	7. Balancer shaft
3. Balancer driven gear	8. Bearing
4. Washer	9. Oil seal
5. Bearing	10. Balancer drive gear washers
11. Balancer drive gear	
12. Spring	
13. Pin	
14. Boss	
15. Bearing	

6. Remove the balancer drive gear assembly, including the inner and outer washers.

7. Remove the oil pump drive gear.

8. Remove the 2 Woodruff keys from the crankshaft.

9. Remove the balancer driven gear nut (B, **Figure 18**).

10. Remove the lockwasher and the balancer driven gear.

11. Remove the Woodruff key from the balancer shaft.

Inspection

1. Clean all parts in solvent. Blow dry with compressed air.

2. Check the primary drive (**Figure 19**), balancer drive (**Figure 20**) and balancer driven (**Figure 21**) gears for:

  a. Broken or chipped teeth.

  b. Heat discoloration and excessive wear.

  c. Worn or damaged center hole.

3. Replace severely worn or damaged washers (**Figure 22**).

5

**Balancer Drive Gear
Disassembly/Reassembly**

1. Push the boss (14, **Figure 16**) out of the balancer drive gear (11, **Figure 16**) and disassemble the gear assembly.

2. Separate the springs and pins. There should a total of 6 springs and 3 pins.

3. Replace worn or damaged components.

4. Refer to **Figure 16** when reassembling the balancer drive gear. Install a spring in every slot and a pin in every other spring. Align the index mark on the gear with the index mark on the boss during reassembly; see **Figure 23**.

Installation

1. Apply clean engine oil to all bearing surfaces prior to installation.

2. Install the balancer driven gear assembly (**Figure 21**) as follows:

   a. Install the flat washer (A, **Figure 24**).

   b. Install the Woodruff key (B, **Figure 24**).

   c. Align the balancer driven gear keyway with the Woodruff key and install the gear onto the shaft (**Figure 25**).

   d. Install the notched lockwasher (**Figure 26**). Insert the notch on the lockwasher into the gear keyway.

   e. Install the balancer driven gear nut (B, **Figure 18**) finger-tight.

3. Install the oil pump drive gear assembly (**Figure 27**) as follows:

   a. Install the Woodruff (half/moon) key into the crankshaft keyway (**Figure 28**).

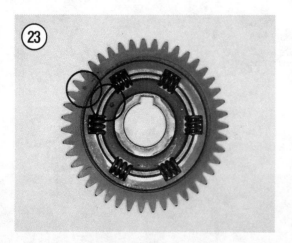

b. Align the oil pump drive gear keyway with the Woodruff key and install the gear onto the shaft (**Figure 29**).

4. Install the balancer drive gear assembly (**Figure 20**) as follows:

    a. Turn the crankshaft so that the square keyway groove faces up.

    b. Install the Woodruff key (**Figure 30**).

    c. Install the 1st large washer (**Figure 31**).

    d. Align the balancer drive gear keyway with the Woodruff key and install the gear. Align the index mark on the balancer drive gear with the index mark on the balancer driven gear (**Figure 32**).

    e. Install the 2nd large washer (**Figure 33**).

5. Install the primary drive gear (**Figure 19**) assembly as follows:

    a. Align the primary drive gear keyway with the Woodruff key and install the gear (**Figure 34**).

5

b. Install the thick washer (A, **Figure 35**).

c. Install the thin lockwasher (B, **Figure 35**).

d. Install the primary drive gear nut (A, **Figure 18**).

NOTE
*When tightening the nuts in the following steps, hold the crankshaft with a wrench on the starter pulley (**Figure 17**).*

6. Tighten the primary drive gear nut (A, **Figure 18**) to the torque specification in **Table 3**. Bend the lockwasher tab over the nut to lock it.

7. Tighten the balancer shaft nut (B, **Figure 18**) to the torque specification in **Table 3**. Bend the lockwasher tab over the nut to lock it.

8. Install the clutch as described in Chapter Six.

OIL PUMP

The oil pump is mounted behind the clutch on the right-hand side of the engine. The oil pump can be removed with the engine mounted in the frame.

Removal

1. Remove the clutch as described in Chapter Six.

2. Remove the balancer drive gear assembly as described in this chapter.

CAUTION
An impact driver with a No. 3 Phillips bit should be used to loosen the oil pump mounting screws in Step 3. Attempting to loosen the screws with a Phillips screwdriver may ruin the screw heads.

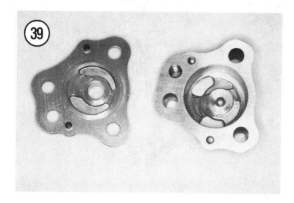

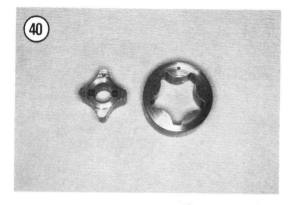

3. Remove the oil pump mounting screws (**Figure 36**) and remove the oil pump and gasket. Discard the gasket.

Oil Pump
Disassembly/Inspection

1. Remove the Phillips head screw (**Figure 37**) securing the pump cover to the pump body and disassemble the oil pump assembly. See **Figure 38**.

2. Remove all gasket residue from the oil pump body and crankcase mating surfaces.

3. Clean all parts in solvent. Blow dry with compressed air.

4. Inspect the oil pump body and cover for cracks (**Figure 39**).

5. Inspect the inner and outer rotors (**Figure 40**) for cracks, scoring or other damage.

6. Install both rotors into the oil pump body with their punch marks facing up; see **Figure 41**.

7. Measure the clearance between the inner rotor tip and the outer rotor with a flat feeler gauge as shown in **Figure 42**. Compare to the tip clearance specification listed in **Table 1**. If the tip clearance is worn to the service limit or greater, replace the oil pump.

8. Measure the side clearance between the outer rotor and the oil pump body with a flat feeler gauge as shown in **Figure 43**. If the side clearance is worn to the service limit or greater, replace the oil pump.

9. Inspect the oil pump drive and driven gears (**Figure 44**) for broken or chipped teeth. Inspect the driven gear shaft for scoring, excessive wear or other damage.

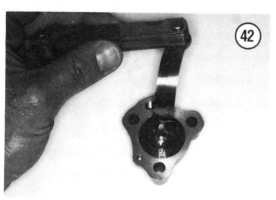

Oil Pump Assembly

1. Coat all parts with clean engine oil prior to assembly.
2. Install the outer cover over the oil pump shaft as shown in A, **Figure 45**.
3. Install the pin (B, **Figure 45**) through the oil pump shaft hole.
4. Align the slot in the inner rotor (**Figure 46**) with the pin and install the inner rotor.
5. Install the outer rotor (**Figure 47**) so that its punch mark faces toward the gear.
6. Align the outer cover dowel pin holes with the oil pump body dowel pins (**Figure 48**) and install the cover. See **Figure 49**.
7. Install the Phillips screw (**Figure 37**), securing the cover to the body, and tighten to the torque specification in **Table 3**.

Oil Pump Installation

1. Install a new oil pump gasket.
2. Install the oil pump onto the crankcase and install the 3 Phillips screws (**Figure 50**).
3. Tighten the Phillips screws to the torque specification in **Table 3**.
4. Install the balancer drive gear assembly as described in this chapter.
5. Install the clutch as described in this chapter.

OIL PIPE

Removal/Installation

1. Remove the clutch as described in Chapter Six.
2. Remove the balancer drive gear assembly as described in this chapter.

3. Loosen, then remove the 2 banjo bolts (**Figure 51**), washers and oil pipe.

4. Clean the oil pipe, banjo bolts and washers (**Figure 52**) in solvent and dry thoroughly.

5. Replace the washers if cracked or otherwise damaged.

6. Check the oil pipe for cracks or other damage. Replace if necessary.

7. Install the oil pipe by reversing these steps, while noting the following.

8. Install a washer on each side of the oil pipe as shown in **Figure 53**.

9. Tighten the oil pipe banjo bolts to the torque specification in **Table 3**.

10. Install the balancer drive gear assembly as described in this chapter.

11. Install the clutch as described in this chapter.

STATOR AND STATOR HOUSING

The stator is installed in the stator housing which is mounted on the left-hand side of the engine.

Stator Housing Removal

Refer to **Figure 54**.

1. Drain the engine oil as described in Chapter Three.

2. Remove the shift lever/left-hand footpeg assembly.

3A. Remove the recoil starter assembly as described in this chapter.

3B. Remove the left-hand crankcase cover.

4. Loosen the starter pulley bolt (**Figure 55**). Then remove the bolt, lockwasher and flat washer.

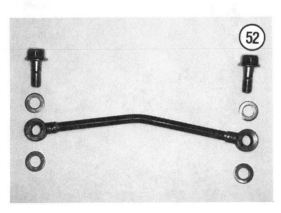

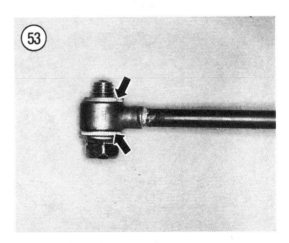

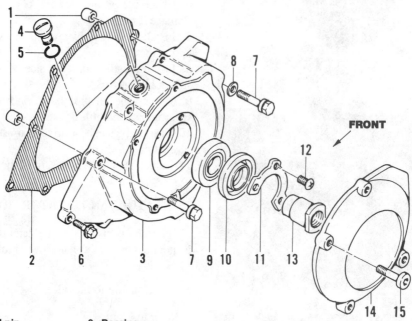

LEFT-HAND SIDE COVER

1. Dowel pin
2. Gasket
3. Stator housing
4. Ignition timing window plug
5. O-ring
6. Bolt
7. Bolt
8. Washer
9. Bearing
10. Oil seal
11. Seal plate
12. Torx screw
13. Starter pulley (1989-on)*
14. Cover (1989-on)*
15. Bolt (1989-on)*

*NOTE: 1987-1988 models were equipped with recoil starter assemblies. To view the starter pulley on these models, refer to *Recoil Starter* in this chapter.

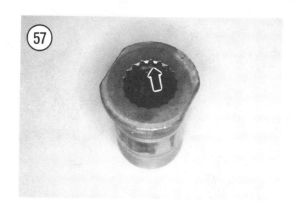

5. Remove the starter pulley (**Figure 56**).

NOTE
*There is an O-ring installed in the starter pulley (**Figure 57**).*

6. Disconnect the stator/CDI electrical connectors.
7. Remove the stator housing (**Figure 58**) mounting bolts and remove the stator housing. See **Figure 59**.
8. Remove the gasket and 2 dowel pins (**Figure 60**).
9. If necessary, remove the stator as described in this chapter.

Stator Testing

Refer to *Stator Testing* in Chapter Nine.

Stator
Removal/Installation

1. Remove the stator housing as described in this section.
2. Remove the source coil wire guide bolts and remove the guide (A, **Figure 61**).
3. Remove the pick-up coil mounting screws (B, **Figure 61**).
4. Remove the stator mounting screws (C, **Figure 61**), lockwashers and flat washers.
5. Remove the stator assembly from the housing. See **Figure 62**.

NOTE
Do not cut the pick-up coil or source coil wires. If a coil is faulty, the stator coil must be replaced as an assembly.

6. If you are going to replace the stator housing oil seal and/or bearing, do so now as described in the following procedure.

7. Clean the stator housing in solvent and dry thoroughly. Do not clean the stator housing in solvent if the stator has not been removed.

8. Install the stator into the housing. Install the stator mounting screws (C, **Figure 61**), lockwashers and flat washers.

9. Align the pick-up coil sensor with the stator coil as shown in **Figure 63**, then install the Phillips screws.

10. Route the source coil wiring harness in the housing. Then push the rubber grommet into the housing notch.

11. Install the source coil wire guide and guide bolts (A, **Figure 61**).

12. Tighten all of the Phillips screws securely.

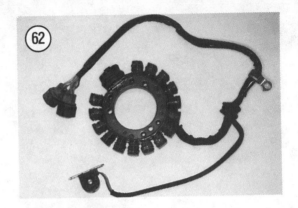

Stator Housing Oil Seal and Bearing Replacement

1. If you are going to replace the bearing, remove the stator as described in the previous procedure.

2. To remove the oil seal (A, **Figure 64**):

> *NOTE*
> *A T-25 Torx screwdriver or socket bit will be required to remove the Torx screws.*

a. Remove the seal plate T-25 Torx screws and remove the seal plate (B, **Figure 64**).

> *WARNING*
> *The seal may be a tight fit in the housing. Safety glasses should be worn in the event the seal pops out and hits you in the face.*

b. Pry the oil seal out of the housing with a large wide-blade screwdriver (**Figure 65**). Support the screwdriver with a rag to avoid damaging the housing. Pry at different points around the seal so it does not bind in its bore.

3. To remove the bearing (**Figure 66**):

a. Support the housing in a press so that inner housing faces up as shown in **Figure 66**.

b. Press the bearing out of the housing.

c. Discard the bearing.

4. To install the new bearing:

a. Support the housing in a press so that the outside of the housing faces up.

b. Align the bearing with the housing so that the manufacturer's name and size code on the bearing is facing up.

c. Press the bearing into the housing until it bottoms. See **Figure 67**.

5. To install the oil seal:

a. Yamaha replacement oil seals come with grease packed between the seal lips as shown in **Figure 68**. If your replacement oil seal does not have grease packed between the seal lips, do so prior to installing the oil seal. Use a waterproof bearing grease.

b. Align the oil seal with the housing so that the manufacturer's name and size code on the oil seal faces out.

c. Press in the oil seal until its outer surface is flush with or slightly below the oil seal bore inside surface (A, **Figure 64**).

6. Install the seal plate (B, **Figure 64**). If the seal plate does not sit flush on the housing, the oil seal is not pressed in far enough. Apply Loctite 242 (blue) to the seal plate mounting bolts prior to installation. Install the T-25 Torx screws (A, **Figure 64**) and tighten securely.

7. If removed, install the stator as described in this chapter.

Stator Housing Installation

Refer to **Figure 54**.

1. Install the 2 dowel pins (**Figure 60**) and a new gasket.

2. Install the stator housing (**Figure 58**) and its mounting bolts. Install the copper washer and the wiring harness guide at the bolt hole shown in **Figure 69**. Tighten the mounting bolts to the torque specification in **Table 3**.

3. Install the starter pulley O-ring, if removed, into the pulley groove as shown in **Figure 57**. Apply a waterproof bearing grease to the oil seal.

4. Install the starter pulley (**Figure 56**).

5. Install the starter pulley bolt, lockwasher and flat washer. Tighten the starter pulley bolt to the torque specification in **Table 3**.

6A. Install the recoil starter assembly as described in this chapter.

6B. Install the left-hand crankcase cover.

7. Install the shift lever/left-hand footpeg assembly. Tighten the footpeg mounting bolts to the torque specification in **Table 3**.

8. Refill the engine oil as described in Chapter Three.

ALTERNATOR ROTOR AND STARTER CLUTCH

The starter clutch is mounted on the backside of the alternator rotor.

Removal

1. Place the vehicle on level ground and set the parking brake.

2. Remove the stator housing as described in this chapter.

3. Pull the idler gear, shaft and bearing (**Figure 70**) out of the crankcase and remove them.

> *NOTE*
> *The Yamaha flywheel puller (part No. YM-01404) or equivalent will be required to remove the alternator; see **Figure 71**.*

4. Screw the flywheel puller body (A, **Figure 72**) onto the alternator rotor until it stops. Then wipe the end of the pressure bolt with grease (B, **Figure 72**) and screw the bolt into the body until it stops.

> *CAUTION*
> *Do not try to remove the rotor without a puller; any attempt to do so will ultimately lead to some form of damage to the engine and/or the rotor. If you can't buy or borrow one, have a dealer remove the rotor.*

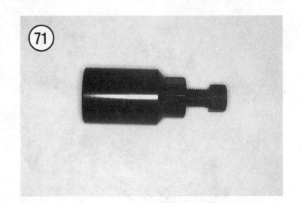

5. Hold the puller body with a wrench and gradually tighten the pressure bolt (**Figure 73**) until the rotor disengages from the crankshaft. See **Figure 74**. Remove the puller from the alternator rotor.

CAUTION
If normal rotor removal attempts fail, do not force the puller as the threads may be stripped off of the rotor causing expensive damage. Take it to a dealer and have them remove it.

6. Remove the Woodruff key (A, **Figure 75**) from the crankshaft groove.

7. Remove the starter driven gear (B, **Figure 75**), needle bearing and washer (**Figure 76**).

8. Remove the starter idler gear assembly (if not removed previously).

Starter Clutch Inspection

1. Wash all parts in solvent. Blow dry with compressed air.

2. Inspect idle gear assembly (**Figure 77**) for:
   a. Broken or chipped gear teeth.
   b. Worn or scored shaft surface.
   c. Worn or damaged needle bearings.
   d. Worn or damaged washer.

3. Inspect starter clutch assembly (**Figure 78**) for:
   a. Broken or chipped gear teeth.
   b. Worn or damaged needle bearing.
   c. Worn or damaged washer.
   d. Worn or damaged starter clutch rollers.

4. To check starter clutch operation, perform the following:
   a. Install the starter wheel gear (**Figure 79**) into the starter clutch.

b. Turn the starter wheel gear counterclockwise. The gear (**Figure 79**) should turn freely.

c. Now try to turn the starter wheel gear clockwise. The gear (**Figure 79**) should engage with the starter clutch and should not turn.

d. If the starter clutch failed to operate as described in sub-step b or c, replace it as described in the following step.

5. To replace the starter clutch, perform the following:

a. Using an impact driver and socket bit, remove the bolts securing the starter clutch housing to the rotor.

b. Note the direction of the sprags in the starter clutch. It must be installed in the same direction.

c. Remove the starter clutch.

d. Remove all Loctite residue from the starter clutch bolts and the bolt threads in the rotor.

e. Install the new starter clutch onto the alternator rotor.

f. Apply Loctite 242 (blue) to the starter clutch mounting bolt threads prior to installation. Install the bolts and tighten to the torque specification listed in **Table 3**.

g. Stake the starter clutch mounting bolts with a punch.

Installation

1. Assemble the idler gear assembly as shown in **Figure 80**. Make sure the circlip(s) is fully seated in the shaft groove(s). Then install the idler gear assembly into the crankcase, engaging the idler gear with the starter motor drive gear; see **Figure 81**.

2. Install the washer and needle bearing (**Figure 76**) onto the crankshaft.

3. Install the starter driven gear with its shoulder facing out (**Figure 82**).

4. Install the Woodruff key (A, **Figure 75**) into the crankshaft keyway.

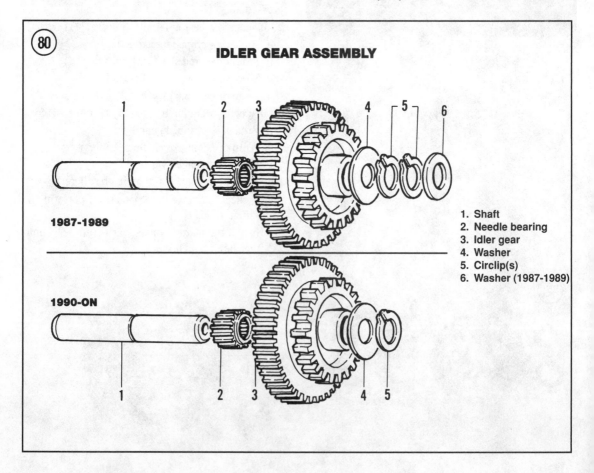

80

IDLER GEAR ASSEMBLY

1987-1989

1990-ON

1. Shaft
2. Needle bearing
3. Idler gear
4. Washer
5. Circlip(s)
6. Washer (1987-1989)

CAUTION
*Carefully inspect the inside of the rotor (**Figure 83**) for small bolts, washers or other metal "trash" that may have been picked up by the magnets. These small metal bits can cause severe damage to the alternator stator plate components.*

5. Align the keyway in the rotor with the Woodruff key and install the rotor (**Figure 84**) onto the crankshaft.

6. Install the starter pulley and its mounting bolt and washers onto the crankshaft. Then hold the starter pulley with a wrench and tighten the bolt (**Figure 85**) hand-tight to push the rotor onto the crankshaft taper. This will help to hold the rotor in place so that it does not slide off the crankshaft while installing the stator housing. Remove the mounting bolt, washers and starter pulley.

CRANKCASE AND CRANKSHAFT

Disassembly of the crankcase—splitting the cases—and removal of the crankshaft assembly requires engine removal from the frame. However, the cylinder head, cylinder and all other attached assemblies should be removed with the engine in the frame.

The crankcase is made in 2 halves of precision diecast aluminum alloy and is of the "thin-walled" type. To avoid damage to them, do not hammer or pry on any of the interior or exterior projected walls. These areas are easily damaged if stressed beyond their designed limits. They are assembled without a gasket; only gasket sealer is used while dowel pins align the crankcase halves when they are bolted together. The crankcase halves are sold as a matched

set only (**Figure 86**). If one crankcase half is severely damaged, both must be replaced.

The crankshaft assembly is made up of 2 full-circle flywheels pressed together on a crankpin. The connecting rod big end bearing on the crankpin is a needle bearing assembly (**Figure 87**). The crankshaft assembly is supported by 2 ball bearings in the crankcase.

The procedure which follows is presented as a complete, step-by-step major lower end overhaul that should be followed if the engine is to be completely reconditioned.

Remember that the right- and left-hand side of the engine relates to the engine as it sits in the frame, not as it sits on your workbench.

Special Tools

When splitting the crankcase assembly, a few special tools will be required. These tools allow easy

disassembly and reassembly of the engine without prying or hammer use. Remember, the crankcase halves can be easily damaged by improper disassembly or reassembly techniques.

a. Yamaha crankcase separating tool (part No. YU-01135) (**Figure 88**). This tool threads into the crankcase and is used to separate the crank-

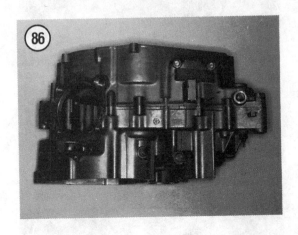

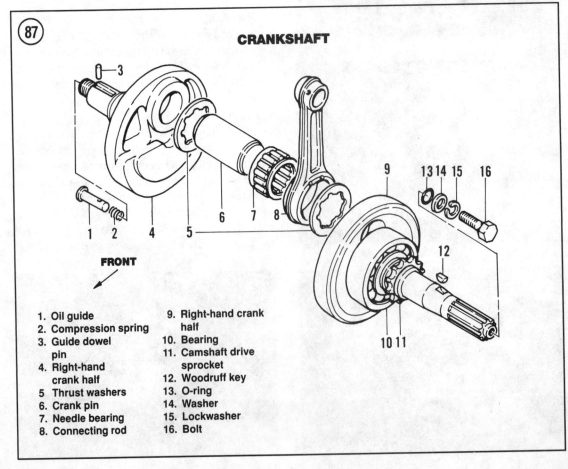

CRANKSHAFT

FRONT

1. Oil guide
2. Compression spring
3. Guide dowel pin
4. Right-hand crank half
5 Thrust washers
6. Crank pin
7. Needle bearing
8. Connecting rod
9. Right-hand crank half
10. Bearing
11. Camshaft drive sprocket
12. Woodruff key
13. O-ring
14. Washer
15. Lockwasher
16. Bolt

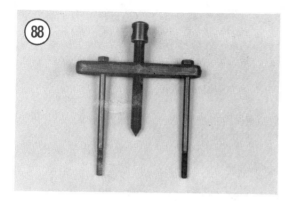

case halves and to press the crankshaft out of the crankcase. The tool is very simple in design and a similar type of tool, such as a steering wheel puller can be substituted.

b. Yamaha crankshaft installing set (part No. YU-90050 [A, **Figure 89**]), Yamaha adapter (part No. YU-1383 [B, **Figure 89**]) and the Yamaha spacer (part No. YM-91044 [C, **Figure 89**]). These tools are used together to pull the crankshaft back into the crankcase assembly.

Crankcase Disassembly

This procedure describes disassembly of the crankcase halves and removal of the crankshaft, transmission, reverse assembly and internal shift mechanism. Disassembly and reassembly of the transmission, reverse assembly and internal shift mechanism assembly is described in Chapter Seven.

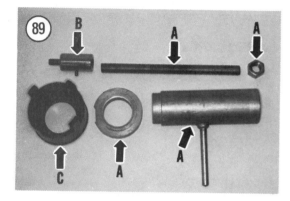

1. Remove all exterior engine assemblies as described in this chapter and other related chapters:

    a. Cylinder head.

    b. Cylinder and piston.

    c. Alternator.

    d. Starter motor.

    e. Clutch.

    f. External shift mechanism.

    g. Oil pump.

    h. Balancer and primary drive gears.

    i. Oil pipe.

2. Remove the reverse shift cam bolt, washer, spring (**Figure 90**) and ball (**Figure 91**).

3. Place the engine assembly on a couple of wood blocks with the left-hand side facing up (**Figure 92**).

4. Loosen all screws securing the crankcase halves together one-quarter turn. To prevent warpage,

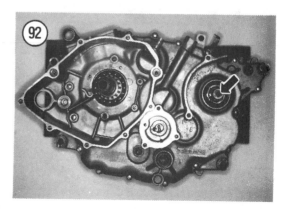

loosen them in the numerical order shown in **Figure 93**, starting with bolt No. 1.

5. Remove all screws loosened in Step 4. Be sure to remove all of them.

> *NOTE*
> *To prevent loss and to ensure proper location during assembly, draw the crankcase outline on cardboard, then punch holes to correspond with screw locations. Insert the screws in their appropriate locations.*

> *CAUTION*
> *Perform this operation over and close down to the work bench as the crankcase halves may easily separate. Do **not** hammer on the crankcase halves as they will be damaged.*

6. Turn the crankcase over so that the right-hand side faces up (**Figure 94**).

> *CAUTION*
> *Do not pry between the crankcase mating surfaces when separating the crank-*

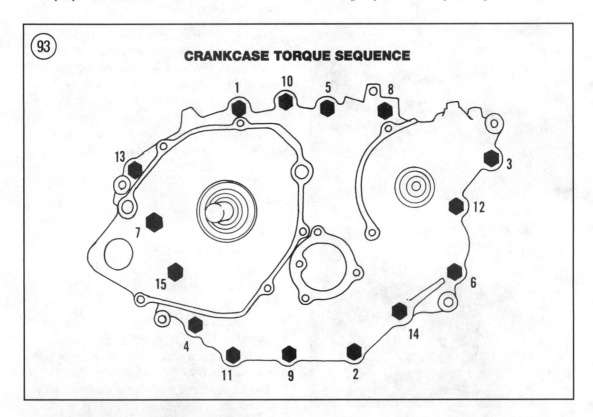

CRANKCASE TORQUE SEQUENCE

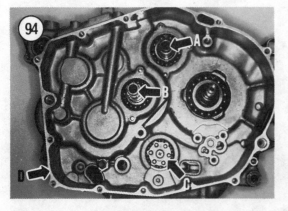

case halves. Doing so will result in oil leaks, requiring replacement of both case halves.

7. See **Figure 94** and tap on the balancer shaft (A), main axle (B) and shift cam (C) while lifting the right-hand crankcase (D) from the engine.

8. Immediately check the bearings in the right-hand crankcase for shims that may be stuck to them. If any are found, install them on their respective axle shaft; see **Figure 95**.

NOTE
Separate the following axles and their gears, bearings, washers, etc. as you remove them in the following steps.

9. Remove the counter axle assembly (**Figure 96**). Do not lose the 2 washers.

10. Remove the reverse axle assembly (A, **Figure 97**). Do not lose the washer installed on top of the gear.

11. Remove the reverse shift fork shaft (B, **Figure 97**).

12. See **Figure 98**. Remove the output axle (A), reverse shift fork (B) and shift cam (C) as an assembly.

13. Remove the 2 shift fork shafts (A, **Figure 99**).

14. Remove the shift cam (B, **Figure 99**).

15. Remove the 3 shift forks.

16. See **Figure 100**. Remove the drive axle (A) and main axle (B) as an assembly. Do not lose the outer washer on the main axle.

17. Remove the balancer shaft (C, **Figure 100**).

18. Remove the oil guide assembly (A, **Figure 101**) from the end of the crankshaft as follows:

a. Remove the guide pin (3, **Figure 87**).

b. Remove the oil guide (1, **Figure 87**) and spring (2, **Figure 87**).

> *NOTE*
> *Store these parts in a plastic bag, sealed and labeled, so that you do not lose them.*

19. Remove the crankshaft (B, **Figure 101**) as follows:

a. Install the Yamaha tool attachment (part No. YM-1382) onto the left-hand side of the crankshaft (**Figure 102**).

b. Install the crankcase separating tool (**Figure 102**) into the threaded holes on the left-hand crankcase. Center the pressure bolt on the end of the crankshaft. Tighten the long separating bolts into the crankcase, making sure the tool body is parallel with the crankcase. If necessary, back out one of the long bolts.

c. Screw the puller *clockwise* and push the crankshaft out of the crankcase.

d. When the crankshaft is free of the crankcase bearing, remove it.

Crankcase Inspection

1. Remove all of the external crankcase oil seals as described under *External Oil Seal Replacement* in this chapter.

2. Using a scraper, remove all sealer and gasket residue from all gasket surfaces.

> *WARNING*
> *When drying the crankcase bearings in Step 3, do not allow the inner bearing race to spin. The bearing will be dry of all lubrication and damage will result. When drying the bearings, hold the inner race with your hand. In addition, when drying bearings with compressed air, never allow the air jet to rotate the bearing. The jet is capable of rotating the bearing at speeds far in excess of those for which they were designed. The likelihood of a bearing disintegrating and causing serious injury and damage is very great.*

3. Clean both crankcase halves inside and out and all crankcase bearings with cleaning solvent. Thoroughly dry with compressed air.

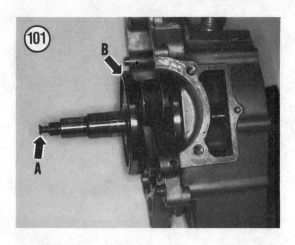

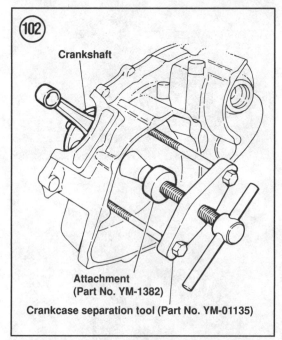

Crankshaft

Attachment
(Part No. YM-1382)

Crankcase separation tool (Part No. YM-01135)

4. Clean all crankcase oil passages with compressed air.

5. Lightly oil the crankcase bearings (**Figure 103**) with engine oil before checking the bearings in Step 6.

6. Check the bearings (**Figure 103**) for roughness, pitting, galling and play by rotating them slowly by hand. If any roughness or play can be felt in the bearing it must be replaced.

NOTE
Always replace opposing bearing at the same time.

7. Replace any worn or damaged bearings as described under *Crankcase Bearing and Oil Seal Replacement* in this chapter.

8. Carefully inspect the cases for cracks and fractures, especially in the lower areas where they are vulnerable to rock damage. **Figure 104** shows typical damage that can occur to the crankcases.

9. Check the areas around the stiffening ribs, around bearing bosses and threaded holes (**Figure 104**) for damage. If any are found, have them repaired by a shop specializing in the repair of precision aluminum castings or replace them.

10. Check the threaded holes in both crankcase halves for thread damage, dirt or oil buildup. If necessary, clean or repair the threads with a suitable size metric tap. Coat the tap threads with kerosene or an aluminum tap fluid before use.

11. Check the shift shaft pin bolt (**Figure 105**) for damage and replace it necessary. During replacement, install a new lockwasher and bend the lockwasher tab over one flat on the pin bolt to lock it.

External Oil Seal Replacement

The oil seals should be replaced whenever the engine is disassembled or when they are leaking or damaged.

External oil seals mounted in the left-hand crankcase are:

    a. Output axle oil seal (A, **Figure 106**).

    b. Shift shaft oil seal (B, **Figure 106**).

External oil seal mounted in the right-hand crankcase is the reverse shift drum oil seal (**Figure 107**).

1. Pry out the oil seals (**Figure 108**) with a screwdriver. Place a rag underneath the screwdriver to avoid damaging the crankcase.

2. If necessary, replace the output axle bearing (**Figure 109**) prior to installing the new oil seal, as described in the following procedure.

3. Clean the oil seal bores.

4. Pack the lip of each oil seal with a waterproof bearing grease prior to installation.

5. Install the oil seals with their manufacturer's name and size code facing out.

6. Press or drive in the oil seal (**Figure 110**) until its outer surface is flush with or slightly below the oil seal bore inside surface. See **Figure 111**, typical.

Internal Oil Seal and Bearing Replacement

Internal oil seals are those installed on the inside of the crankcase, between the bearing and crankcase wall.

A pilot bearing remover (**Figure 112**) will be required to remove the bearings described in this section.

Because bearing removal usually damages the internal oil seal, if applicable, new oil seals should be installed when installing bearings.

When replacing bearings and oil seals in the following steps, note the following:

a. Because of the number of bearings used in the left- and right-hand crankcase (**Figure 103**), make sure to identify bearings before removing them. The size code found on the bearings and oil seals can be used for identification.

b. Refer to *Ball Bearing Replacement* in Chapter One for general information on bearing removal and installation.

c. Prior to removing the oil seal(s), note and record the direction in which the lip of the seal(s) face for proper reinstallation.

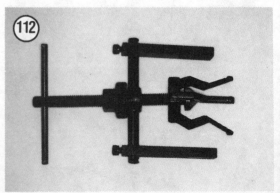

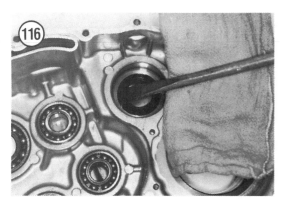

Balancer shaft bearing and oil seal replacement

Refer to A, **Figure 113** and A, **Figure 114**.

1. To replace the left-hand bearing and oil seal (A, **Figure 113**):

   a. Remove the bearing with a bearing remover (**Figure 115**).

   b. Pry the oil seal out of the crankcase with a screwdriver (**Figure 116**). Pad the screwdriver with a rag to avoid damaging the crankcase.

   c. Pack the lip of the oil seal with a waterproof bearing grease prior to installation.

   d. Align the oil seal so that its lip faces in the direction recorded during disassembly.

   e. Press the oil seal in until it is flush with the oil seal bore inside surface as shown in **Figure 117**.

   f. Press the bearing in until it bottoms in the crankcase.

2. To replace the right-hand bearing (A, **Figure 114**):

   a. Remove the bearing plate screws and remove the bearing plate (A, **Figure 118**).

   b. Press bearing from crankcase.

5

c. Press the bearing in until it bottoms in the crankcase.

d. Install the bearing plate.

e. Apply Loctite 242 (blue) to mounting screws prior to installation. Install the screws and tighten securely.

Main axle bearing and oil seal replacement

Refer to B, **Figure 113** and B, **Figure 114**.

1. To replace the left-hand bearing and oil seal (B, **Figure 113**):

a. Remove the bearing with a bearing remover (**Figure 119**).

b. Lift out the oil seal if it didn't come out with the bearing (**Figure 120**).

c. Pack the lip of the oil seal with a waterproof bearing grease prior to installation.

d. Align the oil seal so that its lip faces in the direction recorded during disassembly.

e. Place the new oil seal into the bearing bore (**Figure 121**).

f. Press in the bearing until it bottoms in the crankcase.

2. To replace the right-hand bearing (B, **Figure 114**):

a. Remove the bearing plate screws and remove the bearing plate (B, **Figure 118**).

b. Press bearing out of crankcase.

c. Press the bearing in until it bottoms in the crankcase.

d. Install the bearing plate.

e. Apply Loctite 242 (blue) to mounting screws prior to installation. Install the screws and tighten securely.

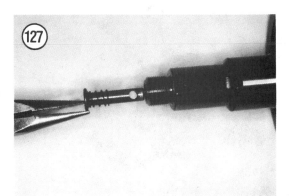

Drive axle bearing and oil seal replacement

Refer to C, **Figure 113** and C, **Figure 114**.

1. To replace the left-hand bearing and oil seal (C, **Figure 113**):
   a. Remove the bearing with a bearing remover (**Figure 122**).
   b. Lift out the oil seal if it didn't come out with the bearing (**Figure 123**).
   c. Pack the lip of the oil seal with a waterproof bearing grease prior to installation.
   d. Align the oil seal so that its lip faces in the direction recorded during disassembly.
   e. Place the new oil seal into the bearing bore (**Figure 124**).
   f. Press in the bearing until it bottoms in the crankcase.
2. To replace the right-hand bearing (C, **Figure 114**):
   a. Remove the bearing with a bearing remover.
   b. Press the bearing in until it bottoms in the crankcase.

Right-hand main bearing, reverse axle and output axle bearing replacement

These bearings do not have oil seals behind them, and are identified as follows:
   a. Main bearings. **Figure 125** shows right-hand bearing. Left-hand bearing (A, **Figure 126**) is removed with crankshaft.

NOTE
*To replace left-hand main bearing, refer to **Crankshaft Sprocket and Main Bearing Replacement** in this chapter.*

   b. Reverse axle bearings. See D, **Figure 113** and D, **Figure 114**.
   c. Output axle bearings. See E, **Figure 113** and E, **Figure 114**.

1A. Remove blind bearings with a bearing remover.
1B. Remove other bearings by pressing out of crankcase.
2. Press each bearing in until it bottoms in the crankcase.

Crankshaft Inspection

1. If not previously done, remove the oil guide retaining pin, oil guide and spring from the crankshaft (**Figure 127**).

2. Clean the crankshaft thoroughly with solvent. Clean the crankshaft oil passageway with compressed air. Dry the crankshaft with compressed air. Then lubricate all bearing surfaces with a light coat of engine oil.

3. Check the crankshaft journals (A, **Figure 128**) for scratches, heat discoloration or other defects.

4. Check flywheel taper, threads and keyway (B, **Figure 128**) for damage. If one crankshaft half is damaged, the crankshaft can be disassembled and the damaged part replaced as described in this chapter.

5. Check crankshaft bearing surfaces for chatter marks and excessive or uneven wear. Minor cases of chatter mark may be cleaned up with 320 grit carborundum cloth. If 320 cloth is used, clean crankshaft in solvent and check surfaces. If they did not clean up properly, disassemble the crankshaft and replace the damaged part.

6. Check the connecting rod big end (C, **Figure 128**) for signs of seizure, bearing or thrust washer damage or connecting rod damage.

7. Check the connecting rod small end (D, **Figure 128**) for signs of excessive heat (blue coloration) or other damage.

8. Slide the connecting rod to one side and check the connecting rod side clearance with a flat feeler gauge (**Figure 129**). Compare to dimensions given in **Table 2**. If clearance is greater than specified, the crankshaft assembly must be disassembled and the connecting rod, thrust washers and bearing replaced.

9. Measure crankshaft width with micrometer and compare so the specifications listed in **Table 2**. Measure around the crankshaft wheel circumference on the outer machined edge—do not measure on cast surfaces. If different measurements are found, have crankshaft trued by a Yamaha dealer.

10. Check crankshaft runout with a dial indicator and V-blocks as shown in **Figure 130**. Retrue the crankshaft if the runout meets or exceeds service limit in **Table 2**.

11. If necessary, overhaul crankshaft as described in this chapter.

Crankshaft Sprocket and Main Bearing Replacement

The camshaft drive sprocket (B, **Figure 126**) and left-hand main bearing (A, **Figure 126**) are pressed onto the crankshaft.

1. Prior to removing the camshaft drive sprocket, note the timing mark on the sprocket. The timing mark (C, **Figure 126**) must align with the center of the crankshaft Woodruff keyway (D, **Figure 126**).

2. Support the camshaft drive sprocket with a bearing remover and press the crankshaft from the sprocket.

3. Support the left-hand main bearing with a bearing remover and press the crankshaft from the sprocket.

4. Clean the crankshaft in solvent and dry with compressed air.

5. Support the crankshaft and press on the left-hand main bearing until its inner race bottoms against the crankshaft.

6. Align the camshaft drive sprocket timing mark with the center of the crankshaft Woodruff keyway and press on the sprocket.

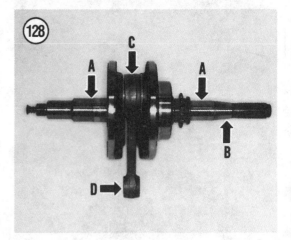

Crankshaft Overhaul

Crankshaft overhaul requires a hydraulic press of 20 ton capacity (minimum), holding jigs, crankshaft alignment jig, dial indicators and a micrometer or vernier caliper. For this reason, crankshaft overhaul should be referred to a Yamaha dealer or motorcycle repair shop familiar with crankshaft rebuilding. When having the crankshaft rebuilt, make sure the crankshaft and crank pin oil passages aligns as shown in **Figure 131**.

Balancer Shaft Inspection

Refer to **Figure 132**.
1. Check the balancer shaft bearing journals (**Figure 133**) for deep scoring, excessive wear, heat discoloration or cracks.
2. Check the keyway in the end of the balancer shaft for cracks or excessive wear.
3. Replace the balancer shaft if necessary.

Transmission and Reverse Assembly Inspection

Refer to Chapter Seven for all disassembly, inspection and reassembly procedures.

Crankcase Assembly

1. Pack all of the crankcase oil seals with a heat durable grease.
2. Apply engine oil to the crankshaft bottom end bearing.
3. Use the following Yamaha tools (**Figure 134**) and install the crankshaft into the left-hand crankcase as follows:

NOTE
*If you do not have access to the Yamaha crankshaft installing set shown in **Figure 134**, a tool can be fabricated using the parts shown in **Figure 135**. It is important to note that the long threaded bolts must have a metric thread size of M10 × 1.25. If you cannot find a metric bolt of this size, purchase a 5/8 in. threaded rod and have one end re-threaded to the metric size M10 × 1.25. This can be done by a machine shop. The long nut used to connect the 2 bolts can be made by drilling and tapping a piece of hex stock.*

CAUTION
If you do not have access to the crankshaft installation tools, have the crankshaft installed by a dealer or machine shop. Do not drive the crankshaft and bearing into the crankcase with a hammer.

a. Apply a light coat of engine oil to the left-hand crankshaft bearing journal.

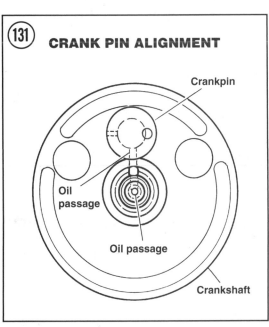

BALANCER SHAFT

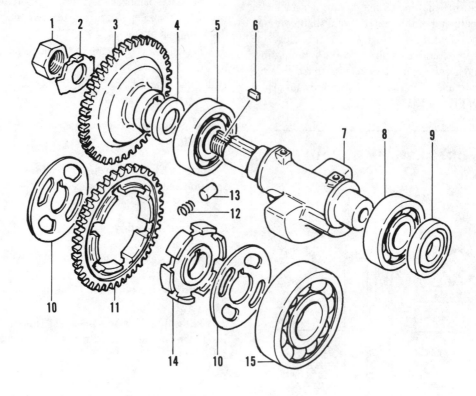

1. Nut
2. Lockwasher
3. Balancer driven
   gear
4. Washer
5. Bearing
6. Key
7. Balancer shaft
8. Bearing
9. Oil seal
10. Balancer drive
    gear washers
11. Balancer drive
    gear
12. Spring
13. Pin
14. Boss
15. Bearing

b. Insert the crankshaft into the main bearing so that the crankshaft assembly is square with the crankcase mating surface (**Figure 136**). Using hand pressure only, push the crankshaft into the crankcase until it stops.

c. Tilt the crankcase assembly up and install the crankshaft installing set (**Figure 134**) as follows. Thread the crankcase adapter (**Figure 137**) into the end of the crankshaft. Then install the adapter (A, **Figure 138**) and the crankcase installer set (B, **Figure 138**).

CAUTION
When installing the crankshaft, make sure to position the connecting rod at
top dead center (TDC) as shown at C, Figure 138. If the connecting rod drops down it could catch onto the side of the crankcase; this would damage the connecting rod and crankcase as the crankshaft is pulled into position.

d. Hold the crankcase installer set body and tighten the nut (**Figure 138**) to pull the crankshaft into the crankcase. Check the crankshaft often to make sure it is being pulled straight in with no side load. Pull the crankshaft until it is completely seated in the crankcase; see **Figure 139**.

e. After installing the crankshaft, remove the crankshaft installer set. Then turn the crankshaft

5

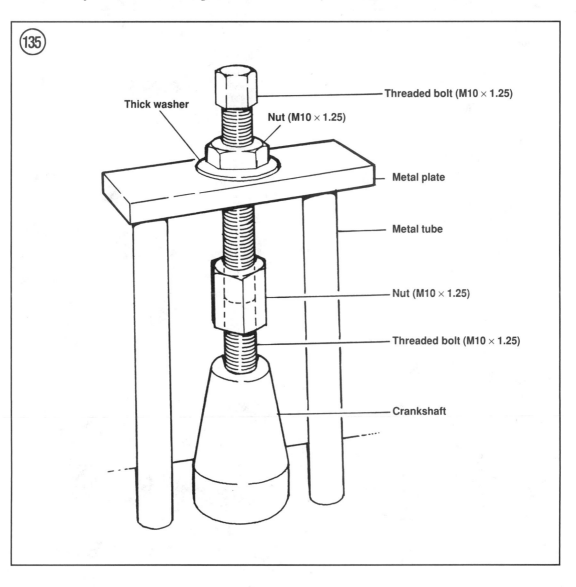

(135)

Thick washer

Threaded bolt (M10 × 1.25)

Nut (M10 × 1.25)

Metal plate

Metal tube

Nut (M10 × 1.25)

Threaded bolt (M10 × 1.25)

Crankshaft

slowly by hand. It should turn freely without any signs of roughness or noise.

4. Place the left-hand crankcase assembly onto wood blocks as shown in **Figure 140**.

5. Apply engine oil to the inner race of all bearings in the left-hand crankcase half.

6. Install the balancer shaft (**Figure 141**).

7. Install the transmission (main axle and drive axle) as follows:

   a. Install washer onto drive axle as shown in **Figure 142**.

   b. Mesh drive axle (A) and main axle (B) together as shown in **Figure 143**.

   c. Install the transmission assembly into the left-hand crankcase bearings. See **Figure 144**.

   d. Check that the washer is still installed onto the drive axle (**Figure 144**).

8. Prior to installing the shift fork assembly (**Figure 145**), note the following:

   a. Each shift fork is embossed with the letter "L" (left-hand), "C" (center) or "R" (right-hand); see **Figure 146**.

   b. The 2 shift fork shafts are different. The shaft with the 2 O-rings is used with the "C" shift fork; see **Figure 147**.

9. Install the shift forks (**Figure 145**) as follows:

   a. Install all of the shift forks with their embossed letter facing up.

   b. Install the "C" shift fork into the main axle 3rd/4th gear; see **Figure 148**.

   c. Install the "L" shift fork into the drive axle 6th gear; see **Figure 149**.

   d. Install the "R" shift fork into the drive axle 5th gear; see **Figure 150**.

10. Install the shift drum as follows:

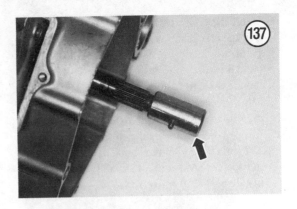

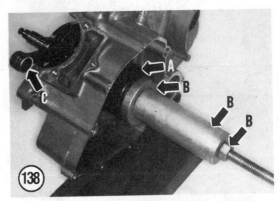

(141)

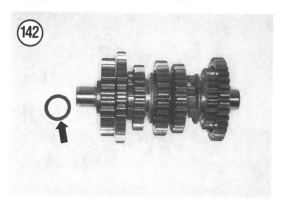

(142)

(143)

(144)

(145)

INTERNAL SHIFT MECHANISM

1. Shift drum
2. Shift fork "C" (center)
3. Shift fork shaft
4. Shift fork "R" (right-hand)
5. Shift fork "L" (left-hand)
6. Shift fork shaft
7. Reverse shift fork shaft
8. Reverse shift fork
9. Bolt
10. Washer
11. Spring
12. Detent ball
13. Reverse shift drum

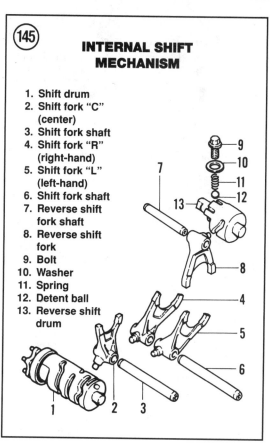

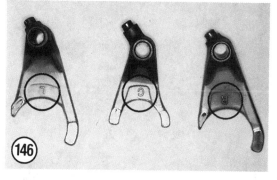

(146)

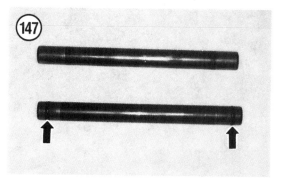

(147)

a. Install the shift drum into the blind hole in the case (**Figure 151**).

b. Engage the "L" shift fork pin into the bottom shift drum groove.

c. Engage the "C" shift fork pin into the center shift drum groove.

d. Engage the "R" shift fork pin into the upper shift drum groove.

11. Install the shift fork shafts as follows:

a. Apply engine oil to the 2 shift fork shaft O-rings (**Figure 147**).

b. Install the shift fork shaft with the 2 O-rings through the "C" shift fork; see A, **Figure 152**.

c. Install the other shift fork shaft through the "R" and "L" shift forks; see B, **Figure 152**.

d. Make sure both shift forks are seated completely in the blind holes in the crankcase.

NOTE
Step 12 is best done with the aid of a helper as the assemblies are loose and do not want to spin very easily. Have the helper spin the transmission shaft while you turn the shift drum through all the gears.

12. Spin the transmission shafts and shift through the gears using the shift drum. Make sure you can

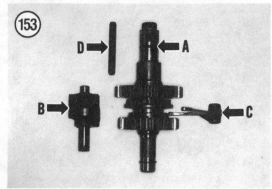

shift into all gears. This is the time to find that something may be installed incorrectly—not after the crankcase is completely assembled.

13. After making sure the transmission shifts into all of the gears correctly, shift the transmission assembly into NEUTRAL.

14. Set the crankcase assembly on 2 wood blocks or a wood holding fixture.

15. See **Figure 153**. Install the output axle (A), reverse shift drum (B), reverse shift fork (C) and shift fork shaft (D) as follows:

   a. Apply engine oil to the output axle O-ring (A, **Figure 154**).

   b. Install the reverse shift fork onto the output axle dog clutch groove as shown at B, **Figure 154**.

   c. Install the output axle and reverse shift fork into the left-hand crankcase as shown in **Figure 155**.

   d. Install the reverse shift drum (**Figure 156**) into the blind hole in the crankcase. Engage the shift fork pin with the shift drum groove.

   e. Install the shift fork shaft (**Figure 157**) through the shift fork and into the blind crankcase hole.

16. Install the reverse axle as follows:

   a. Install the washer onto the reverse axle (**Figure 158**).

   b. Install the reverse axle (**Figure 159**).

17. Install the counter axle assembly (**Figure 160**) as follows:

  a. Prior to installation, lubricate the counter axle needle bearings, thrust washers and axle with engine oil.

NOTE
The 2 counter axle washers are identical.

  b. Place the 1st washer onto the crankcase blind hole (**Figure 161**).

  c. Install the counter axle gear cluster so that the larger gear (**Figure 162**) faces up.

NOTE
*When installing the counter axle, the notch on the axle must align with the notch machined into the left-hand crankcase; see **Figure 163**.*

  d. Insert the counter axle through the gear cluster (**Figure 164**) and insert it into the crankcase until you feel it bottom out. You should not be able to turn the axle when it is properly installed.

  e. Install the 2nd washer (**Figure 165**).

18. Install the 2 locating dowels (**Figure 166**).

NOTE
*Prior to installing gasket sealer, check forward and reverse shifting as described under **Forward and Reverse Shifting Check** in this chapter.*

19. When forward and reverse shifting is correct, continue with Step 20.

NOTE
Make sure the left- and right-hand crankcase surfaces are clean and free of

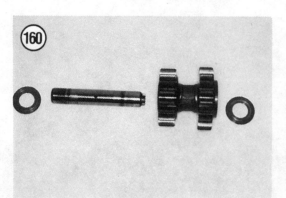

all old gasket material. This is to make sure you get a leak free seal.

20. Apply a light coat of *non-hardening liquid gasket* sealer, such as Yamabond No. 4 or equivalent, onto the mating surfaces of both crankcase halves (**Figure 167**).

21. Align the right-hand crankcase with the axle shafts and crankshaft install it (**Figure 168**). Push it down squarely into place until it engages the dowel pins and then seats completely against the lower case half. See **Figure 169**.

CAUTION
If everything is lined up properly, the right-hand crankcase half should be easy to install. Force should not be required. If the crankcase halves do not fit together completely, do not attempt to pull them together with the crankcase screws. Separate the crankcase halves and investigate the cause of the interference. If the transmission and/or reverse assemblies were disassembled, recheck to make sure that a gear is not installed backwards. Crankcase halves are a matched set and are very expensive. Do not risk damage by trying to force them together.

22. Turn all of the exposed axle shafts, crankshaft and shift drums (forward and reverse). There should be no tightness. If everything turns okay, continue with Step 23.

23. Turn the engine over so that the left-hand crankcase faces up. Install all of the crankcase mounting bolts finger-tight (**Figure 170**). Install the wire clamp onto screw No. 8.

24. Tighten the crankcase mounting bolts in 2-3 stages in the numerical order shown in **Figure 170** to the final torque specification listed in **Table 3**.

25. Rotate the axle shafts, crankshaft and shift drums to make sure there is no binding. If there is any binding, remove the crankcase mounting bolts and the right-hand crankcase half and correct the problem.

26. Install the reverse shift cam detent assembly (**Figure 171**) as follows:

    a. Install the detent ball (**Figure 172**) so that it rests in the shift drum detent ramp.

    b. Install the spring, washer and reverse shift cam bolt (**Figure 173**). Tighten the bolt to the torque specification in **Table 3**.

27. Install all exterior engine assemblies as described in this chapter and other related chapters:

    a. Oil pipe.

    b. Balancer and primary drive gears.

    c. Oil pump.

    d. External shift mechanism.

    e. Clutch.

    f. Starter motor.

    g. Alternator.

    h. Cylinder and piston.

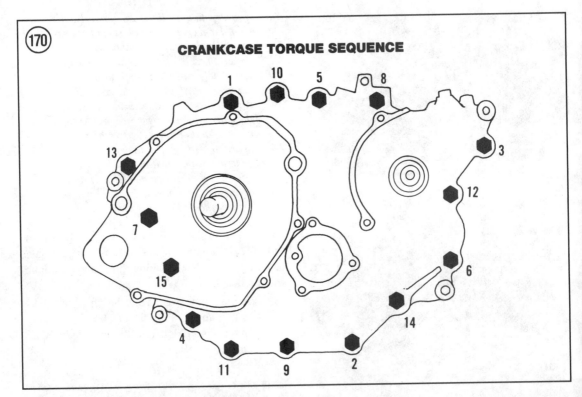

CRANKCASE TORQUE SEQUENCE

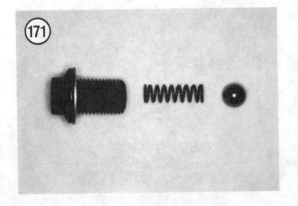

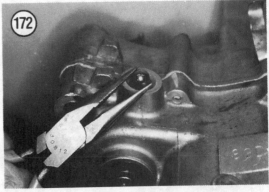

i. Cylinder head.

Forward and Reverse Shifting Check

Forward and reverse shifting should be checked prior to reassembling the engine.

1. If you are in the process of reassembling the engine, install the crankcase 2 dowel pins (**Figure 166**). Then install the right-hand crankcase (without gasket sealer) and secure it with 3-4 mounting bolts. Tighten the bolts finger-tight.

2. Install the reverse shift cam detent assembly (**Figure 171**) as follows:

    a. Install the detent ball (**Figure 172**) so that it rests in the shift drum detent ramp.

    b. Install the spring, washer and reverse shift cam bolt (**Figure 173**). Tighten the bolt to the torque specification in **Table 3**.

3. Install the shift drum stopper lever, spring and mounting bolt (**Figure 174**). Tighten the stopper lever bolt to the torque specification in **Table 3**.

4. To check forward shifting:

    a. Shift the transmission into NEUTRAL. **Figure 174** shows the shift drum/stopper arm assembly in NEUTRAL. You can confirm NEUTRAL by connecting an ohmmeter (set on R × 1) between the neutral switch and ground (**Figure 175**). The ohmmeter will show continuity when the transmission is in NEUTRAL.

    b. Turn the main axle (A, **Figure 169**) counter-clockwise and turn the shift drum (B, **Figure 169**) to engage each gear. While turning main axle, check output axle rotation with other hand. Output axle (**Figure 176**) should turn *counter-clockwise* in each gear. Check engagement and rotation of each gear.

5. To check reverse shifting:

    a. Shift transmission into NEUTRAL (**Figure 174**).

    b. Connect an ohmmeter (set on R × 1) between the reverse switch and ground; see **Figure 177**. The ohmmeter will show continuity when the transmission is in REVERSE.

    c. Turn the reverse shaft clockwise with a 10 mm wrench (**Figure 178**). The transmission should now be in reverse.

    d. Now turn main axle (A, **Figure 169**) counter-clockwise and check that output axle (**Figure 176**) turns clockwise.

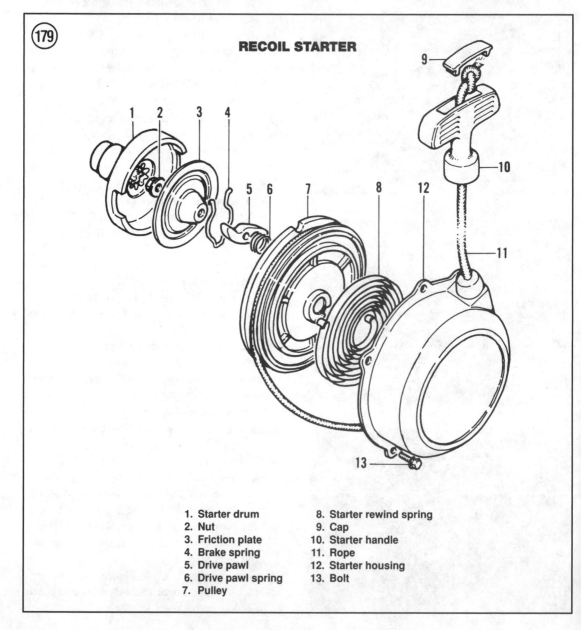

RECOIL STARTER

1. Starter drum
2. Nut
3. Friction plate
4. Brake spring
5. Drive pawl
6. Drive pawl spring
7. Pulley
8. Starter rewind spring
9. Cap
10. Starter handle
11. Rope
12. Starter housing
13. Bolt

6. If the transmission failed to operate as described in Steps 4 and 5, remove transmission and reverse gear assemblies and examine installed gears as described in Chapter Seven.

7. If engine shifts into forward and reverse correctly, remove parts previously installed (Steps 1-3) and complete engine reassembly, starting with Step 19 under *Crankcase Reassembly* in this chapter.

RECOIL STARTER

All 1987-1988 models are equipped with a rope-operated recoil starter assembly. The same starter assembly can be installed on 1989 and later models. See **Figure 179**.

The rewind starter assembly is mounted in a housing that is bolted onto the left side of the engine next to the alternator. Pulling the handle attached to the rope causes the pulley to rotate against spring tension. The drive pawl attached to the pulley is moved to engage the starter drum that is attached to the engine crankshaft. After the pawls engage the starter drum, additional rotation of the starter pulley will turn the crankshaft to start the engine.

When the starter handle is released, the rewind spring turns the pulley in the reverse direction. As the pulley returns to its original position, the rope is wound back into the groove of the pulley.

Rewind starters are relatively trouble-free. The most common malfunctions are a broken rope, or a broken rewind spring.

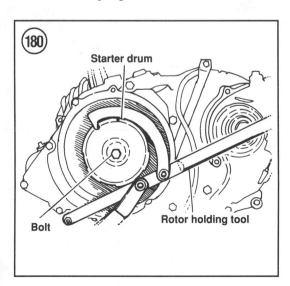

Starter Housing
Removal/Installation

1. Park the vehicle on level ground and set the parking brake.
2. Remove the bolts that hold the starter housing to the engine, then remove the starter housing.
3. Install by reversing these steps. Torque the starter housing mounting bolts to the specifications in **Table 3**.

Starter Drum
Removal/Installation

The starter drum is bolted onto the left-hand end of the crankshaft.
1. Remove the starter housing as described in this chapter.
2. Hold the starter drum with the Yamaha rotor holding tool (part No. YU-01235) or equivalent and loosen the alternator rotor and starter pulley mounting bolt (**Figure 180**). Then, remove the bolt, lockwasher and flat washer.
3. Remove the starter drum (**Figure 180**).

NOTE
There is an O-ring installed inside the starter drum.

4. Install by reversing these removal steps. Tighten the alternator rotor (starter drum) mounting bolt to the torque specification in **Table 3**.

Starter Housing Disassembly

WARNING
The starter rewind spring is under pressure and may jump out when disassembling the starter. The spring is not very strong, but it may cause eye injury and is often sharp enough to cut fingers and hands. Safety glasses should be worn when disassembling the starter.

1. Remove the starter housing as described in this chapter.
2. Pull the handle partway out and hold the sheave drum with your thumb as shown in **Figure 181** to prevent the sheave drum from unwinding.
3. Pull the rope partway out from between the starter housing and the pulley as shown in **Figure**

181. The rope should be exiting the notch in the pulley as shown.

4. Hold onto the rope near the pulley notch, keep the rope in the notch and prevent the pulley from rewinding.

5. Release your thumb and allow the pulley to unwind slowly.

6. Remove the starter handle as follows:

   a. Pry the cap (9, **Figure 179**) from the handle.

   b. Slide the rope through the handle and untie the knot.

   c. Remove the starter handle.

7. Remove the starter shaft nut (A, **Figure 182**), then remove the following parts.

   a. Friction plate (B, **Figure 182**).

   b. Drive pawl (**Figure 183**).

   c. Drive pawl spring (**Figure 184**).

> *WARNING*
> *The starter rewind spring may remain wound in the starter housing or it may fly out as the pulley is removed in step 8. Watch out and protect yourself accordingly.*

8. Slowly lift the pulley (**Figure 185**) and attached rope from the housing.

9. If necessary, carefully remove the starter spring (**Figure 186**) from the housing as follows:

   a. Place the starter housing on the floor with the spring side down. Tap the housing lightly while holding it tightly to the floor. The spring will unwind as it falls from the cavity in the starter housing.

   b. Pick the spring and starter housing up from the floor.

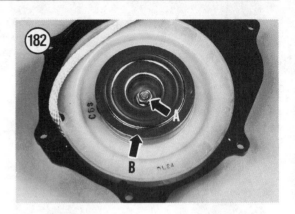

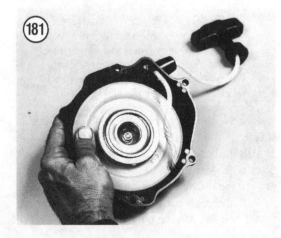

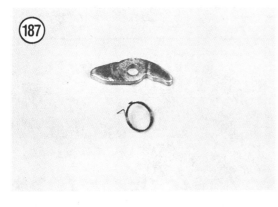

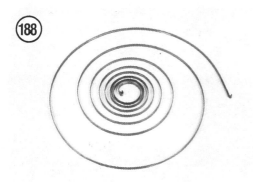

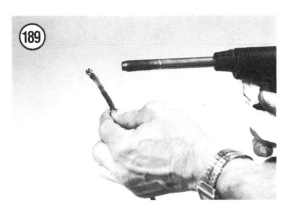

Rewind Starter Inspection

1. Clean all parts, except the rope, in solvent and dry thoroughly.

2. Check the starter shaft in the starter housing. If the shaft is cracked, worn excessively or loose in the housing, replace the entire starter housing.

3. Check the guide where the rope passes through the starter housing for wear or roughness that would damage the rope. Install a new housing if damaged.

4. Inspect the pulley for damage at the center hub where rewind spring attaches and where pawl attaches. Check the top and bottom surfaces of the pulley for cracks or other damage.

5. Inspect the drive pawl (**Figure 187**) for damage, especially near the ends.

6. Check the friction plate (3, **Figure 179**). Install new friction plate if it is cracked, warped or severely worn.

7. Install a new rope if it is frayed or broken. Carefully measure the diameter and length of the old rope to make sure that replacement is identical.

WARNING
Be careful when cleaning and inspecting the rewind spring, because the edges may be sharp enough to cut cleaning cloths and hands.

8. Check the starter spring (**Figure 188**). Make sure that neither end is broken off, cracked or otherwise damaged. Clean the entire length of the spring and check for cracks, bends or other damage. Install a new spring if damaged in any way.

Attaching Rope to Pulley

NOTE
The ends of the starter rope can be heated with a lighter, candle or a torch (as shown in Figure 189) to prevent fraying and to keep knots from untying.

1. Remove and disassemble the starter assembly as described in this chapter.

2. Insert one end of the rope through the hole in pulley.

3. Tie the knot shown in **Figure 190** in the rope end.

NOTE
Make sure that knot is both tight and small enough to fit into pocket of sheave pulley as shown in **Figure 191**.

4. Coil the rope clockwise tightly into the pulley groove 4 1/2 turns and through the notch as shown in **Figure 191**. Cut rope about 45 cm (18 in.) beyond the notch.

5. Heat the cut end of the rope to prevent fraying and to make it easier to thread end through the starter housing and handle.

6. Refer to Assemble Starter in this chapter.

Installing Rewind Spring

WARNING
Safety glasses should be worn when installing the rewind spring and while assembling the remainder of the starter.

1. Remove and disassemble the starter assembly as described in this chapter.

2. Install the rewind spring in the starter housing as follows:

   a. Lubricate the entire length of the rewind spring and the inside of the cavity in starter housing with water proof grease.

   b. Attach the hooked outer end of the rewind spring to the slot in starter housing.

   c. Wind the spring into the housing in a clockwise direction as shown in **Figure 186**.

NOTE
The spring should lay flat in the housing as shown in **Figure 186**.

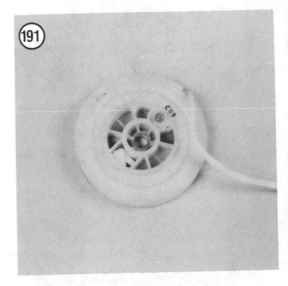

Assemble Rewind Starter

1. Install the rewind spring and starter rope as described in this chapter.

2. Install the pulley over the shaft in starter housing (**Figure 192**). Keep the rope coiled into the pulley groove and exiting through the notch.

3. Engage the inner end of spring with the notch in pulley center hub. Make sure that pulley is fully seated in the starter housing and that spring is attached to the hub.

4. Turn pulley clockwise while holding rope in notch to check for spring pressure. Carefully release spring pressure after checking while keeping the

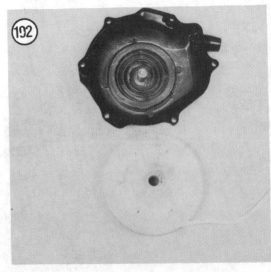

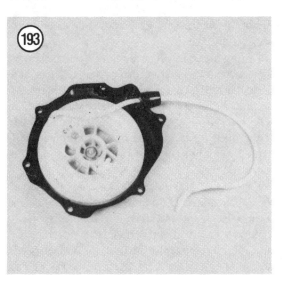

rope in the pulley notch. The rope should still be coiled 4 1/2 turns around the pulley (**Figure 193**).

5. Install the pawl spring and drive pawl as follows:
  a. Insert the long end of the pawl spring into the hole in pulley (**Figure 194**).
  b. Install the drive pawl into the spring so that the short end of the pawl spring fits into the drive pawl notch (See **Figure 183**).
  c. Preload the drive pawl spring by turning it one turn counterclockwise, then push the drive pawl into the cutout in pulley.

6. Make sure that brake spring clip (**Figure 195**) is correctly installed in the friction plate.

7. Install the brake spring clip and friction plate as shown in **Figure 196**.

8. Install retaining nut (2, **Figure 179**) securely.

NOTE
There should still be 4 1/2 turns of the starter rope wrapped into the pulley groove. When preloading the rewind spring in the following step, do not unwind rope from the pulley groove.

9. Grasp the starter rope where it exits the notch in pulley and preload the rewind spring by rotating the pulley 3 turns clockwise.

10. Hold pulley to stop it from turning and feed about 30 cm (1 foot) of the rope through the rope guide of the starter housing.

11. Tie a loose knot in the rope to prevent the rope from rewinding into the housing. Be sure to leave enough room to attach the handle.

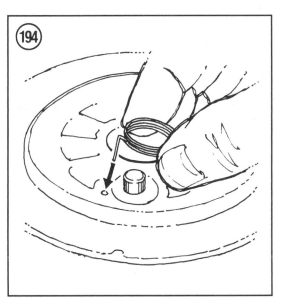

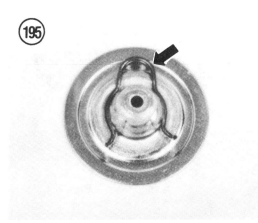

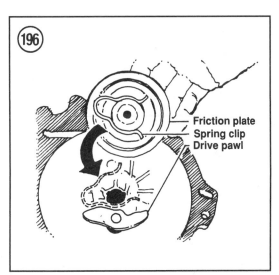

Friction plate
Spring clip
Drive pawl

12. Feed the free end of the rope through the handle and tie the knot shown in **Figure 190**. Pull knot down into the handle.

13. Untie the loose knot and let the rope rewind around the pulley.

14. Test assembly by pulling the handle, then releasing it to rewind the rope around the pulley.

15. If the rope does not rewind completely, add additional preload as follows:
   a. Pull the rope up into the notch as shown in **Figure 181**.
   b. Hold rope at notch and turn pulley clockwise one additional turn.
   c. Guide rope out of notch and into line with pulley groove.
   d. Recheck starter operation.

16. Operate starter and check that pawl extends properly. If pawl does not extent, the friction plate, brake spring, pawl, or pawl spring may be damaged or installed incorrectly.

BREAK-IN PROCEDURE

If the rings were replaced, a new piston installed, the cylinder rebored or honed or major lower end work performed, the engine should be broken-in just as though it were new. The performance and service life of the engine depends greatly on a careful and sensible break-in.

During break-in, oil consumption will be higher than normal. It is therefore important to check and correct the oil level frequently (Chapter Three). At no time during the break-in or later should the oil level be allowed to drop below the minimum level. If the oil level is low, the oil will become overheated resulting in insufficient lubrication and increased wear.

For the first 300 miles (500 km), do not operate the engine above 4,000 rpm. Yamaha recommends to stop the engine and allow it to cool for approximately 5 to 10 minutes after each one hour of operation. Prolonged steady running at one speed, no matter how moderate, is to be avoided as well as hard acceleration.

Between 300-600 miles (500-1,000 km) do not operate the engine above 5,000 rpm or use full throttle at any time.

After 600 miles (1,000 km), change the engine oil and filter and clean the oil strainer as described in Chapter Three. It is essential to perform this service to ensure that all of the particles produced during break-in are removed from the lubrication system. The small added expense may be considered a smart investment that will pay off in increased engine life.

After 600 miles (1,000 km) the engine may be operated at full throttle.

Table 1 OIL PUMP SERVICE SPECIFICATIONS

	mm	in.
Tip clearance	0.15	0.006
Side clearance	0.04-0.09	0.002-0.004

Table 2 CRANKSHAFT SERVICE SPECIFICATIONS

	New mm (in.)	Service limit mm (in.)
Crank width	58.95-59.00 (2.321-2.323)	— —
Runout limit	— —	0.06 (0.002)
Connecting rod side clearance	0.35-0.85 (0.014-0.0335)	—
Small end free play limit	0.8-1.0 (0.0315-0.0394)	—

Table 3 ENGINE TIGHTENING TORQUES

	N•m	ft.-lb.
Balancer shaft nut	60	43
Alternator rotor bolt	50	36
Cam sprocket bolt	60	43
Chain guide (intake side)	10	7.2
Oil pump Phillips screws	7	5.1
Engine drain plug	32	23
Oil filter cover	10	7.2
Crankcase mounting bolts	10	7.2
Stator housing flange bolts	10	7.2
Clutch nut	80	59
Primary drive gear nut	80	59
Drive sprocket nut	75	55
Cam chain tensioner		
Mounting bolts	10	7.2
Blind bolt	38	27
Recoil starter bolts	10	7.2
Starter motor	10	7.2
Neutral switch	20	14
Reverse switch	20	14
Stopper lever bolt	14	10
Reverse shift cam bolt	10	7.2
Upper front engine mounting bracket	33	24
Front engine mounting bolt	33	24
Rear upper & lower engine mount bolts	33	24
Oil pipe banjo bolt	16	11
Footpeg mounting bolts	55	40
Starter clutch mounting bolts	30	22
Starter pulley bolt	50	36
Recoil starter housing mounting bolts	10	7.2

5

CLUTCH AND EXTERNAL SHIFT MECHANISM

This chapter describes service procedures for the following sub-assemblies:

    a. Clutch.

    b. Clutch release mechanism.

    c. External shift mechanism.

    d. Clutch cable.

These sub-assemblies can be removed with the engine in the frame. General clutch specifications are listed in **Table 1**. **Tables 1-3** are found at the end of the chapter.

CLUTCH COVER

The clutch release mechanism is mounted in the clutch cover.

Removal/Installation

1. Remove the right-hand footpeg cover.

2. Disconnect the master cylinder pushrod at the rear brake pedal (A, **Figure 1**).

3. Disconnect the rear brake pedal spring and remove the right-hand footpeg mounting bolts and remove the footpeg (B, **Figure 1**).

4. Drain the engine oil as described in Chapter Three.

5. Loosen the clutch cable locknut (A, **Figure 2**) at the clutch release lever and disconnect the cable from its mounting bracket. Then disconnect the cable (B, **Figure 2**) from the release lever.

NOTE
To obtain additional clutch cable slack, loosen clutch cable adjuster at handlebar and disconnect cable.

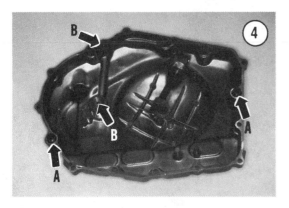

6. Remove the clutch cover mounting bolts. Note the copper washer installed on the long mounting bolt. Then remove the clutch cover (**Figure 3**).

7. Remove the 2 dowel pins (A, **Figure 4**) and gasket.

8. Remove all gasket residue from the cover and crankcase gasket surfaces.

9. Installation is the reverse of these steps. Note the following.

10. Clean the oil holes in the clutch cover (B, **Figure 4**) with compressed air.

11. Install the clutch cover. Center the end of the release lever between the 2 embossed marks on the crankcase as shown in **Figure 5**.

12. Install the clutch cover mounting bolts. Install the long bolt and copper washer into the bolt hole shown in **Figure 6**.

13. Tighten the clutch cover mounting bolts to the torque specification listed in **Table 3**.

14. Refill the engine oil as described in Chapter Three.

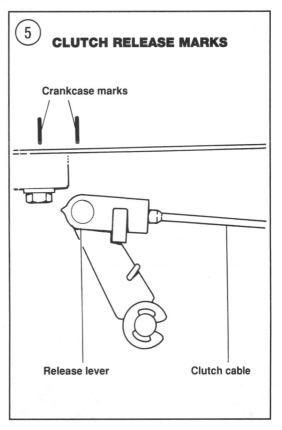

CLUTCH RELEASE MARKS

Crankcase marks

Release lever   Clutch cable

CLUTCH RELEASE MECHANISM

Refer to **Figure 7** when servicing the clutch release mechanism assembly.

Removal/Installation

1. Remove the clutch cover as described in this chapter.

2. Record the installed (spline) position of the clutch release lever (**Figure 8**) in relation to the pinion gear (A, **Figure 9**) and lower pushrod (B, **Figure 9**).

3. Remove the E-clip (C, **Figure 9**) and washer (**Figure 10**) at the bottom of clutch release shaft.

4. Remove the clutch release shaft and spring assembly from the clutch cover (A, **Figure 11**).

5. To remove the short pushrod (A, **Figure 12**) from the clutch cover:

   a. Insert a metal rod through the release shaft holes in the clutch cover as shown at B, **Figure 12**.

   b. Carefully pry the short pushrod out of its bore with a screwdriver as shown at C, **Figure 12**.

   c. Remove the metal rod.

6. To remove the clutch release lever (A, **Figure 13**):

   a. Make a punch mark on the clutch release shaft that aligns with the index mark on the clutch release lever.

   b. Remove the E-clip and remove the lever, spring and washer.

Inspection

1. Clean all parts in solvent and dry thoroughly.

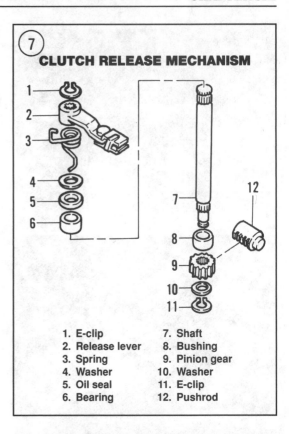

⑦ CLUTCH RELEASE MECHANISM

1. E-clip	7. Shaft
2. Release lever	8. Bushing
3. Spring	9. Pinion gear
4. Washer	10. Washer
5. Oil seal	11. E-clip
6. Bearing	12. Pushrod

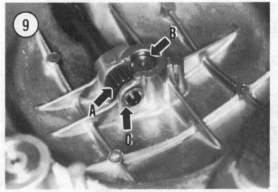

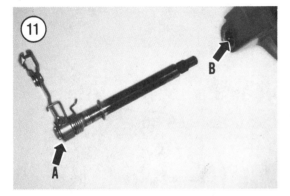

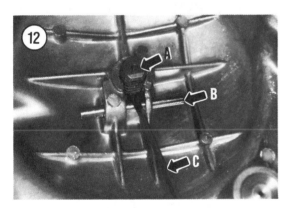

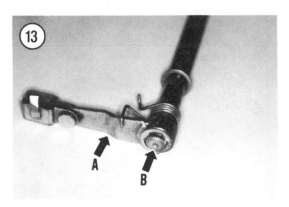

2. Replace the clutch cover oil seal (B, **Figure 11**) if leaking or damaged.

3. Inspect all of the clutch release mechanism parts for severe wear or damage. Check the gears for chipped or broken gear teeth. Replace damaged parts.

Installation

1. Install the washer, spring and clutch release lever onto the shaft (**Figure 14**), while noting the following:

   a. Align the index mark on the lever (A, **Figure 14**) with the punch mark on the shaft.

   b. Install the E-clip (B, **Figure 13**) into the shaft groove.

   c. Engage the spring arm into the lever groove as shown at B, **Figure 14**.

2. Install the lower pushrod (**Figure 15**) into the clutch cover, then install the clutch release lever shaft (A, **Figure 16**) partway into the clutch cover.

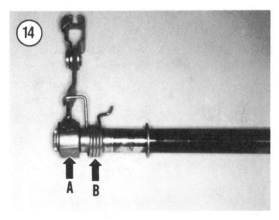

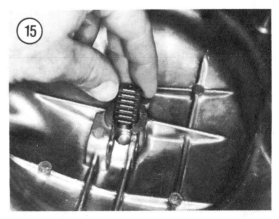

3. Install the pinion gear (B, **Figure 16**), engaging it with the lower pushrod and shaft so that the same relationship recorded during disassembly is maintained.

4. Install the lower washer (**Figure 10**) and E-clip (C, **Figure 9**).

CLUTCH

The clutch is a wet multiplate type which operates immersed in the oil supply it shares with the engine

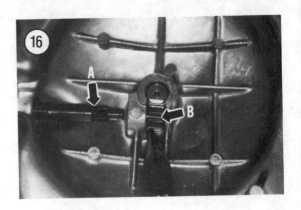

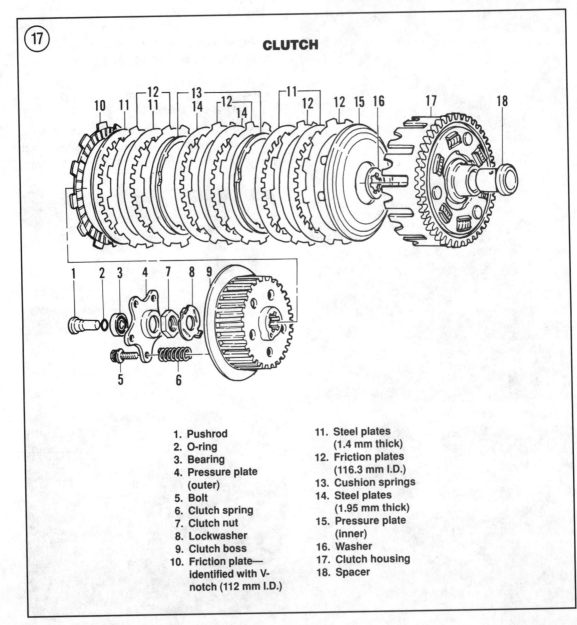

CLUTCH

1. Pushrod
2. O-ring
3. Bearing
4. Pressure plate (outer)
5. Bolt
6. Clutch spring
7. Clutch nut
8. Lockwasher
9. Clutch boss
10. Friction plate— identified with V-notch (112 mm I.D.)
11. Steel plates (1.4 mm thick)
12. Friction plates (116.3 mm I.D.)
13. Cushion springs
14. Steel plates (1.95 mm thick)
15. Pressure plate (inner)
16. Washer
17. Clutch housing
18. Spacer

and transmission. The clutch boss is splined to the transmission main axle and the clutch housing can rotate freely on the main axle. The clutch housing is geared to the primary drive gear attached to the crankshaft.

The clutch can be removed with the engine in the frame.

Removal

Refer to **Figure 17** for this procedure.
1. Remove the clutch cover as described in this chapter.
2. Remove the clutch release bearing and pushrod (A, **Figure 18**).
3. Loosen the clutch spring bolts (A, **Figure 19**) in a crisscross pattern. Then remove the bolts, pressure plate (B, **Figure 19**) and clutch springs.
4. Pry the lockwasher tab away from the clutch nut.
5. Hold the clutch boss with the Yamaha rotor holding tool (part No. YU-01235) and loosen the clutch nut (A, **Figure 20**). Insert the rotor holding tool pins into the 2 clutch boss holes (B, **Figure 18**).

CAUTION
Do not hold the pressure plate bolt tabs with a wrench or other tool when loosening the clutch nut. These tabs are fragile and will break easily. If you do not have a suitable tool, you can make a holding tool with a flat piece of metal, 2 bolts and 2 nuts as shown in Figure 21.

6. Remove the clutch nut and lockwasher.
7. Remove the clutch boss (B, **Figure 20**) and clutch plates.
8. Remove the washer (A, **Figure 22**) and clutch housing (B, **Figure 22**).
9. Remove the spacer (**Figure 23**).
10. Separate the clutch plates in the order shown in **Figure 17**.

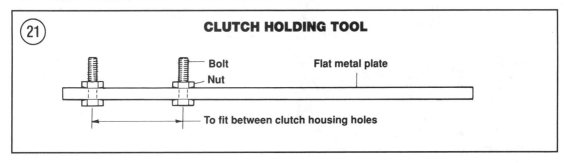

CLUTCH HOLDING TOOL

Bolt
Nut
Flat metal plate
To fit between clutch housing holes

Inspection

Clutch service specifications and wear limits are listed in **Table 2**.

1. Clean all parts in solvent and dry with compressed air.

2. Measure the free length of each clutch spring (**Figure 24**) with a vernier caliper. Replace the springs as a set if any one spring is too short.

3. **Table 1** lists the number of friction plates (**Figure 25**) used in the stock clutch. Note that there are 6 friction plates with an inside diameter of 116.3 mm (4.58 in.) and 1 friction plate with an inside diameter of 112 mm (4.41 in.); see **Figure 26**. The friction material is bonded onto an aluminum plate for warp resistance and durability. Measure the thickness of each friction plate at several places around the disc (**Figure 27**) with a vernier caliper. Replace all friction plates if any one is too thin. Do not replace only 1 or 2 plates (unless it is the 112 mm I.D. plate).

4. **Table 1** lists the number of clutch metal plates (**Figure 28**) used in the stock clutch. Place each clutch metal plate on a surface plate or a thick piece of glass and check for warpage with a feeler gauge (**Figure 29**). If any plate is warped more than speci-

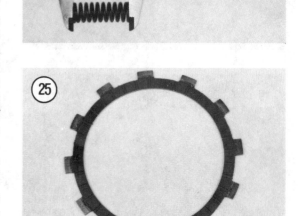

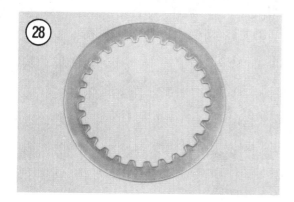

fied, replace the entire set of plates. Do not replace only 1 or 2 plates.

5. The clutch metal plate inner teeth mesh with the clutch boss splines (A, **Figure 30**). Check the splines for cracks or galling. They must be smooth for chatter-free clutch operation. If the clutch boss splines are worn, check the clutch metal plate teeth for wear or damage.

6. Inspect the clutch boss shaft splines (B, **Figure 30**) for scoring or other damage.

7. The friction plates have tabs that slide in the clutch housing grooves (**Figure 31**). Inspect the tabs for cracks or galling in the grooves. The tabs (A, **Figure 32**) must be smooth for chatter-free clutch operation. Light damage can be repaired with an oilstone. Replace the clutch housing if damage is severe.

8. Check the clutch housing bearing bore (B, **Figure 32**) for cracks, deep scoring, excessive wear or heat discoloration. If the bearing bore is damaged, check the main axle for damage. Replace worn or damaged parts.

9. Check the spacer and spacer bore in the clutch housing (**Figure 33**) for scoring, excessive wear or other damage. Replace damaged parts.

10. Inspect the inner pressure plate bolt studs (A, **Figure 34**) for thread damage or cracks at the base of the studs. Thread damage may be repaired with the correct size metric tap. Replace the pressure plate if a bolt stud is cracked or otherwise damaged.

11. Inspect the outer pressure plate (B, **Figure 34**) for warpage or other damage.

12. Inspect the clutch release bearing (C, **Figure 34**) for damage. Hold the outer bearing race and turn the inner race by hand. The bearing should turn smoothly with no roughness or excessive noise.

13. Inspect the pushrod (D, **Figure 34**) for severe wear or damage. Replace the pushrod O-ring if damaged.

14. Lay a cushion spring on a flat surface and measure the spring height at each raised point with a scale as shown in **Figure 35**. Replace the cushion spring if the height measurement is less than the specification in **Table 2**. Repeat for each cushion spring.

15. If there is any doubt about the condition of any part, replace it with a new one.

Assembly

Refer to **Figure 17** when installing the clutch assembly.

1. Coat all clutch parts and the main axle shaft with engine oil prior to assembly.

2. Slide the spacer (**Figure 23**) onto the main axle with its shoulder facing inward.

3. Slide the clutch housing onto the main axle and over the spacer, engaging the clutch housing gear with the primary drive gear; see **Figure 36**.

4. Install the splined washer onto the main axle (**Figure 37**) and seat it against the clutch housing.

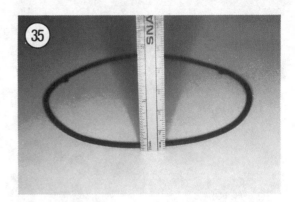

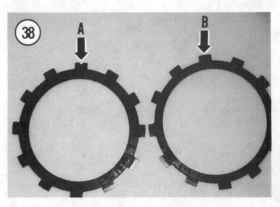

The main axle splines will end before the washer reaches the clutch housing. The washer will then spin on the main axle. This condition is normal.

5. Prior to installing the clutch plate assembly, note the following:

  a. There are 2 different types of friction plates. The friction plate installed against the clutch boss has an inner diameter of 112 mm (4.41 in.); this plate can be identified with the V-notch cut into one plate tab (A, **Figure 38**). The remaining 6 friction plates have an inner diameter of 116.3 mm (4.58 in.); these plates do not have a V-notch (B, **Figure 38**).

  b. There are 2 different types of steel plates. See 11, **Figure 17** and 14, **Figure 17**.

6. Install the clutch plates as follows:

  a. Place the clutch boss on the workbench so that the spline end faces up (**Figure 39**).

  b. Prior to installation, apply new engine oil to all of the clutch plates.

  c. Install the friction plate with the 112 mm (4.41 in.) inner diameter; see **Figure 40**.

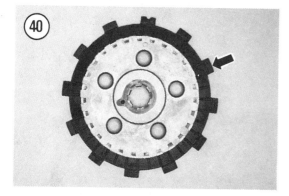

*Remember, this friction plate can be identified by the V-notch (**Figure 41**) machined into one of the plate's tabs.*

  d. Install a steel plate (**Figure 42**).

  e. Install a friction plate (**Figure 43**).

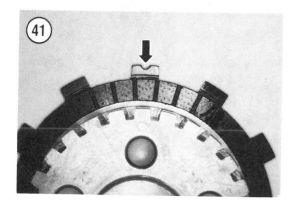

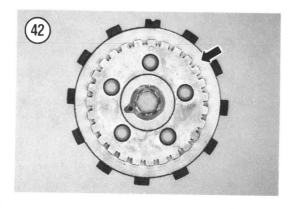

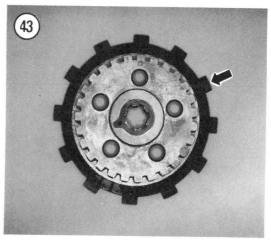

f. Install a cushion spring (**Figure 44**). The cushion spring should fit inside the friction plate as shown in **Figure 45**.

g. Install a steel plate (14, **Figure 17**).

h. Continue to install the clutch plates in the order shown in **Figure 17**. The last plate installed should be a friction plate.

> *NOTE*
> *Be sure the cushion springs and clutch plates (14, Figure 17) are installed in the order shown in Figure 17.*

7. Align the V-notch on the friction plate tab with the arrow mark on the clutch boss; see **Figure 46**. Then align all of the friction plate tabs.

8. Install the inner pressure plate as follows:

a. Align the pressure plate index mark (A, **Figure 47**) with the clutch boss index mark (B, **Figure 47**) when installing the pressure plate.

b. Align the index marks (sub-step a) and install the pressure plate onto the clutch boss (**Figure 48**).

> *NOTE*
> *Make sure the pressure plate sits flush against the outer friction plate. If not, check the index marks and realign the pressure plate.*

9. Install one clutch spring and clutch spring bolt (**Figure 49**) to hold the clutch assembly together.

> *NOTE*
> *Make sure to maintain friction plate alignment or the clutch plates will be difficult to install into the clutch housing. Confirm that the V-notch is still aligned with the clutch boss arrow mark (Figure 46).*

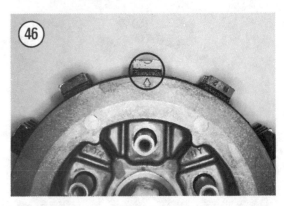

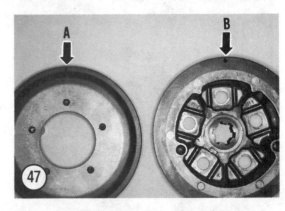

10. Align the clutch boss splines with the main axle splines and the friction plate tabs with the clutch housing grooves and slide the clutch plate assembly into the clutch housing. When doing so, center the clutch boss index mark (A, **Figure 50**) between the 2 clutch housing index marks (B, **Figure 50**). See **Figure 51**.

11. Install a new lockwasher, engaging the lockwasher tab into the clutch boss notch (**Figure 52**).

12. Thread the clutch nut, with its chamfered side facing outward, onto the main axle (A, **Figure 53**).

13. Hold the clutch with the same tool used during disassembly (B, **Figure 53**) and tighten the clutch nut to the torque specification in **Table 3**. Bend the lockwasher so that one tab seats against one flat of the clutch nut.

NOTE
*Prior to removing the clutch bolt and spring (**Figure 52**) to complete clutch assembly, insert a wide-blade screwdriver between the pressure plate and clutch housing as shown in **Figure 54**. Then carefully move the clutch plate assembly toward you and hold in this position until all of the clutch springs, outer pressure plate and clutch spring bolts have been installed (and 2 of the bolts tightened). This prevents the pressure plate (A, Figure 55) from slipping off the back of the clutch boss (B, **Figure 55**). If the pressure plate does slip off, there will be too much clutch plate clearance. This will cause clutch slippage and possible pressure plate damage.*

6

14. Remove the bolt and install the remaining clutch springs (**Figure 56**).

15. Install the outer pressure plate (**Figure 57**) with its bearing recess facing inward. The install 2 clutch spring bolts (**Figure 57**) and tighten them sufficiently to compress the springs and hold the clutch plates/pressure plate assembly against the clutch boss; see **Figure 58**. Remove the screwdriver.

16. Install the remaining clutch spring bolts (**Figure 59**) and tighten all bolts in a crisscross pattern to the torque specification in **Table 3**.

NOTE
Now check that the clutch plates, clutch boss and pressure plate are properly installed. There should be no clearance at the back of the clutch. If you can move the clutch plates by hand, remove the clutch plates and reinstall.

17. Slide the pushrod through the clutch release bearing and apply engine oil to the pushrod O-ring (**Figure 60**).

18. Install the bearing/pushrod assembly into the outer pressure plate (**Figure 61**).

19. Install the clutch cover as described in this chapter.

EXTERNAL SHIFT MECHANISM

The external shift mechanism is located on the same side of the crankcase as the clutch assembly and can be removed with the engine in the frame. To remove the shift drum and shift forks it is necessary to remove the engine and split the crankcases (see Chapter Five).

Removal

Refer to **Figure 62** for this procedure.

1. Remove the clutch as described in this chapter.

2. Remove the pinch bolt (15, **Figure 62**) and slide the shift lever boss off of the shift shaft.

6

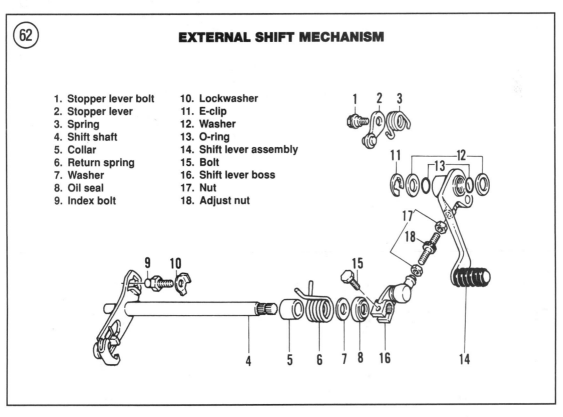

EXTERNAL SHIFT MECHANISM

1. Stopper lever bolt
2. Stopper lever
3. Spring
4. Shift shaft
5. Collar
6. Return spring
7. Washer
8. Oil seal
9. Index bolt
10. Lockwasher
11. E-clip
12. Washer
13. O-ring
14. Shift lever assembly
15. Bolt
16. Shift lever boss
17. Nut
18. Adjust nut

3. Remove the shift shaft (**Figure 63**) and washer (**Figure 64**).

4. Remove the shift drum stopper lever bolt (A, **Figure 65**), then remove the stopper lever (B, **Figure 65**) and spring (C, **Figure 65**).

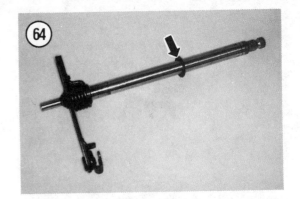

Inspection

1. Remove all thread sealer residue from the stopper lever bolt and crankcase threads.

2. Clean all parts in solvent and dry thoroughly.

3. Check the shift shaft (**Figure 66**) for cracks or bending. Check the splines on the end of the shaft for damage.

4. Check the shift shaft return spring (A, **Figure 67**) and collar (5, **Figure 62**). The return spring arms should be centered on the shift shaft arm as shown at A, **Figure 67**. Replace the return spring if it shows signs of fatigue or is damaged. Replace the collar if severely worn or damaged.

5. Check the small shift drum arm spring (B, **Figure 67**) for weakness or damage. If this spring is damaged, the shift shaft will have to be replaced as the spring is not available as a separate item.

6. Check the stopper lever assembly (**Figure 68**) for the following:

    a. Weak or damaged spring.

    b. Bent or damaged stopper lever and roller.

    c. Damaged shoulder bolt.

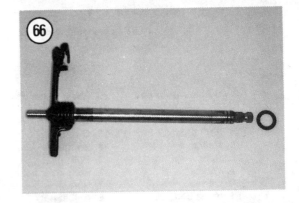

Installation

1. Apply Loctite 242 (blue) to the stopper lever mounting bolt prior to installation. Assemble the stopper lever assembly and install it as shown in **Figure 65**, making sure the shoulder on the stopper lever bolt is installed all the way through the stopper lever. Note how the spring fits around the stopper

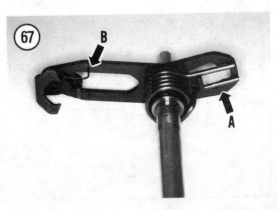

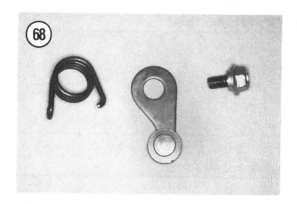

lever in C, **Figure 65**. Tighten the stopper lever bolt to the torque specification in **Table 3**.

2. Slide the washer (**Figure 64**) onto the shift shaft.

3. Slide the shift shaft into the crankcase, centering the return spring over the bolt stud as shown in **Figure 69**.

4. Slide the shift lever bars (**Figure 70**) onto the shift shaft. Install the pinch bolt and tighten securely.

5. Install the clutch as described in this chapter.

CLUTCH CABLE

Replacement

1. Remove the fuel tank as described in Chapter Eight.

2. Pull the clutch/brake cable adjuster cover away from the handlebar cable adjusters.

3. Loosen the clutch cable adjuster locknut (A, **Figure 71**) and screw the adjuster (B, **Figure 71**) in.

4. Loosen the clutch cable adjuster locknuts (A, **Figure 72**) and disconnect the clutch cable from the clutch release lever (B, **Figure 72**).

5. Disconnect the clutch cable from the clutch lever at the handlebar.

NOTE
Prior to removing the cable, make a drawing of the cable routing through the frame. It is very easy to forget its routing after it has been removed. Replace the cable exactly as it was, avoiding any sharp turns.

6. Pull the cable out of any retaining clips on the frame.

7. Remove the clutch cable from the vehicle.

8. Lubricate the new cable as described in Chapter Three.

9. Install the new cable by reversing these removal steps. Make sure it is correctly routed with no sharp turns. Adjust the clutch cable as described in Chapter Three.

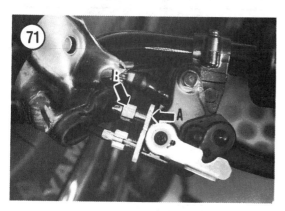

Table 1 GENERAL CLUTCH SPECIFICATIONS

Clutch spring quantity	5
Friction plate quantity	
V-notch	1
All other	6
Clutch plate quantity	
Thick	2
Thin	4

Table 2 CLUTCH SERVICE SPECIFICATIONS

	New mm (in.)	Service limit mm (in.)
Friction plate thickness		
V-notch plate	2.94-3.06	2.8
	(0.116-0.120)	(0.110)
All other plates	2.74-2.86	2.64
	(0.107-0.113)	(0.104)
Clutch plate*		
Thickness		
Thick	1.9-2.1	—
	(0.075-0.083)	—
Thin	1.5-1.7	—
	(0.059-0.066)	—
Warp limit	—	0.2
	—	(0.008)
Clutch spring free length	47.8	46.5
	(1.882)	(1.831)
Cushion spring height	3.15-3.45	—
	(0.124-0.136)	—

*See text for thick and thin clutch plate identification.

Table 3 TIGHTENING TORQUES

	N•m	ft.-lb.
Clutch cover bolts	10	7.2
Clutch spring bolts	8	6
Clutch nut	80	59
Primary drive gear	80	59
Drive sprocket	75	55
Stopper lever bolt	14	10
Reverse shift cam stopper bolt	10	7.2

CHAPTER SEVEN

TRANSMISSION AND INTERNAL SHIFT MECHANISM

7

The transmission on all models provides six speeds forward and one speed in reverse. To gain access to the transmission and internal shift mechanism it is necessary to remove the engine and split the crankcase (Chapter Five). Once the crankcase has been split, removal of the transmission, reverse gears, shift drums and forks is a simple task of pulling the assemblies up and out of the crankcase.

Transmission gear ratios are listed in **Table 1**. Transmission service specifications are listed in **Table 2**. Both tables are found at the end of the chapter.

TRANSMISSION/REVERSE SYSTEM IDENTIFICATION

With the forward and reverse systems, there are 10 different assemblies in the transmission that will be covered in this chapter. The different assemblies are identified in **Figure 1** and listed as follows:

a. Reverse shift drum.

b. Reverse shift fork shaft.

c. Output axle.

d. Reverse axle.

e. Counter axle.

f. Drive axle.

g. Main axle.

h. Shift fork.

i. Shift fork.

j. Forward shift drum.

TRANSMISSION TROUBLESHOOTING

Refer to Chapter Two.

TRANSMISSION/REVERSE OVERHAUL

Removal/Installation

Remove and install the transmission and internal shift assemblies as described under *Crankcase Disassembly and Crankcase Assembly* in Chapter Five.

Transmission Service Notes

1. A divided container such as an egg carton can be used to help maintain correct alignment and position of the parts as they are removed from the transmission and reverse axles.

2. The circlips are a tight fit on the transmission axles. All circlips removed during disassembly should be discarded and new circlips installed.

3. Circlips will turn and fold over, making removal and installation difficult. To ease replacement, open the circlip with a pair of circlip pliers while at the same time holding the back of the circlip with a pair of pliers and remove it. See **Figure 2**.

Main Axle
Disassembly/Assembly

A hydraulic press (**Figure 3**) and a bearing splitter (**Figure 4**) will be required to disassemble and reassemble the main axle. If you do not have access to a press, have the main axle rebuilt by Yamaha dealer or machine shop.

Refer to **Figure 5** for this procedure.

1. Place the assembled axle into a large can or plastic bucket and thoroughly clean with solvent and stiff brush. Dry with compressed air or let sit on rags to drip dry.

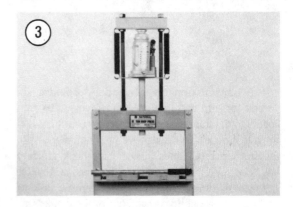

NOTE
When using a press and bearing splitter to disassemble the main axle in Step 2, follow the manufacturer's instructions and guidelines when using their equipment. It is recommended to wear safety glasses when using press equipment.

2. Press off main axle second gear (23, **Figure 5**) as follows:

   a. Measure width of installed gears on main axle with vernier caliper (**Figure 6**) and record measurement. Then measure clearance between main axle 2nd and 6th gears with feeler gauge

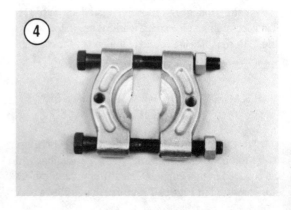

TRANSMISSION

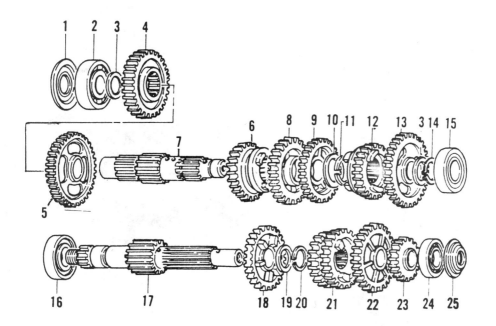

7

1. Oil seal
2. Bearing
3. Washer
4. Counter axle drive gear
5. Drive axle 1st gear
6. Drive axle 5th gear
7. Drive axle
8. Drive axle 3rd gear
9. Drive axle 4th gear
10. Washer
11. Circlip
12. Drive axle 6th gear
13. Drive axle 2nd gear

14. Circlip
15. Bearing
16. Bearing
17. Main axle/1st gear
18. Main axle/5th gear
19. Washer
20. Circlip
21. Main axle 3rd/4th gear
22. Main axle 6th gear
23. Main axle 2nd gear
24. Bearing
25. Oil seal

(**Figure 7**) and record measurement. These measurements will be used to reassemble main axle.

b. Because 2nd gear is symmetrical—either side can be installed first on axle—mark outside of gear with a grease pencil so that gear can be installed facing in its original position.

c. Install a bearing splitter below main axle 2nd gear (**Figure 8**) and tighten it. Then install main axle in press bed (**Figure 9**).

d. Press off main axle 2nd gear (**Figure 9**). Make sure to catch the axle assembly to prevent it from falling onto the shop floor.

e. Remove main axle 2nd gear (**Figure 10**).

3. Slide off 6th gear.
4. Slide off 3rd/4th gear combination.
5. Remove circlip and washer and slide off 5th gear.

NOTE
*Main axle 1st gear (**Figure 11**) is an integral part of main axle.*

6. Inspect main axle parts as described under *Transmission Inspection* in this chapter.

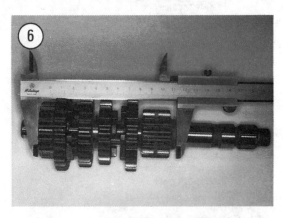

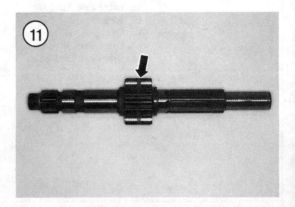

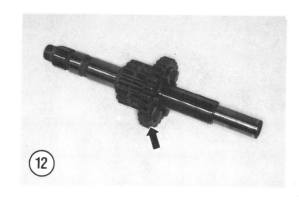

12

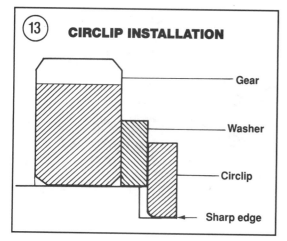

13 **CIRCLIP INSTALLATION**

— Gear

— Washer

— Circlip

← Sharp edge

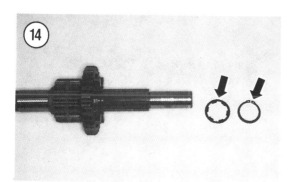

14

15

7. Slide on 5th gear (**Figure 12**) so that gear dogs face away from 1st gear.

NOTE
*Install circlip in Step 8 so that its flat edge faces away from the washer (**Figure 13**).*

8. Install spline washer and circlip (**Figure 14**). Seat circlip in axle groove next to 5th gear (**Figure 15**). Position circlip so that gap aligns with axle groove as shown in **Figure 16**.

9. Slide on 3rd/4th gear combination so that larger gear (4th) faces away from 5th gear; see **Figure 17**.

10. Slide on 6th gear so that gear dogs face toward 4th gear; see **Figure 18**.

11. Press 2nd gear (**Figure 10**) onto main axle as follows:

a. Apply light coat of assembly oil to inside of 2nd gear.

NOTE
If installing original 2nd gear, install gear facing in same direction as marked prior to removal. If installing new 2nd gear, gear can be installed with either side installed first as gear is symmetrical.

7

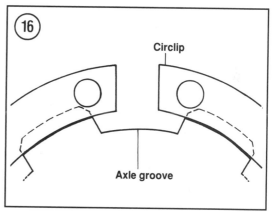

16

Circlip

Axle groove

17

b. Slide 2nd gear (**Figure 19**) over main axle until it stops.

c. Place main axle in press bed with 2nd gear (A, **Figure 20**) facing up.

d. Install a hollow driver over main axle and center on 2nd gear (B, **Figure 20**).

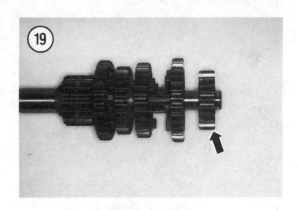

CAUTION
Driver inside diameter must be large enough and deep enough so that it does not contact main axle. Otherwise, main axle will be damaged during press operation.

e. Carefully press 2nd gear onto main axle. Periodically, stop and check assembled gear length with vernier caliper. Check final positioning with feeler gauge (**Figure 20**). Refer to the measurements taken prior to disassembly.

f. Assembly is complete when assembled gear length is same as that recorded during disassembly.

12. After assembly is complete refer to **Figure 21** for correct placement of main axle gears.

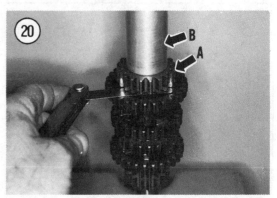

Drive Axle
Disassembly/Assembly

Refer to **Figure 5** for this procedure.

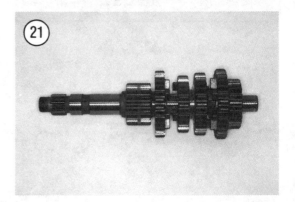

1. Place the assembled axle into a large can or plastic bucket and thoroughly clean with solvent and stiff brush. Dry with compressed air or let it sit on rags to drip dry.

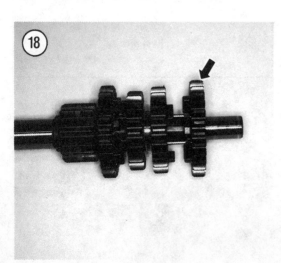

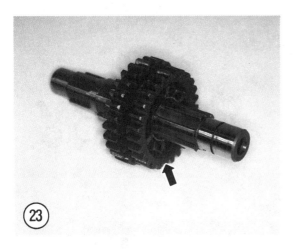

(23)

2. Remove the washer and remove the counter axle drive gear (4, **Figure 5**).

3. Slide off 1st and 6th gears.

4. Remove the circlip and washer and slide off 2nd gear (13, **Figure 5**) and 6th gear.

5. Remove the circlip and washer and slide off 4th and 3rd gears.

6. Inspect drive axle assembly as described under *Transmission Inspection* in this chapter.

7. Slide on 3rd gear (A, **Figure 22**) so that its longer shoulder faces in the direction indicated by B, **Figure 22**.

8. Slide on 4th gear (**Figure 23**) so that its gear dog slots face away from 3rd gear.

NOTE
Install circlip in Step 9 so that its flat edge faces away from the washer as shown in **Figure 24**.

9. Install the flat washer and circlip (**Figure 25**). Seat circlip in groove next to 4th gear (**Figure 26**). Position circlip so that gap aligns with axle groove as shown in **Figure 27**.

7

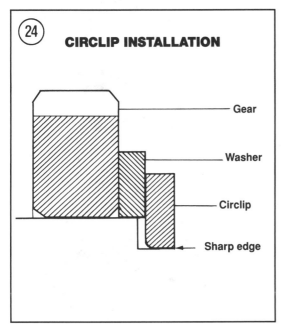

(24)

CIRCLIP INSTALLATION

Gear

Washer

Circlip

Sharp edge

(26)

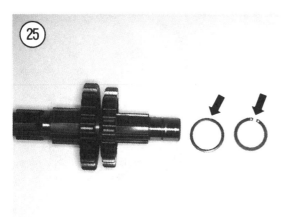

(25)

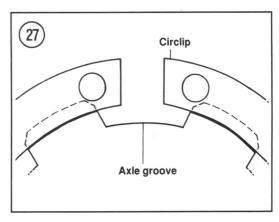

(27)

Circlip

Axle groove

10. Slide on 6th gear (**Figure 28**) so that its shift fork groove faces toward 4th gear.

11. Slide on 2nd gear (**Figure 29**) so that its longer shoulder faces toward 6th gear.

NOTE
Install circlip in Step 12 so that its flat edge faces away from the washer as shown in ***Figure 24***.

12. Install the flat washer and circlip (**Figure 30**). Seat circlip in groove next to 2nd gear (**Figure 31**).

13. Slide on 5th gear (**Figure 32**) so that its shift fork groove faces toward 3rd gear.

14. Slide on 1st gear (**Figure 33**) so that its longer shoulder faces toward 5th gear.

15. Slide on counter axle drive gear (**Figure 34**) so that its longer shoulder faces away from 1st gear.

16. Install flat washer (**Figure 35**) so that it seats against counter axle drive gear.

17. After assembly is complete refer to **Figure 35** for the correct placement of all gears. Make sure all circlips are seated correctly in the axle grooves.

OUTPUT AXLE

Output axle assembly is shown in **Figure 36**.

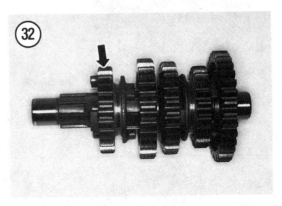

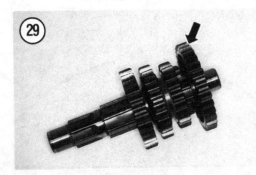

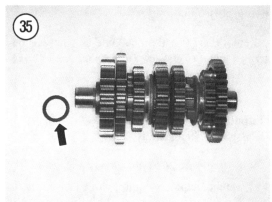

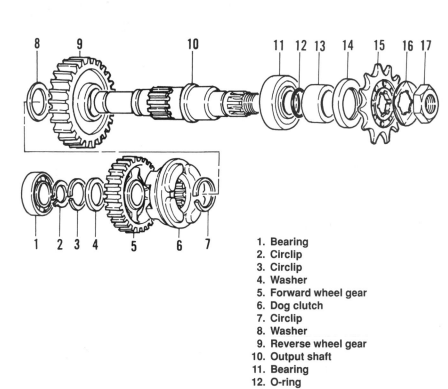

OUTPUT AXLE

1. Bearing
2. Circlip
3. Circlip
4. Washer
5. Forward wheel gear
6. Dog clutch
7. Circlip
8. Washer
9. Reverse wheel gear
10. Output shaft
11. Bearing
12. O-ring
13. Spacer
14. Oil seal
15. Drive sprocket
16. Lockwasher
17. Nut

Removal/Installation

Remove and install output axle assembly as described under *Crankcase Disassembly and Crankcase Assembly* in Chapter Five.

Output Axle
Disassembly/Reassembly

Refer to **Figure 36** for this procedure.

1. Place the output axle into a large can or plastic bucket and thoroughly clean with solvent and stiff brush. Dry with compressed air or let it sit on rags to drip dry.

2. Remove outer circlip (2, **Figure 36**).

3. Remove circlip (3, **Figure 36**) and washer installed next to forward wheel gear.

4. Remove forward wheel gear and dog clutch.

5. Remove circlip and washer and slide off reverse wheel gear.

6. Inspect output axle assembly as described under *Transmission Inspection* in this chapter.

7. Install reverse wheel gear so that dog slots face in direction shown in **Figure 37**.

8. Install flat washer and circlip (**Figure 38**). Seat circlip in groove next to reverse wheel gear (**Figure 39**). Position circlip so that gap aligns with axle groove as shown in **Figure 40**.

9. Slide the dog clutch onto the output axle as shown in **Figure 41**.

10. Slide on forward wheel gear (**Figure 42**) so that dog slots face toward dog clutch.

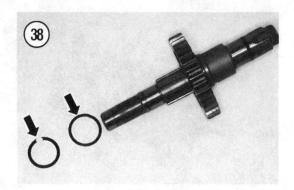

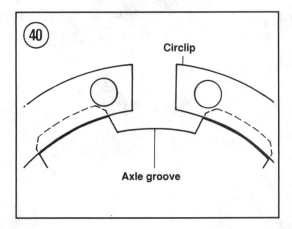

Circlip

Axle groove

NOTE
*Install circlip in Step 11 so that its flat edge faces away from the washer as shown in **Figure 43**.*

11. Install flat washer and circlip (**Figure 44**). Seat circlip in groove next to forward wheel gear (**Figure 45**).

12. Install outer circlip (**Figure 46**) in outer output axle groove (B, **Figure 46**). Position circlip so that its flat edge faces inward (toward forward wheel gear).

13. After assembly is complete refer to **Figure 47** for correct placement of all gears. Make sure all circlips are seated correctly in output axle grooves.

COUNTER WHEEL GEAR ASSEMBLY

The counter wheel gear assembly consists of the gear combination, 2 needle bearings, 2 washers and counter axle. Refer to **Figure 48** when servicing the counter wheel gear assembly.

CIRCLIP INSTALLATION

- Gear
- Washer
- Circlip
- Sharp edge

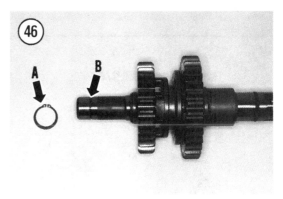

7

Removal/Installation

Remove and install the counter wheel gear assembly as described under *Crankcase Disassembly and Crankcase Assembly* in Chapter Five.

Counter Wheel Gear Assembly Inspection

1. Clean all parts (**Figure 49**) in solvent. Blow dry with compressed air.
2. Check combination gear for broken or chipped teeth.
3. Check counter axle for burrs, excessive wear or damage.
4. Check washers for galling or other damage.
5. Check needle bearings (**Figure 50**) for loose or damaged needles. Check bearing cage for galling or other damage. If necessary, replace bearings as described in following procedure.

Counter Wheel Gear Needle Bearing Replacement

1. Mount a blind bearing remover onto one bearing as shown in **Figure 51**.

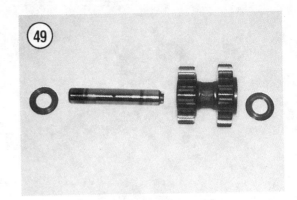

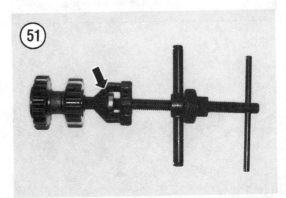

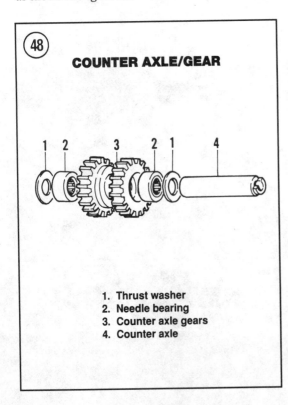

COUNTER AXLE/GEAR

1. Thrust washer
2. Needle bearing
3. Counter axle gears
4. Counter axle

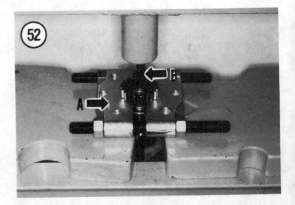

NOTE
Because of bearing's mounting position in gear, you may not be able to grasp bottom of bearing in order to remove it. Instead, install bearing remover so that the tool's arms wedge themselves into the bearing. Then tighten puller securely and continue with Step 2.

2. Mount gear side opposite bearing puller into a bearing splitter and install splitter (A, **Figure 52**) into press bed so that puller is installed at bottom.

3. Insert a rod through top of gear and center on bearing remover arms as shown at B, **Figure 52**. Now press out bottom bearing; see **Figure 53**.

4. Repeat to remove opposite bearing.

5. Discard both bearings.

6. Clean gear in solvent. Dry with compressed air.

NOTE
Install new bearings with manufacturer's marks facing outward.

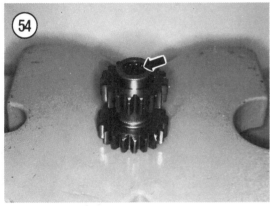

7. Place gear in press and center new bearing in gear bore (**Figure 54**). Center a hollow pipe over bearing and press bearing into gear until it bottoms.

8. Turn gear over and repeat to install opposite bearing.

9. Check condition of both bearings.

REVERSE GEAR

The reverse gear is shown in **Figure 55**.

Removal/Installation

Remove and install reverse gear as described under *Crankcase Disassembly and Crankcase Assembly* in Chapter Five.

Disassembly/Reassembly

1. Remove the washer and reverse gear from the reverse axle.

2. If necessary, remove circlip (4, **Figure 55**) from groove in reverse axle.

3. Inspect reverse gear as described under *Transmission Inspection* in this chapter.

4. If removed, install circlip (**Figure 56**) in reverse axle groove. Position circlip so that gap aligns with axle groove as shown in **Figure 57**.

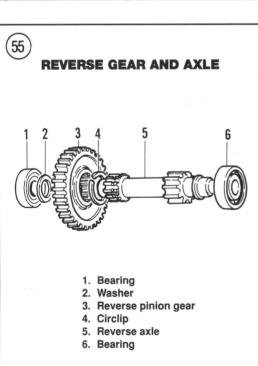

REVERSE GEAR AND AXLE

1. Bearing
2. Washer
3. Reverse pinion gear
4. Circlip
5. Reverse axle
6. Bearing

5. Slide on reverse gear so that longer shoulder on gear faces side opposite circlip as shown in A, **Figure 58**.

6. Install washer (B, **Figure 58**) so that it rests against gear.

TRANSMISSION INSPECTION

1. Clean all parts in solvent. Dry with compressed air.

> *NOTE*
> *Maintain alignment of disassembled axles and gears when cleaning and drying them.*

2. Check all axle splines for wear, cracks or other damage. Identify transmission axles as follows:
   a. Main axle (**Figure 59**).
   b. Drive axle (**Figure 60**).
   c. Output axle (**Figure 61**).
   d. Reverse axle (**Figure 62**).

3. Check the main axle 1st gear (**Figure 59**). If gear is damaged, replace main axle.

4. Replace output axle O-ring (**Figure 61**).

5. Place each axle on V-blocks and check runout with a dial indicator (**Figure 63**). If runout exceeds service limit in **Table 2**, replace axle.

6. Check each gear for excessive wear, burrs, pitting, or chipped or missing teeth.

7. Check each stationary gear bore (A, **Figure 64**) for scoring, cracks or other damage.

8. Check the gear dogs (B, **Figure 64**) for severe wear or damage.

9. Check each sliding gear groove (C, **Figure 64**) for wear, cracks or other damage.

10. Make sure that all gears slide or turn on their respective axles smoothly and without any binding.

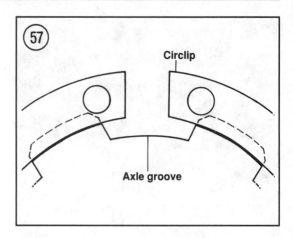

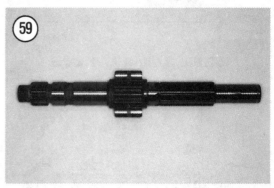

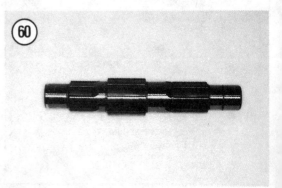

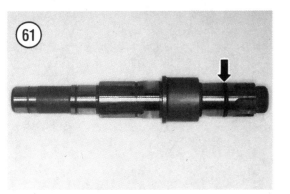

NOTE
Defective gears should be replaced, and it is a good idea to replace the mating gear even though it may not show as much wear or damage.

11. Replace all circlips during reassembly. In addition, check the washers for burn marks, scoring or cracks. Replace if necessary.

FORWARD SHIFT MECHANISM

The forward shift mechanism is shown in **Figure 65** (parts No. 1-6).

Removal/Installation

Remove and install the transmission assembly as described under *Crankcase Disassembly and Crankcase Assembly* in Chapter Five.

7

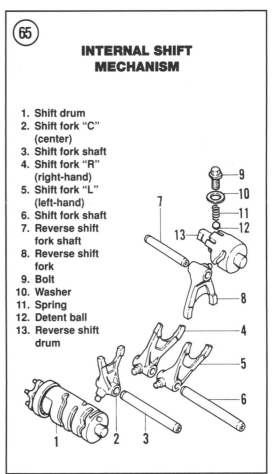

INTERNAL SHIFT
MECHANISM

1. Shift drum
2. Shift fork "C" (center)
3. Shift fork shaft
4. Shift fork "R" (right-hand)
5. Shift fork "L" (left-hand)
6. Shift fork shaft
7. Reverse shift fork shaft
8. Reverse shift fork
9. Bolt
10. Washer
11. Spring
12. Detent ball
13. Reverse shift drum

Shift Fork
Inspection

Refer to **Figure 65** for this procedure.

1. Inspect each shift fork (**Figure 66**) for signs of wear or damage. Examine the shift forks at the points where they contact the slider gear (**Figure 67**). This surface should be smooth with no signs of wear or damage.

2. Check for any arc-shaped wear or burn marks on the shift forks. This indicates that the shift fork has come in contact with the gear. The shift fork fingers have become excessively worn and the shift fork must be replaced.

3. Check the shift fork shafts (**Figure 68**) for bending or other damage. Check that each shift fork slides smoothly on its respective shaft.

4. Replace severely worn or damaged parts.

Shift Drum
Inspection

While the shift drum can be partially disassembled, Yamaha does not list part numbers for the separate shift drum parts. However, if the shift drum bearing is damaged, you may be able to cross-reference the bearing through a bearing supply company and replace it without having to purchase the complete shift drum assembly. Instructions for shift drum disassembly and reassembly are found in this section.

Refer to **Figure 65** for this procedure.

1. Check the grooves in the shift drum (A, **Figure 69**) for wear or roughness.

2. Check the bearing (B, **Figure 69**) for roughness or damage. If bearing is damaged, refer to *Disassembly/Reassembly* in this chapter.

3. Check the shift drum pins (C, **Figure 69**) for severe wear or damage.

4. Oil the bearing with clean engine oil.

Disassembly/Reassembly

1. Prior to disassembling the shift drum, write down the bearing number (A, **Figure 70**) and attempt to cross-reference it through a bearing supply company. If you can find a replacement bearing, continue with Step 2. If not, you will have to purchase a new shift drum assembly through a Yamaha dealer.

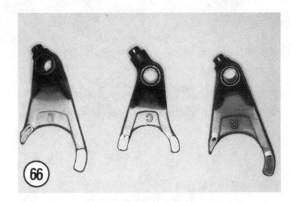

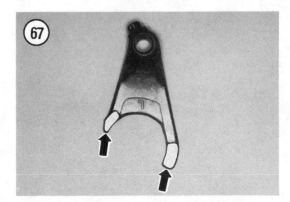

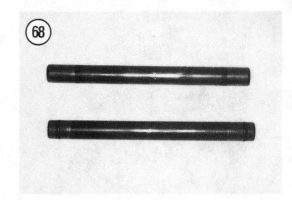

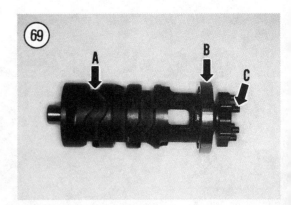

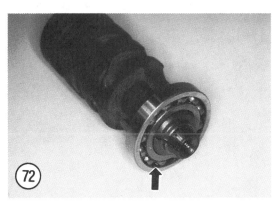

An impact driver with a No. 2 Phillips bit will be required to loosen the shift drum screw in Step 2.

2. Loosen, then remove the Phillips screw (B, **Figure 70**) from the shift drum.

3. Remove the screw, washer, pin plate and key from the shift drum (**Figure 71**).

4. Press bearing off of shift drum.

5. Remove all thread sealer residue from the shift drum and Phillips screw threads.

6. Clean all parts in solvent. Dry with compressed air.

7. Press new bearing (**Figure 72**) onto shift drum until it bottoms.

8. Install key into shift drum groove (A, **Figure 73**). Then align keyway in pin plate and install plate (B, **Figure 73**) onto shift drum. Check that key is positioned in keyway properly; see **Figure 74**.

9. Install washer (C, **Figure 70**) into pin plate recess.

10. Apply Loctite 242 (blue) to the Phillips screw and thread screw into shift drum (B, **Figure 70**). Tighten screw securely.

REVERSE SHIFT MECHANISM

The reverse shift mechanism is shown in **Figure 65** (parts No. 7-13).

Removal/Installation

Remove and install the transmission assembly as described under *Crankcase Disassembly and Crankcase Assembly* in Chapter Five.

Shift Fork
Inspection

Refer to **Figure 65** for this procedure.

1. Inspect the reverse shift fork (**Figure 75**) for signs of wear or damage. Check the shift fork where it contacts the dog clutch installed on the output axle. This surface should be smooth with no signs of wear or damage.

2. Check for any arc-shaped wear or burn marks on the shift fork. This indicates that the shift fork is bent and must be replaced.

7

3. Check the shift fork shaft (**Figure 75**) for bending or other damage. Check that the reverse shift fork slides smoothly on the shaft.

4. Replace severely worn or damaged parts.

Shift Drum
Inspection

Refer to **Figure 65** for this procedure.

1. Check the reverse shift drum groove (A, **Figure 76**) for wear or roughness.

2. Check detent ball grooves (B, **Figure 76**) in the shift drum for excessive wear or other damage.

3. Replace the shift drum if severely worn or damaged.

4. Check the reverse shift drum detent assembly (**Figure 77**) for damaged parts. Compare the new

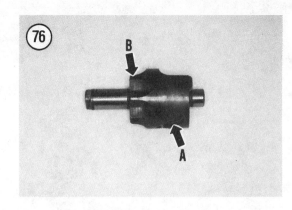

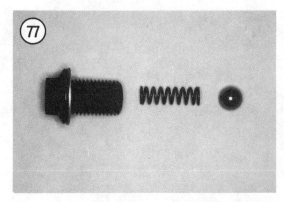

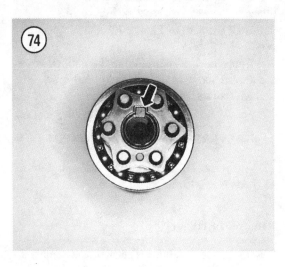

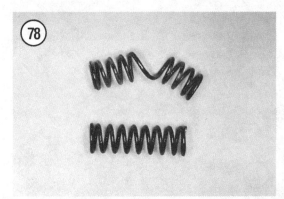

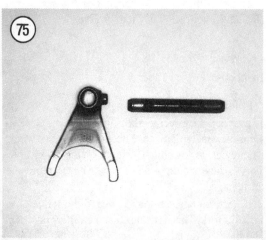

and damaged detent spring shown in **Figure 78**. Replace damaged parts as required.

REVERSE SHIFT LEVER ADJUSTMENT

Adjustment
(1988-1989)

1. Shift the reverse shift lever into its forward position (**Figure 79**).

2. Measure the rod's length as shown in **Figure 80**. The clearance at dimension A and B should be equal.

3. If necessary, loosen the shift lever rod locknuts and turn the rod as required. Tighten the locknuts and recheck.

Adjustment
(1987 and 1990-on)

Yamaha does not provide reverse shift lever specifications for these models. If the shift lever rod length has been changed, loosen the rod's locknuts and readjust the rod as required to obtain correct operation into forward and reverse gears.

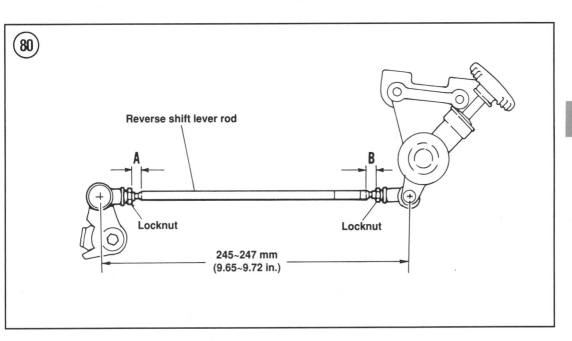

⑧⁰

Reverse shift lever rod

A   B

Locknut   Locknut

245~247 mm
(9.65~9.72 in.)

7

Table 1 TRANSMISSION GEAR RATIOS

Transmission type	Constant mesh, 6-speed forward, 1-speed reverse
Primary reduction ratio	76/24 (3.167:1)
Secondary reduction ratio	40/13 (3.077:1)
Gear ratio	
1st	$36/16 \times 20/27 \times 29/18$ (2.685:1)
2nd	$33/20 \times 20/27 \times 29/18$ (1.969:1)
3rd	$29/33 \times 20/27 \times 29/18$ (1.505:1)
4th	$27/26 \times 20/27 \times 29/18$ (1.239:1)
5th	$25/28 \times 20/27 \times 29/18$ (1.066:1)
6th	$23/29 \times 20/27 \times 29/18$ (0.947:1)
Reverse	$33/16 \times 11/10$ (6.806:1)

Table 2 TRANSMISSION SERVICE SPECIFICATIONS

Axle runout limit	0.01 mm (0.0004 in.)

CHAPTER EIGHT

FUEL AND EXHAUST SYSTEMS

The fuel system consists of the fuel tank, fuel shutoff valve, a single carburetor and an air filter.

The exhaust system consists of an exhaust pipe and muffler assembly.

This chapter includes service procedures for all parts of the fuel system and exhaust system. Air filter service is covered in Chapter Three.

Carburetor specifications are covered in **Table 1**. **Tables 1-4** are at the end of the chapter.

CARBURETOR OPERATION

An understanding of the function of each of the carburetor components and their relation to one another is a valuable aid for pinpointing a source of carburetor trouble.

The carburetor's purpose is to supply and atomize fuel and mix it in correct proportions with air that is drawn in through the air intake. At the primary throttle opening (idle), a small amount of fuel is siphoned through the pilot jet by the incoming air. As the throttle is opened further, the air stream begins to siphon fuel through the main jet and needle jet. The tapered needle increases the effective flow capacity of the needle jet as it is lifted, in that it occupies progressively less of the area of the jet.

At full throttle, the carburetor venturi is fully open and the needle is lifted far enough to permit the main jet to flow at full capacity.

The choke circuit is a "bystarter" system in which the choke lever opens a valve rather than closing a butterfly in the venturi area as on many carburetors. In the open position, the slow jet discharges a stream of fuel into the carburetor venturi, to enrich the mixture when the engine is cold.

CARBURETOR

Removal/Installation

1. Place the vehicle on level ground and set the parking brake.
2. Remove the seat.
3. Remove the fuel tank as described in this chapter.

4. Loosen the rear carburetor hose clamp screw (**Figure 1**). Slide the clamp away from the carburetor.

5. Remove the 2 front carburetor mounting nuts (**Figure 2**).

6. Note the routing of the carburetor vent and overflow tubes prior to removing the carburetor.

7. Slide the carburetor back to free it from the intake manifold, and then remove it from the air box boot.

8. Remove the carburetor side cover screws and remove the side cover (**Figure 3**).

9. Lift the throttle lever (**Figure 4**) and disconnect the throttle cable (**Figure 5**). Do not lose the ball from the end of the cable (**Figure 5**).

10. Loosen the throttle cable locknut (**Figure 6**) and unscrew the throttle cable adjuster from cable guide on the carburetor. Then slide the cable out of the cable guide.

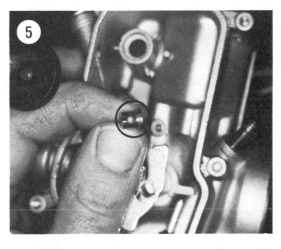

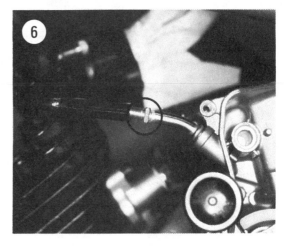

8

11. On 1988-1992 models, remove the top cover screws (**Figure 7**) and remove the cover and piston valve (**Figure 8**).

> *NOTE*
> *On 1988-1992 models, wrap the piston valve in a clean paper towel to protect the valve and jet needle from damage.*

12. Remove the carburetor assembly.

13. Place a clean shop cloth into the intake manifold and air box boot openings to prevent the entry of foreign matter.

14. Install by reversing these removal steps, while noting the following.

15. On 1988-1992 models, perform the following:

  a. Replace the carburetor top cover gasket (**Figure 9**) if damaged. To install the new gasket, or to reapply a used gasket, apply Gasgacinch to the top gasket surface and mount the gasket to the bottom of the top cover as shown in **Figure 9**.

  b. Insert the piston valve (**Figure 8**) into the carburetor, making sure to align the jet needle with the needle jet. See **Figure 10**.

  c. Install the cover and cover screws (**Figure 7**). Tighten the screws securely.

16. To reconnect the throttle cable at the throttle lever:

  a. Insert the cable through the cable guide and thread the cable adjuster onto the cable guide; see **Figure 6**. Do not tighten the locknut at this time.

  b. Pull the throttle cable down (**Figure 11**) and install the cable end onto the end of the cable (**Figure 5**).

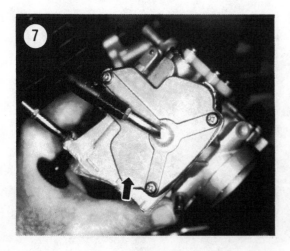

c. Push the throttle lever up and connect the cable end to the throttle lever as shown in **Figure 4**. The throttle cable must be installed on the inside of the throttle lever as shown in **Figure 4**.

d. Operate the throttle lever at the handlebar a few times, making sure the throttle lever at the carburetor moves up and down smoothly with no binding and that the cable end does not pop out.

17. Replace the carburetor side cover O-ring (**Figure 12**), if damaged, and install the side cover (**Figure 3**). Tighten the side cover screws securely.

18. Install the carburetor front O-ring (**Figure 13**) if removed.

19. Install the carburetor and tighten the mounting nuts (**Figure 2**) to the torque specification in **Table 4**.

20. Reverse removal procedure to complete installation.

Piston Valve
Removal/Installation
(1987 and 1993-on)

Refer to **Figure 14**.

1. Remove the carburetor cap and gasket.

8

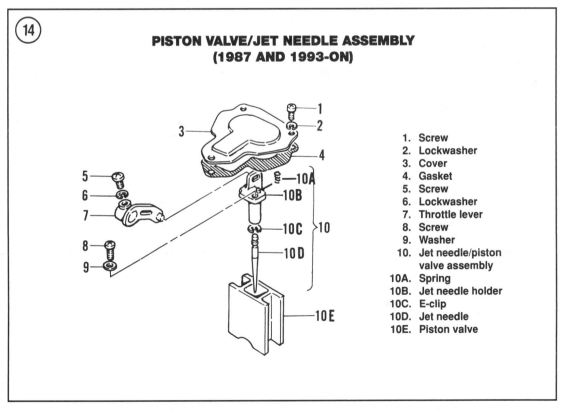

PISTON VALVE/JET NEEDLE ASSEMBLY
(1987 AND 1993-ON)

1. Screw
2. Lockwasher
3. Cover
4. Gasket
5. Screw
6. Lockwasher
7. Throttle lever
8. Screw
9. Washer
10. Jet needle/piston valve assembly
10A. Spring
10B. Jet needle holder
10C. E-clip
10D. Jet needle
10E. Piston valve

2. Remove the throttle lever screw and lift out the piston valve assembly.

3. Remove the 2 jet needle holder screws. Then remove the jet needle holder and jet needle.

4. Install by reversing these steps, plus the following.

5. Replace the carburetor top cover gasket (**Figure 9**) if damaged. To install the new gasket, or to reapply a used gasket, apply Gasgacinch to the top gasket surface and mount the gasket to the bottom of the top cover as shown in **Figure 9**.

6. Insert the piston valve (**Figure 8**) into the carburetor, making sure to align the jet needle with the needle jet. See **Figure 10**.

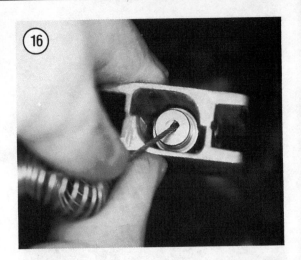

PISTON VALVE/JET NEEDLE ASSEMBLY
(1988-1992)

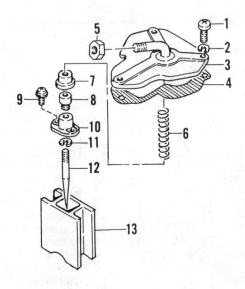

1. Screw
2. Lockwasher
3. Cover
4. Gasket
5. Nut
6. Spring
7. Spring seat
8. Guide
9. Screw
10. Jet needle holder
11. E-clip
12. Jet needle
13. Piston valve

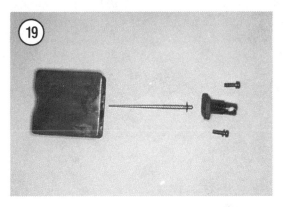

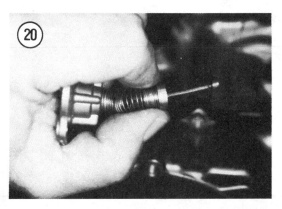

7. Tighten the throttle lever screw securely.

8. Install the cover and cover screws. Tighten the screws securely.

Piston Valve/Jet Needle Removal/Installation (1988-1992)

Refer to **Figure 15**.

1. Remove the top cover screws (**Figure 7**) and remove the cover and piston valve (**Figure 8**).

2. Compress the spring and disconnect the throttle cable from the jet needle holder (**Figure 16**).

3. Relax the spring. Then remove the spring and spring seat (**Figure 17**).

4. Remove the 2 jet needle holder screws (A, **Figure 18**) and remove the jet needle holder (B, **Figure 18**) and jet needle. See **Figure 19**.

5. Install by reversing these steps, plus the following.

6. Replace the carburetor top cover gasket (**Figure 9**) if damaged. To install the new gasket, or to reapply a used gasket, apply Gasgacinch to the top gasket surface and mount the gasket to the bottom of the top cover as shown in **Figure 9**.

7. To reconnect the throttle cable, compress the spring seat and spring as shown in **Figure 20**. Then slip the end of the cable into the jet needle holder ball groove and release the spring seat (**Figure 16**) and spring (**Figure 8**).

8. Insert the piston valve (**Figure 8**) into the carburetor, making sure to align the jet needle with the needle jet. See **Figure 10**.

9. Install the top cover and its mounting screws. Tighten the screws securely.

Disassembly

Refer to the exploded view drawing for your model when disassembling the carburetor:

    a. **Figure 21** (1987).
    b. **Figure 22** (1988-1992).
    c. **Figure 23** (1993-on).

Table 1 lists carburetor specifications and I.D. mark numbers. The I.D. mark number is listed on each carburetor; see **Figure 24**.

1. Remove the carburetor as described in this chapter.

2. Remove the piston valve from the carburetor as described in this chapter.

8

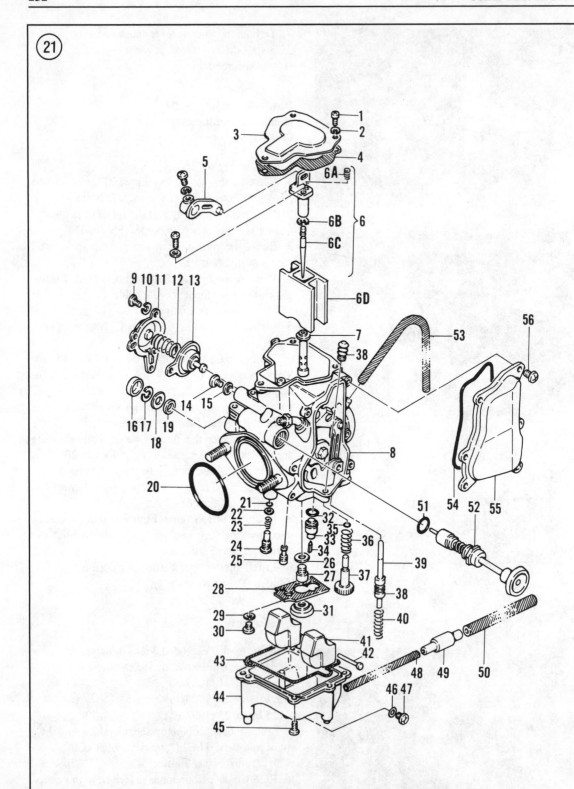

CARBURETOR (1987)

1. Screw	16. Cap	37. Idle speed
2. Lockwasher	17. Clip	adjust screw
3. Cover	18. Gasket	38. Boot
4. Gasket	19. Seal	39. Accelerator rod plunger
5. Throttle lever	20. O-ring	40. Spring
6. Jet needle/piston	21. O-ring	41. Floats
valve assembly	22. Washer	42. Float pin
6A. Spring	23. Spring	43. O-ring
6B. E-clip	24. Pilot air screw	44. Float bowl
6C. Jet needle	25. Pilot jet	45. Screw
6D. Piston valve	26. Washer	46. Washer
7. Needle jet	27. Main jet	47. Screw
8. Housing	28. Plate	48. Hose
9. Screw	29. Washer	49. Pipe
10. Lockwasher	30. Screw	50. Hose
11. Cover	31. Main jet washer	51. O-ring
12. Spring	32. O-ring	52. Enrichener valve
13. Coasting enrichener	33. Fuel valve seat	53. Hose
diaphragm	34. Fuel valve	54. O-ring
14. Screw	35. O-ring	55. Cover
15. Washer	36. Spring	56. Screw

8

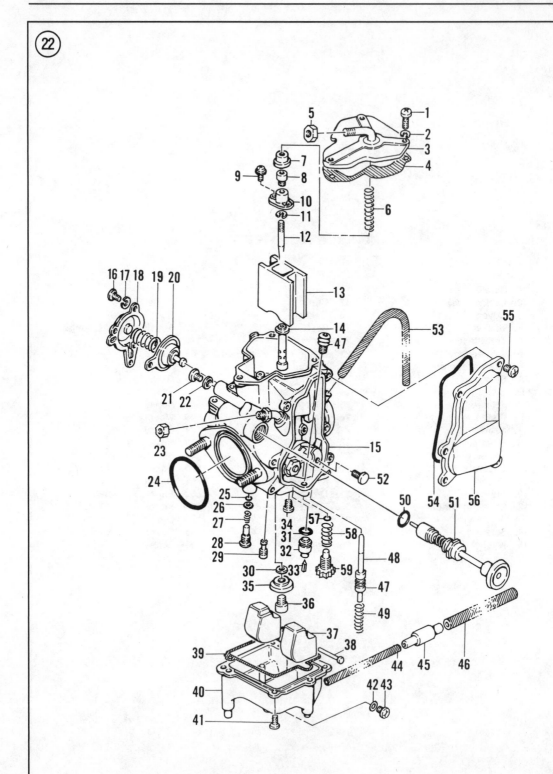

CARBURETOR (1988-1992)

1. Screw
2. Lockwasher
3. Cover
4. Gasket
5. Nut
6. Spring
7. Spring seat
8. Guide
9. Screw
10. Jet needle holder
11. E-clip
12. Jet needle
13. Piston valve
14. Needle jet
15. Housing
16. Screw
17. Lockwasher
18. Cover
19. Spring
20. Coasting enrichener diaphragm
21. Screw
22. Washer
23. Nut
24. O-ring
25. O-ring
26. Washer
27. Spring
28. Pilot air screw
29. Pilot jet
30. Main jet washer
31. O-ring
32. Fuel valve seat
33. Fuel valve
34. Screw
35. Main jet washer
36. Main jet
37. Floats
38. Float pin
39. O-ring
40. Float bowl
41. Screw
42. Washer
43. Screw
44. Hose
45. Pipe
46. Hose
47. Boot
48. Accelerator rod plunger
49. Spring
50. O-ring
51. Enrichener valve
52. Screw
53. Hose
54. O-ring
55. Screw
56. Cover
57. O-ring
58. Spring
59. Idle speed adjust screw

8

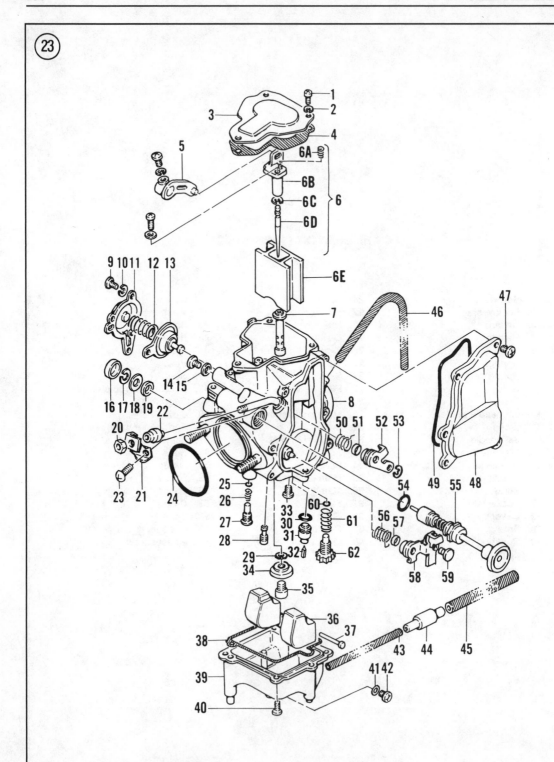

CARBURETOR (1993-ON)

1. Screw
2. Lockwasher
3. Cover
4. Gasket
5. Throttle lever
6. Piston valve/jet needle assembly
6A. Spring
6B. Jet needle holder
6C. E-clip
6D. Jet needle
6E. Piston valve
7. Needle jet
8. Housing
9. Screw
10. Lockwasher
11. Cover
12. Spring
13. Coasting enrichener diaphragm
14. Screw
15. Washer
16. Cap
17. Clip

18. Gasket
19. Seal
20. Nut
21. Plate
22. Cover
23. Screw
24. O-ring
25. O-ring
26. Spring
27. Pilot air screw
28. Pilot jet
29. Main jet washer
30. O-ring
31. Fuel valve seat
32. Fuel valve
33. Screw
34. Main jet washer
35. Main jet
36. Floats
37. Float pin
38. O-ring
39. Float bowl
40. Screw

41. Washer
42. Screw
43. Hose
44. Pipe
45. Hose
46. Hose
47. Screw
48. Cover
49. O-ring
50. Spring
51. Seal
52. Arm
53. E-clip
54. O-ring
55. Enrichener valve
56. Spring
57. Seal
58. Arm
59. Throttle cable ball
60. O-ring
61. Spring
62. Idle speed adjust screw

8

3. Remove the idle speed screw, spring and O-ring from the carburetor body.

4. Remove the O-ring (A, **Figure 25**).

5. Loosen the enrichener valve nut and remove the enrichener valve assembly (B, **Figure 25**).

6. Remove the plug screw and washer (A, **Figure 26**) if used.

7. Remove the coasting enrichener system as follows:

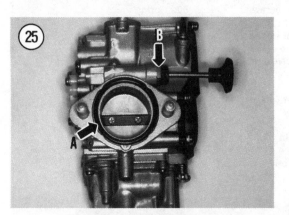

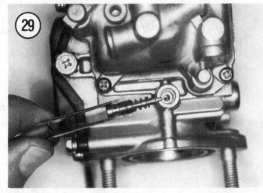

a. Remove the cover screws and cover (B, **Figure 26**).

b. Remove the spring and diaphragm (**Figure 27**).

8. Lightly seat the pilot air screw (**Figure 28**), counting the number of turns required for reassembly reference, then back screw out and remove from carburetor with spring (**Figure 29**).

9. Remove the float bowl screws and lift off the float bowl (**Figure 30**).

10. Remove the accelerator plunger spring (**Figure 31**).

11. Remove the main jet washer (**Figure 32**).

12. Remove the float pin (**Figure 33**).

13. Lift the float and needle valve (**Figure 34**) out of the main body.

14. On 1987 models, remove the screw, washer and plate (28, **Figure 21**).

15. Remove the main jet (**Figure 35**) and washer (**Figure 36**).

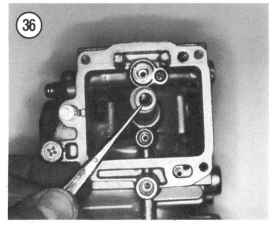

8

16. Push the needle jet (A, **Figure 37**) out through the top of the carburetor. See **Figure 38**.

17. Remove the pilot jet (**Figure 39**).

18. Remove the Phillips screw (B, **Figure 37**) and remove the fuel valve seat and O-ring (C, **Figure 37**). See **Figure 40**.

19. Remove the accelerator rod plunger (**Figure 41**) and boot (**Figure 42**).

> *NOTE*
> *Further disassembly is neither necessary nor recommended. Do not remove the throttle shaft or butterfly (**Figure 43**) as these parts are not available separately.*

20. Clean and inspect all parts as described in this chapter.

Cleaning and Inspection

1. Initially clean all parts in a petroleum based solvent. Then clean in hot soap and water and rinse with cold water. Blow dry with compressed air.

> *CAUTION*
> *Do not dip the carburetor body or any of the O-rings in a carburetor cleaner or other solution that can damage the rubber parts and seals.*

> *CAUTION*
> *If compressed air is not available, allow the parts to air dry or use a clean lint-free cloth. Do **not** use a paper towel to dry carburetor parts, as small paper particles may plug openings in the carburetor body or jets.*

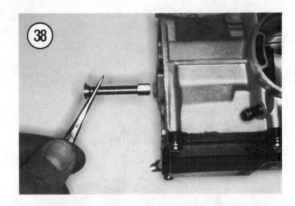

CAUTION
*Do **not** use wire or drill bits to clean jets as minor gouges in the jet can alter flow rate and upset the fuel/air mixture.*

2. Make sure the float bowl overflow tube (**Figure 44**) is clear. Blow out with compressed air if necessary.

3. Inspect the float bowl O-ring gasket for damage or deterioration; replace if necessary. O-ring gaskets tend to become hardened after prolonged use and heat and therefore lose their ability to seal properly.

4. Inspect the coasting enricher diaphragm (**Figure 45**) for cracks or other deterioration; replace if necessary.

5. Inspect the accelerator plunger assembly (**Figure 46**) for damage. Replace damaged parts.

6. Inspect the fuel valve assembly (**Figure 47**) as follows:

  a. Check the O-ring (A) for severe wear, hardness, cracks or other damage.

  b. Inspect the end of the fuel valve needle (B) for wear or damage.

  c. Check the inside of the fuel valve body (seat) (C) for steps, uneven wear or other damage.

8

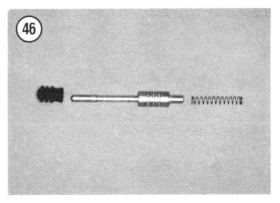

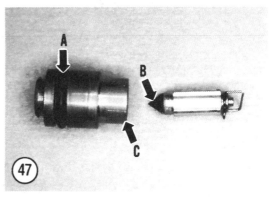

d. If the fuel valve needle and/or body (seat) are damaged, replace the fuel valve needle assembly as a set. Damage to these parts will allow the fuel valve to leak. This will cause a rich fuel mixture and/or carburetor flooding.

7. Inspect the pilot air screw (**Figure 48**) and spring for damage. Replace the screw if the tip or threads are damaged.

8. Inspect the idle speed screw O-ring (**Figure 49**) for severe wear, hardness, cracks or other damage. Replace if necessary.

9. Inspect the enrichener valve assembly (**Figure 50**) for wear, damage or deterioration.

10. Inspect the float for deterioration or damage. If the float is suspected of leakage, place it in a water filled container and push it down. If the float sinks or if bubbles appear (indicating a leak), the float must be replaced.

11. Make sure the butterfly screws (**Figure 43**) are tight. Tighten if necessary.

12. Move the throttle lever back and forth from stop-to-stop and check for free movement. If it does not move freely or if it sticks in any position, replace the carburetor body.

13. Make sure all openings in the carburetor body are clear. Clean out if they are plugged in any way.

14. Do not loosen or remove the 2 Torx screws (**Figure 51**) securing the piston valve bore to the carburetor body.

Assembly

Refer to the exploded view drawing for your model when assembling the carburetor:
a. **Figure 21** (1987).
b. **Figure 22** (1988-1992).
c. **Figure 23** (1993-on).

1. Install the accelerator boot (**Figure 42**) and accelerator rod plunger (**Figure 41**).

2. Push the fuel valve seat (with O-ring) into the carburetor body until it bottoms (C, **Figure 37**). Install the Phillips screw (B, **Figure 37**) and tighten securely.

3. Install the pilot jet (**Figure 39**).

4. Insert the needle jet through the carburetor body (**Figure 38**) and seat it into body as shown in A, **Figure 37**.

5. Install the washer (**Figure 36**) and main jet (**Figure 35**).

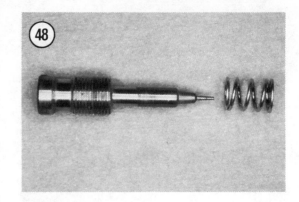

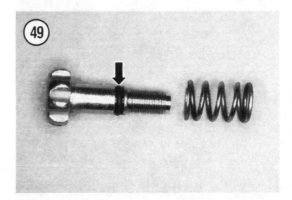

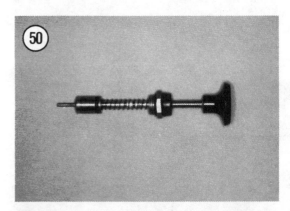

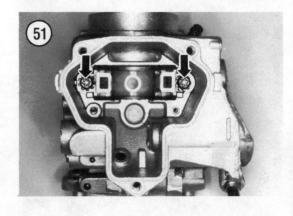

6. On 1987 models, install the plate (28, **Figure 21**), washer and screw.

7. Attach the fuel valve to the float as shown in **Figure 52**. Then install the fuel valve into the fuel valve seat (**Figure 34**) and install the pin through the float (**Figure 33**).

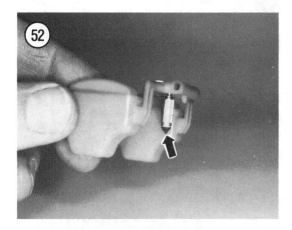

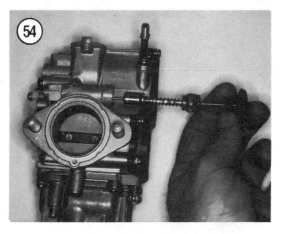

8. Check float height as described in this chapter.
9. Slide main jet washer over main jet (**Figure 32**).
10. Install accelerator plunger spring onto plunger (**Figure 31**).
11. Install O-ring gasket into float bowl groove (**Figure 53**). Then install float bowl on carburetor (**Figure 30**) and secure with mounting screws.
12. Install the pilot air screw and spring (**Figure 29**) and lightly seat it. Then back out number of turns recorded during removal or set to the stock adjustment setting listed in **Table 2**.
13. Install the coasting enrichener system as follows:
   a. Install the diaphragm and spring as shown in **Figure 27**.
   b. Install the cover and cover screws (B, **Figure 26**). Tighten screws securely.
14. Install the plug screw and washer (A, **Figure 26**), if used, and tighten securely.
15. Carefully align and install the enrichener valve (**Figure 54**). Thread the valve's nut into the carburetor and tighten securely. See B, **Figure 25**.
16. Install the O-ring into the carburetor groove.
17. Install the throttle stop screw, spring and O-ring into the carburetor body.
18. Install the carburetor as described in this chapter.
19. After assembly and installation are completed, adjust the carburetor as described in this chapter.

CARBURETOR ADJUSTMENTS

Idle speed and pilot air screw adjustment are covered in Chapter Three.

Float Adjustment

The fuel valve and float maintain a constant fuel level in the carburetor float bowl. Because the float level affects the fuel mixture throughout the engine's operating range, the level must be maintained within factory specifications.

The carburetor assembly has to be removed and partially disassembled for this adjustment.
1. Remove the carburetor as described in this chapter.
2. Remove the screws (**Figure 55**) securing the float bowl and remove float bowl.
3. Hold the carburetor so the float arm is just touching the fuel valve—not pushing it down. Use a float level gauge, vernier caliper or small ruler (**Figure**

56) and measure the distance from the carburetor body gasket surface (gasket removed) to the float. The correct height is listed in **Table 3**.

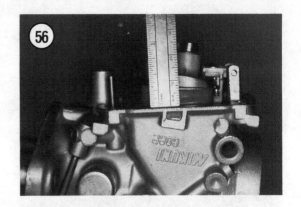

4. If the float height is incorrect, adjust as follows:

   a. Push out the float pin (**Figure 57**) and remove the float and fuel valve (**Figure 58**). Remove the fuel valve (**Figure 52**) from the float arm.

   b. Carefully bend the float arm (**Figure 59**) with a screwdriver to adjust the float level.

   c. Install the fuel valve onto the float arm and install the float and float pin.

   d. Recheck the float level as described in Step 3. Repeat until the float level adjustment is correct.

5. Reassemble and install the carburetor.

Jet Needle Adjustment

The position of the jet needle can be adjusted to affect the fuel/air mixture for medium throttle openings.

1. Remove the piston valve and jet needle (**Figure 60**) as described in this chapter.

NOTE
Record the clip position prior to removal.

2. Raising the needle (lowering the clip) will enrich the mixture during mid-throttle opening, while lowering the needle (raising the clip) will lean the mixture. Refer to **Figure 61**.

3. Refer to **Table 1** for the standard jet needle clip position.

4. Install the jet needle and piston valve as described in this chapter.

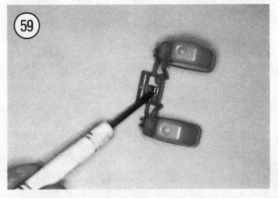

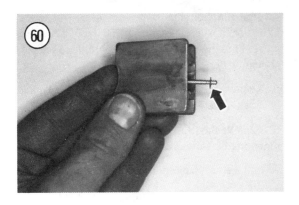

60

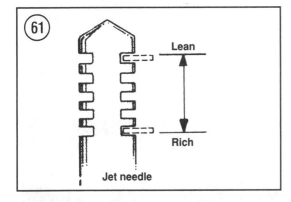

61

Lean

Rich

Jet needle

62

A B

A B

63

THROTTLE CABLE REPLACEMENT

On 1987 and 1993-on models, a single throttle cable is used. On 1988-1992 models, the throttle cable consists of 3 different cables. If any one cable is damaged, the throttle cable must be replaced as an assembly.

1. Place the vehicle on level ground and set the parking brake.

2. Remove the seat.

3. Remove the front fender as described in Chapter Thirteen.

4. Remove the fuel tank as described in this chapter.

5. Disconnect the throttle cable(s) at the carburetor as described under *Carburetor Removal/Installation* in this chapter. On 1988-1992 models, disconnect the throttle cable from the carburetor cap.

6. Disconnect the throttle cable at the throttle lever as follows:

    a. Slide the rubber boot (A, **Figure 62**) off of the cable adjuster.

    b. Remove the throttle cover screws and remove the cover (B, **Figure 62**).

    c. Loosen the throttle cable adjuster (A, **Figure 63**) to provide as much cable slack as possible.

    d. Disconnect the throttle cable from the throttle arm (B, **Figure 63**). If you can't disconnect the cable end, remove the throttle arm nut, washer, lever and spring and disconnect the cable.

    e. Withdraw the throttle cable from the throttle housing.

7. Disconnect the throttle cable from any clips holding the cable to the frame.

8. On 1988-1992 models, disconnect the throttle cable junction box from the frame (**Figure 64**).

9. Make a note of the cables routing path through the frame, then remove it.

8

64

10. Lubricate the new cable(s) as described in Chapter Three.

11. Reverse Steps 1-8 to install the new cable assembly, noting the following.

12. On 1988-1992 models, connect the 2 rear cables as follows:

 a. Throttle valve cable. See A, **Figure 65** and **Figure 66**.

 b. Piston valve cable. See B, **Figure 65** and **Figure 67**.

13. On all models, reconnect throttle cable(s) at carburetor as described under *Carburetor Removal/Installation* in this chapter.

14. Apply grease to the cable end in the throttle lever housing.

15. Operate the throttle lever and make sure the carburetor throttle linkage is operating correctly and with no binding. If operation is incorrect or there is binding, carefully check that the cable is attached correctly and there are no tight bends in the cable.

16. Adjust the throttle cable(s) as described in Chapter Three.

17. Test ride the vehicle and make sure the throttle is operating correctly.

FUEL TANK

Removal/Installation

Refer to **Figure 68** for this procedure.

1. Place the vehicle on level ground and set the parking brake.

2. Remove the seat.

3. Disconnect the battery negative lead (**Figure 69**).

4. Turn the fuel shutoff valve (**Figure 70**) to the OFF position and disconnect the fuel line at the valve. Plug the open end of the fuel line to prevent contamination.

5. Remove the fuel tank cover mounting bolts and cover (**Figure 71**).

6. Remove the front (**Figure 72**) and rear fuel tank mounting bolts, washers and collars.

7. Pull the fuel tank to the rear and remove it.

8. Inspect the rubber cushion on each side of the fuel tank where the tank is held in place. Replace as a set if either is damaged or starting to deteriorate.

9. Install by reversing these removal steps, check for fuel leakage after installation is completed. Tighten fuel tank mounting bolts securely.

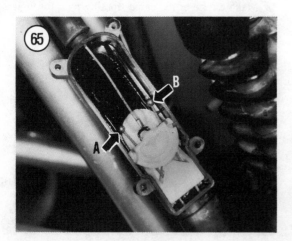

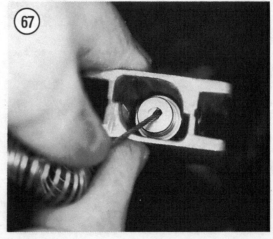

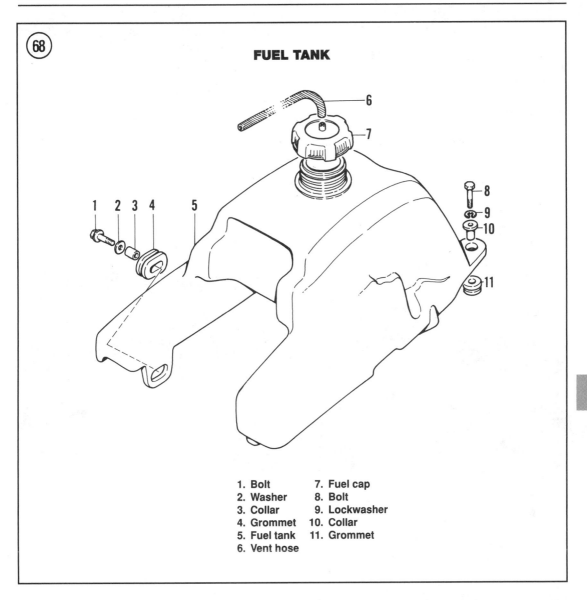

FUEL TANK

1. Bolt
2. Washer
3. Collar
4. Grommet
5. Fuel tank
6. Vent hose
7. Fuel cap
8. Bolt
9. Lockwasher
10. Collar
11. Grommet

8

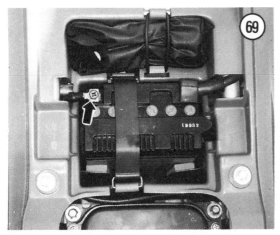

FUEL SHUTOFF VALVE

The fuel shutoff valve is shown in **Figure 73** (1987-1989) and **Figure 74** (1990-on).

Removal/Installation

1. Remove the fuel tank as described in this chapter.
2. Drain the fuel tank of all gas. Store the fuel in a can approved for gasoline storage.
3. Remove the screws securing the fuel shutoff valve to the fuel tank and remove the valve (**Figure 75**) and gasket.
4. To replace the fuel valve O-ring:

a. Remove the 2 cover screws (**Figure 76**) and disassemble the valve in the order shown in **Figure 73** or **Figure 74**.

b. Replace the O-ring and reassemble the valve.

5. Install by reversing these steps. Install a new fuel shutoff valve O-ring gasket. Tighten the screws securely.

6. Check for fuel leakage after installation is completed.

AIR FILTER AIR BOX

The air box is mounted underneath the seat.

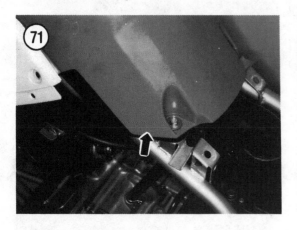

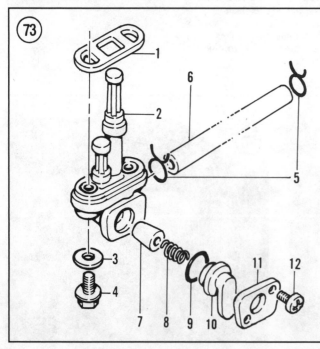

FUEL VALVE (1987-1989)

1. O-ring gasket
2. Fuel valve
3. Washer
4. Screw
5. Clip
6. Fuel hose
7. Spring seat
8. Spring
9. O-ring
10. Lever
11. Plate
12. Screw

FUEL VALVE
(1990-ON)

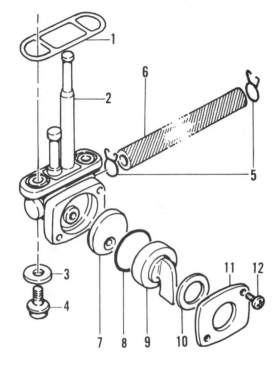

1. O-ring gasket
2. Fuel valve
3. Washer
4. Screw
5. Clip
6. Fuel hose
7. Valve
8. O-ring
9. Lever
10. Wave washer
11. Plate
12. Screw

8

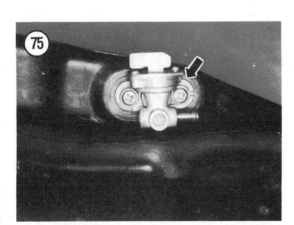

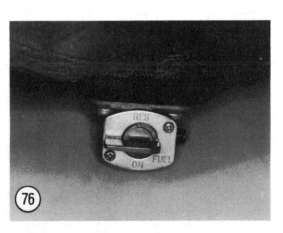

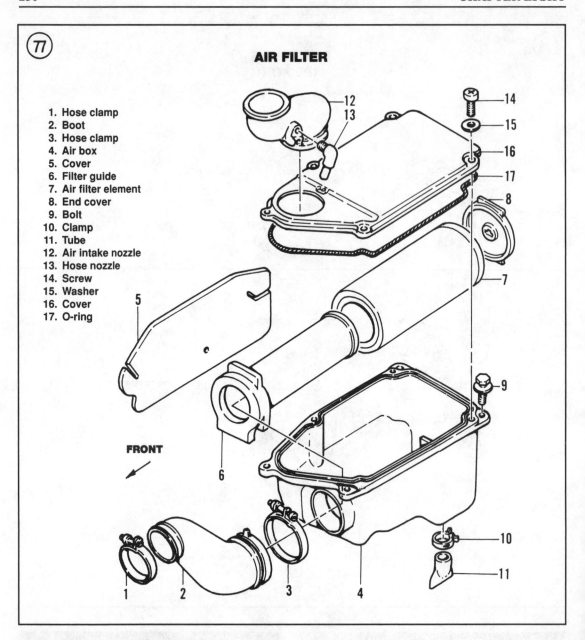

AIR FILTER

1. Hose clamp
2. Boot
3. Hose clamp
4. Air box
5. Cover
6. Filter guide
7. Air filter element
8. End cover
9. Bolt
10. Clamp
11. Tube
12. Air intake nozzle
13. Hose nozzle
14. Screw
15. Washer
16. Cover
17. O-ring

FRONT

Removal/Installation

Refer to **Figure 77** for this procedure.

1. Place the vehicle on level ground and set the parking brake.
2. Remove the seat as described in Chapter Thirteen.
3. Remove the fuel tank as described in this chapter.
4. Loosen the hose clamp securing the air box to the carburetor (A, **Figure 78**).
5. Disconnect the crankcase breather hose at the air box (B, **Figure 78**).
6. Remove the air box mounting bolts (**Figure 79**) and lift the air box out of the frame and remove it.
7. Plug the carburetor opening to prevent dust from entering the carburetor.
8. Inspect all rubber components of the air box assembly and replace any that are damaged or starting to deteriorate.

9. Install by reversing these removal steps, noting the following.

10. Make sure the carburetor-to-air box hose clamp is seated properly and tightened securely.

EXHAUST SYSTEM

Check the exhaust system for deep dents and fractures and repair or replace parts as required. Check the muffler frame mounting flanges for fractures and loose bolts. Check the cylinder head mounting flange for tightness. A loose exhaust pipe connection will cause excessive exhaust noise and rob the engine of power.

The stock exhaust system consists of the exhaust pipe, muffler, gaskets and mounting fasteners (**Figure 80**).

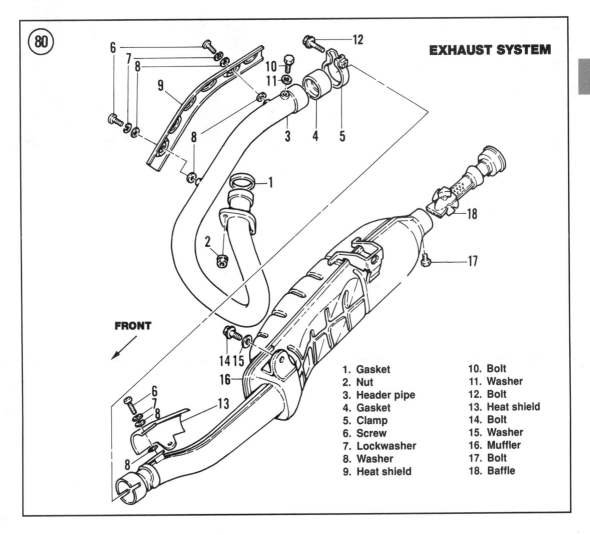

(80) **EXHAUST SYSTEM**

8

FRONT

1. Gasket
2. Nut
3. Header pipe
4. Gasket
5. Clamp
6. Screw
7. Lockwasher
8. Washer
9. Heat shield
10. Bolt
11. Washer
12. Bolt
13. Heat shield
14. Bolt
15. Washer
16. Muffler
17. Bolt
18. Baffle

Removal/Installation

1. Place the vehicle on level ground and set the parking brake.

2. Remove the seat and the rear fender as described in Chapter Thirteen.

3. Loosen the muffler mounting bolts.

4. Loosen the exhaust pipe-to-muffler clamp bolt.

5. Remove the muffler mounting bolts and remove the muffler.

6. Remove the nuts (**Figure 81**) securing the exhaust pipe to the cylinder head and remove the exhaust pipe.

7. Install by reversing these removal steps, noting the following.

8. Inspect the gasket at the front of the exhaust pipe where it attaches to the exhaust port. Replace the gasket if damaged or leaking. See **Figure 82**.

9. Replace the exhaust pipe-to-muffler gasket if damaged or leaking.

10. To minimize the chances of an exhaust leak at the cylinder head, tighten bolts in the following order to the tightening torque listed in **Table 4**:

    a. Exhaust pipe-to-cylinder head nuts (**Figure 81**).

    b. Muffler mounting bolts.

    c. Exhaust pipe-to-muffler clamp bolt.

11. After installation is complete, start the engine and make sure there are no exhaust leaks.

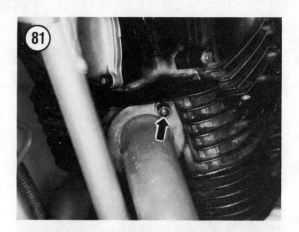

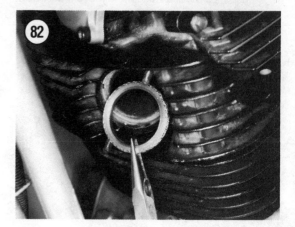

Table 1 MIKUNI CARBURETOR SPECIFICATIONS*

	1987	1988-on
Carburetor model No.	BTM36SH	BTM36SH
Identification mark	1UY00	2XK-00 or 3GD-00
Main jet	145	145
Main air jet	0.6	0.6
Jet needle/clip position	5J18/3	5J18/3
Needle jet	0-6	0-6
Pilot jet	42.5	42.5
Pilot air jet		
No. 1	1.0	1.0
No. 2	0.7	0.7
Valve seat	2.5	2.5
Starter jet	#55	#62.5

*Jet specifications for 1998-on California models may differ. Check with a Yamaha dealership for jet specifications.

Table 2 CARBURETOR ADJUSTMENT SPECIFICATIONS

Engine idle speed	1,450-1,550 rpm
Pilot air screw adjustment	
1987-1989	1 1/4 turns out
1990-on	2 turns out
Vacuum @ idle speed	33.3 kPa (9.84 in. Hg)

Table 3 CARBURETOR FLOAT HEIGHT

	mm	in.
Float height		
1987	11.9-12.9	0.468-0.508
1998-on	11.4-13.4	0.45-0.53

Table 4 TIGHTENING TORQUES

	N•m	ft.-lb.
Carburetor mounting nuts	16	12
Carburetor clamp hose	2	18 in.-lb.
Exhaust system		
Exhaust pipe-to-cylinder head nut	12	106 in.-lb.
Muffler mounting bolts	27	20
Exhaust pipe-to-muffler clamp bolt	20	14

CHAPTER NINE

ELECTRICAL SYSTEM

This chapter contains service and test procedures for all electrical and ignition components.

ELECTRICAL COMPONENT REPLACEMENT

Most motorcycle dealerships and parts suppliers will not accept the return of any electrical part. If you cannot determine the exact cause of any electrical system malfunction, have a Yamaha delaership retest that specific system to verify your test results. If you purchase a new electrical component(s), install it, and then find that the system still does not work properly, you will probably be unable to return the unit for a refund

Consider any test results carefully before replacing a component that tests only slightly out of specification, especially resistance. A number of variables can affect test results dramatically. These include: the testing meter's internal circuitry, ambient temperature and conditions under which the machine has been operated. All instructions and specifications have been checked for accuracy; however, successful test results depend to a great extent upon individual accuracy.

Since this type of vehicle may be subjected to moisture and water, it is important to keep all electrical connections completely coupled to each other. Consider applying dielectric grease (available from automotive parts stores) to all electrical connectors whenever they are disconnected and reconnected to prevent corrosion of the electrical connector terminals.

Refer to Chapter Three for the battery and spark plugs.

Specifications are in **Tables 1-7** at the end of this chapter.

CHARGING SYSTEM

The typical charging system consists of the battery, alternator, fuse and a voltage regulator/rectifier (**Figure 1**).

Alternating current generated by the alternator is rectified to direct current. The voltage regulator maintains the voltage to the battery and additional electrical loads (lights, ignition, etc.) at a constant voltage regardless of variations in engine speed and load. Refer to the specific diagram at the back of the manual when troubleshooting.

Charging System Output Test

Whenever a charging system trouble is suspected, make sure the battery is fully charged and in good condition before going any further. Clean and test the battery as described under *Battery Testing* in Chapter Three.

Also make sure all electrical connectors within the charging system are tight and free of corrosion prior to making this test.

1. Remove the seat.

2. Check the main fuse. Locate the fuse holder adjacent to the battery. Open the fuse holder and

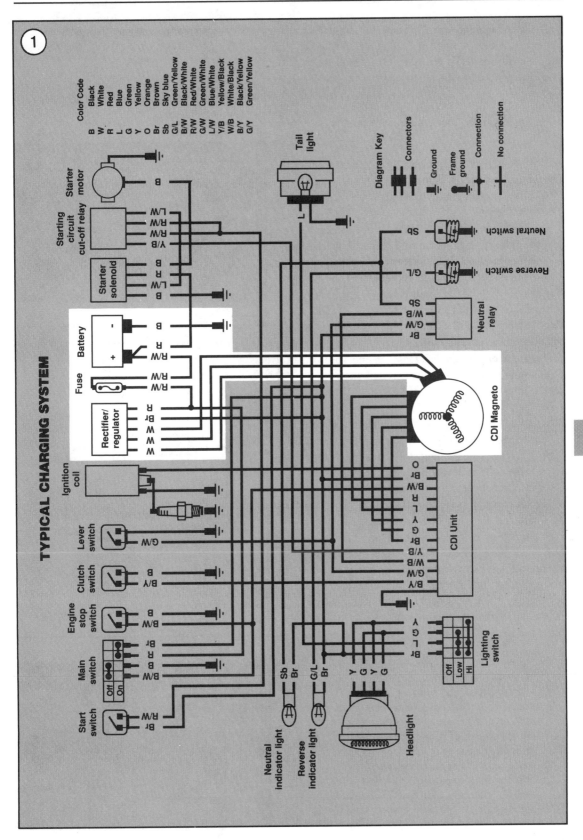

pull the fuse out and visually inspect it (**Figure 2**). If the fuse is blown, refer to *Fuse* in this chapter. If the main fuse is okay, reinstall it, or install a new one, then proceed to the next step.

> *NOTE*
> *Make sure the fuse is secure in its holder.*

3. Test the battery specific gravity as described under *Battery* in Chapter Three. Note the following:
   a. If the specific gravity reading is correct, perform Step 4.
   b. If the specific gravity reading is not within the prescribed range, clean and recharge the battery as required. If the battery is damaged or if it will not hold a charge, replace it.

4. Connect a 0-20 DC voltmeter to the battery terminals as shown in **Figure 3**. Connect an inductive tachometer to the spark plug following the manufacturer's instructions.

5. Start the engine and increase engine speed to 5,000 rpm. Read the voltage indicated on the voltmeter. It should be between 14-15 volts. Note the following:
   a. Charging voltage correct: The charging system is operating properly.
   b. Charging voltage incorrect: Test the stator charge coils as described under *Alternator*. Replace the stator coils if faulty. If the charging coils are okay, perform Step 6.

6. Check the charging system wiring harness and connectors for dirty or loose-fitting terminals; clean and repair as required. If the wiring harness and connectors are okay, and you have not found the problem after performing the previous tests, the regulator/rectifier is probably faulty. Install a regulator/rectifier unit that is known to be in working order and retest.

> *NOTE*
> *Most ATV dealers and parts suppliers will not accept the return of any electrical part. If you have been unable to determine the cause of the charging system malfunction, have a Yamaha dealer retest the charging system to verify your test results. If you purchase a new regulator/rectifier, install it, and then find that the charging system still does not work properly, you will, in most cases, be unable to return the unit for a refund.*

> *Note also that Yamaha does not provide any service specifications for testing the regulator/rectifier unit.*

7. After the test is completed, disconnect the voltmeter and tachometer.

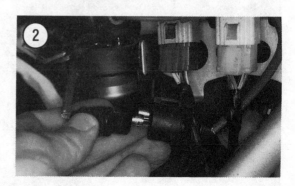

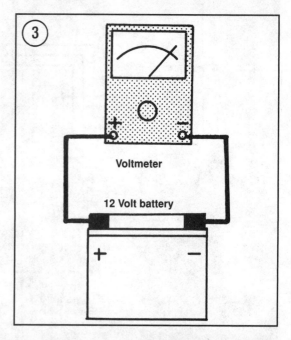

Voltmeter

12 Volt battery

8. Install the seat.

ALTERNATOR
(STATOR CHARGE COIL)

Alternator rotor and stator assembly (**Figure 4**) removal and installation procedures are covered in Chapter Five.

Stator Charge Coil Testing

It is not necessary to remove the stator coil to perform the following tests. In order to get accurate resistance measurements the stator assembly and coil must be warm (minimum temperature is 20° C [68° F]. If necessary, start the engine and let it warm up to normal operating temperature.

1. Remove the seat.

2. Disconnect the white 3-pin electrical connector from the alternator.

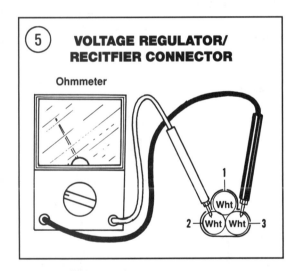

3. Use an ohmmeter set at R × 1 and check resistance between each white wire (**Figure 5**) on the alternator side of the connector.

4. The specified resistance is listed in **Table 3** If there is continuity (indicated resistance) and it is within the specified resistance, the coil is good. If there is no continuity (infinite resistance) or the resistance is less than specified, the coil is bad and the stator assembly must be replaced (the individual coil cannot be replaced).

5. Apply dielectric grease (available from an automotive parts store) to the electrical connector prior to reconnecting it. This will help seal out moisture.

6. Make sure the electrical connectors are free of corrosion and are completely coupled to each other.

VOLTAGE REGULATOR/RECTIFIER

Testing

Yamaha does not provide any service specifications for testing the voltage regulator/rectifier.

Removal/Installation

1. Place the vehicle on level ground and set the parking brake.

2. Disconnect the voltage regulator/rectifier electrical connectors.

3. Remove the voltage regulator/rectifier mounting bolts and remove the unit from underneath the rear fender; see **Figure 6**.

4. Install by reversing these removal steps, noting the following.

5. Apply dielectric grease to the electrical connectors prior to reconnecting them. This will help seal out moisture.

6. Make sure all electrical connectors are free of corrosion and are completely coupled to each other.

CAPACITOR DISCHARGE IGNITION

All vehicle models are equipped with a capacitor discharge ignition system, a solid-state system that uses no breaker points.

The ignition system is shown in **Figures 7-9**.

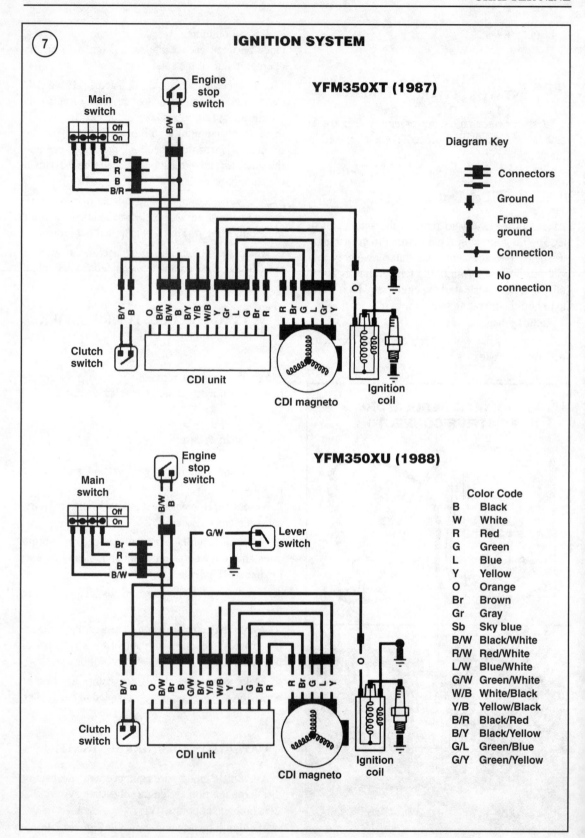

IGNITION SYSTEM

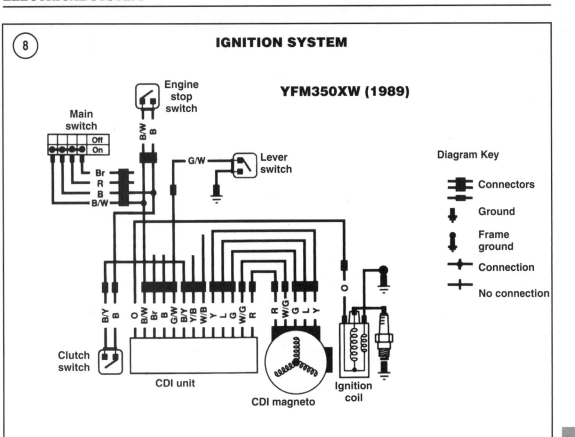

YFM350XW (1989)

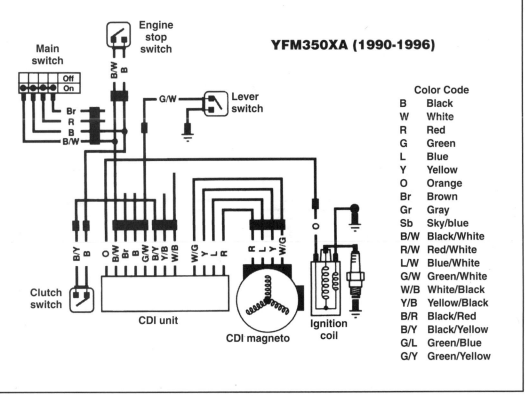

YFM350XA (1990-1996)

9

Color Code

B	Black
W	White
R	Red
G	Green
L	Blue
Y	Yellow
O	Orange
Br	Brown
Gr	Gray
Sb	Sky/blue
B/W	Black/White
R/W	Red/White
L/W	Blue/White
G/W	Green/White
W/B	White/Black
Y/B	Yellow/Black
B/R	Black/Red
B/Y	Black/Yellow
G/L	Green/Blue
G/Y	Green/Yellow

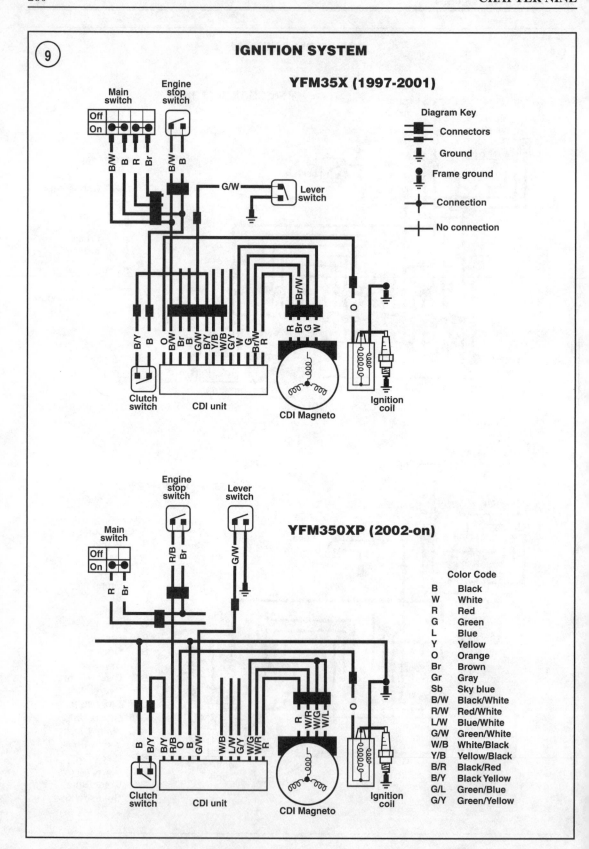

IGNITION SYSTEM

YFM35X (1997-2001)

YFM350XP (2002-on)

CDI Precautions

Certain measures must be taken to protect the capacitor discharge system. Damage to the semiconductors in the system will occur if the following precautions are not observed.

1. Never disconnect any of the electrical connections while the engine is running.

2. Apply dielectric grease to all electrical connectors prior to reconnecting them. This will help seal out moisture.

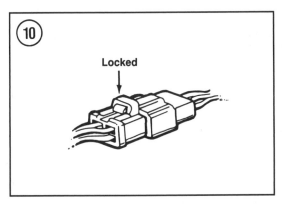

Locked

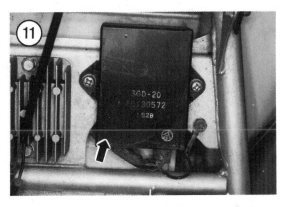

3. Make sure all electrical connectors (**Figure 10**) are free of corrosion and are completely coupled to each other.

4. The CDI unit is mounted within a rubber vibration isolator. Always be sure that the isolator is in place when installing the unit.

CDI Troubleshooting

Refer to Chapter Two.

CDI Unit Testing

Yamaha does not provide any service specifications for testing the CDI unit. They only provide test procedures for the components within the ignition system.

CDI Unit Replacement

1. Place the vehicle on level ground and set the parking brake.

2. Disconnect the CDI unit electrical connectors.

3. Remove the CDI unit mounting bolts and remove the CDI unit from underneath the rear fender; see **Figure 11**.

4. Install by reversing these steps, plus the following.

5. Apply dielectric grease to the electrical connectors prior to reconnecting them. This will help seal out moisture.

6. Make sure all electrical connectors are free of corrosion and are completely coupled to each other.

IGNITION COIL

Testing

The ignition coil (**Figure 12**) is a form of transformer which develops the high voltage required to jump the spark plug gap. The only maintenance required is that of keeping the electrical connections clean and tight and occasionally checking to see that the coil is mounted securely.

If the condition of the coil is doubtful, there are several checks which may be made.

First as a quick check of coil condition, disconnect the high voltage lead from the spark plug. Remove the spark plug from the cylinder head. Connect a

262 CHAPTER NINE

new or known good spark plug to the high voltage
lead and place the spark plug base on a good ground
like the engine cylinder head (**Figure 13**). Position
the spark plug so you can see the electrode.

> *NOTE*
> *WARNING*
> *If it is necessary to hold the high volt-*
> *age lead, do so with an insulated pair*
> *of pliers. The high voltage generated*
> *by the CDI could produce serious or*
> *fatal shocks.*

Turn the engine over with the starter or pull starter.
If a fat blue spark occurs the coil is in good condition; if not proceed as follows. Make sure that you
are using a known good spark plug for this test. If
the spark plug used is defective the test results will
be incorrect.

Reinstall the spark plug in the cylinder head.

> *NOTE*
> *In order to get accurate resistance meas-*
> *urements the coil must be warm (mini-*
> *mum temperature is 20° C—68° F).*

1. Remove the front fender as described in Chapter
Thirteen.
2. Disconnect the spark plug cap (secondary lead)
at the spark plug.
3. Disconnect the primary electrical connector (orange wire) at the ignition coil (**Figure 12**).
4. Test spark plug cap as follows:
  a. Carefully remove the spark plug cap from the
    high voltage lead.
  b. Measure the spark plug cap resistance using an
    ohmmeter set at R × 1,000. Measure between
    each end of the cap as shown in **Figure 14**. The
    correct resistance is listed in **Table 4**.
  c. Replace the spark plug cap if the resistance
    exceeds the specification in **Table 4**.
  d. Reinstall the spark plug cap.

> *NOTE*
> *When switching between ohmmeter*
> *scales, always cross the test leads*
> *and zero the needle to assure a cor-*
> *rect reading.*

5. Measure the coil primary resistance using an
ohmmeter set at R × 1. Measure resistance between
the primary terminal and the ignition coil body (**Figure 15**). See **Table 4** for test specifications.

6. With the spark plug cap connected to the high
voltage lead (spark plug lead), measure the secondary resistance using an ohmmeter set at R × 1,000.
Measure the resistance between the secondary lead
(spark plug lead) and the primary lead (**Figure 15**).
See **Table 4** for test specifications.
7. If the coil resistance does not meet either of these
specifications, the coil must be replaced. If the coil
exhibits visible damage, it should be replaced.
8. Reconnect the ignition coil leads.

Removal/Installation

1. Place the vehicle on level ground and set the
parking brake.

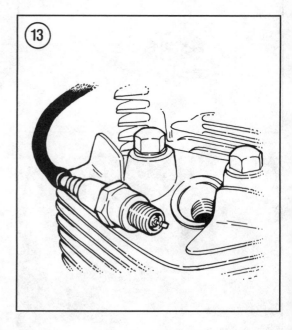

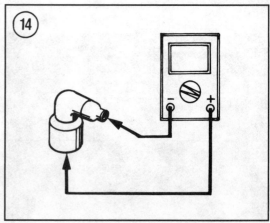

2. Remove the front fender as described in Chapter Thirteen.

3. Disconnect the spark plug cap (secondary lead) at the spark plug.

4. Disconnect the primary electrical connector (orange wire) at the ignition coil (**Figure 12**).

5. Remove the mounting screws and ground wire, then remove the ignition coil (**Figure 12**) from the frame.

6. Install by reversing these removal steps, making sure all electrical connections are tight and free of corrosion.

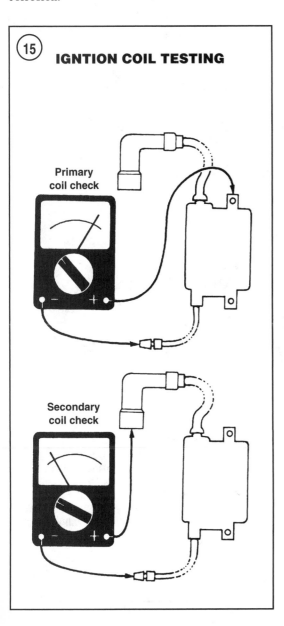

15

IGNTION COIL TESTING

Primary coil check

Secondary coil check

ALTERNATOR (STATOR SOURCE AND PICKUP COILS)

Alternator rotor and stator assembly (**Figure 4**) removal and installation procedures are covered in Chapter Five.

Source and Pickup Coil Testing

It is not necessary to remove the stator coils to perform the following tests. In order to get accurate resistance measurements the stator assembly and coil must be warm (minimum temperature is 20° C [68° F]).

1. Remove the seat.

2. Disconnect the CDI magneto electrical connector from the alternator. See wiring diagram for your model at end of book for connector identification and wire colors.

3. Set an ohmmeter on the R × 100 scale.

4. Refer to **Table 3** for connections and test values for the source and pickup coils and compare the meter reading to the stated value. If any of the meter readings differ from the stated valves, replace the stator coil assembly as described in Chapter Five. Individual stator coils cannot be replaced.

5. Apply dielectric grease to the electrical connector prior to reconnecting it. This will help seal out moisture.

6. Make sure the electrical connector is free of corrosion and is completely coupled to each other.

STARTING SYSTEM

The starting system consists of the starter motor, starter gears, solenoid and the starter button.

Electrical diagrams for 1987-1996 starting systems are shown in **Figure 16** and **Figure 17**. Refer to the wiring diagrams at the back of the manual for 1997-on models. When the starter button is pressed, it engages the starter solenoid switch that completes the circuit allowing electricity to flow from the battery to the starter motor.

> *CAUTION*
> *Do not operate the starter for more than 5 seconds at a time. Let it rest approximately 10 seconds, then use it again.*

The starter gears are covered in Chapter Five.

9

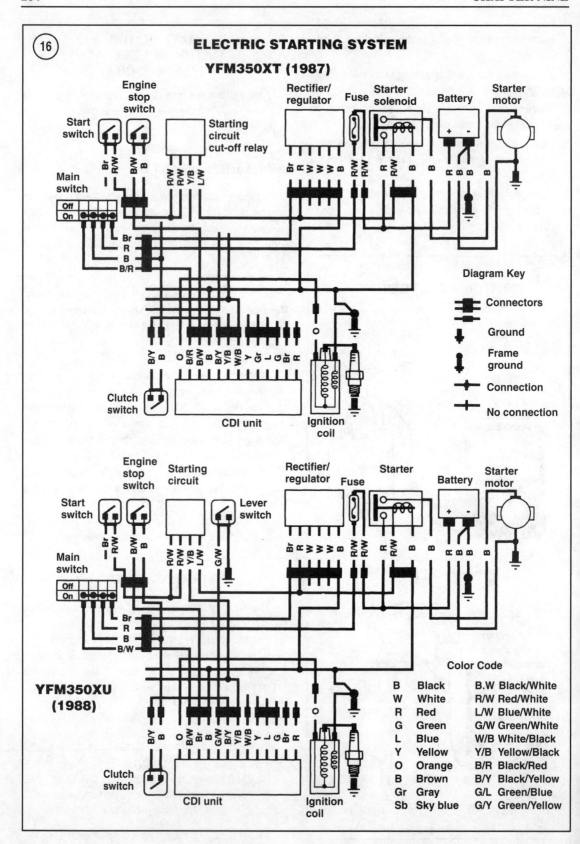

ELECTRIC STARTING SYSTEM

YFM350XT (1987)

YFM350XU (1988)

Diagram Key

Connectors

Ground

Frame ground

Connection

No connection

Color Code

B	Black	B.W	Black/White
W	White	R/W	Red/White
R	Red	L/W	Blue/White
G	Green	G/W	Green/White
L	Blue	W/B	White/Black
Y	Yellow	Y/B	Yellow/Black
O	Orange	B/R	Black/Red
B	Brown	B/Y	Black/Yellow
Gr	Gray	G/L	Green/Blue
Sb	Sky blue	G/Y	Green/Yellow

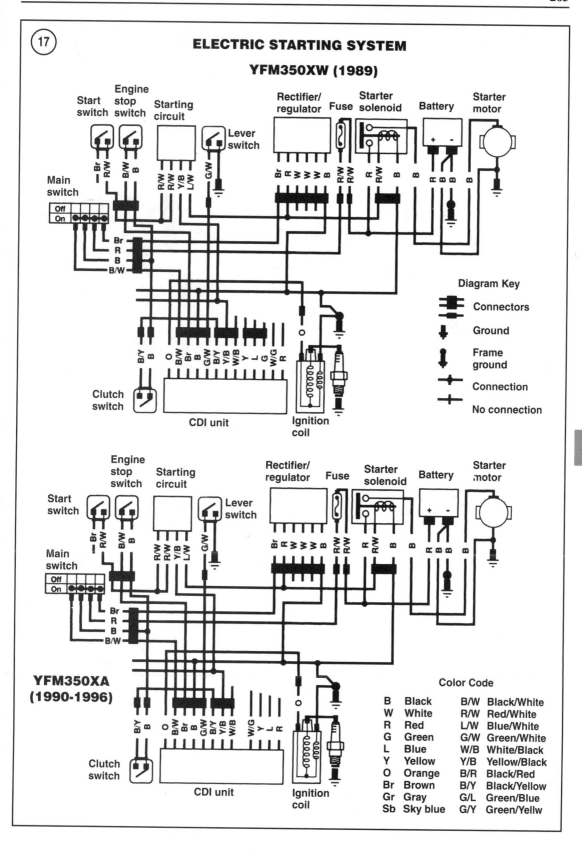

ELECTRIC STARTING SYSTEM

YFM350XW (1989)

YFM350XA (1990-1996)

Color Code

B	Black	B/W	Black/White
W	White	R/W	Red/White
R	Red	L/W	Blue/White
G	Green	G/W	Green/White
L	Blue	W/B	White/Black
Y	Yellow	Y/B	Yellow/Black
O	Orange	B/R	Black/Red
Br	Brown	B/Y	Black/Yellow
Gr	Gray	G/L	Green/Blue
Sb	Sky blue	G/Y	Green/Yellw

Diagram Key
- Connectors
- Ground
- Frame ground
- Connection
- No connection

Troubleshooting

Refer to Chapter Two.

Starter
Removal/Installation

1. Place the vehicle on level ground and set the parking brake.

2. Remove the seat.

3. Disconnect the battery negative lead (**Figure 18**).

4. Pull back the rubber boot (A, **Figure 19**) on the electrical connector.

5. Disconnect the black electric starter cable from the starter (A, **Figure 19**).

6. Remove the bolts (B, **Figure 19**) securing the starter to the crankcase.

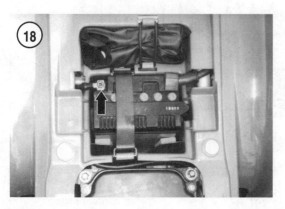

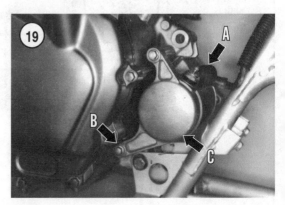

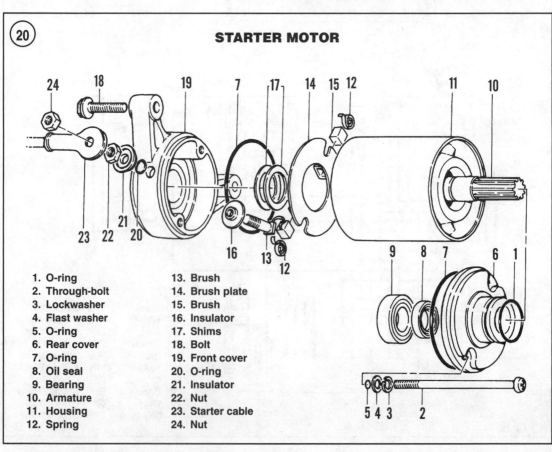

STARTER MOTOR

1. O-ring	13. Brush
2. Through-bolt	14. Brush plate
3. Lockwasher	15. Brush
4. Flast washer	16. Insulator
5. O-ring	17. Shims
6. Rear cover	18. Bolt
7. O-ring	19. Front cover
8. Oil seal	20. O-ring
9. Bearing	21. Insulator
10. Armature	22. Nut
11. Housing	23. Starter cable
12. Spring	24. Nut

7. Pull the starter (C, **Figure 19**) toward the right-hand side and remove it from the engine.

8. Install by reversing these removal steps. Make sure the electrical connector is free of corrosion and is tight.

Disassembly

Refer to **Figure 20** for this procedure.

1. Scribe an alignment mark across both end covers and the armature housing for reassembly.

2. Remove the 2 case bolts, washers, lockwashers and O-rings (**Figure 21**).

> *NOTE*
> *Write down the thickness and number of shims used on the shaft next to the front and rear covers as they are removed in the following steps. Be sure to install these shims in their same position when reassembling the starter.*

> *NOTE*
> *The number of shims used in each starter varies. The starter you are working on may use a different number of shims from that shown in the following photographs.*

3. Remove the rear cover (**Figure 22**) and shim(s) (**Figure 23**).

4. Slide the front cover (**Figure 24**) off of the armature. Remove the shim(s).

5. Slide brush plate (**Figure 25**) off armature shaft and remove front cover and brush plate together.

6. Slide armature (**Figure 26**) out of housing and remove it.

7. Clean all grease, dirt and carbon from the armature, case and end covers.

> *CAUTION*
> *Do not immerse the wire windings in the case or the armature coil in solvent as the insulation may be damaged. Wipe the windings with a cloth lightly moistened with solvent and thoroughly dry.*

Inspection

Starter motor specifications are listed in **Table 5**.

1. Pull the spring away from each brush and pull the brushes (A, **Figure 27**) out of their guides.

2. Measure the length of each brush with a vernier caliper (**Figure 28**). If the length is equal to or less than the service limit in **Table 5**, replace both brushes as a set. Refer to *Starter Brush Replacement* in this chapter.

3. Inspect the brush springs (B, **Figure 27**) for damage or weakness. If necessary, replace brush springs as follows:

   a. Make a drawing of the brush springs as they are installed on the brush holder, noting the direction in which the spring coils turn.

   b. Remove and replace both brush springs as a set.

4. Inspect the commutator (**Figure 29**). The mica in a good commutator is below the surface of the copper bars. On a worn commutator the mica and copper bars may be worn to the same level (**Figure 30**). If necessary, have the commutator serviced by a dealer or electrical repair shop.

5. Inspect the commutator copper bars for discoloration. If a pair of bars are discolored, grounded armature coils are indicated.

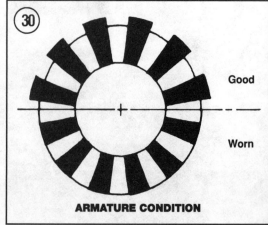

ARMATURE CONDITION

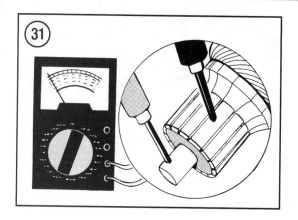

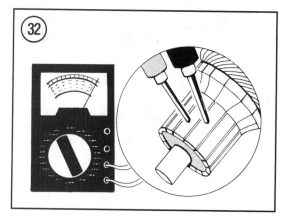

6. Use an ohmmeter and perform the following:

a. Check for continuity between the commutator bars (**Figure 31**); there should be continuity (indicated resistance) between pairs of bars.

b. Check for continuity between the commutator bars and the shaft (**Figure 32**); there should be no continuity (infinite resistance).

c. If the unit fails either of these tests, the starter assembly must be replaced. The armature cannot be replaced individually.

7. Measure the commutator outer diameter (**Figure 33**). If the commutator outer diameter is equal to or less than the service limit in **Table 5**, replace the starter motor.

8. Use an ohmmeter and perform the following:

a. Check for continuity between the starter cable terminal and the front cover; there should be continuity (indicated resistance).

b. Check for continuity between the starter cable terminal and the brush black wire terminal; there should be no continuity (infinite resistance).

c. If the unit fails either of these tests, the starter assembly must be replaced. The case/field coil assembly cannot be replaced individually.

9. Inspect the oil seal and needle bearing (**Figure 34**) in the front cover for wear or damage. If either is damaged, replace the starter assembly as these parts are not available separately.

10. Inspect the bushing (**Figure 35**) in the rear cover for wear or damage. If it is damaged, replace the starter assembly as this part is not available separately.

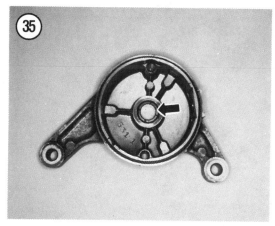

9

11. Inspect the starter housing (**Figure 36**) for cracks or other damage. Then inspect for loose, chipped or damaged magnets.

12. Inspect all of the starter O-rings for deterioration, flat spots or other damage. Replace as required.

Starter Brush Replacement

Replace both brushes as a set.

1. Remove the terminal nut (**Figure 37**). Then slide off the insulator and O-ring (**Figure 38**).

2. Push the terminal (**Figure 39**) through the starter housing and remove the brush plate assembly.

3. The terminal bolt and brush (A, **Figure 40**) are replaced as an assembly. Remove the terminal bolt and brush and replace it.

4. The other brush (B, **Figure 40**) is soldered to the brush plate. To replace it:

   a. Heat the brush connection with a soldering iron or gun and remove it.

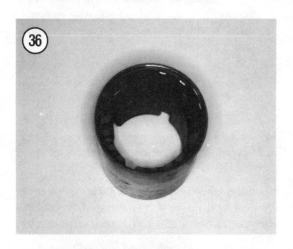

b. Install the new brush so that its wire is routed in the same direction; see B, **Figure 40**.

c. Solder the new brush in place with rosin core solder.

5. Reverse Steps 1 and 2 to install the brush plate assembly. Tighten the terminal nut (**Figure 37**) securely.

Assembly

1. If removed, install the brushes into their holders and secure the brushes with the springs.

2. Insert the armature into the housing as shown in **Figure 26**.

> *NOTE*
> ***Figure 41*** *shows the correct installation position of the front and rear covers.*

3. Mount the armature in a vise (with soft jaws) so that the commutator end faces up (**Figure 42**).

4. Install the washer(s) over the armature shaft (**Figure 43**).

5. Compress the brushes and slide the brush plate over the commutator (**Figure 44**). Release the brushes.

6. Align the notch in the brush plate with the tab on the housing as shown in **Figure 45**. Then remove the starter from the vise and install the front cover over the armature as shown in **Figure 46**. Align the alignment marks on the front cover and housing made prior to disassembly. Then hold the front cover in place.

7. Install the shim(s) onto the armature shaft (**Figure 47**).

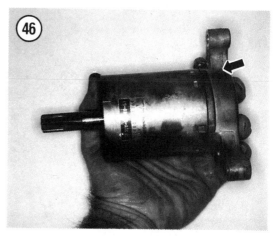

8. Install the rear cover (**Figure 48**) onto the housing, aligning the index marks made prior to disassembly.

9. Make sure the O-rings are installed on the starter mounting bolts (**Figure 49**) and install the bolts through the rear cover and thread into the front cover; see **Figure 50**. If the bolts will not pass through the starter motor, the end covers and/or brush plate are installed incorrectly. Tighten the bolts securely.

STARTER SOLENOID

The starter solenoid is mounted underneath the rear fender on the left-hand side; see A, **Figure 51**.

System Test

System testing of the starter solenoid is found under *Engine Starting System* in Chapter Two.

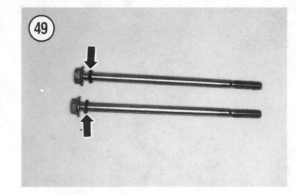

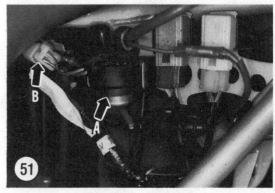

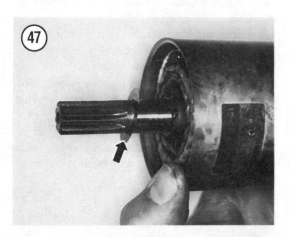

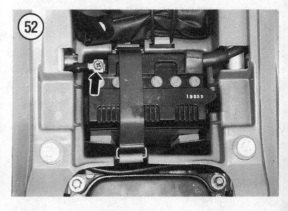

Starter Solenoid
Resistance Test

The starter solenoid can be tested with an ohmmeter as follows.

1. Turn the ignition switch OFF.
2. Disconnect the starter solenoid electrical connector (B, **Figure 51**).
3. Switch an ohmmeter to R × 1 and connect its leads across the 2 starter solenoid connector pins (on the solenoid side). The ohmmeter should read 3.4 ohms (±10%).
4. Replace the starter solenoid if the resistance reading is incorrect.
5. Reconnect the solenoid electrical connector.

Removal/Installation

1. Remove the seat.
2. Disconnect the battery negative lead (**Figure 52**).
3. Disconnect the starter solenoid electrical connector (B, **Figure 51**).
4. Disconnect the red (from battery) and black (from starter motor) solenoid leads on top of the solenoid (A, **Figure 51**).

5. Remove the solenoid from the rubber mount on the frame.
6. Replace by reversing these removal steps, noting the following.
7. Install both electrical wires to the solenoid and tighten the nuts securely.
8. Make sure the electrical connectors are on tight and that the rubber boot is properly installed to keep out moisture.

LIGHTING SYSTEM

The lighting system consists of a headlight, taillight and indicator lights. **Table 6** lists replacement bulbs for these components.

Always use the correct wattage bulb as indicated in this section. The use of a larger wattage bulb will give a dim light and a smaller wattage bulb will burn out prematurely.

Headlight Bulb Replacement

Refer to **Figure 53** (1987-1992) or **Figure 54** (1993-on) for this procedure.

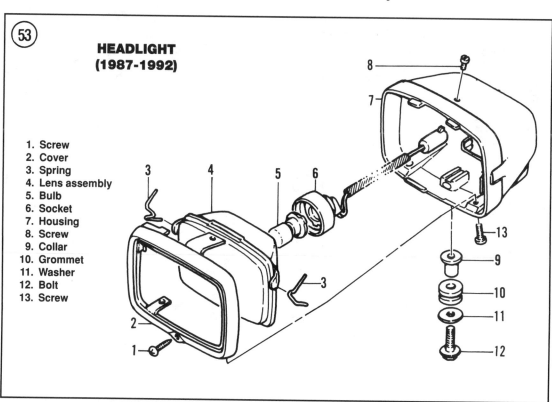

(53)

**HEADLIGHT
(1987-1992)**

1. Screw
2. Cover
3. Spring
4. Lens assembly
5. Bulb
6. Socket
7. Housing
8. Screw
9. Collar
10. Grommet
11. Washer
12. Bolt
13. Screw

CAUTION
All models are equipped with quartz-halogen bulbs. Do not touch the bulb glass with your fingers because traces of oil on the bulb will drastically reduce the life of the bulb. Clean any traces of oil or other chemicals from the bulb with a cloth moistened in alcohol or lacquer thinner.

WARNING
If the headlight has just burned out or turned off, it will be hot! Do not touch the bulb until it cools off.

1. Remove the headlight guard (**Figure 55**), if so equipped.

2. Remove the headlight mounting screw(s) and pull the headlight out of its housing.

3. Remove the bulb holder and remove the bulb.

4. Install by reversing these steps.

Headlight Adjustment

The headlight is equipped with only a vertical adjust screw located at the base of the headlight below the grille.

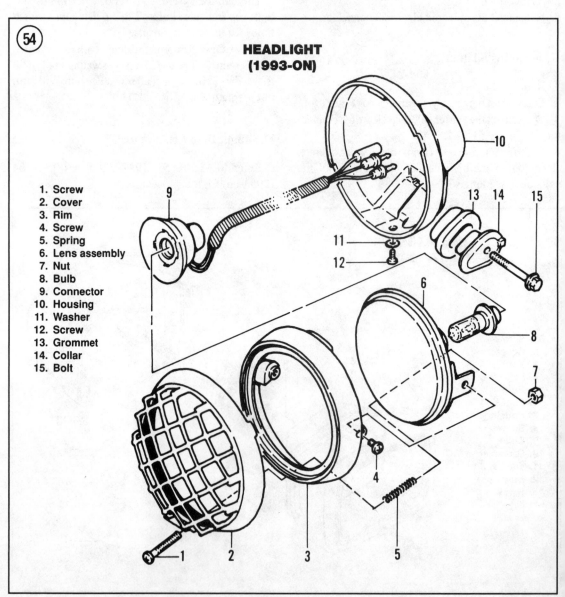

HEADLIGHT
(1993-ON)

1. Screw
2. Cover
3. Rim
4. Screw
5. Spring
6. Lens assembly
7. Nut
8. Bulb
9. Connector
10. Housing
11. Washer
12. Screw
13. Grommet
14. Collar
15. Bolt

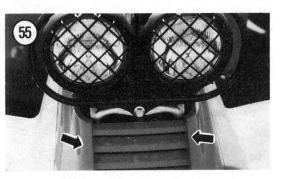

To adjust the headlight vertically, turning the screw clockwise will move the light up and counter-clockwise will move the light down.

Taillight Bulb and Lens Replacement

Refer to **Figure 56** for this procedure.

1. Remove the 2 Phillips screws (**Figure 57**) and pull the lens assembly out of its housing (**Figure 58**).

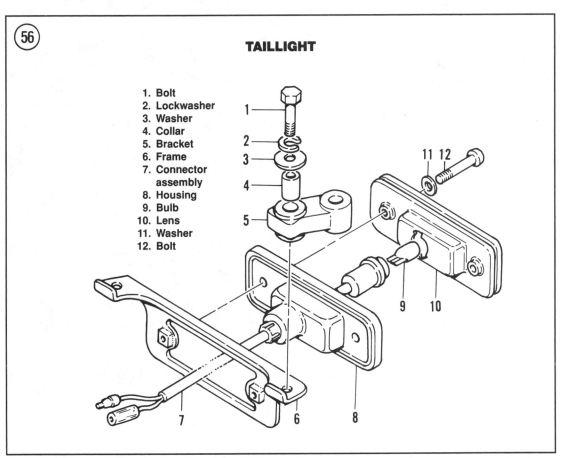

TAILLIGHT

1. Bolt
2. Lockwasher
3. Washer
4. Collar
5. Bracket
6. Frame
7. Connector assembly
8. Housing
9. Bulb
10. Lens
11. Washer
12. Bolt

9

2. Separate the lens from the housing and remove the bulb (**Figure 59**).

3. Replace the bulb.

4. Install by reversing these steps, while noting the following.

5. Make sure the rubber gasket seal is seated all the way around the lens when assembling the lens and housing.

Indicator Lights Lamp Replacement

Reverse and neutral indicator lights (**Figure 60**) are used on all models.

1. Pull up on the handlebar cover (**Figure 60**) to unsnap it from the handlebar.

2. Turn the cover over and locate the bulb holders (**Figure 61**).

3. Carefully withdraw the bulb holder and remove the blown bulb (**Figure 62**).

4. Install the new bulb and install the bulb holder into the cover.

5. Align the handlebar cover with the handlebar and snap the cover into place. Check that the bulb wires and connectors are routed properly.

SWITCHES

Testing

Switches can be tested for continuity with an ohmmeter (see Chapter One) or a test light at the switch connector plug by operating the switch in each of its operating positions and comparing results with its switch operating diagram. For example, **Figure 63** shows a continuity diagram for the starter switch. It shows which terminals should show continuity when the switch is in a given position.

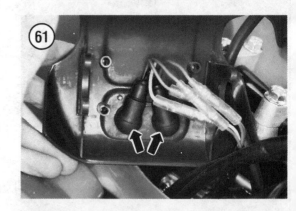

When the starter switch is in the ON position, there should be continuity between the brown and red/white terminals. This is indicated by the line on the continuity diagram. An ohmmeter connected between these 2 terminals should indicate little or no resistance or a test light should light. When the starter switch is OFF, there should be no continuity between the same terminals.

When testing switches, note the following:

a. First check the fuse as described under *Fuse* in this chapter.

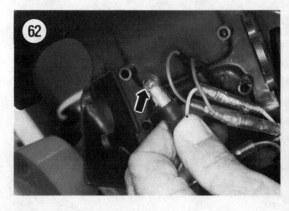

63

STARTER SWITCH

Position \ Color	Brown	Red/ white
Off		
On	•——————•	

64

ENGINE STOP SWITCH

Position \ Color	Black/ white	Black
Off	•——————•	
Run		

65

LIGHTS (DIMMER) SWITCH

Position \ Color	Brown	Blue	Green	Yellow
Off				
Low	•——————•——————•			
Hi	•——————•——————————•			

66

MAIN SWITCH (1987)

Position \ Color	Black/ red	Black/ white	Red	Brown
Off				
On	•——————•		•——————•	

67

MAIN SWITCH (1988-ON)

Position \ Color	Black/ white	Black	Red	Brown
Off	•——————•			
On			•——————•	

b. Check the battery as described under *Battery* in Chapter Three; if necessary, charge or replace the battery.

c. Disconnect the battery negative lead (**Figure 52**) from the battery if the switch connectors are not disconnected in the circuit.

CAUTION
Do not attempt to start the engine with the battery disconnected.

d. When separating 2 connectors, pull on the connector housings and not the wires.

e. After locating a defective circuit, check the connectors to make sure they are clean and properly connected. Check all wires going into a connector housing to make sure each wire is properly positioned and that the wire end is not loose.

f. To reconnect connectors properly, push them together until they click or snap into place.

If the switch or button does not perform properly, replace it. Refer to the following figures when testing the switch:

a. Starter switch: **Figure 63**.

b. Engine stop switch: **Figure 64**.

c. Light switch: **Figure 65**.

d. Main switch: **Figure 66** (1987) or **Figure 67** (1988-on).

NOTE
Neutral, reverse and clutch switch testing will be described later in this section.

Right-hand Handlebar Switch Housing Replacement

The right-hand handlebar switch housing is equipped with the following switches:

a. Light switch (A, **Figure 68**).
b. Engine stop switch (B, **Figure 68**).
c. Starter switch (C, **Figure 68**).

NOTE
The switches mounted in the right-hand handlebar switch housing are not available separately. If one switch is damaged, the housing will have to be replaced as an assembly.

1. Remove the front fender assembly as described in Chapter Thirteen.
2. Remove or cut any clamps securing the switch wiring harness to the handlebar.
3. Disconnect the right-hand switch electrical connector.
4. Remove the screws securing the switch to the handlebar and remove the switch assembly (**Figure 69**).
5. Install by reversing these steps.

Main Switch
Replacement

The main switch (**Figure 70**) is mounted in the front panel.
1. Loosen the main switch plastic nut.
2. Remove the front panel as described in Chapter Thirteen.
3. Remove the plastic nut and remove the main switch.
4. Disconnect the main switch electrical connector and remove the switch.
5. Install a new main switch by reversing these removal steps.

Clutch Switch
Testing/Replacement

The clutch switch (**Figure 71**) is mounted in the clutch lever housing.
1. Disconnect the clutch switch electrical connector.
2. Test the clutch switch as follows:
   a. Connect an ohmmeter to the switch side of the switch's black/yellow and black wire terminals.
   b. There should be continuity with the clutch lever pulled in and no continuity with the lever released.

c. If the switch failed to operate as described, replace it as described in the following steps.

3. Using a small straight-tipped screwdriver, push the clutch switch locking tab away from the hole in the clutch lever housing (**Figure 72**) and pull the switch out. See **Figure 73**.

4. Install the new switch by reversing these steps, plus the following.

5. Push the clutch switch firmly into the clutch lever housing until it clicks into place.

Neutral Switch
Testing/Replacement

The neutral switch is mounted in the left-hand crankcase, below the oil filter (**Figure 74**).

1. Disconnect the neutral switch electrical connector at the switch (**Figure 74**). Connect an ohmmeter (set on R × 1) between the neutral switch lead (on the switch) and ground as shown in **Figure 75**. With the transmission in NEUTRAL, the ohmmeter should show continuity (0 ohms). With the transmission in gear, the ohmmeter should read infinity. If the meter reading is incorrect for one or both tests, neutral switch is faulty and should be replaced.

2. To replace neutral switch:
   a. Drain the engine oil as described in Chapter Three.
   b. Loosen, then remove the neutral switch (**Figure 74**).
   c. Install the neutral switch and tighten to the torque specification in **Table 7**.

3. Reconnect the neutral switch wire at the switch.

4. Refill the engine oil as described in Chapter Three.

Reverse Switch
Testing/Replacement

The reverse switch is mounted in the top of the left-hand crankcase (**Figure 76**).

1. Disconnect the reverse switch green/white wire from the wiring harness. The reverse switch is

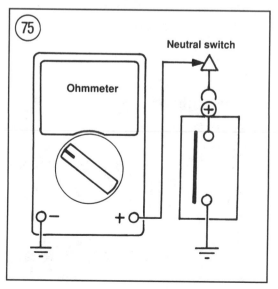

shown in **Figure 76**. Connect an ohmmeter (set on R × 1) between the switch lead and ground as shown in **Figure 77**. With the reverse lever (**Figure 78**) in the forward position, the ohmmeter should show continuity (0 ohms). With the reverse lever in the reverse position, the ohmmeter should show infinity. If the meter reading is incorrect for one or both tests, reverse switch is faulty and should be replaced.

2. To replace reverse switch:
   a. Disconnect the wire connector at the reverse switch.
   b. Loosen, then remove the reverse switch (**Figure 76**).
   c. Install the reverse switch and tighten to the torque specification in **Table 7**.
3. Reconnect the wire connector(s).

REVERSE SWITCH RELAY
(1987-1988)

The reverse switch relay is mounted underneath the rear fender on the right-hand side; see **Figure 79**.

Testing

1. Disconnect the electrical connector at the reverse switch relay (**Figure 79**) and remove the relay from the frame.
2. Perform the following:
   a. Attach an ohmmeter set to the R × 1 scale to the reverse switch relay contacts as shown in **Figure 80** and read resistance indicated on the ohmmeter. It should be 0 ohms.
   b. Leave the ohmmeter connected and connect a 12-volt battery to the reverse switch relay contacts as shown in **Figure 80** and read resistance

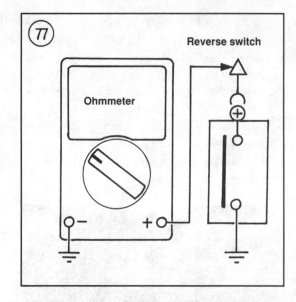

⑦⑦ Reverse switch

Ohmmeter

⑦⑧

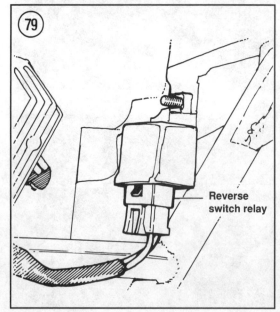

⑦⑨

Reverse switch relay

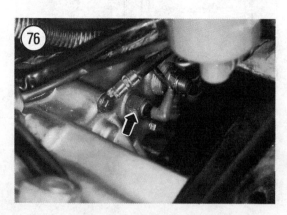

⑦⑥

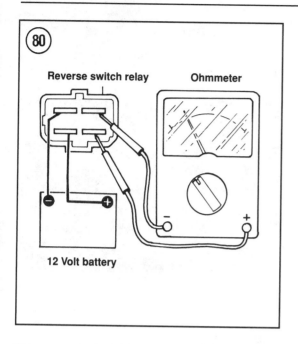

(80)

Reverse switch relay   Ohmmeter

12 Volt battery

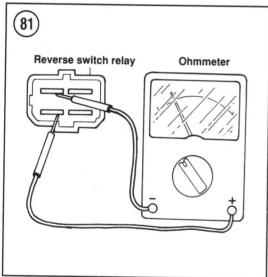

(81)

Reverse switch relay   Ohmmeter

indicated on the ohmmeter. It should be infinity (high resistance).

c. Disconnect the ohmmeter and battery from the relay.

d. If the readings were correct, perform Step 3. If not, replace the reverse switch relay.

3. Attach an ohmmeter set to the R × 100 scale to the reverse switch relay brown and green/yellow contacts as shown in **Figure 81**. Ohmmeter should read between 72-88 ohms. If the resistance reading was not within the prescribed range, the reverse relay is faulty and must be replaced.

4. If the resistance readings were correct in all tests, check for dirty or loose-fitting terminals; clean and repair as required.

5. Reverse the procedure to install the reverse switch relay.

STARTING CIRCUIT CUT-OFF RELAY

The starting circuit cut-off relay is mounted underneath the rear fender on the left-hand side; see A, **Figure 82**.

System Test

System testing of the starting circuit cut-off relay is found under *Engine Starting System* in Chapter Two.

Removal/Installation

1. Disconnect the electrical connector from the starting circuit cut-off relay (A, **Figure 82**) and remove it from its mounting pad.

2. Reverse the procedure to install.

NEUTRAL SWITCH RELAY

The neutral switch relay is mounted underneath the rear fender on the left-hand side; see B, **Figure 82**.

Removal/Installation

1. Disconnect the electrical connector from the neutral switch relay (B, **Figure 82**) and remove it from its mounting pad.

2. Reverse to install.

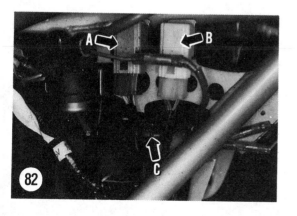

(82)

FUSE

All models are equipped with a 15 amp main fuse that is located next to the battery (C, **Figure 82**). To replace the fuse, pull the fuse holder off of its holder and remove one end (**Figure 83**). Replace the blown fuse and install the fuse holder.

NOTE
Always carry a spare fuse.

Whenever the fuse blows, find out the reason for the failure before replacing the fuse. Usually, the trouble is a short circuit in the wiring. This may be caused by worn-through insulation or a discon-nected wire shorted to ground.

WIRING DIAGRAMS

Wiring diagrams for all models are located at the end of this book.

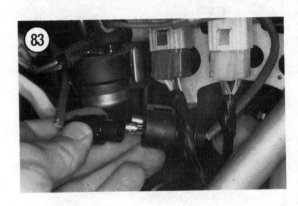

Table 1 ELECTRICAL SYSTEM SPECIFICATIONS

Battery	
Type	GM12CZ-4A
Capacity	12 volts, 12 amp hour
Charging system	Flywheel magneto
Ignition system	Capacitor discharge ignition (CDI)

Table 2 CHARGING SYSTEM TEST SPECIFICATIONS

Charging output voltage	14-15 volts @ 5,000 rpm

Table 3   STATOR COIL TEST SPECIFICATIONS

Charging Coil Resistance	Resistance (ohms-Ω)[1]
All Models	
1987-2000	
White to white	0.70-0.86 Ω
2001-on	
White to white	0.51-0.63 Ω
Pickup Coil Resistance	
1987	
Gray to blue	195-205 Ω
1988	
Yellow to green, green to blue	180-220 Ω
1989	
Yellow to green, yellow to blue	170-209 Ω
1990-1996	
Yellow to blue	171-209 Ω
1997-2001	
Red to white	459-561 Ω
2002-on	
White/Red to White/Green	459-561 Ω
Source Coil	
1987	
Brown to red	297-303 Ω
(continued)	

Table 3 STATOR COIL TEST SPECIFICATIONS (continued)

Charging Coil Resistance	Resistance (ohms-Ω)[1]
Source Coil (continued)	
1988	
Brown to red	270-330 Ω
1989	
White/green to red	270-330 Ω
1990-1996	
White/green to red	220-330 Ω
1997-2001	
Brown to green	270-330 Ω
Charging/Rotor rotation direction coil[2]	
2002-on	
Red to white/blue	0.083-0.101 Ω

1 Tests should be made with components at 20°C (68°F). Do not test when the engine is hot.
2 This component replaces the source coil from previous models to aid in the safe operation of the vehicle. It works in conjunction with the CDI unit to limit the speed of the engine when the parking brake is applied or the transmission is in reverse.

Table 4 IGNITION COIL TEST SPECIFICATIONS*

Primary Resistance	
1987-1988	0.72-0.98 Ω
1989-2001	0.36-0.48 Ω
2002-on	0.18-0.28 Ω
Secondary Resistance	
1987-1988	5.06-6.84 Ω
1989-2001	5.44-7.36 Ω
2002-on	6.32-9.48 Ω
Spark plug cap resistance	10 KΩ

* Tests should be made with components at 20°C (68°F). Do not test when the engine is hot

Table 5 STARTER MOTOR SPECIFICATIONS

Armature coil resistance	0.011-0.013 ohms @ 20°C (68°F)
Brush length	
Standard	12 mm (0.47 in.)
Minimum	
1987	3.5 mm (0.14 in.)
1988-on	8.5 mm (0.33 in.)
Brush spring pressure	
1987	800 g (28.2 oz.)
1988-on	650-950 g (22.9-33.5 oz.)
Commutator diameter	
Standard	28 mm (1.10 in.)
Minimum	27 mm (1.06 in.)
Mica undercut	0.6 mm (0.024 in.)

Table 6 REPLACEMENT BULBS

Item	Voltage/wattage
Headlight	12V 25W/25W
Taillight	12V 3.8W
Neutral light	12V 3.4W
Reverse light	12V 3.4W

Table 7 ELECTRICAL SYSTEM TIGHTENING TORQUES

	N•m	ft.-lb.	in.-lb.
Alternator rotor bolt	50	37	–
Starter motor mounting bolts	10	–	88
Neutral switch	20	15	–
Reverse switch	20	15	–

9

FRONT SUSPENSION AND STEERING

This chapter describes repair and maintenance of the front wheels, hubs, front suspension arms and steering components.

Refer to **Table 1** for general front suspension and steering specifications. **Tables 2-4** lists service specifications and torque specifications. **Tables 1-4** are located at the end of this chapter.

FRONT WHEEL

Removal/Installation

1. Place the vehicle on level ground and set the parking brake.

2. Mark the front tires with an "L" (left side) or "R" (right side) so that they can be installed onto the same side of the vehicle from which they were removed.

3. Loosen but do **not** remove the lug nuts (**Figure 1**) securing the wheel to the front hub.

4. Jack up the front of the vehicle with a small hydraulic or scissor jack. Place the jack under the frame with a piece of wood between the jack and the frame.

5. Place wood block(s) under the frame to support the vehicle securely with the front wheels off the ground.

6. Remove the wheel nuts and washers (loosened in Step 3) and remove the front wheel.

7. Remove the outer disc cover (**Figure 2**), if required.

8. Clean the lug nuts in solvent and dry thoroughly.

9. Inspect the wheel for cracks, bending or other damage. If damage is severe, replace wheel as described under *Tires and Wheels* in this chapter.

10. Install the outer disc cover (**Figure 2**) and front wheel.

11. Install the washers and nuts (**Figure 1**). Finger tighten the nuts until the wheel is positioned squarely against the front hub.

> *WARNING*
> *Always tighten the lug nuts to the correct torque specification or the nuts may work loose and the wheel could fall off.*

12. Use a torque wrench and tighten the lug nuts in a crisscross pattern to the torque specification listed in **Table 4**.

13. After the wheel is installed completely, rotate it; apply the front brake several times to make sure that the wheel rotates freely and that the brake is operating correctly.

14. Measure wheel runout with a dial indicator as described under *Front Hub* in this chapter.

15. Jack up the front of the vehicle up a little and remove the wood block(s).

16. Let the jack down and remove the jack and wood block.

FRONT HUB

The front hub consists of 2 oil seals, 2 ball bearings and a tapered center hub spacer. The front brake disc is bolted to the front hub. Refer to **Figure 3**

10

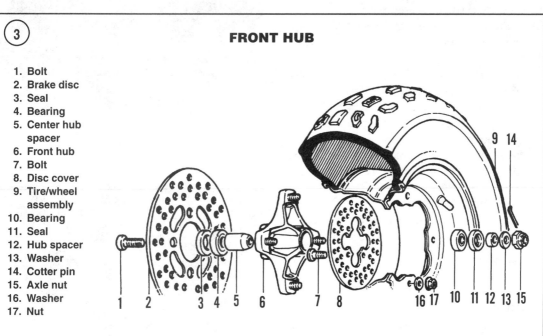

FRONT HUB

1. Bolt
2. Brake disc
3. Seal
4. Bearing
5. Center hub spacer
6. Front hub
7. Bolt
8. Disc cover
9. Tire/wheel assembly
10. Bearing
11. Seal
12. Hub spacer
13. Washer
14. Cotter pin
15. Axle nut
16. Washer
17. Nut

when servicing the front hub assembly in the following sections.

Inspection
(Hub Installed)

Inspect each wheel bearing prior to removing it from the wheel hub.

> ### CAUTION
> *Do not remove the wheel bearings for inspection purposes as they can be damaged during the removal process. Remove the wheel bearings only if they are to be replaced.*

1. Check that lug nuts (**Figure 1**) are tightened to the torque specification in **Table 4**.
2. Place the vehicle on level ground and set the parking brake. Block the rear wheels so the vehicle will not roll in either direction.
3. Jack up the front of the vehicle with a small hydraulic or scissor jack. Place the jack under the frame with a piece of wood between the jack and the frame.
4. Place wood block(s) under the frame to support the vehicle securely with the front wheels off the ground.
5. Mount a dial indicator against the rim as shown in **Figure 4** to measure radial and lateral runout. Turn tire slowly by hand and read movement indicated on dial indicator. See **Table 2** for runout limits. Note the following:
   a. If runout limit is excessive, first check condition of wheel assembly. If wheel is bent or otherwise damaged, it may require replacement.
   b. If wheel condition is okay but runout is excessive, remove wheel and turn hub (**Figure 2**) by hand. Hub should turn smoothly with no sign of roughness, excessive play or other abnormal conditions. If hub does not turn smoothly, remove hub and check bearings.
6. Remove dial indicator and lower vehicle to ground, or proceed with following section.

Hub Removal

Refer to **Figure 3** for this procedure.
1. Remove the front wheel as described in this chapter.

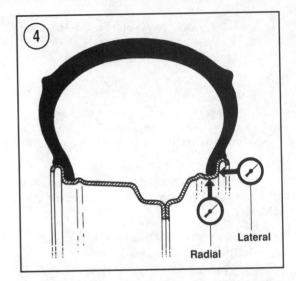

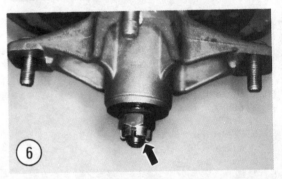

2. Remove the 2 brake caliper mounting bolts (**Figure 5**) and lift the caliper off of the brake disc. Hang the caliper from the vehicle with a stiff wire hook.

> *NOTE*
> *Insert a piece of vinyl tubing or plastic between the brake pads in the caliper, in place of the brake disc. That way if the brake lever is inadvertently squeezed, the piston will not be forced out of the cylinder. If this does happen, the caliper may have to be disassembled to reseat the piston. This will require bleeding of both front brakes. By blocking the brake pads, the piston cannot be forced out and bleeding the system should not be required.*

3. Remove and discard the axle nut cotter pin.
4. Loosen and remove the axle nut (**Figure 6**).
5. Slide the front hub (**Figure 7**) off the steering knuckle and remove it.

Inspection
(Hub Removed)

1. Remove the hub spacer (**Figure 8**) from the outer oil seal.
2. Inspect the oil seals. Replace if they are deteriorating or starting to harden.
3. Inspect the threaded studs on the front hub. Replace as necessary.
4. If necessary, remove the oil seals as described under *Disassembly* in this chapter.
5. Turn each bearing inner race (**Figure 9**) with your fingers. The bearing should turn smoothly with no roughness, binding or excessive noise.
6. Inspect the play of the inner race (**Figure 10**) of each hub bearing. Check for excessive lateral and radial play. Replace the bearings if play is excessive.
7. Always replace both bearings in the hub at the same time. When replacing the bearings, write down the bearing manufacturer's code numbers (found on

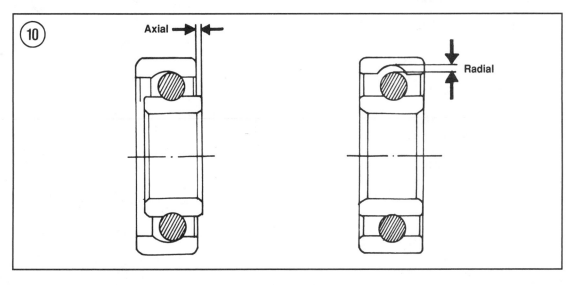

the outside of each bearing) and take them with you to ensure a perfect match up.

Disassembly

The front hub bearings (**Figure 3**) are installed with a press fit and force will be required to remove them.

This section describes 2 methods on removing the front hub bearings. The first method (Step 2A) is recommended by Yamaha. However, because of the close fit between the bearings and hub spacer, this method can be difficult, as it is possible to damage the center hub spacer's machined surface when removing the first bearing. The second method (Step 2B), while easier and results with less chance of damaging the spacer, requires the use of a wheel bearing remover set.

Remove the bearings only if the bearings must be replaced. Note that the inner and outer bearings and the inner and outer oil seals are different. Prior to removing the oil seals and bearings, write down the size code on each part so that the replacement parts can be installed correctly.

1. Remove the oil seals by prying them out of the hub with a wide-blade screwdriver (**Figure 11**). Support the screwdriver with a rag to avoid damaging the hub or brake disc.

> *CAUTION*
> *When removing the bearings in the following steps, support the front hub carefully so that you do not damage the brake disc (**Figure 12**).*

2A. To remove the front hub bearings without special tools:

   a. Using a long drift, tilt the center hub spacer away from one side of the outer bearing as shown in **Figure 13**.

> *NOTE*
> *Try not to damage the hub spacer's machined surface when positioning and driving against the long drift. You may have to grind a clearance groove in the drift to enable it to grab hold of the bearing while clearing the spacer.*

   b. Tap the bearing out of the hub with a hammer, working around the perimeter of the bearing's inner race.

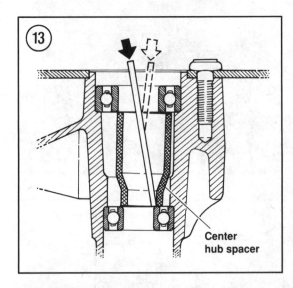

Center hub spacer

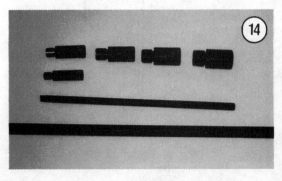

c. Remove the center hub spacer from the hub, noting the direction in which the spacer is installed in the hub, for reassembly reference.

d. Using a large socket or bearing driver, drive the opposite bearing out of the hub.

NOTE
*The Kowa Seiki Wheel Bearing Remover set shown in **Figure 14** can be ordered by a Yamaha dealer through K & L Supply Co. in Santa Clara, CA.*

2B. To remove the hub bearings with the Kowa Seiki Wheel Bearing Remover set:

a. Select the correct size remover head tool and insert it into the outer bearing; see A, **Figure 15**.

b. From the opposite side of the hub, insert the remover shaft into the slot in the backside of the remover head; see B, **Figure 15**. Position the hub so that the remover head tool (A, **Figure 15**) is resting against a solid surface and tap the remover shaft to force it into the slit in the remover head. This will wedge the remover head against the inner bearing race.

c. Position the hub and tap on the end of the remover shaft with a hammer and drive the bearing out of the hub. Remove the bearing and tool. Tap on the remover head to release it from the bearing.

d. Remove the center hub spacer from the hub, noting the direction in which the spacer is installed in the hub, for reassembly reference.

e. Using a large socket or bearing driver, drive the opposite bearing out of the hub.

3. Clean the hub and center hub spacer in solvent and dry thoroughly.

Assembly

Single row, deep groove ball bearings are used in the front hub. Depending on model year, unshielded (open) or single shielded bearings are used. Prior to installing new bearings and oil seals, note the following:

a. As noted during disassembly, the inner and outer oil seals and bearings are different. Refer to the drawing in **Figure 16** when assembling the front hub in the following steps.

b. When installing bearings in following steps, install unshielded bearings so that the manufacturer's code marks and numbers face out. Install single shielded bearings so that open side faces out (**Figure 9**).

c. Install bearings by pressing them into hub with a socket or bearing driver that seats against the outer bearing race only (**Figure 17**).

d. Install oil seals with their closed side facing out.

10

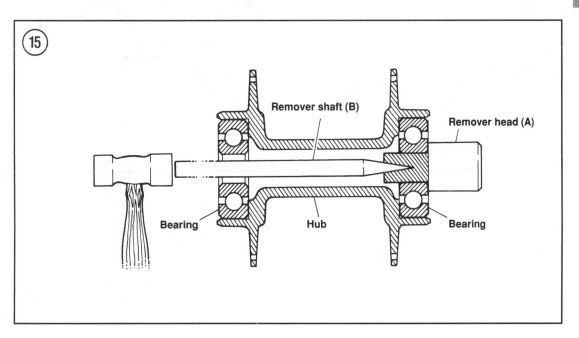

1. Pack the bearings with a good quality bearing grease. Work the grease in between the balls thoroughly. Turn the bearing by hand to make sure the grease is seated evenly inside the bearing.

2. Blow any dirt or foreign matter out of the hub and center hub spacer prior to installing the bearings.

3. Press in the inner bearing (**Figure 18**) until it bottoms in the hub bearing bore.

4. Turn the hub over and install the center hub spacer so that its larger inner diameter seats against the inner bearing as shown in **Figure 16**.

5. Press in the outer bearing (**Figure 19**) until it bottoms in the hub bearing bore.

NOTE
Yamaha factory replacement front hub oil seals are pre-greased at the factory.

6. If your replacement oil seals are not pre-greased, pack the lip of each seal with a waterproof bearing grease.

7. Press in the inner oil seal (A, **Figure 20**) until its outer surface is flush with the oil seal bore inside surface as shown in **Figure 21**.

8. Press in the outer oil seal (B, **Figure 20**) until its outer surface is flush with the oil seal bore inside surface as shown in **Figure 22**.

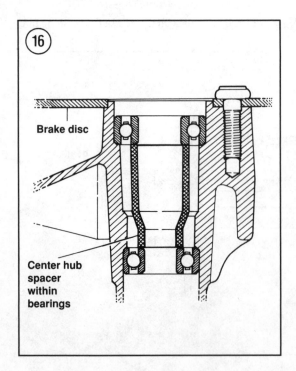

Brake disc

Center hub spacer within bearings

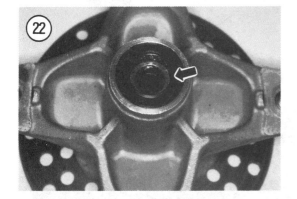

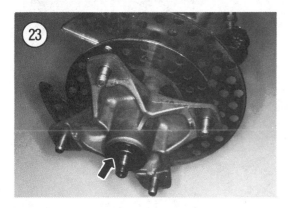

Installation

1. Clean the steering knuckle bearing surface, threads and axle nut with solvent or contact cleaner. Blow dry with compressed air.

2. Install the hub spacer into the front hub outer oil seal as shown in **Figure 8**.

3. Slide the front hub onto the steering knuckle (**Figure 23**).

4. Install the flat washer onto the steering knuckle.

5. Hand-thread the axle nut onto the steering knuckle. Then tighten axle nut (**Figure 24**) to the torque specification in **Table 4**. Now check that one of the axle nut's grooves is aligned with the cotter pin hole in the steering knuckle. If not, align the groove by tightening the axle nut. Do *not* loosen the axle nut to align the groove.

> *WARNING*
> *Always install a new cotter pin.*

6. Insert the new cotter pin through the nut groove and steering knuckle hole and then bend its arms to lock it as shown in **Figure 25**.

7. Remove the spacer from between the brake pads and slide the brake caliper over the brake disc. Install the 2 brake caliper mounting bolts (**Figure 26**) and

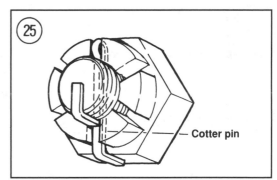

Cotter pin

10

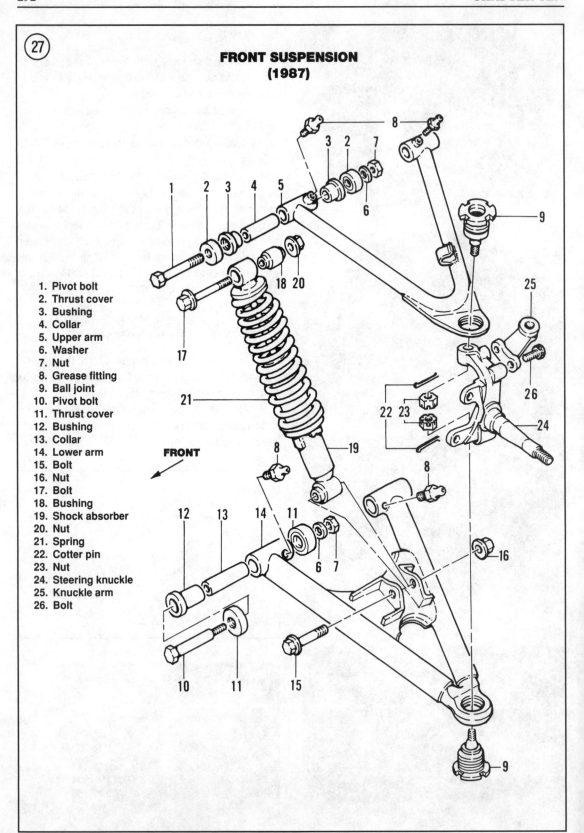

**FRONT SUSPENSION
(1987)**

1. Pivot bolt
2. Thrust cover
3. Bushing
4. Collar
5. Upper arm
6. Washer
7. Nut
8. Grease fitting
9. Ball joint
10. Pivot bolt
11. Thrust cover
12. Bushing
13. Collar
14. Lower arm
15. Bolt
16. Nut
17. Bolt
18. Bushing
19. Shock absorber
20. Nut
21. Spring
22. Cotter pin
23. Nut
24. Steering knuckle
25. Knuckle arm
26. Bolt

FRONT

tighten to the torque specification in **Table 4**. Apply the front brake lever a few times to seat the pads against the disc.

8. Install the front wheel as described in this chapter.

FRONT SUSPENSION

Figure 27 (1987) and **Figure 28** (1988-on) show the front suspension system. The 2 Y-shaped control arms are bolted to mounting brackets welded to the

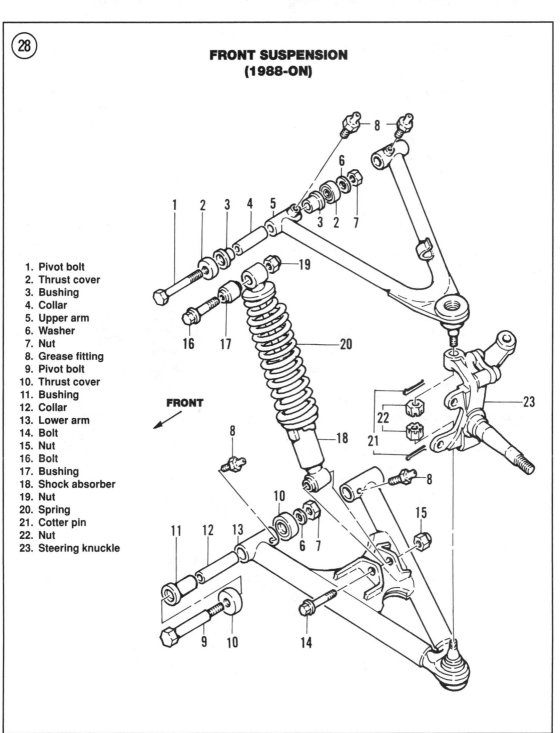

**FRONT SUSPENSION
(1988-ON)**

1. Pivot bolt
2. Thrust cover
3. Bushing
4. Collar
5. Upper arm
6. Washer
7. Nut
8. Grease fitting
9. Pivot bolt
10. Thrust cover
11. Bushing
12. Collar
13. Lower arm
14. Bolt
15. Nut
16. Bolt
17. Bushing
18. Shock absorber
19. Nut
20. Spring
21. Cotter pin
22. Nut
23. Steering knuckle

FRONT

10

frame. Ball joints connect both control arms to the steering knuckle. On 1987 models, the ball joints are a thread fit into the control arms and can be replaced separately. On 1988 and later models, the ball joints are an integral part of the control arms and cannot be replaced separately.

Steering is controlled by tie rods connected to the steering shaft and steering knuckle.

Front Suspension Tools

CAUTION
The threads of the tie rods and ball joints are easily damaged. If you have difficulty separating the tie rods or ball joints from the steering knuckle, have a dealer perform this operation. Using a forked tool ("pickle fork") will usually damage the boot.

Along with common hand tools, pullers will be required to separate both control arms and tie rod from the steering knuckle. Likewise, a puller will be required to separate the tie rod from the steering shaft. The pullers shown in **Figure 29** can be used to separate all of the ball joints on your Yamaha:

a. A universal 2-jaw puller (A, **Figure 29**) can be used to separate the tie rod from the steering knuckle and steering shaft.
b. Separating the control arms from the steering knuckle is a bit more difficult because of the confined working area. However, a special removal tool can be made quite easily. The tool

shown in B, **Figure 29** was made from a discarded motorcycle flywheel puller, a 2 1/4 in. length of 1/2-13 threaded rod and two 1/2-13 nuts. The flywheel puller body was drilled and tapped to accept national coarse (USS) 1/2-13 threads. Basic dimensions for the tool are shown in **Figure 30**.

NOTE
If you are going to machine the tool body from a piece of steel, either machine it with hex or square stock or cut 2 opposite flats onto a round piece of metal so that you can hold it with a wrench when using it.

SHOCK ABSORBER

Refer to **Figure 27** or **Figure 28** when servicing the shock absorbers.

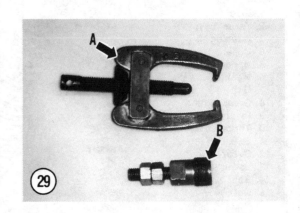

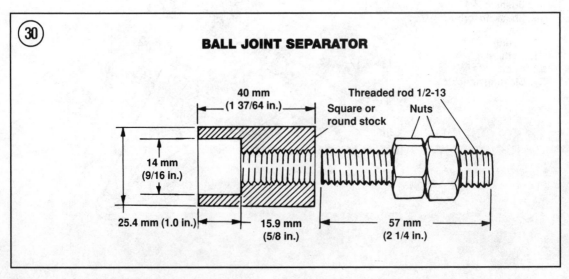

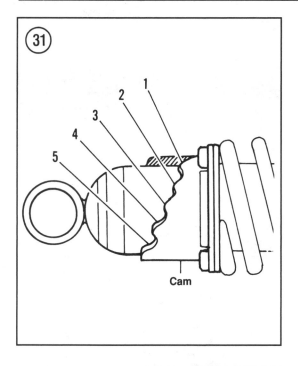

Cam

Spring Preload Adjustment

The front shock absorber springs are provided with 5 preload positions. See **Figure 31**. The No. 1 position is soft and the No. 5 position is hard. The spring preload can be changed by rotating the cam at the end of the spring. Set both front shock absorbers to the same preload position.

Removal/Installation

1. Remove the front wheel(s) as described in this chapter.
2. Remove the upper and lower shock absorber mounting nuts and bolts and remove the shock absorber. See **Figure 27** or **Figure 28**.
3. Install by reversing these removal steps, while noting the following.
4. Inspect each damper unit (**Figure 32**) for fluid leakage or other damage. Replace the shock if leaks are found.

> *WARNING*
> *Do not attempt to disassemble the damper unit. Disassembly can release gas that is under pressure and cause injury.*

5. Clean the upper and lower mounting bolts and nuts in solvent and dry thoroughly.
6. Apply a waterproof grease to the upper and lower mounting bolts prior to installation.
7. Install the shock mounting bolts from the front side as shown in **Figure 27** or **Figure 28**.
8. Tighten the upper and lower shock mounting bolts and nuts to the torque specification in **Table 4**.
9. Repeat for the other side as required.

Spring Removal/Installation

The shock is spring-controlled and hydraulically damped. The shock damper unit is sealed and cannot be serviced. Service is limited to removal and replacement of the damper unit, spring and mounting bushings.

Table 1 lists stock spring rate specifications for all 1987-on stock shock absorbers.

> *NOTE*
> *Yamaha does not list replacement springs (**Figure 33**) for the front shock absorbers. If replacement springs are needed, consult an aftermarket supplier.*

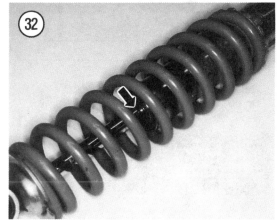

10

1. Mount the lower shock mount in a vise with soft jaws and turn the spring adjuster (**Figure 34**) to its softest position.

> *WARNING*
> *Do not remove the spring without a spring compressor. The spring is under considerable pressure and may fly off and cause injury.*

2. Mount a spring compressor onto the shock absorber and compress the spring. Then remove the upper spring seat and remove the spring.

3. Measure the spring free length (**Figure 35**). Replace the spring if it has sagged to the service limit in **Table 1**.

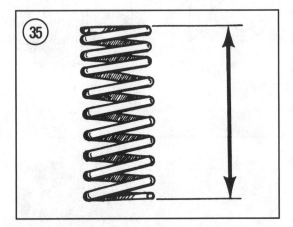

> *NOTE*
> *The damper unit cannot be rebuilt; it must be replaced as a unit.*

4. Check the damper unit for leakage and make sure the damper rod is straight. Replace the damper unit if necessary.

5. Check the shock bushings (**Figure 36**) for deterioration, severe wear or other damage. If necessary, replace bushings as follows:

   a. Support damper unit in a press and press out damaged bushing.
   b. Clean shock bushing bore to remove dirt, rust and other debris.
   c. Press in the new bushing until its outer surface is flush with the bushing bore inside surface as shown in **Figure 36**.

6. Assemble the shock by reversing these steps, while noting the following.

7. If installing progressive rate springs, install spring with closer wound coils toward top of shock.

8. Make sure the spring seat is properly seated in the spring (**Figure 37**).

9. Turn the spring adjuster to adjust spring pre-load (**Figure 31**).

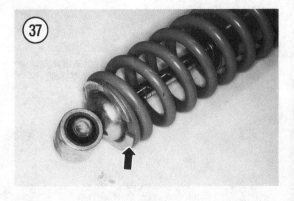

> *NOTE*
> *Adjust both shocks to the same spring pre-load setting.*

STEERING KNUCKLE

Refer to **Figure 27** or **Figure 28** when servicing the steering knuckle.

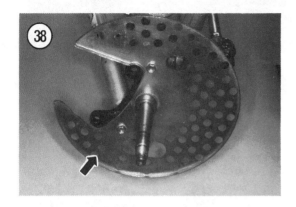

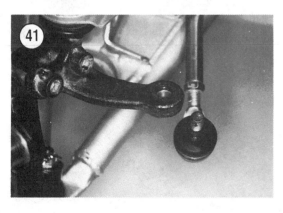

Removal

1. Remove the front hub as described in this chapter.

2. Remove the inner disc cover bolts and remove the disc cover (**Figure 38**).

3. Slide the brake hose out of the upper control arm clamp.

4. Remove the shock absorber as described in this chapter.

CAUTION
Do not hammer on any ball joint when trying to remove it. Doing so will damage the ball joint stud and threads. This will require a new ball joint (if available separately) or complete replacement of the tie rod or control arm(s) assembly.

5. To disconnect the tie rod ball joint from the steering knuckle:

   a. Remove the cotter pin from the tie rod ball joint stud nut. Discard the cotter pin.

   b. Remove the castellated nut from the tie rod ball joint stud (**Figure 39**).

NOTE
When installing the puller, make sure you do not damage the ball joint rubber seal. If the angled arms on the puller are too thick, they can damage the seal.

   c. Attach a 2-jaw puller to the steering knuckle and center the puller's pressure bolt against the ball joint stud as shown in **Figure 40**.

   d. Operate the puller to apply pressure against the ball joint stud, checking that the puller is not cocked to one side. When the ball joint stud is under pressure, strike the top of the puller with a hammer to free the ball joint from the steering knuckle (**Figure 41**).

6. To disconnect the upper and lower control arm ball joints from the steering knuckle:

   a. Remove the cotter pins from the upper (A, **Figure 42**) and lower (B, **Figure 42**) control arm ball joint stud nuts. Discard the cotter pins.

   b. Remove the castellated nuts that hold the ball joint in each control arm to the steering knuckle.

10

> *NOTE*
> *Refer to **Front Suspension Tools** under **Front Suspension** in this chapter for a description of the tool used to separate the control arm ball joints from the steering knuckle.*

c. To separate the lower control arm, attach the special tool between upper and lower control arm ball joint studs as shown in **Figure 43**. Center the tool's pressure bolt against the lower control arm stud. Tighten the tool's pressure bolt (**Figure 44**) to apply pressure against the ball joint stud. Continue until the ball joint pops free.

d. To separate the upper control arm, attach the special tool between the control arm ball joint stud and steering knuckle arm as shown in **Figure 45**. Center the tool's pressure bolt against the upper control arm stud. Tighten the tool's pressure bolt (**Figure 46**) to apply pressure against the ball joint stud. Continue until the ball joint pops free.

7. Lower the upper control arm and remove the steering knuckle.

Inspection

1. Clean the steering knuckle in solvent and dry with compressed air.

> *NOTE*
> *On 1987 models, the knuckle arm bolts and arm (25, **Figure 27**) can be removed from the knuckle assembly. On 1988-on models, the knuckle arm bolts (A, **Figure 47**) are spot welded to the knuckle assembly; do not attempt to separate the knuckle arm (B, **Figure 47**) from the knuckle assembly.*

2. Inspect the steering knuckle (**Figure 48**) for bending, thread damage, cracks or other damage.

3. Inspect the spindle portion where the front wheel bearings ride for wear or damage. A hard spill or collision may cause the spindle portion to bend or fracture. If the spindle is damaged in any way, replace the steering knuckle.

4. Check the hole at the end of the spindle where the cotter pin fits. Make sure there are no fractures or cracks leading out toward the end of the steering knuckle. If any are present, replace the steering knuckle.

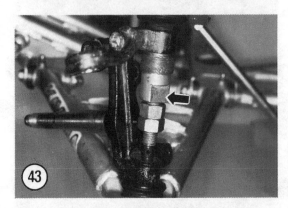

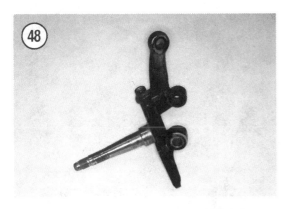

5. If replacing the knuckle arm (25, **Figure 27**) on 1987 models, tighten the knuckle arm Allen bolts to 38 N•m (27 ft.-lb.).

Installation

1. Position the steering knuckle between the control arms. Then install the upper and lower control arm ball joint studs (**Figure 49**) through the steering knuckle. See **Figure 50**.

2. Thread the castellated nuts onto the upper and lower ball joint studs (**Figure 42**). Then tighten both nuts to the torque specification in **Table 4**. Tighten the nuts, if necessary, to align the cotter pin hole with the nut slot.

3. Install the tie rod ball joint (**Figure 41**) through the steering knuckle as shown in **Figure 39**. Install the castellated nut and tighten to the torque specification in **Table 4**. Tighten the nut, if necessary, to align the cotter pin hole with the nut slot.

4. Install new cotter pins through all ball joint studs. Open cotter pins arms to lock them in place.

5. Install shock absorber as described in this chapter.

6. Turn handlebar from side to side, check that steering knuckle (**Figure 51**) moves smoothly with no binding or roughness.

10

7. Install inner disc brake cover (**Figure 38**) and its mounting bolts. Tighten bolts securely.

8. Install front hub and front wheel as described in this chapter.

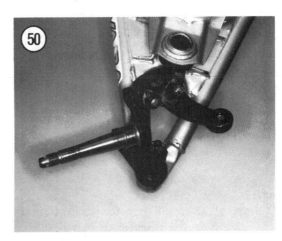

CONTROL ARMS

Refer to **Figure 27** or **Figure 28** when servicing the upper and lower control arms.

Removal

1. Disconnect the control arm(s) from the steering knuckle as described under *Steering Knuckle* in this chapter.

> *NOTE*
> *On 1987 models, you do not need to remove the control arm(s) in order to replace the ball joint. Refer to **Ball Joint Inspection and Replacement (1987)** in this section.*

2. Remove the nut from each pivot bolt (**Figure 52**) that secures the upper control arm to the frame. Remove the pivot bolt, control arm, thrust covers and bushings.

3. Remove the nut from each pivot bolt (**Figure 53**) that secures the lower control arm to the frame. Remove the pivot bolt, control arm, thrust covers and bushings.

Control Arm
Cleaning and Inspection

> *NOTE*
> *Do not intermix the pivot bolts, nuts, bushings and thrust covers when disassembling and cleaning the upper and lower control arms. Separate the parts so that they can be installed in their original mounting positions.*

1. Remove the thrust covers and collars from the upper (**Figure 54**) and lower (**Figure 55**) control arms.

> *NOTE*
> *When cleaning the control arms, do not wash the ball joints (**Figure 56**) in solvent. Handle the ball joints carefully to avoid contaminating the grease or damaging them.*

2. Clean parts in solvent and dry with compressed air.

3. Inspect both control arms for cracks, fractures and dents. If damage is severe, replace the control

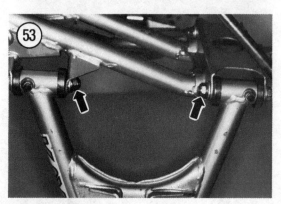

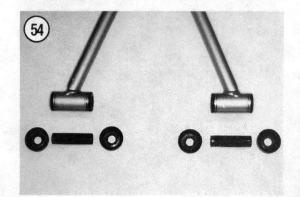

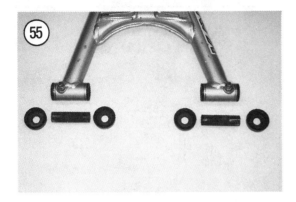

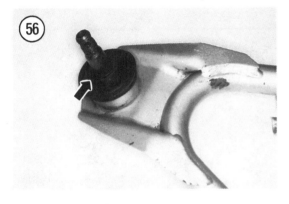

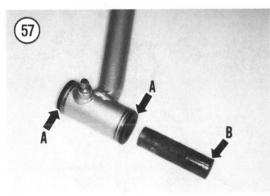

arm. Never try to straighten a damaged or dented control arm as it cannot be straightened properly.

4. Inspect each bushing (A, **Figure 57**) and collar (B, **Figure 57**) set for severe wear or damage. Replace damaged parts.

5. To replace the control arm bushings (A, **Figure 57**):

    a. Support the control arm and drive or press out the bushing. Repeat this step for each bushing.

    b. Clean the control arm bushing bores in solvent and dry thoroughly. Remove all rust and dirt residue.

    c. Support control arm and press bushing into bore until bushing shoulder bottoms.

6. Inspect the rubber seal in each thrust cover for severe wear or damage. Replace the thrust cover if damage is severe.

7. Inspect pivot bolts for bending or other damage. Replace damaged bolts.

8. Inspect ball joints (**Figure 56**) as described under *Ball Joints Inspection and Replacement* in this chapter.

Ball Joint
Inspection and Replacement
(1987)

A single ball joint (9, **Figure 27**) is mounted on each control arm. The ball joints on these models (1987 only) are threaded and can be replaced as a single unit. Replacement parts of the ball joint (ball joint, cover and spring) are not available separately.

1. Inspect the ball joint rubber boot. The swivel joint is packed with grease. If the rubber boot or ball joint is damaged, replace ball joint as follows.

2. Install the control arm onto the vehicle if previously removed. This will make it easier to hold the control arm when loosening and tightening the ball joint.

NOTE
*The Yamaha ball joint wrench (part No. YM-01405 [**Figure 58**]) or an equivalent tool will be required to loosen and install ball joints.*

3. Loosen, then remove ball joint with ball joint wrench (**Figure 59**).

4. Clean control arm threads.

5. If reinstalling ball joint, clean ball joint threads thoroughly.

10

6. Hand thread ball joint into control arm. Then torque ball joint with ball joint wrench and torque wrench to the torque specification in **Table 4**.

Ball Joints
Inspection and Replacement
(1988-on)

A single ball joint (**Figure 56**) is mounted on each control arm. The ball joints on these models are an integral part of the control arm and cannot be replaced separately.

Inspect the ball joint rubber boot. The swivel joint is packed with grease. If the rubber boot or ball joint is damaged, replace control arm as the ball joint cannot be replaced.

Installation

1. Prior to installation, apply a waterproof grease to each of the following components (**Figure 60** and **Figure 61**):
    a. Collar outer diameter.
    b. Thrust cover rubber seal.
    c. Pivot bolts.
2. Install the collars and thrust covers; see **Figure 60** and **Figure 61**.
3. Position the lower control arm between its mounting brackets and install the pivot bolts, washers and nuts (**Figure 53**). Tighten both nuts to the torque specification in **Table 4**.
4. Position the upper control arm between its mounting brackets and install the pivot bolts, washers and nuts (**Figure 52**). Tighten both nuts to the torque specification in **Table 4**.
5. Raise and lower both control arms (**Figure 62**) by hand. Control arms should pivot smoothly with no roughness or binding.
6. Connect control arm ball joints to steering knuckle as described under *Steering Knuckle* in this chapter.

HANDLEBAR

Removal

> *CAUTION*
> *Cover the seat, fuel tank and front fender with a heavy cloth or plastic tarp to protect them from the acciden-*

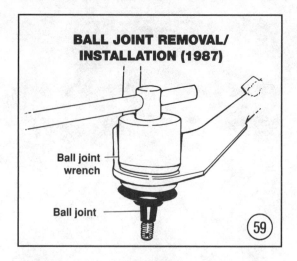

BALL JOINT REMOVAL/ INSTALLATION (1987)

Ball joint wrench

Ball joint

59

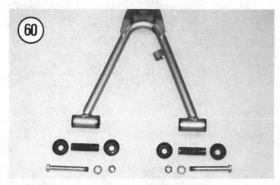

60

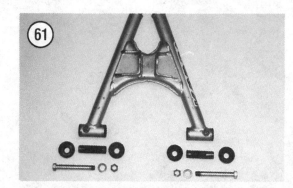

61

62

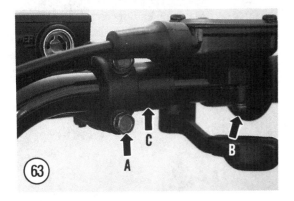

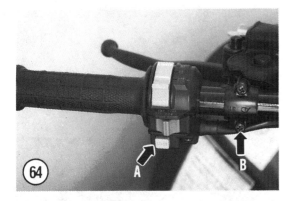

tal spilling of brake fluid. Wash any spilled brake fluid off any painted or plated surface immediately as it will destroy the finish. Use soapy water and rinse thoroughly.

1. Remove the bolts (A, **Figure 63**) securing the front master cylinder to the handlebar and rest it on the front fender. Keep the reservoir in the upright position to keep air from entering the brake system. Do not remove the brake line from the master cylinder unless you are going to remove the master cylinder from the vehicle.

CAUTION
Do not allow the master cylinder to hang by its hose. This could damage the hose.

2. Remove the screws and clamp securing the throttle assembly (B, **Figure 63**) to the handlebar and remove the assembly. Lay the assembly over the front fender. Be careful that the cable does not get crimped or damaged.

3. Remove all wire bands holding the left-hand switch housing wires to the handlebar.

4. Remove the screws securing the left-hand switch assembly (A, **Figure 64**). Then separate the switch housing and remove from the handlebar.

5. Remove the screws and clamp (B, **Figure 64**) securing the left-hand clutch and parking brake assembly to the handlebar and remove the assembly. Position the assembly so that the cables do not get crimped or damaged.

6. Remove the handlebar crossbar cover (A, **Figure 65**) from the handlebar.

7. Pull the handlebar cover off of the handlebar. See B, **Figure 65**, typical.

8. Remove the bolts securing the handlebar upper holders and remove the holders (**Figure 66**).

9. Remove the handlebar.

10. To maintain a good grip on the handlebar and to prevent it from slipping, clean the knurled section of the handlebar with a wire brush. It should be kept rough so it will be held securely by the holders. The holders should also be kept clean and free of any metal that may have been gouged loose by handlebar slippage.

10

Installation

1. Position the handlebar on the lower handlebar holders and hold it in place.

> *NOTE*
> *The upper handlebar holders are directional; they are machined with one side offset from the other (A, **Figure 67**). The front side is marked with a punch mark (B, **Figure 67**). To ensure correct handlebar installation, the upper holders must be installed as described in Step 2.*

2. Install the upper handlebar holders with their punch mark (B, **Figure 67**) facing toward the front. See **Figure 68**.

3. Install the handlebar holder bolts. Tighten the forward bolts first and then the rear bolts; tighten to the torque specification listed in **Table 4**.

> *NOTE*
> *If you are installing a new handlebar, do not forget to install the master cylinder spacer (C, **Figure 63**) onto the handlebar before installing the left-hand grip.*

4. If you installed a new handlebar, install new grips now. Follow manufacturer's directions for installing and sealing grips to handlebar.

5. Position the left-hand switch housing (A, **Figure 64**) onto the handlebar and seat it next to the grip as shown. Tighten the switch screws securely.

6. Secure housing wiring harness to handlebar with clamps. Make sure harness is routed with no sharp bends.

7. Position left-hand clutch and parking brake assembly on handlebar and install clamp and 2 screws (B, **Figure 64**). Check clutch lever position while sitting on seat, then tighten 2 clamp screws securely.

8. Position throttle assembly (B, **Figure 63**) onto handlebar and secure with clamp and 2 screws.

9. Slide master cylinder spacer along handlebar and seat groove in spacer into notch on throttle housing; see **Figure 69**.

10. Install master cylinder onto handlebar and secure with clamp and 2 bolts (A, **Figure 64**). Install clamp so that arrow faces up. Slide master cylinder

toward throttle housing until it contacts master cylinder spacer (**Figure 69**). Then check front brake lever position while sitting on seat and tighten master cylinder mounting bolts to torque specification in **Table 4**.

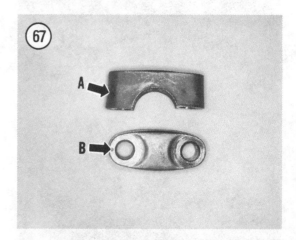

11. Install handlebar cover (B, **Figure 65**).

12. Install handlebar crossover bar pad (A, **Figure 65**).

13. After all assemblies have been installed, test each one to make sure it operates correctly with no binding. Correct any problem at this time.

TIE RODS

Figure 70 and **Figure 71** are exploded views of the steering shaft and tie rod assemblies. The tie rods are comprised of an inner end and outer end. All of the individual parts that make up the tie rod can be replaced separately.

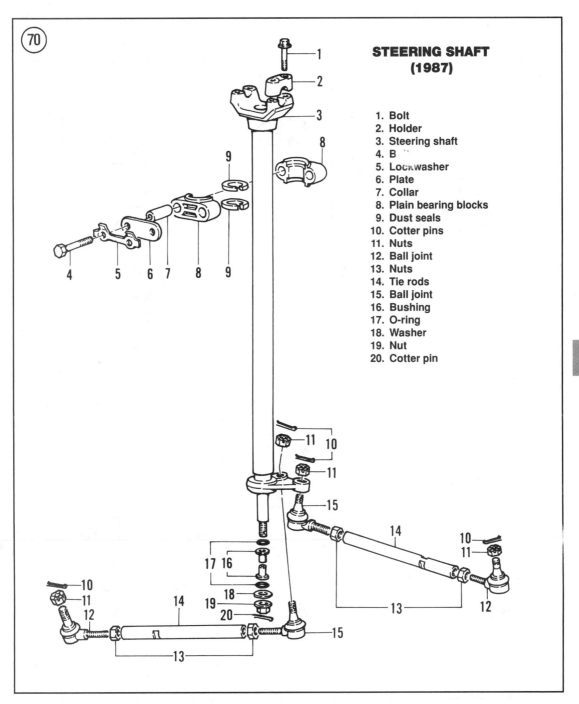

STEERING SHAFT (1987)

1. Bolt
2. Holder
3. Steering shaft
4. B
5. Lockwasher
6. Plate
7. Collar
8. Plain bearing blocks
9. Dust seals
10. Cotter pins
11. Nuts
12. Ball joint
13. Nuts
14. Tie rods
15. Ball joint
16. Bushing
17. O-ring
18. Washer
19. Nut
20. Cotter pin

10

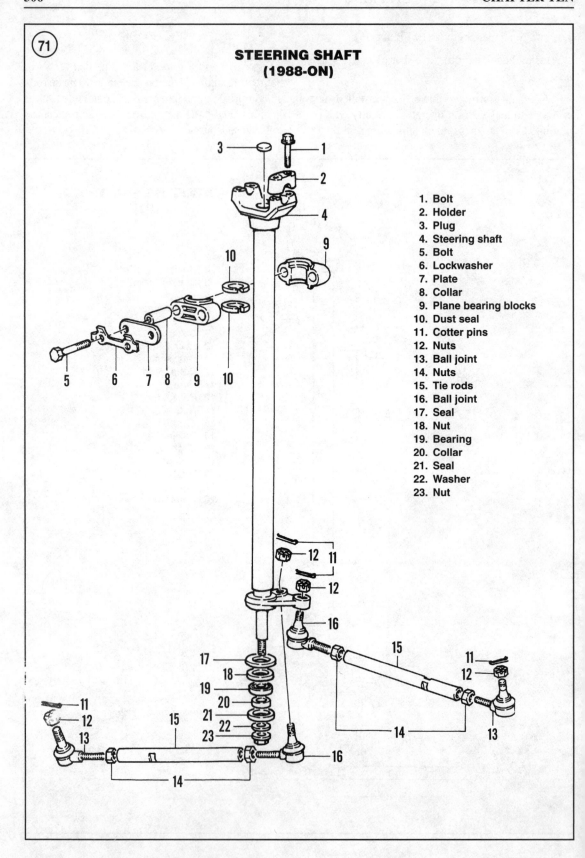

**STEERING SHAFT
(1988-ON)**

1. Bolt
2. Holder
3. Plug
4. Steering shaft
5. Bolt
6. Lockwasher
7. Plate
8. Collar
9. Plane bearing blocks
10. Dust seal
11. Cotter pins
12. Nuts
13. Ball joint
14. Nuts
15. Tie rods
16. Ball joint
17. Seal
18. Nut
19. Bearing
20. Collar
21. Seal
22. Washer
23. Nut

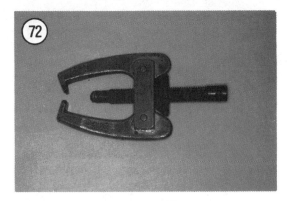

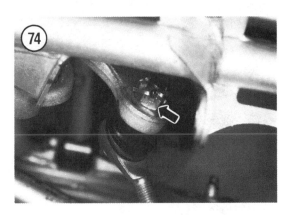

A 2-jaw puller (**Figure 72**) will be required to separate the tie rod from the steering knuckle and steering shaft.

Removal

You can replace the outer tie rod end (**Figure 73**) without having to disconnect the tie rod from the steering shaft.

When replacing the inner tie rod end (**Figure 74**), it is best to remove the tie rod from the vehicle so that the inner tie rod can be properly adjusted.

1. Support the vehicle and remove the front wheel(s) as described in this chapter.

> *CAUTION*
> *Do not hammer on any ball joint when trying to remove it. Doing so will damage the ball joint stud and threads. This will require a new ball joint.*

2. To disconnect the tie rod ball joint from the steering knuckle:

   a. Remove the cotter pin from the tie rod ball joint stud nut. Discard the cotter pin.

   b. Remove the castellated nut from the ball joint stud (**Figure 73**).

> *NOTE*
> *When installing the puller, make sure you do not damage the ball joint rubber seal. If the angled arms on the puller are too thick, they can damage the seal.*

   c. Attach a 2-jaw puller to the steering knuckle and center the puller's pressure bolt against the ball joint stud as shown in **Figure 75**.

   d. Tighten the puller to apply pressure against the ball joint stud, checking that the puller is not cocked to one side. When the ball joint stud is under pressure, strike the top of the puller with a hammer to free the ball joint from the steering knuckle (**Figure 76**).

> *NOTE*
> *If you are going to replace the outer tie rod ball joint, refer to **Tie Rod Disassembly/Reassembly** in this chapter.*

10

NOTE
*Prior to disconnecting the inner tie rod from the steering shaft, it is necessary to make room for the puller by removing the brake lines (**Figure 77**) from the frame mounting brackets as described in Step 3.*

3. To remove the brake lines:
   a. Push the spring clamp (**Figure 78**) away from the brake line and lift the brake line out of the mounting bracket. Do not disconnect the brake lines.
   b. Repeat for the opposite side.
   c. Carefully position the brake lines to make room for your puller when performing Step 4. Do not pinch or otherwise damage the brake lines.
4. To disconnect the tie rod ball joint from the steering shaft:
   a. Remove the cotter pin from the tie rod ball joint stud nut. Discard the cotter pin.
   b. Remove the castellated nut from the ball joint stud (**Figure 74**).

NOTE
When installing the puller, make sure you do not damage the ball joint rubber seal. If the angled arms on the puller are too thick, they can damage the seal.

   c. Attach a 2-jaw puller to the steering knuckle and center the puller's pressure bolt against the ball joint stud as shown in **Figure 79**.
   d. Tighten the puller to apply pressure against the ball joint stud, checking that the puller is not cocked to one side. Continue to apply pressure with the puller until the ball joint pops free from the steering shaft.
5. Remove the tie rod.

Inspection

NOTE
If you clean the tie rod with a solvent, work carefully to prevent the solvent from contaminating the grease in the rubber boot.

1. Inspect the tie rod shaft (A, **Figure 80**) for damage. There should be no creases or bends along the shaft. Check with a straightedge placed against the tie rod shaft.

2. Inspect the rubber boot at each end of the tie rod end swivel joint (**Figure 81**). The swivel joints are permanently packed with grease. If the rubber boot is damaged, dirt and moisture can enter the swivel joint and destroy it. If the boot is damaged in any way, disassemble the tie rod and replace the tie rod end(s). Refer to *Tie Rod Disassembly/Reassembly* in the following procedure.

3. Pivot the tie rod end (**Figure 81**) back and forth by hand. If the tie rod end moves roughly or with excessive play, replace it as described in the following procedure.

Tie Rod
Disassembly/Reassembly

Refer to **Figure 82** when performing this procedure.

1. Hold the tie rod with a wrench across the shaft flat (B, **Figure 80**) and loosen the locknut for the ball joint being replaced.

NOTE
The locknut securing the outside tie rod end (C, Figure 80) has left-hand threads. The inside tie rod end locknut (D, Figure 80) has right-hand threads.

2. Unscrew and remove the damaged tie rod end(s).
3. Clean mating shaft and tie rod end threads with contact cleaner.
4. Identify the new tie rod end with the drawing in **Figure 82**. The outside (E, **Figure 80**) and inside (F, **Figure 80**) tie rods are different. Likewise, the left- and right-hand tie rod shafts are different; the right-hand tie rod shaft is marked with a white paint mark as shown in **Figure 82**.
5. Thread the tie rod (with locknut) into the tie rod shaft.

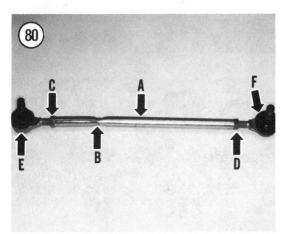

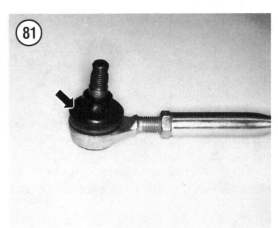

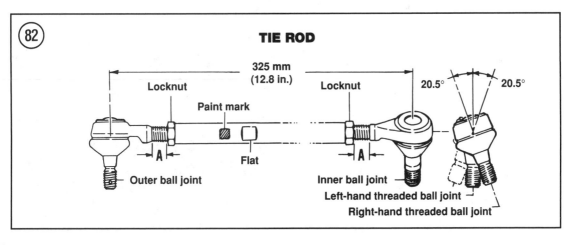

6. Adjust the tie rod length and position the ball joints as follows, referring to **Figure 82**:

  a. Adjust the tie rod ball joints to obtain the tie rod length measurement shown in **Figure 82**.

> *NOTE*
> *When adjusting the ball joints in the following steps, note that dimension A in **Figure 82** must be equal for both ends.*

  b. Align both ball joints, then continue with substep c.

  c. For the left-hand tie rod assembly, turn the right-hand threaded ball joint 20.5° counterclockwise form the left-hand threaded ball joint. For the right-hand tie rod assembly, turn the right-hand threaded ball joint 20.5° clockwise from the left-hand threaded ball joint. See **Figure 82**.

  d. Tighten the locknuts securely. Then check that dimension A in **Figure 82** is equal for both sides.

Installation

> *NOTE*
> *The left- and right-hand tie rod assemblies are different. The right-hand tie rod assembly has a white dot mark painted onto its shaft; see **Figure 82**.*

1. Position the tie rod assembly so the end with the flat on the shaft (**Figure 83**) is attached to the steering knuckle.

2. Attach the tie rod assembly to the steering shaft (**Figure 74**) and to the steering knuckle (**Figure 84**).

3. Thread the castellated nut onto each ball joint stud and tighten to the torque specification in **Table 4**. Tighten the nut(s), if necessary, to align the cotter pin hole with the nut slot.

4. Install new cotter pins through all ball joint studs. Open and bend the cotter pin arms to lock them in place.

5. Reposition the brake lines into the frame mounting brackets and secure with the spring locks as shown in **Figure 78**.

> *NOTE*
> *If you disconnected the brake line(s), you will have to bleed the brakes. Refer to **Brake Bleeding** in Chapter Twelve.*

6. Install the front wheels as described in this chapter.

7. Check the toe-in adjustment, and adjust if necessary, as described in Chapter Three.

STEERING SHAFT

Figure 70 and **Figure 71** are exploded views of the steering shaft and the components that are connected to it. The steering shaft pivots on split bearing blocks at the top and a bushing assembly (1987) or ball bearing (1988-on) at the lower end. Adjustable tie rods connect the steering shaft to the steering knuckle.

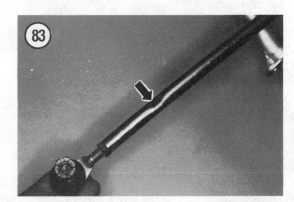

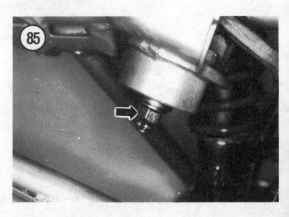

Removal

1. Remove the front fender assembly as described in Chapter Thirteen.

2. Remove both front wheels as described in this chapter.

> *CAUTION*
> *Cover the frame with a heavy cloth or plastic tarp to protect it from the acci-dental spilling of brake fluid. Wash any spilled brake fluid off any painted or plated surface immediately as it will destroy the finish. Use soapy water and rinse thoroughly.*

3. Loosen the bolts (**Figure 66**) that hold the handlebar to the steering shaft. Remove the bolts and upper handlebar holders.

4. Move the handlebar assembly back and off the steering shaft and place it on the frame. Keep the master cylinder in an upright position to minimize loss of brake fluid and to keep air from entering the brake system. It is not necessary to remove the hydraulic brake line from the master cylinder.

5. Disconnect both tie rods from the steering shaft as described under *Tie Rods* in this chapter.

6. Remove the cotter pin, nut and washer that secure the bottom of the steering shaft to the frame. See **Figure 85**, typical.

7. Make a diagram of the cables and wiring harnesses as they pass around the steering shaft for reassembly reference.

8. Pry the lockwasher tabs away from the bolts securing the upper bearing blocks to the frame.

9. Remove the bolts (**Figure 86**) that hold the upper bearing blocks to the frame. Then remove the outer block, collars, split dust seals and inner block assembly.

10. Carefully lift the steering shaft (**Figure 87**) out of the lower frame mount and remove it from the frame. On 1987 models, remove the 2 O-rings (17, **Figure 70**) from the lower frame mount.

Inspection

1. Wash all parts in solvent and dry thoroughly.

2. Inspect the steering shaft (**Figure 88**), especially if the vehicle has been involved in a collision or spill. If the shaft is bent or twisted in any way it must be replaced. If a damaged shaft is installed in the vehicle, it will cause rapid and excessive wear to the bearings as well as place undue stress on other components in the frame and steering system. If shaft straightness is questionable, check with set of V-blocks and dial indicator (**Figure 89**). Yamaha does not provide runout limits.

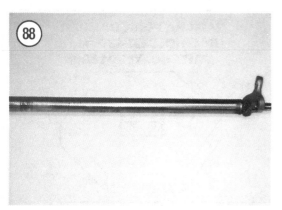

10

NOTE
Figure 90 *shows the type of damage that can occur to a bent steering shaft. The area where the upper bearing block rides (see arrow in **Figure 90**) is severely worn.*

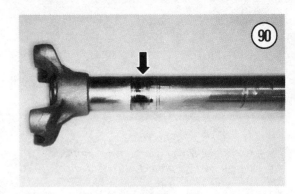

3. Inspect the tie rod attachment holes (A, **Figure 91**) in the lower section of the steering shaft. Check for hole elongation, cracks or wear. Replace the steering shaft if necessary.

4. Inspect the upper bearing assembly (**Figure 92**) for:

   a. Severely worn or damaged dust seals (A, **Figure 92**).

   b. Worn or damaged bearing block halves (B, **Figure 92**).

   c. Bent or damaged bolts and collars.

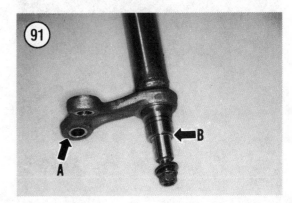

5. Inspect the lower steering shaft bushing (1987) or bearing (1988-on) surfaces; see B, **Figure 91**. If the machined surfaces are severely scored or damaged, replace the steering shaft and the bushing or bearing assembly.

6A. On 1987 models, inspect the steering shaft bushings (16, **Figure 70**). If the bushings are severely worn or damaged, replace both bushings as described later in this chapter. Inspect the steering shaft O-rings (17, **Figure 70**). If the O-rings are worn, flattened, cut or swollen, replace both O-rings during reassembly.

6B. On 1988-on models, inspect the steering bearing oil seals (17 and 21, **Figure 71**). If the oil seals are severely worn, leaking or damaged, replace both oil seals as described in this chapter.

6C. On 1988-on models, inspect the steering bearing (19, **Figure 71**) by turning its inner race with your finger. If the bearing turns roughly or has excessive play, replace the bearing as described in this chapter.

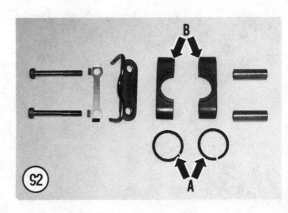

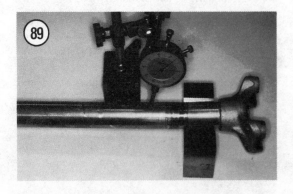

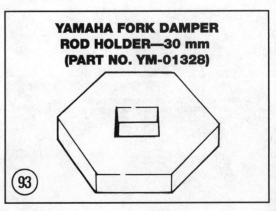

YAMAHA FORK DAMPER ROD HOLDER—30 mm (PART NO. YM-01328)

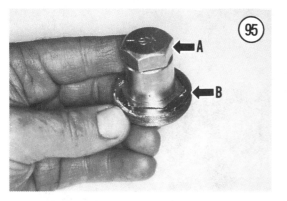

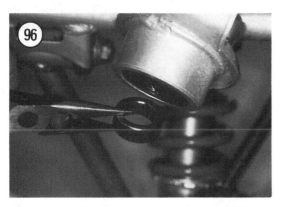

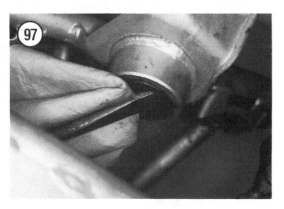

Steering Shaft Bushing Replacement
(1987)

These models are equipped with 2 bushings (16, **Figure 70**).

1. Carefully drive the upper and lower bushings out of the frame.

2. Clean the frame bushing mounting area thoroughly.

NOTE
The upper bushing and lower bushing are identical.

3. Install the upper and lower bushings into the frame. Due to the cramped working area, you can pull the bushings into place with some threaded rod, large washers and nuts. Pull the bushings into place until they bottom against the frame.

Steering Shaft Oil Seal and Bearing Replacement
(1988-on)

A 30 mm hex driver will be required to remove and install the bearing retainer in the following steps. You can use the Yamaha fork damper rod holder (part No. YM-01327 [**Figure 93**]) along with a ratchet and extension or you can make a tool with a 30 mm bolt or nut similar to the one shown in **Figure 94**. **Figure 95** shows how the tool (A) fits into the bearing retainer (B).

1. Remove the collar from the lower oil seal (**Figure 96**).

2. Pry the upper and lower oil seals out of the frame tube with a wide-blade screwdriver. Pad the screwdriver to avoid damaging the frame. See **Figure 97**. Discard both oil seals.

3. Use the 30 mm hex driver (**Figure 98**) and remove the bearing retainer that holds the bearing in

10

the frame. Then remove the tool and bearing retainer and lift out the bearing (**Figure 99**).

4. Clean the bearing retainer and collar in solvent and dry thoroughly.

5. Clean bearing retainer threads (**Figure 100**) in frame.

6. Place bearing in frame with manufacturer's name and size code facing up (**Figure 101**). Make sure bearing seats squarely in bore.

7. Thread the bearing retainer—shoulder side facing down (**Figure 102**)—into the frame. Hand tighten retainer against bearing (**Figure 103**). Torque bearing retainer to specification in **Table 4**.

8. Install upper and lower oil seals as follows:

   a. Upper oil seal (A, **Figure 104**) is larger than lower oil seal (B, **Figure 104**).

   b. Install both oil seals so that closed side faces out (away from bearing).

   c. Pack the lip of each oil seal with a waterproof grease prior to installation.

   d. Drive in the lower oil seal until its outer surface is flush with or slightly below the oil seal bore inside surface as shown in **Figure 105**.

   e. Install the upper oil seal with a piece of threaded rod, 2 large washers and 2 nuts (**Figure 106**). Assemble these pieces as shown in **Figure 107**

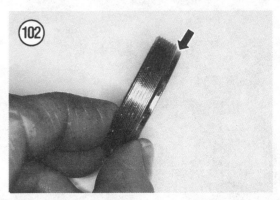

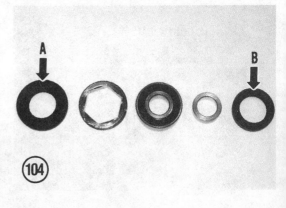

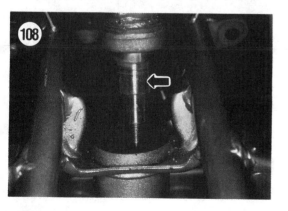

and press in the oil seal until its outer surface is flush with the oil seal bore inside surface. Hold lower nut and turn upper nut to install seal.

9. Insert the collar (**Figure 96**) into the lower oil seal.

Installation

1. On 1987 models, coat the 2 O-rings (17, **Figure 70**) with grease and install them into the frame. Make sure the O-rings are correctly seated. Then apply grease to both bushing inner diameters.

2. Apply a coat of grease to the steering shaft where it fits into the bushing or bearing assembly.

3. Install the steering shaft into the frame—with the tie rod brackets toward the back—and carefully align it with the lower bushing or bearing assembly. See **Figure 108**. Then turn steering shaft and insert into bushing or bearing until shaft bottoms. On 1988-on models, check that the collar is in place and did not drop out.

4. Loosely install the washer and nut (**Figure 109**) that holds the steering shaft to the frame.

5. Assemble and install the upper bearing assembly (**Figure 110**) as follows:

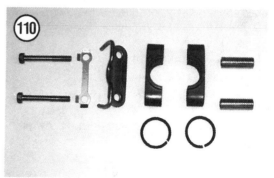

10

a. Grease the inner diameter of both bearing block halves.

b. Grease the dust seals and install them into one of the bearing block halves (**Figure 111**).

NOTE
The inner and outer bearing block halves are identical.

c. Install the inner bearing block between the frame and steering shaft, along with the dust seals, and align with the 2 frame mounting holes (**Figure 112**). Reposition the dust seals, if necessary, so that they sit flush in the bearing block grooves.

d. Install the outer bearing block, engaging the block grooves with the dust seals. Then align and install the 2 collars (**Figure 113**) through both bearing block halves until flush with the outer block.

e. Loosely install the bolts and the washers that hold the bearing block assembly to the frame (**Figure 114**).

f. Torque the steering shaft nut (**Figure 109**) to the specification in **Table 4**. Install a new cotter pin through the steering shaft hole. Bend the cotter pin arms around the steering shaft to lock it in place. After bending the cotter pin arms, make sure the cotter pin is a tight fit.

g. Torque the 2 steering shaft bearing block bolts to the specification in **Table 4**.

6. Turn the steering shaft from side to side. The steering shaft should turn smoothly with no binding, roughness or excessive play.

7. Bend the lockwasher tabs that secure the bearing block bolts (**Figure 114**) around the bolt heads.

8. Install the handlebar assembly onto the steering shaft and tighten as described under *Handlebar* in this chapter.

9. Connect both tie rods onto the steering shaft lower end as described in this chapter.

10. Install the front fender and seat as described in Chapter Thirteen.

11. Check toe-in as described in Chapter Three.

TIRES AND WHEELS

The vehicle is equipped with tubeless, low pressure tires designed specifically for off-road use only. Rapid tire wear will occur if the vehicle is ridden on paved surfaces. Due to their low pressure require-

ments, they should be inflated only with a hand-operated air pump instead of using an air compressor or the compressed air available at service stations.

CAUTION
*Do not overinflate the stock tires as they will be permanently distorted and damaged. If overinflated they will bulge out similar to an inner tube that is not within the constraints of a tire and **will not** return to their original contour.*

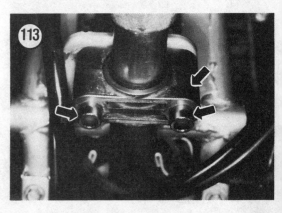

Additional inflation pressure in the stock tires will not improve the ride or the handling characteristics of the vehicle. For improved handling, aftermarket tires will have to be installed.

It's a good idea to carry a cold patch tire repair kit and hand held pump in the tow vehicle. Removing the tire from the rims is different than on a motorcycle or automobile wheel.

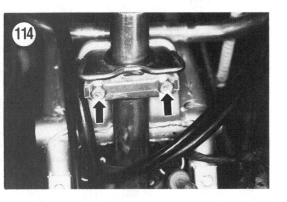

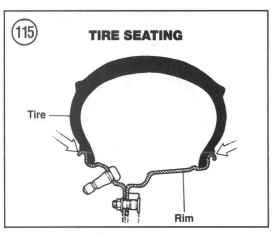

TIRE SEATING

Tire

Rim

CAUTION
Do not *use conventional motorcycle tire irons for tire removal as the tire sealing bead will be damaged when forced away from the rim flange.*

Tire Changing

The front and rear tire rims used on all models are of the 2-piece type and have a very deep built-in ridge (**Figure 115**) to keep the tire bead seated on the rim under severe riding conditions. Unfortunately it also tends to keep the tire on the rim during tire removal as well.

A special tool *is required* for tire changing on these models. A typical tool is shown in **Figure 116**.

1. Remove the valve stem cap and core and deflate the tire. Do not reinstall the core at this time.

2. Lubricate the tire bead and rim flanges with a liquid dish detergent or any rubber lubricant. Press the tire sidewall/bead down to allow the liquid to run into and around the bead area. Also apply lubricant to the area where the bead breaker arm will come in contact with the tire sidewall.

3. Position the wheel into the tire removal tool (**Figure 116**).

4. Slowly work the tire tool, making sure the tool is up against the inside of the rim, and break the tire bead away from the rim.

5. Using your hands, press down on the tire on either side of the tool and try to break the rest of the bead free from the rim.

6. If the rest of the tire bead cannot be broken loose, raise the tool, rotate the tire/rim assembly and repeat Steps 4 and 5 until the entire bead is broken loose from the rim.

7. Turn the wheel over and repeat to break the opposite loose.

8. Remove the tire rims from the tire.

9. Inspect the rim sealing surface of the rim. If the rim has been severely hit it will probably cause an air leak. Repair or replace the rim as required.

10. Inspect the tire for cuts, tears, abrasions or any other defects.

11. Clean the rims and tire sealing surfaces.

12. Inspect the large O-ring seal (**Figure 117**). If it is starting to harden or deteriorate replace it with a new one.

13. Set the tire into position on the outer rim.

10

14. Apply a light coat of grease to the large O-ring seal and place it in the groove in the rim (**Figure 117**).

15. Install the inner rim into the tire and onto the outer rim. Align the bolt holes.

16. Install the wheel onto its hub and install the lug nuts and washers. Tighten the lug nuts to the torque specification in **Table 4**.

17. Install the valve stem core.

18. Apply tire mounting lubricant to the tire bead and inflate the tire to the pressure value listed in **Table 3**.

19. Deflate the tire and let it sit for about one hour.

20. Inflate the tire to the recommended air pressure, refer to **Table 3**.

21. Check the rim line molded into the tire around the edge of the rim. It must be equally spaced all the way around. If the rim line spacing is not equal the tire bead is not properly seated. Deflate the tire and unseat the bead completely. Lubricate the bead and reinflate the tire.

22. Check for air leaks and install the valve cap.

Cold Patch Repair

This is the preferred method of patching a tire. The rubber plug type of repair is recommended only for an emergency repair, or until the tire can be patched correctly with the cold patch method.

Use the manufacturer's instructions for the tire repair kit you are going to use. If there are no instructions, use the following procedure.

1. Remove the tire as described in this chapter.

2. Prior to removing the object that punctured the tire, mark the location of the puncture with chalk or crayon on the outside of the tire.

3. On the inside of the tire, roughen the area around the hole slightly larger than the patch. Use the cap from the tire repair kit or pocket knife. Do not scrape too vigorously or you may cause additional damage.

4. Clean the area with a non-flammable solvent. Do not use an oil base solvent as it will leave a residue rendering the patch useless.

5. Apply a small amount of special cement to the puncture and spread it with your finger.

6. Allow the cement to dry until tacky—usually 30 seconds or so is sufficient.

7. Remove the backing from the patch.

CAUTION
Do not touch the newly exposed rubber with your fingers or the patch will not stick firmly.

8. Center the patch over the hole. Hold the patch firmly in place for about 30 seconds to allow the cement to dry. If you have a roller use it to help press the patch into place.

9. Dust the area with talcum powder.

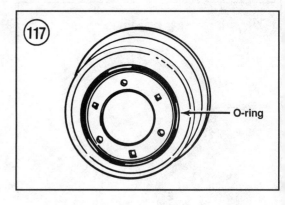

O-ring

Table 1 FRONT SUSPENSION AND STEERING GENERAL SPECIFICATIONS

Steering system	
Caster angle	7°
Trail	30 mm (1.2 in.)
Front suspension	Double wishbone
Front wheel travel	200 mm (7.9 in.)
Front shock absorber	
Type	Coil spring/oil damper type
Stroke	
1987-1988	88 mm (3.46 in.)
1989-on	90 mm (3.54 in.)
Shock absorber spring	
Free length	
1987-1989	236.5 mm (9.31 in.)
1990-on	224.0 mm (8.82 in.)
Spring rate/stroke	
1987-1989	4.0 kg/mm (224 lb.-in.)/0-45 mm (0-1.77 in.)
	4.5 kg/mm (252 lb.-in.)/45-108 mm (1.77-4.25 in.)
1990-on	4.0 kg/mm (224 lb.-in.)/0-109.5 mm (0-4.31 in.)

Table 2 TIRE AND WHEEL SPECIFICATIONS

Tires	
Type	Tubeless
Size	
Front	
1987-1989	AT21 × 8-10
1990-on	AT21 × 7-10
Rear	
1987-1989	AT22 × 11-9
1990-on	AT22 × 10-9
Wheels	
Type	Panel wheel
Material	Aluminum
Front rim size	10 × 6
Rear rim size	9 × 8.25
Rim runout	
Radial and lateral limit	2.0 mm (0.08 in.)

Table 3 TIRE INFLATION PRESSURE

	Standard psi (kPa)	Minimum psi (kPa)
Front		
1987-1989	4.3 (29)	3.8 (26.5)
1990-on	4.4 (30)	3.6 (25)
Rear		
1987-1989	3.6 (25)	3.1 (21.6)
1990-on	3.6 (25)	3.2 (22)

Table 4 TIGHTENING TORQUES

	N·m	ft.-lb.
Front wheel lug nuts	45	32
Axle nut (1)	85	61
Ball joint @ upper and lower arm		
1987	85	61
1988-on	—	—
Steering shaft bearing retainer @ frame		
1987	—	—
1988-on	40	29
Steering knuckle @ knuckle arm bolts (2)	38	27
Steering knuckle @ brake caliper bolt (3)	28	20
Disc brake @ front hub bolt	28	20
Ball joint @ steering knuckle nut	25	18
Ball joint @ knuckle arm nut	25	18
Ball joint @ steering shaft nut	25	18
Ball joint @ tie rod nut	30	22
Steering shaft nut	30	22
Upper handlebar holder bolt	20	14
Steering shaft bearing block @ frame	23	27
Upper & lower control arm @ frame	45	32
Front shock absorber bolts	45	32
Front bumper bolts	23	17
Front brake caliper mounting bolts	28	20
Front master cylinder mounting bolts	10	7.2

(1) M14 × 1.5 thread
(2) M10 × 1.25 thread
(3) M8 × 1.25 thread

REAR SUSPENSION

This chapter contains repair and replacement procedures for the rear wheel and hub and rear suspension components. Service to the rear suspension consists of periodically checking bolt tightness, lubrication of all pivot points, swing arm bushing replacement and rear shock service.

Rear suspension specifications are listed in **Table 1**. Drive chain size and link numbers are listed in **Table 2**. Tightening torques are listed in **Table 3**. **Tables 1-4** are found at the end of this chapter.

REAR WHEELS

Refer to **Figure 1** (1988) or **Figure 2** (1989-on) when servicing the rear wheel.

Removal

1. Park the vehicle on level ground and set the parking brake. Block the front wheels so that the vehicle will not roll in either direction.

2. Lift the vehicle so that both rear wheels are off the ground. Support the vehicle with jackstands or wood blocks.

3A. To remove the tire/wheel assembly only, remove the wheel nuts (A, **Figure 3**) that hold the rear wheel to the hub. Remove the reinforcement plate (1987) and tire/wheel assembly from the rear hub.

3B. To remove the tire/wheel and hub, remove the cotter pin, axle nut (B, **Figure 3**) and washer that hold the rear hub to the rear axle. Remove the tire/wheel and hub assembly from the rear axle.

4. Install by reversing these removal steps, noting the following.

5A. If only the tire/wheel reassembly was removed, perform the following:

    a. Place the tire/wheel assembly onto the rear hub studs.

    b. On 1987 models, install the reinforcement plate (27, **Figure 1**).

    c. Install the wheel nuts (A, **Figure 3**) that secure the rear wheel to the rear hub. Finger tighten the

11

nuts at first. Then torque to the specification in **Table 3**.

5B. If the tire/wheel assembly and the axle hub were removed, perform the following:

a. Slide the axle hub and wheel assembly onto the rear axle splines.

b. Install the washer and the axle nut (B, **Figure 3**) that secure the axle hub to the rear axle.

c. Torque the rear axle nut to the specification in **Table 3**. Tighten the nut, if necessary, to align the cotter pin hole with the nut slot.

d. Insert a new cotter pin through the nut groove and axle hole and then bend its arms around the nut to lock it; see **Figure 4**.

REAR AXLE

Figure 1 and **Figure 2** show the rear axle, brake disc and driven sprocket in relation to the rear axle housing. This section describes complete service to these components. Service to the axle housing is described later in this chapter.

The driven sprocket and rear brake disc can be removed with the rear axle installed on the vehicle.

On early models, ring nuts (**Figure 5**) were used to secure the rear axle to the axle housing. Late models are equipped with hex nuts (**Figure 6**). Replacement ring nuts are no longer available through Yamaha dealers. If ring nuts are ordered, the part number will be superseded and you will receive hex nuts. Because the ring nuts are difficult to remove

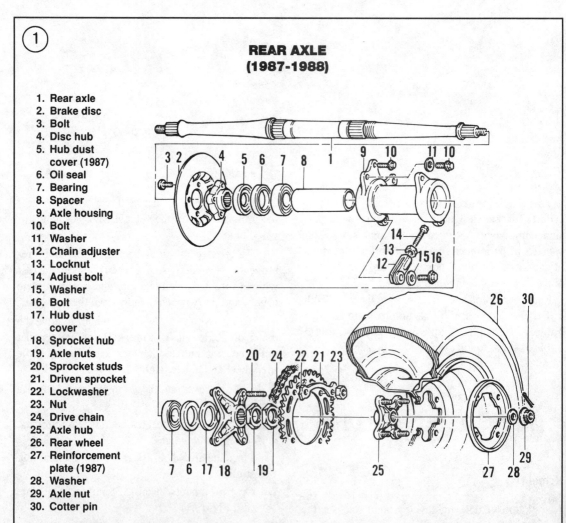

REAR AXLE (1987-1988)

1. Rear axle
2. Brake disc
3. Bolt
4. Disc hub
5. Hub dust cover (1987)
6. Oil seal
7. Bearing
8. Spacer
9. Axle housing
10. Bolt
11. Washer
12. Chain adjuster
13. Locknut
14. Adjust bolt
15. Washer
16. Bolt
17. Hub dust cover
18. Sprocket hub
19. Axle nuts
20. Sprocket studs
21. Driven sprocket
22. Lockwasher
23. Nut
24. Drive chain
25. Axle hub
26. Rear wheel
27. Reinforcement plate (1987)
28. Washer
29. Axle nut
30. Cotter pin

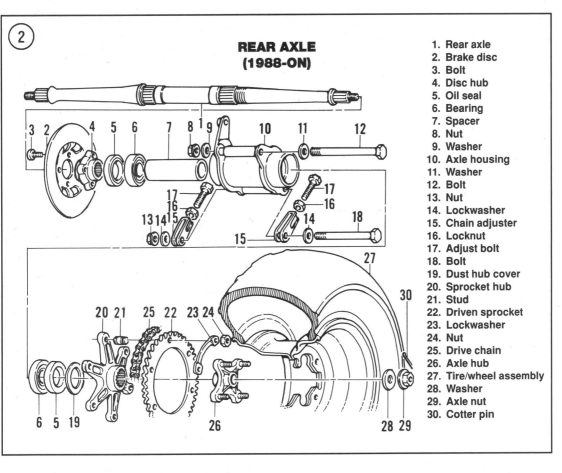

② **REAR AXLE (1988-ON)**

1. Rear axle
2. Brake disc
3. Bolt
4. Disc hub
5. Oil seal
6. Bearing
7. Spacer
8. Nut
9. Washer
10. Axle housing
11. Washer
12. Bolt
13. Nut
14. Lockwasher
15. Chain adjuster
16. Locknut
17. Adjust bolt
18. Bolt
19. Dust hub cover
20. Sprocket hub
21. Stud
22. Driven sprocket
23. Lockwasher
24. Nut
25. Drive chain
26. Axle hub
27. Tire/wheel assembly
28. Washer
29. Axle nut
30. Cotter pin

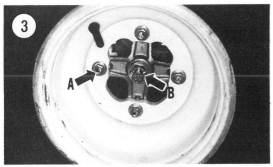

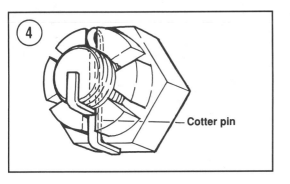

Cotter pin

11

and tighten, it suggested that you discard the ring nuts and install hex nuts during reassembly.

When removing and installing the rear axle, a special wrench will be required to loosen and tighten the axle housing nuts. Use the Yamaha axle nut wrench (part No. YM-37132 [**Figure 7**]) or an equivalent wrench that can be used with a torque wrench. Proper tightening of the axle housing nuts is critical in preventing the nuts from backing off and the axle from loosening in the housing.

To avoid starting a procedure that you may be unable to complete, read the following sections through before starting work. Note any tool that you may need and acquire it before starting.

Removal

1. Park the vehicle on level ground and set the parking brake. Shift transmission into 1st gear.
2. Support the vehicle and remove both rear wheels as described in this chapter.
3. Remove the axle hub from the axle as follows:
   a. Remove and discard the axle nut cotter pin.
   b. Loosen the nut (A, **Figure 8**) securing the axle hub to the rear axle. Then remove the nut and washer.
   c. Slide the axle hub (B, **Figure 8**) off the axle and remove it. If the axle hub is stuck, remove it with a puller as shown in **Figure 9**.

> *CAUTION*
> *The axle hub is designed to be a sliding fit on the axle. However, corrosion built up on the mating hub and axle splines (**Figure 10**) can make hub removal difficult. Do not drive the axle hub off of the axle with a hammer as the force may bend one of the hub arms. Use a puller as previously described.*

4. Remove the axle nuts from the axle as follows:

> *CAUTION*
> *The inner and outer axle nuts have had a thread locking compound applied to their threads during assembly and are tightened to a high torque valve (170 ft.-lb.[240 N•m]). The ring nuts are difficult to remove. Do not heat the axle nuts in order to remove them, as the heat may ruin the heat-treated hardness of the axle.*

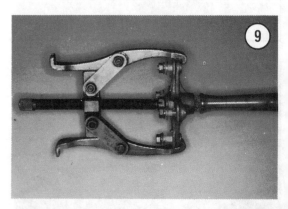

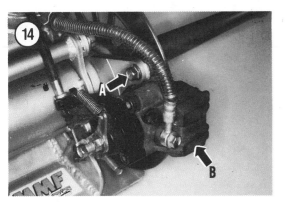

a. Clean the exposed axle threads with contact cleaner and dry with compressed air.

NOTE
Because the thread sealing compound applied to the axle nuts may spread to the sides of the nuts when they are tightened, hold the inner axle nut when loosening the outer axle nut.

WARNING
Safety glasses must be worn when removing the ring nuts with a punch and hammer.

b. On models with ring nuts, loosen and remove the outer ring nut with a large punch and hammer. Clean the exposed axle threads and then spray the axle threads with a penetrating lubricant (**Figure 11**).

c. On models with hex nuts, loosen and remove the outer nut with the Yamaha rear axle nut wrench (**Figure 12**) and a breaker bar. Clean the exposed axle threads (**Figure 13**) and then spray the axle threads with a penetrating lubricant.

d. Loosen and remove the inside axle nut.

5. Remove the drive chain as described in this chapter.

6. Release the parking brake at the handlebar.

7. Remove the bolts (A, **Figure 14**) holding the rear brake caliper to the axle housing. Then slide the brake caliper (B, **Figure 14**) off the brake disc. Make a hook out of a piece of stiff wire and hang the caliper from it so that weight is not placed on the brake hose.

NOTE
Insert a wood or plastic spacer in the caliper between the brake pads. That way, if the brake lever is inadvertently pressed, the piston will not be forced out of the caliper bore. If this does happen, the caliper will probably have to be partially disassembled to reseat the piston and the rear brake will have to be bled.

8. Slide the driven sprocket and its collar (**Figure 15**) off of the axle and remove it.

9. Drive the rear axle out of the axle housing as follows:

a. Make sure the vehicle is secured on a stand.

11

b. Slide the left-hand axle hub (A, **Figure 16**) onto the axle.

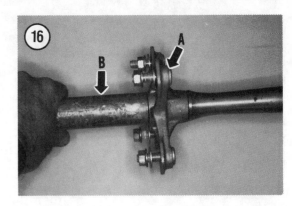

> *WARNING*
> *Safety glasses must be worn when driving the axle out in the following steps.*

> *CAUTION*
> *When removing the rear axle, never hit directly against the axle with a hammer as this will damage the axle. Use a piece of pipe as described in the following procedure.*

c. Center a piece of pipe against the axle hub as shown in B, **Figure 16**. Hammer against the pipe and drive the axle out of the bearing housing.

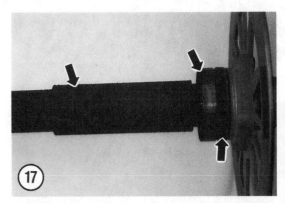

> *NOTE*
> *If the axle housing oil seals and bearings have not been properly serviced, the axle may be difficult to remove. What normally happens is that the center axle housing spacer (8, Figure 1) becomes rusted to the axle shaft. Then, when removing the axle, the spacer, rusted to the axle, forces the right-hand bearing and oil seal out of the axle housing. See Figure 17. If this happens, refer to Axle Disassembly to remove the spacer, bearing, oil seal and brake disc.*

d. When the axle is free of the axle housing, remove the left-hand axle hub (A, **Figure 16**) and carefully slide the axle out of the axle housing and remove it. See **Figure 18**.

e. Slide the brake disc assembly (**Figure 19**) off of the axle and remove it.

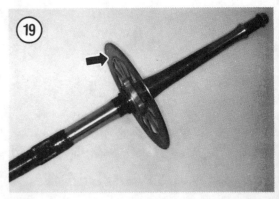

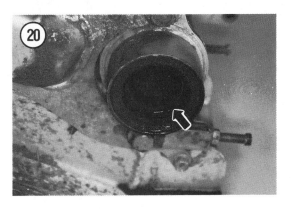

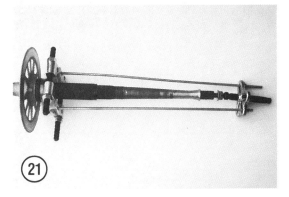

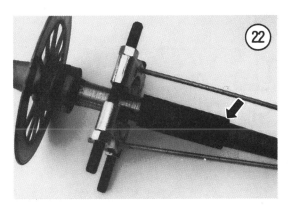

10. Inspect the axle housing oil seals (**Figure 20**) and bearings as described under *Rear Axle Housing* in this chapter.

11. Inspect the axle as described in this chapter.

Axle Disassembly

If the axle housing spacer, right-hand bearing and right-hand oil seal (**Figure 17**) came off with the axle when the axle was removed, remove them as follows:

1. Assemble a bearing splitter and puller onto the axle as shown in **Figure 21**. Then tighten the puller to pull the spacer (**Figure 22**) off of the axle and remove it.

> *CAUTION*
> *When pressing out the axle in Step 2, it will fall to the floor when the right-hand bearing is free of the axle. Support the axle so that it does not fall.*

2. Support the axle assembly in a press (**Figure 23**) and press the axle off of the right-hand bearing and the right-hand oil seal.

3. Remove the axle from the press and slide off the brake disc assembly.

Inspection

1. Wash the axle in solvent and dry thoroughly. Handle the axle carefully to avoid scoring the bearing surfaces and splines on the axle.

2. Inspect the axle for signs of fatigue, fractures and other damage. Inspect the splines (**Figure 24**) for wear or damage.

3. Check the hole at each end of the axle where the cotter pin fits. Make sure there are no fractures or

11

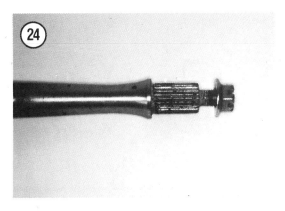

cracks leading out toward the end of the axle. If any are found, replace the axle.

4. Check the bearing machined surfaces (**Figure 25**) on the axle for scoring, cracks or other damage.

5. Check the axle for straightness using a set of V-blocks and a dial indicator as shown in **Figure 26**. Axle runout must not exceed 1.5 mm (0.06 in.). If axle runout is excessive, replace the axle.

> *WARNING*
> *Do not attempt to straighten a bent axle.*
> *Axle failure may occur during riding*
> *and cause loss of control and severe*
> *personal injury.*

6. Inspect the axle nuts (**Figure 27**) for wear or damage. Replace the axle nuts if the threads are damaged or if the hex portion of the nut is rounded over or damaged.

7. Inspect the driven sprocket hub (**Figure 28**) and brake disc hub (A, **Figure 29**) splines for severe wear or damage. Replace the hub(s) if necessary.

8. Inspect the dust hub cover (A, **Figure 30**) mounted on the driven sprocket hub. If the dust hub cover is loose, bent or cracked, replace it.

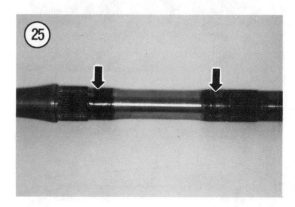

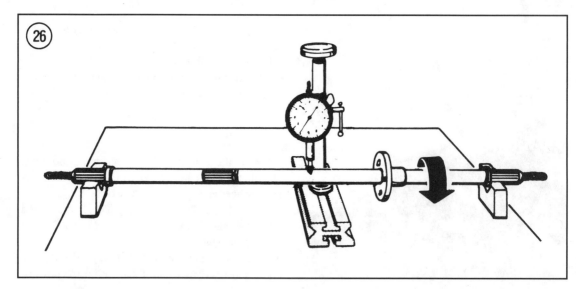

9. On 1987 models, inspect the hub dust cover (5, **Figure 1**) mounted inboard of the brake disc hub. If the hub dust cover is bent or cracked, replace the cover.

Installation

1. Apply a light coat of wheel bearing grease to the lips of both axle housing oil seals (**Figure 31**).
2. Apply a light coat of grease onto the brake disc hub shoulder (B, **Figure 29**). Then slide the brake disc hub onto the axle and seat it against the right-hand axle shoulder as shown in **Figure 32**.
3. Working from the right-hand side, slide the rear axle assembly into the axle housing until it stops (**Figure 33**).
4. Slide the right-hand wheel hub onto the end of the axle as shown in **Figure 34**.

> *WARNING*
> *Safety glasses must be worn when driving the axle into the axle housing in the following steps.*

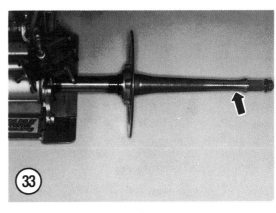

11

CAUTION
When installing the rear axle, never hit directly against the axle with a hammer as this will damage the axle. Use a piece of pipe as described in the following procedure.

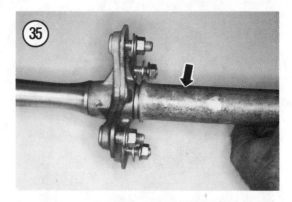

5. Center a piece of pipe against the axle hub as shown in **Figure 35**. Hammer against the pipe and drive the axle's left-hand bearing race through the right-hand bearing. Then stop and slide the axle inward until the right-hand axle bearing race (**Figure 36**) contacts the right-hand bearing. Then hammer against the pipe and drive the left- and right-hand axle bearing races into their respective bearings. Continue until the shoulder on the brake disc hub bottoms out against the right-hand bearing. See **Figure 37**.

6. Spin the axle by hand. It should turn smoothly with no roughness, binding or excessive noise.
7. Apply a light coat of wheel bearing grease onto the driven sprocket hub shoulder (B, **Figure 30**). Then slide the driven sprocket hub onto the axle splines (**Figure 38**) and push it into the axle housing until it bottoms. See **Figure 39**.
8. Remove the plastic spacer from between the brake pads in the brake caliper.
9. Slide the brake caliper (**Figure 40**) over the brake disc. Install the 2 bolts holding the brake caliper to the axle housing. Torque the brake caliper bolts to the specification in **Table 3**.

NOTE
To make sure the brake pads are seated against the brake disc, depress the brake pedal several times.

10. Set the parking brake.
11. Using the Yamaha rear axle nut wrench (YM-37132) and a torque wrench, tighten the rear axle nuts as follows:
   a. Apply Loctite 271 (red) to the threads on the rear axle.
   b. Install the inside nut (**Figure 41**) and tighten hand tight.

NOTE
The Yamaha rear axle nut wrench (YM-37132) or an equivalent tool will be required to tighten the rear axle nuts. Because the rear axle nut wrench is a horizontal adapter, it will effectively lengthen the torque wrench; the torque

value indicated on the torque wrench will not be the same amount of torque actually applied to the axle nuts. When using a torque wrench with a horizontal adapter, it is necessary to recalculate the torque readings. To calculate the amount of torque indicated at the torque wrench when applying a specific amount of torque to the axle nuts, you must know: The lever length of the torque wrench, the center-to-center length of the torque adapter, and the correct amount of actual torque desired at the axle nuts. **Figure 42** *shows how to do this. The actual torque readings for the inside and outside axle nuts are listed in the following steps.*

c. Using the information in **Figure 42**, determine the indicated torque valves for the following 3 torque specifications: (1) 55 N•m (40 ft.-lb.); (2) 190 N•m (140 ft.-lb.); and (3) 240 N•m (170 ft.-lb.).

d. Mount the rear axle nut wrench onto a torque wrench.

e. Tighten the inside axle nut to 55 N•m (40 ft.-lb.). See **Figure 43**.

NOTE
In **Figure 43**, *note how the axle nut wrench extends straight from the end of the torque wrench. This position is critical to ensure the accuracy of the computed torque reading. If the axle nut wrench is angled on the torque wrench, the torqued applied to the nut will be incorrect.*

11

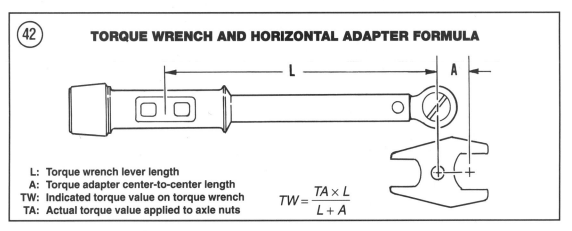

TORQUE WRENCH AND HORIZONTAL ADAPTER FORMULA

L

A

L: Torque wrench lever length
A: Torque adapter center-to-center length
TW: Indicated torque value on torque wrench
TA: Actual torque value applied to axle nuts

$$TW = \frac{TA \times L}{L + A}$$

f. Install the outside axle nut (A, **Figure 44**) and hand tighten it against the inside axle nut (B, **Figure 44**).

g. Hold the inside nut (B, **Figure 44**) and tighten the outside nut (A, **Figure 44**) to 190 N•m (140 ft.-lb.).

h. Draw a straight line across the inside and outside axle nuts as shown in **Figure 45**.

i. Hold the outside axle nut (A, **Figure 44**) and turn the inside axle nut (B, **Figure 44**) back—turn torque wrench counterclockwise—against

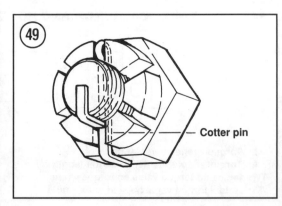

Cotter pin

the outside nut to a torque reading of 240 N•m (170 ft.-lb.).

j. Now measure the distance between the 2 straight lines made in sub-step h; see **Figure 46**. If the measured distance is less than 3 mm (0.12 in.), retighten the inside nut against the outside nut as described in sub-step i. Then remeasure the distance once again, and retighten as required to obtain a distance of 3 mm (0.12 in.). See **Figure 47**.

12. Install the drive chain as described in this chapter.

13. Slide the axle hub (**Figure 48**) onto the axle.

14. Install the large flat washer onto the axle shaft.

15. Hand-thread the axle nut onto the axle. Then tighten the axle nut (**Figure 48**) to the torque specification in **Table 3**. Tighten the axle nut, if necessary, to align the cotter pin hole with the nut slot.

WARNING
Always install a new cotter pin.

16. Insert the new cotter pin through the nut groove and rear axle hole and then bend its arms to lock it as shown in **Figure 49**.

17. Install the rear wheels as described in this chapter.

REAR AXLE HOUSING

The rear axle housing is bolted to the rear swing arm. Four bolts are used on 1987-1988 models. On 1989 and later models, 2 long bolts are used. These bolts are loosened during chain adjustment and should be checked periodically for looseness or damage.

The rear axle housing is equipped with 2 ball bearings, 2 oil seals and a center spacer. The bearings are pressed into the rear axle housing and should be installed with a hydraulic press and suitable bearing drivers.

Figure 50 and **Figure 51** shows the axle housing and its components in relationship to the rear axle and axle hub components.

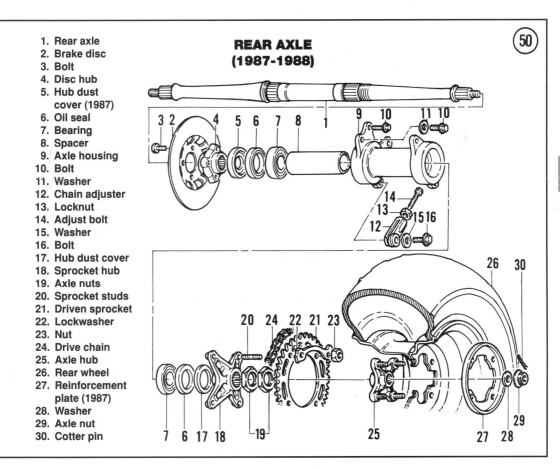

1. Rear axle
2. Brake disc
3. Bolt
4. Disc hub
5. Hub dust cover (1987)
6. Oil seal
7. Bearing
8. Spacer
9. Axle housing
10. Bolt
11. Washer
12. Chain adjuster
13. Locknut
14. Adjust bolt
15. Washer
16. Bolt
17. Hub dust cover
18. Sprocket hub
19. Axle nuts
20. Sprocket studs
21. Driven sprocket
22. Lockwasher
23. Nut
24. Drive chain
25. Axle hub
26. Rear wheel
27. Reinforcement plate (1987)
28. Washer
29. Axle nut
30. Cotter pin

REAR AXLE (1987-1988)

50

11

Bearing Preliminary Inspection

Before removing the rear axle housing, check the bearings as follows:

1. Remove the rear axle as described in this chapter.
2. Wipe off all excessive grease from both bearings.
3. Inspect each bearing (**Figure 52**) for visual damage. Check for overheating, a broken or cracked cage and corrosion. If the oil seals are damaged, moisture will have entered the axle housing, producing corrosion on the bearing, axle and center spacer.
4. Turn each bearing (**Figure 52**) by hand. The bearings should turn smoothly with no roughness, catching, binding or excessive noise. Some axial play (end play) is normal, but radial play (side play) should be negligible; see **Figure 53**.
5. Replace the bearings, if necessary, as described in this chapter.

Removal

1. Remove the rear axle as described in this chapter.

2. Remove the bolts and the washers that hold the rear axle housing to the rear swing arm; see **Figure 50** or **Figure 51**.

3. Slide the rear axle housing (**Figure 54**) away from the swing arm and remove it. Remove the 2 chain adjusters.

CAUTION
Double shielded bearings are used. Do not wash these bearings in solvent or any other chemical as the chemical may enter the bearing and contaminate the grease.

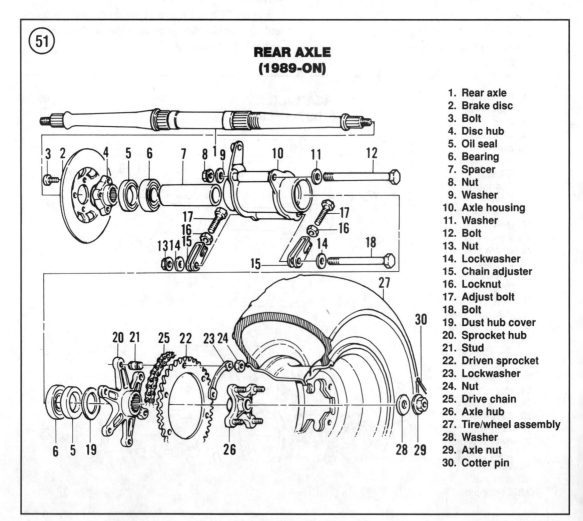

(51)

REAR AXLE
(1989-ON)

1. Rear axle
2. Brake disc
3. Bolt
4. Disc hub
5. Oil seal
6. Bearing
7. Spacer
8. Nut
9. Washer
10. Axle housing
11. Washer
12. Bolt
13. Nut
14. Lockwasher
15. Chain adjuster
16. Locknut
17. Adjust bolt
18. Bolt
19. Dust hub cover
20. Sprocket hub
21. Stud
22. Driven sprocket
23. Lockwasher
24. Nut
25. Drive chain
26. Axle hub
27. Tire/wheel assembly
28. Washer
29. Axle nut
30. Cotter pin

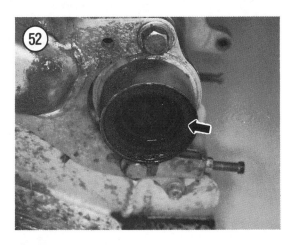

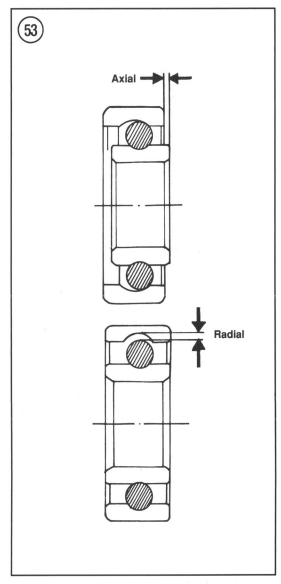

Axial

Radial

Disassembly

NOTE
*If the right-hand bearing and center spacer came off with the rear axle (**Figure 17**), remove them as described under **Axle Disassembly**; see **Rear Axle** in this chapter.*

1. Pry the oil seals out of the axle housing with a wide-blade screwdriver as shown in **Figure 55**. Pad the screwdriver to prevent it from damaging the axle housing bore.
2. Insert a drift into one side of the axle housing.
3. Push the center spacer over to one side and place the drift on the inner race of the opposite bearing.
4. Tap the bearing out of the hub with a hammer, working around the perimeter of the bearing's inner race to prevent the bearing from binding in the housing bore.
5. Remove the bearing and the center spacer.
6. Tap out the opposite bearing with a suitable driver inserted through the axle housing.

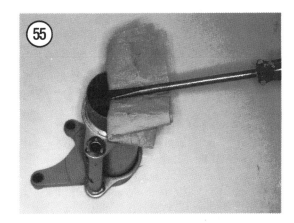

Inspection

1. Clean the axle housing in solvent and dry with compressed air.

2. Remove all corrosion and rust from the center spacer with a steel brush or a wire wheel mounted in a drill. Then clean the spacer and dry with compressed air.

3. Check the center spacer for cracks, distortion or other damage. Replace if necessary.

4. Check the axle housing bores (**Figure 56**) for cracks or other damage. Remove any burrs or nicks with a file or fine sandpaper.

> *NOTE*
> *If one or both bearings were loose in their respective housing bore, do not center punch or rough up the area to increase its bore size. Installing the bearing will flatten these areas, causing the bearing to run loose once again. If the axle housing bearing bores are severely worn or damaged, replace the axle housing.*

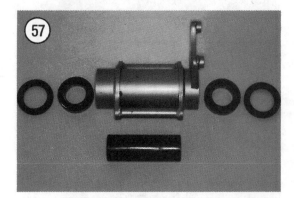

Reassembly

Single row, deep groove ball bearings (**Figure 57**) are used in the axle housing. Both bearings are double shielded. Prior to installing new bearings and oil seals, note the following:

   a. Install bearings with their manufacturer's code marks and numbers facing out.

   b. Install bearings by pressing them into axle housing with a socket or bearing driver that seats against the outer bearing race only.

   c. Install oil seals with their closed side facing out.

   d. Refer to *Ball Bearing Replacement* in Chapter One for additional information.

1. Blow any dirt or foreign matter out of the housing and out of the center hub spacer prior to installing the bearings.

2. Press in the first bearing until it bottoms in the axle housing bearing bore (**Figure 58**).

3. Turn the axle housing over and install the center spacer (A, **Figure 59**).

4. Press in the second bearing (B, **Figure 59**) until it bottoms in the axle housing bearing bore or just contacts the center spacer.

5. Remove the axle housing and check that both bearings (**Figure 60**A) turn smoothly.

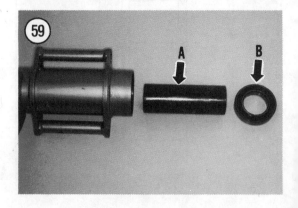

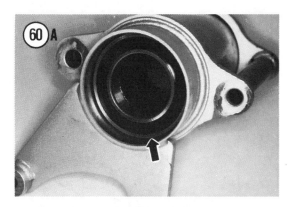

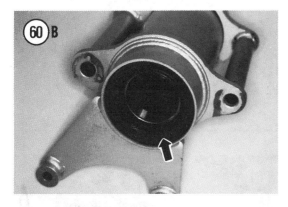

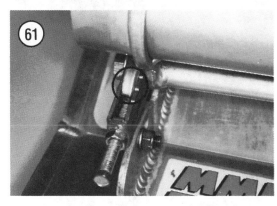

6. Pack the lip of each oil seal with a waterproof bearing grease.

7. Press in the first oil seal until its outer surface is flush with or slightly below the oil seal bore inside surface as shown in **Figure 60**B.

8. Repeat Step 7 to install the second oil seal.

Installation

1. Install the axle housing (**Figure 54**) into the swing arm.

2. Install the chain adjusters so that they are positioned between the swing arm and axle housing. Adjustment marks on chain adjusters must be facing up as shown in **Figure 61**.

3A. On 1987-1988 models, install the bolts and washers securing the axle housing to the swing arm as shown in **Figure 50**.

3B. On 1989-on models, install the 2 bolts, washers and nuts securing the axle housing to the swing arm. Install the bolts from the left-hand side (**Figure 62**).

4. Install the rear axle as described in this chapter.

5. Install the drive chain as described in this chapter.

6. Adjust the drive chain as described in Chapter Three. Then tighten the upper and lower bolts/nuts that secure the axle housing to the swing arm to the torque specification listed in **Table 3**.

DRIVE CHAIN

A 520 O-ring drive chain was originally installed on all models. O-ring drive chains are equipped with rubber O-rings between each side plate. The master link is equipped with 4 removable O-rings (**Figure 63**). O-ring chains are internally lubricated at the time of manufacture and assembly. The O-rings are designed to seal in the chains lubricant while keeping dirt and moisture out.

Table 2 lists drive chain specifications.

Removal/Installation

1. Support the vehicle with both rear wheels off the ground.

2. Turn the rear axle and drive chain until the master link is accessible.

3. Remove the master link spring clip with a pair of pliers.

4. Use a chain breaker to separate the side plate from the master link (**Figure 64**). Then remove the side plate and the 2 outside O-rings (**Figure 63**).

5. Push out the connecting link and remove the 2 inside O-rings (**Figure 63**).

6. Pull the drive chain off of the drive sprocket and remove it.

7. Install by reversing these removal steps while noting the following.

8. Assemble the drive chain and install the master link as follows:

    a. Install an O-ring on each connecting link pin (**Figure 63**).

    b. Insert the connecting link through the chain to join it together.

    c. Install the remaining 2 O-rings onto the connecting link pins (**Figure 63**).

    d. Push the side plate onto the connecting link as far as it will go. Then press the side plate into position with a press-fit chain tool like the one shown in **Figure 65**.

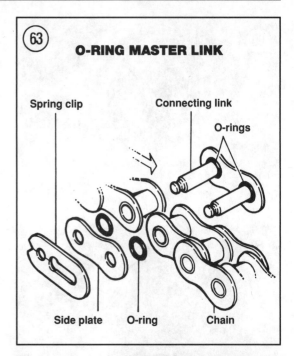

63

O-RING MASTER LINK

Spring clip   Connecting link

O-rings

Side plate   O-ring   Chain

NOTE
Most commercial press-fit chain tools are designed to press the side plate onto the connecting link to its correct depth. If the side plate is pressed on too far, it will bind the chain where it joins the master link. If the side plate is not pressed on far enough, the spring clip cannot be installed correctly and may come off. What you are looking to do is to press the side plate onto the connecting link so that the slide plate is flush with both pin seating grooves in the connecting link.

64

CAUTION
Attempting to assemble a press-fit master link without the proper tools may cause you to damage the master link and drive chain.

    e. Install the spring clip on the master link so that the closed end of the clip is facing the direction of chain travel (**Figure 66**).

9. Adjust the drive chain as described in Chapter Three.

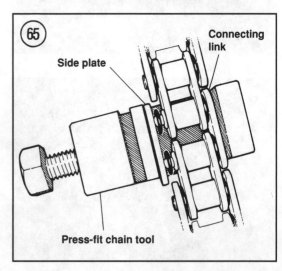

65

Connecting link

Side plate

Press-fit chain tool

Cutting A Drive Chain To Length

Table 2 lists the correct number of chain links required for stock gearing. If your replacement drive chain is too long, cut it to length as follows.

1. Remove the new chain from its box and stretch it out on your workbench. Set the master link aside for now.

2. Refer to **Table 2** for the correct number of links for your chain, then count the links out on the new chain. Make a chalk mark on the 2 chain pins where you want to cut it. Count the chain links one more time just to make sure you are correct.

WARNING
A bench grinder or hand-operated high-speed grinding tool will be required to grind the chain pins when cutting the chain. When using this equipment, safety glasses must be worn.

3. Grind the head of two pins flush with the face of the side plate with a grinder or suitable grinding tool.

4. Next, use a chain breaker or a punch and hammer and lightly tap the pins out of the side plate; support the chain carefully when doing this. If the pins are

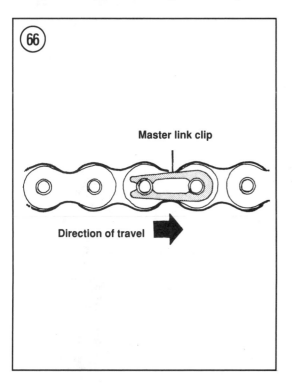

still tight, grind more material from the end of the pins and then try again.

5. Remove the side plate and push out the connecting link.

Drive Chain Cleaning/Lubrication

CAUTION
The O-rings can be easily damaged by improper cleaning and handling of the drive chain. Do not use a steam cleaner, a high-pressure washer or any solvent that may damage the rubber O-rings.

1. Remove the drive chain as described in this chapter.

2. Immerse the chain in a pan of kerosene and allow it so soak for about half an hour. Move it around and flex it during this period so that the dirt between the links, pins, rollers and O-rings may work its way out.

CAUTION
In the next step, do not use a wire brush to clean the chain or the O-rings will be damaged and the drive chain must be replaced.

3. Lightly scrub the rollers with a soft brush and rinse away loosened dirt. Do not scrub hard or use a hard brush as the O-rings may be damaged. Rinse the chain a couple of times in kerosene to make sure all dirt and grit are washed out. Hang the chain up over a pan and allow the chain to dry thoroughly.

4. After cleaning the chain, examine it carefully for wear or damage. Check the O-rings for damage. Replace the chain if necessary.

5. Externally lubricate the chain with SAE 30-50 weight motor oil or a good grade of chain lubricant (non-tacky) specifically formulated for O-ring chains, following the manufacturer's instructions.

CAUTION
Do not use a tacky chain lubricant on O-ring chains. Dirt and other abrasive materials that stick to the lubricant will grind away at the O-rings and damage them. Remember, an O-ring chain is pre-lubricated during its assembly at the factory. External oiling is only re-

quired to prevent chain rust and to keep the O-rings pliable.

DRIVEN SPROCKET

The driven sprocket rides on a hub that is mounted on the rear axle. The driven sprocket can be removed without having to remove the rear axle from the vehicle. See **Figure 50** or **Figure 51**.

Inspection

Check the sprocket teeth for severe wear, undercutting or other damage. If the sprocket is damaged, replace both sprockets and chain at the same time. Installing a new chain over severely worn or damaged sprockets will cause rapid chain wear.

Removal/Installation

1. Remove the left-hand axle hub as described under *Rear Axle* in this chapter.
2. Remove the drive chain as described under *Drive Chain* in this chapter.
3. Pry the lockwasher tabs away from the sprocket nuts. Then remove the nuts that hold the sprocket to the hub and remove the sprocket (**Figure 67**).
4. Install by reversing these steps, while noting the following.
5. Replace weak or damaged lockwashers.
6. One side of the sprocket is stamped with the number of teeth on the sprocket. Install the sprocket with the stamped side facing out.
7. Tighten the sprocket nuts securely. Then bend the lockwasher tabs over one nut flat to lock the nuts in position.

TIRE CHANGING AND TIRE REPAIRS

Refer to Chapter Ten.

SHOCK ABSORBER

All models use a single rear shock absorber and spring unit with a remote nitrogen gas/oil reservoir for better fade resistance.

Table 1 lists shock and spring specifications.

Rebound Damping Adjustment

Rebound damping affects the rate of speed at which the shock absorber is able to return to the fully extended position after compression. This adjustment will not affect the action of the shock absorber

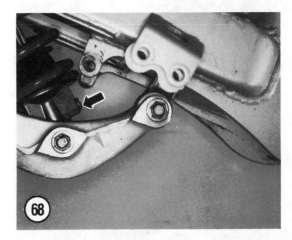

on compression. But if the rebound is too slow, the rear wheel may bottom on subsequent bumps.

Rebound damping can be adjusted to 20 different settings. The adjuster screw is located at the bottom of the shock absorber (**Figure 68**). A clicker adjuster is used; each click of the adjuster screw represents one adjustment change.

For the standard setting, turn the adjuster screw clockwise until it stops, then turn it counterclockwise the number of clicks (standard) listed in **Table 4**. When the standard setting has been set, the 2 index marks on the adjuster will line up. Repeat to set the minimum setting.

> *CAUTION*
> *Do not turn the adjuster screw more than 20 clicks counterclockwise from its fully turned in position.*

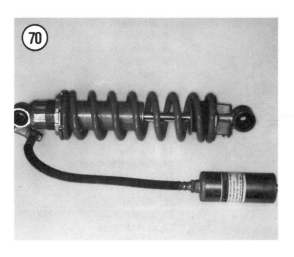

For the maximum setting, turn the adjuster screw clockwise until it stops.

To increase the rebound damping, turn the adjuster screw clockwise.

To decrease the rebound damping, turn the adjuster screw counterclockwise.

The rebound setting should be adjusted to personal preference to accommodate rider weight and operating conditions. Make sure the adjuster wheel is located in one of the detent positions and not in between any 2 settings.

Shock Spring Pre-load Adjustment

By varying the position of the spring adjuster on the shock body (**Figure 69**), spring pre-load can be changed to best suit rider weight and riding conditions.

Spring pre-load can be adjusted on all models. Initially, remove the shock as described in this chapter and measure the spring's installed length (**Figure 70**) on the shock absorber, then reinstall the shock. Write down the spring's installed length measurement so that you can refer to it when adjusting spring pre-load with the shock mounted on the vehicle.

1. Support the vehicle with both rear wheels off the ground.

2. Clean the threads at the top of the shock absorber (A, **Figure 71**).

> *NOTE*
> *Shock pre-load is adjusted by changing the position of the adjuster on the shock absorber.*

3. Measure the existing spring length (**Figure 70**) with a tape measure.

> *NOTE*
> *Use the spanner wrench provided in your owner's tool kit or a similar tool to turn the locknut and adjuster on the shock absorber.*

4. To adjust, loosen the locknut (B, **Figure 71**) and turn the adjuster (C, **Figure 71**) in the desired direction, making sure to maintain the spring length within the dimensions listed in **Table 1**. Tightening the adjust nut increases spring pre-load and loosening it decreases pre-load. One complete turn

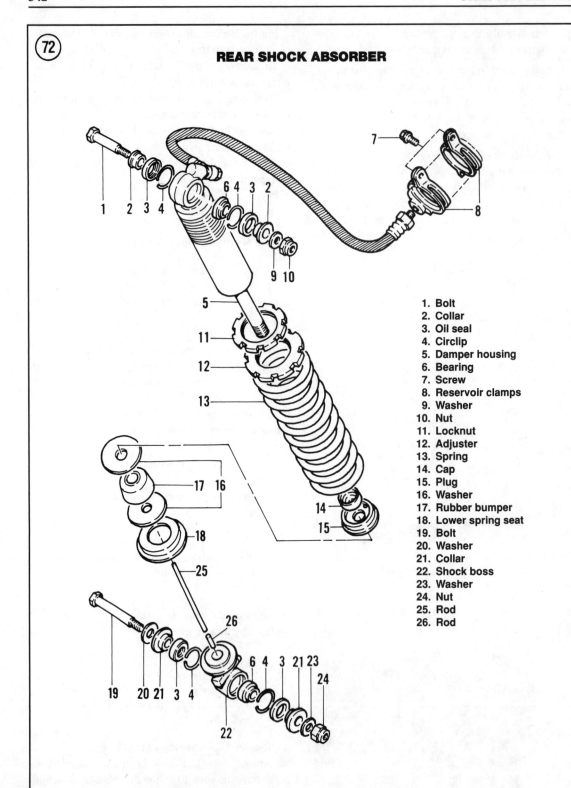

⑦

REAR SHOCK ABSORBER

7
8
6 4 3 2
1 2 3 4
9 10
5
11
12
13
14
15
17 16
18
25
26
19 20 21 3 4
6 4 3 21 23
24
22

1. Bolt
2. Collar
3. Oil seal
4. Circlip
5. Damper housing
6. Bearing
7. Screw
8. Reservoir clamps
9. Washer
10. Nut
11. Locknut
12. Adjuster
13. Spring
14. Cap
15. Plug
16. Washer
17. Rubber bumper
18. Lower spring seat
19. Bolt
20. Washer
21. Collar
22. Shock boss
23. Washer
24. Nut
25. Rod
26. Rod

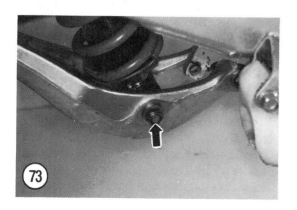

73

74

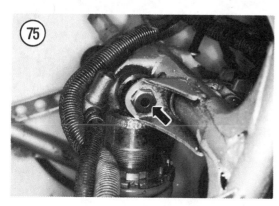

75

76

(360°) of the adjuster moves the spring 1.5 mm (1/16 in.).

5. After the desired spring pre-load is achieved, tighten the locknut to 54 N•m (39 ft.-lb.).

Nitrogen Pressure Adjustment

Refer all nitrogen pressure adjustment to a Yamaha dealer or suspension specialist. Maintain the nitrogen pressure within the specification listed in **Table 1**.

Shock Absorber
Removal/Installation

Refer to **Figure 72**.
1. Support the vehicle with both rear wheels off the ground.
2. Remove the nut, washers and bolt (**Figure 73**) that hold the lower end of the shock absorber to the relay arm.
3. Loosen the hose clamp bolts that secure the shock reservoir (**Figure 74**) to the frame clamps.
4. Remove the nut, washer and bolt (**Figure 75**) that hold the upper end of the shock absorber to the frame.
5. Slide the reservoir (**Figure 74**) through the clamps. Then remove the shock absorber/reservoir assembly from the vehicle.
6. Remove the collars (**Figure 76**) that are located on each side of the shock absorber bearings. Note that the upper and lower collars are different sizes.
7. Install by reversing these steps. Note the following.
8. Clean the shock bolts, nuts, washers and collars in solvent. Dry thoroughly.
9. Inspect and service the dust seals and shock bearings as described in this section.
10. Apply bearing grease to the shock bearings and collars. Then install a collar into each shock absorber oil seal.
11. Apply a light coat of bearing grease onto each shock absorber mounting bolt.

11

12. Position the upper end of the shock absorber in the frame so that the reservoir hose is positioned toward the back as shown in **Figure 75**. Then install the upper shock mounting bolt from the right-hand side. Install the washer and nut.

13. Position the lower end of the shock absorber in the relay arm (**Figure 73**). Then install the large washer on the lower shock mounting bolt and install the bolt from the right-hand side. Install the washer and nut.

14. When installing the reservoir, route the reservoir hose around the brake hose as shown in **Figure 75**.

15. Torque the upper and lower shock absorber mounting nuts to the torque specification in **Table 3**.

Dust Seal and Bearing Inspection/Replacement

The bearings are centered in the shock mounts and secured with a circlip on each side. Oil seals are installed on both sides of each bearing to protect the bearings from damage and dirt contamination. See **Figure 72**.

1. Remove the collar (**Figure 76**) from each oil seal.

2. Inspect the dust seals (A, **Figure 77**) for cracks, age deterioration or other damage. Replace if necessary.

3. Pivot the bearing with your hand. The bearing should pivot smoothly with no roughness or binding. Visually check the bearing for rust or other types of contamination.

4. To replace the bearing(s):

> *WARNING*
> *Safety glasses should be worn when removing and installing the bearing circlips in the following steps.*

  a. Pry the oil seals (A, **Figure 77**) out of the shock absorber.

  b. Remove the bearing circlips from both sides of the bearing. See 4, **Figure 72**.

  c. Support the shock absorber and press out the bearing.

  d. Clean the bearing mount thoroughly.

  e. Support the shock absorber and press in the new bearing. Center the bearing between the 2 circlip grooves.

  f. Install a circlip in the groove on each side of the bearing. Make sure each circlip is fully seated in its groove.

  g. Lubricate the bearing with bearing grease.

  h. Check that the bearing pivots smoothly.

  i. Repeat for the opposite bearing if necessary.

5. To install the rear shock absorber oil seals (B, **Figure 77**):

  a. Pack the lip of each oil seal with bearing grease prior to installation.

  b. Install the oil seals with their closed side facing out.

  c. Press in the oil seal until its outer surface is flush with the bearing bore inside surface as shown in B, **Figure 77**.

Shock Inspection

> *WARNING*
> *The shock absorber damper unit and remote reservoir contain nitrogen gas.*

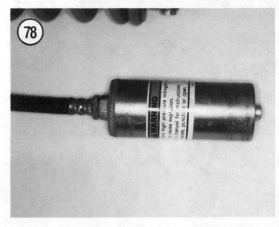

Do not tamper with or attempt to open the damper unit or disconnect the reservoir hose from either unit. Do not place it near an open flame or other extreme heat. Do not dispose of the damper assembly yourself. Take it to a dealer where it can be deactivated and disposed of properly. Never attempt to remove the valve core from the base of the reservoir. Read the WARNING label fixed to the reservoir (Figure 78).

1. Inspect the shock absorber (**Figure 70**) for gas and oil leaks.

2. Check the damper rod for bending, rust or other damage.

3. Check the reservoir for dents or other damage.

4. Remove and inspect the spring as described in the following procedure.

Spring
Removal/Installation

In addition to the standard shock spring, you can purchase replacement shock springs, from aftermarket suspension specialists, in a variety of spring rates. To replace a spring, perform the following.

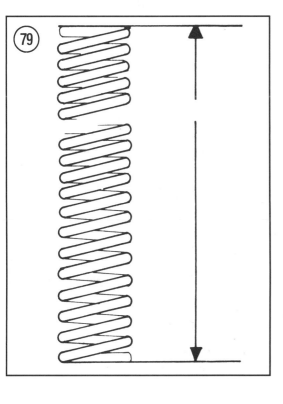

1. Remove the shock absorber as described in this chapter.

2. If you are satisfied with the existing spring pre-load setting and want to maintain it, measure and record the spring pre-load position as described under *Shock Spring Pre-load Adjustment* in this chapter.

3. Clean the shock threads (A, **Figure 71**).

4. Secure the shock absorber upper mount in a vise with soft jaws.

5. Loosen the spring locknut (B, **Figure 71**) with a spanner wrench and turn it all the way down. Then do the same for the adjust nut (C, **Figure 71**) to reduce spring pre-load. There should be no pre-load on the spring.

6. Slide the rubber shock bumper down the shock shaft.

7. Secure the spring with a shock spring tool and remove the spring retainer, spring seat and spring from the shock.

8. Measure spring free length with a tape measure or caliper (**Figure 79**). Replace the spring if it is appreciably shorter than the free length listed in **Table 1**. Yamaha does not list wear limits for spring free length.

9. Install by reversing these steps, while noting the following.

10. Install the spring, spring guide and spring retainer. Check that the spring guide and spring retainer seat flush against the spring.

11. Adjust the spring pre-load as described under *Shock Pre-load Adjustment* in this chapter.

SUSPENSION LINKAGE

11

Figure 80 shows the rear suspension linkage assembly. The relay arm is bolted to the frame, rear shock absorber and connecting rod. The connecting rod is bolted to the rear swing arm and relay arm. The relay arm and connecting rod pivot on solid bushings, steel collars and pivot bolts. Dust seals are mounted outside of each bushing to prevent the entry of dirt and moisture. Grease fittings are installed at each bushing position. For the rear swing arm and linkage assembly to operate properly, all pivot areas must be removed, cleaned and lubricated periodically.

Removal

1. Support the vehicle with both rear wheels off the ground.

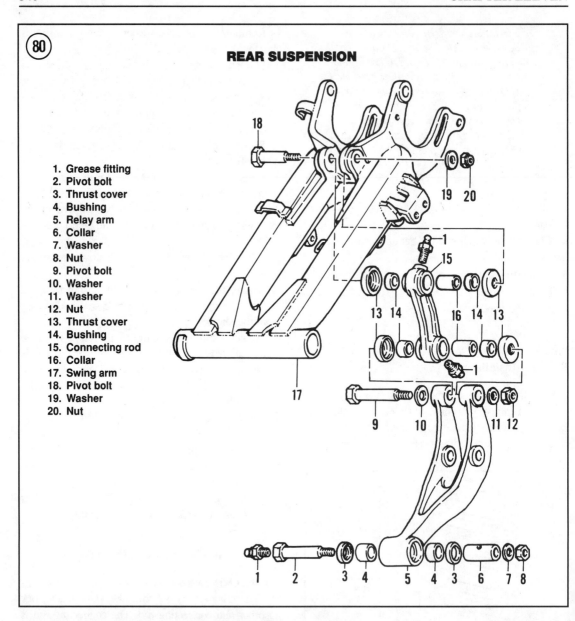

REAR SUSPENSION

1. Grease fitting
2. Pivot bolt
3. Thrust cover
4. Bushing
5. Relay arm
6. Collar
7. Washer
8. Nut
9. Pivot bolt
10. Washer
11. Washer
12. Nut
13. Thrust cover
14. Bushing
15. Connecting rod
16. Collar
17. Swing arm
18. Pivot bolt
19. Washer
20. Nut

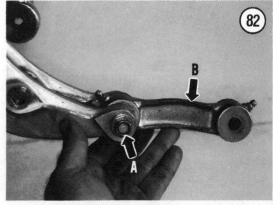

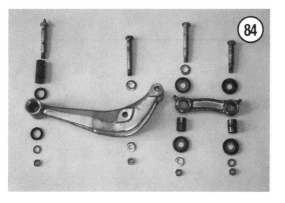

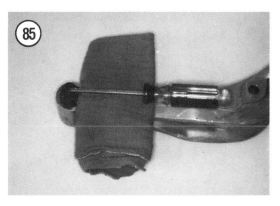

2. Remove the nut, washers and bolt (**Figure 73**) that hold the lower end of the shock absorber to the relay arm.

3. Remove the nut, washer and bolt (**Figure 81**) that hold the connecting rod to the rear swing arm. Then pull the connecting rod out of the rear swing arm mounting brackets.

4. Suspend the rear swing arm to the frame with a stiff wire hook or prop it up with wood blocks.

5. Remove the nut, washers and bolt (A, **Figure 82**) that hold the connecting rod to the relay arm. Then remove the connecting rod (B, **Figure 82**).

6. Remove the nut, washer and bolt (A, **Figure 83**) that hold the relay arm to the frame. Then remove the relay arm (B, **Figure 83**) from the frame.

7. Remove the rear swing arm, if necessary, as described later in this chapter.

Connecting Rod and Relay Arm
Disassembly/Inspection/Reassembly

Store the connecting rod and relay arm collars, bushings and pivot bolt assemblies in separate containers so that they can be installed in their original locations. See **Figure 80** and **Figure 84**.

1. Remove the dust seals from the connecting rod.

2. Prior to removing the collars from their bushings, turn each collar slowly with your fingers. Each collar should turn smoothly with no roughness or binding. If any roughness or binding is noted, examine the bushing and collars as described in the following steps.

3. Remove the connecting rod and relay arm collars.

4. Pry the oil seals out of the relay arm with a wide-blade screwdriver as shown in **Figure 85**. Pad the screwdriver to avoid damaging the relay arm bushing bore.

5. Wash parts in solvent and dry thoroughly with compressed air.

6. Check the pivot bolts and collars for scoring, cracks or severe wear. If the collars are severely worn or damaged, they should be replaced along with the bushings. Rusted pivot bolts can be cleaned with a wire wheel mounted in a drill. Replace scored or excessively worn pivot bolts.

7. Visually check the connecting rod (**Figure 86**) and relay arm (**Figure 87**) bushings for severe wear, looseness, cracks or other damage. Refer to *Bushing Replacement* in the following section.

8. Inspect the relay arm (**Figure 88**) for cracks, distortion or other damage. Check the rear shock

11

absorber and connecting rod pivot holes for cracks or other damage.

9. Inspect the connecting rod (**Figure 86**) for severe wear or damage.

10. To install the relay arm oil seals:

   a. Pack the lip of each oil seal with bearing grease prior to installation.

   b. Install the oil seals with their closed side facing out.

   c. Press in the oil seal until its outer surface is flush with the bushing bore inside surface as shown in **Figure 89**.

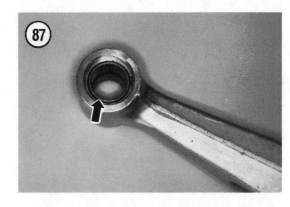

Bushing Replacement

If the connecting rod bushings (**Figure 86**) or the relay arm bushing (**Figure 87**) must be replaced, perform the following.

1. Purchase the replacement bushings prior to removing the damaged bushing(s).

2. Remove the 2 grease fittings install in the connecting rod; see **Figure 86**.

3. Support the connecting rod or relay arm in a press and press out the old bushing.

4. Clean the bushing bores and the replacement bushings in solvent. Dry with compressed air.

5. When replacing the connecting rod bushings, align the grease hole in the bushing with the hole in the connecting rod.

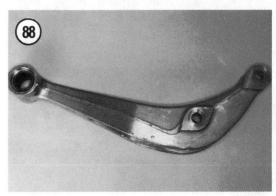

6A. Press in the connecting rod bushing until its outer surface is flush with the connecting rod bushing bore inside surface as shown in **Figure 86**. Repeat for the other bushing.

6B. Press in the relay arm bushing until its outer surface is flush with the relay arm bushing bore inside surface as shown in **Figure 87**.

7. Install the 2 connecting rod grease fittings (**Figure 86**).

8. Install the relay arm oil seals as described in the previous section.

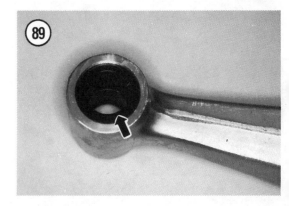

Installation

1. Lubricate the following components with bearing grease:

   a. Bushing inside diameters.

   b. Collars.

   c. Pivot bolt shafts.

2. Install the relay arm assembly (**Figure 90**) as follows:

   a. Install the collar into the relay arm bushing.

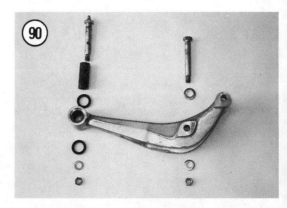

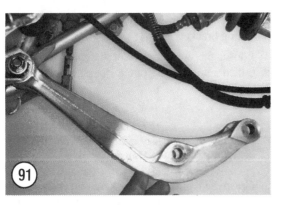

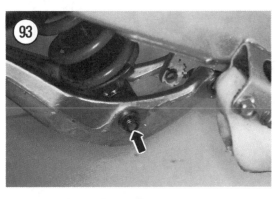

b. Position the relay arm between the frame mounting brackets as shown in **Figure 91**.

c. Install the front pivot bolt through the relay arm from the right-hand side. Then install the flat washer and nut. Torque the relay arm nut to the specification in **Table 3**.

d. Check that the relay arm pivots up and down smoothly.

3. Install the connecting rod assembly (**Figure 92**) onto the relay arm as follows:

a. Install the collars and dust seals onto the connecting rod.

b. Position the connecting rod between the relay arm as shown in **Figure 82**—the grease fittings must be facing up.

c. Install the pivot bolt and washer through the connecting rod from the right-hand side (**Figure 82**). Then install the flat washer and nut. Torque the connecting rod-to-relay arm pivot bolt to the specification in **Table 3**.

4. Pivot the connecting rod up and install it between the swing arm mounting brackets as shown in **Figure 81**. Install the pivot bolt through the connecting rod from the right-hand side. Then install the flat washer and nut. Torque the connecting rod-to-rear swing arm pivot bolt to the specification in **Table 3**.

5. Check that the 2 collars (**Figure 93**) are pushed into the shock absorber lower end.

6. Pivot the rear swing arm up and install the shock absorber lower end into the relay arm (**Figure 94**). Install the large washer on the lower shock pivot bolt and install the bolt from the right-hand side. Install the washer and nut and torque to the specification in **Table 3**.

7. Lower the vehicle so that both wheels contact the ground.

REAR SWING ARM

Figure 95 is an exploded view of the rear swing arm. Needle bearings are pressed into both sides of the swing arm. A center collar is installed between the needle bearings. Oil seals are installed on the outside of each needle bearing to prevent dirt and moisture from entering the bearings. Steel thrust covers are installed on the outside of each oil seal. A nylon chain roller is installed on the swing arm left-hand side to prevent the chain from damaging the swing arm. The hollow pivot shaft is installed through the swing arm from the right-hand side.

Plate washers—2.05 mm (0.081 in.) thick—are installed between the outer thrust covers and oil seals to maintain swing arm side play. Yamaha does not provide swing arm side play specifications or provide procedures on adjusting side play.

Swing Arm Bearing Inspection

The swing arm needle bearings and bushings should be inspected periodically for excessive play, roughness or damage.

1. Remove the rear axle as described in this chapter.
2. Remove the nut, washers and bolt (**Figure 73**) that hold the lower end of the shock absorber to the relay arm.
3. Remove the nut, washer and bolt (**Figure 81**) that hold the connecting rod to the rear swing arm. Then pull the connecting rod out of the rear swing arm mounting brackets.

4. Loosen the swing arm pivot shaft nut (11, **Figure 95**), then retorque the nut to the specification in **Table 3**.

NOTE
Have an assistant steady the vehicle when performing Step 5.

5. Grasp the rear end of the swing arm (**Figure 96**) and try to move it from side to side in a horizontal arc. There should be no noticeable side play.

6. Grasp the rear of the swing arm once again and pivot it up and down through its full travel. The swing arm should pivot smoothly with no roughness or binding.

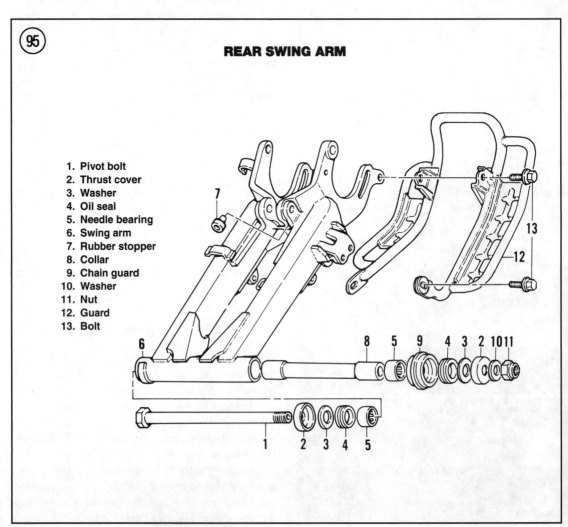

95

REAR SWING ARM

1. Pivot bolt
2. Thrust cover
3. Washer
4. Oil seal
5. Needle bearing
6. Swing arm
7. Rubber stopper
8. Collar
9. Chain guard
10. Washer
11. Nut
12. Guard
13. Bolt

7. If play is evident and the pivot bolt nut is tightened correctly, remove the swing arm and inspect the needle bearings as described in the following sections.

8. Reverse Steps 1-3 if you are not going to remove the swing arm. See **Table 3** for tightening torques.

Removal

1. Support the vehicle with both rear wheels off the ground.

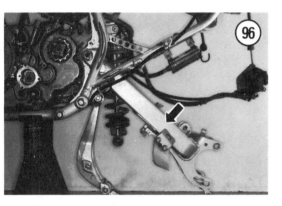

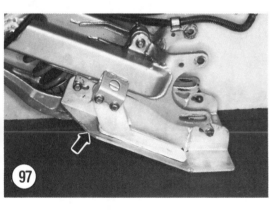

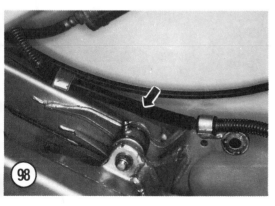

2. Remove the drive sprocket cover.

NOTE
You do not have to remove the rear axle from the axle housing when performing Step 3.

3. Remove the rear axle housing as described in this chapter.

4. Remove the bolts that hold the wheel hub cover (**Figure 97**) to the rear swing arm. Then remove the wheel hub cover.

5. Remove the nut, washers and bolt (**Figure 73**) that hold the lower end of the shock absorber to the relay arm.

6. Remove the nut, washer and bolt (**Figure 81**) that hold the connecting rod to the rear swing arm. Then pull the connecting rod out of the rear swing arm mounting brackets.

7. Suspend the rear swing arm to the frame with a stiff wire hook or prop it up with wood blocks.

8. Remove the nut, washers and bolt (A, **Figure 82**) that hold the connecting rod to the relay arm. Then remove the connecting rod (B, **Figure 82**).

9. Remove the nut, washer and bolt (A, **Figure 83**) that hold the relay arm to the frame. Then remove the relay arm (B, **Figure 83**) from the frame.

10. Remove the brake hose (**Figure 98**) from its guide clamps on the swing arm. Support the brake caliper with a heavy wire hook.

11. Loosen the swing arm pivot shaft nut (11, **Figure 95**). Then remove the nut and washer.

12. Remove the pivot bolt (1, **Figure 95**) from the right-hand side. If the pivot bolt is tight, tap it out with a brass or aluminum drift. Tap on the pivot bolt carefully, however, as you may damage the threads on the end of the bolt.

13. Pull back on the swing arm (**Figure 96**), free it from the frame and remove it.

14. If you are not going to remove the swing arm thrust cover and bearing assemblies, cover the left- and right-hand bearing assemblies with plastic bags. Secure the plastic bags with tape or lock ties. The bags will prevent the bearing assemblies from falling out.

11

Swing Arm
Disassembly/Inspection/Reassembly

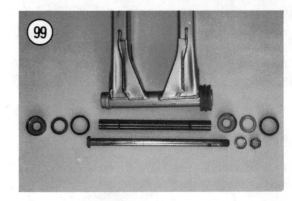

Store the left- and right-hand bearing assemblies in separate containers so that they can be installed in their original locations. Refer to **Figure 95**.

1. Remove the chain guide mounting bolts and remove the chain guide from the swing arm.

2. Remove the dust seals, plate washers and collar from the swing arm as shown in **Figure 99**. Do not remove the needle bearings from the swing arm.

3. Wash parts in solvent and dry thoroughly with compressed air.

4. Wipe off any excess grease from the needle bearings at each end of the swing arm. Needle bearing wear is difficult to measure. Turn each bearing (**Figure 100**) with your figure. The bearings should turn smoothly with no roughness or excessive play. Check the rollers for evidence of wear, pitting or rust. Then repeat with the collar installed in the swing arm.

5. Check the collar (8, **Figure 95**) for scoring, cracks or severe wear. If the collar is severely worn, replace the collar and bearings as a set.

6. Replace severely worn or damaged needle bearings as described under *Swing Arm Needle Bearing Replacement* in this chapter.

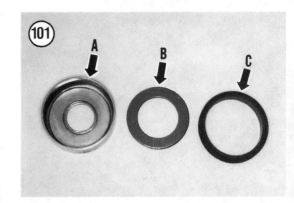

7. Check the outer dust covers and oil seals (**Figure 101**) for sever wear or damage.

8. Check the plate washers (3, **Figure 95**) for galling, cracks or other damage.

9. Replace the oil seals if severely worn or damaged. Install new seals when replacing bearings.

10. Replace the chain slider if severely worn or damaged.

11. Check the swing arm (**Figure 102**) for cracks, bending or other damage. Check the axle housing mounts for damage. Refer repair to a Yamaha dealer or welding shop or replace the swing arm.

12. Check for a bent, cracked or scored pivot bolt. Replace if necessary.

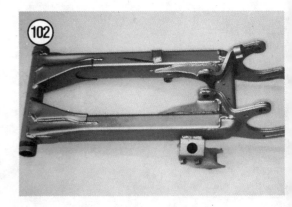

13. Lubricate the following parts with bearing grease prior to assembly.
   a. Needle bearings (**Figure 100**).
   b. Plate washers (3, **Figure 95**).
   c. Collar (8, **Figure 95**).
   d. Oil seals.

14. Slide the collar through the needle bearings in the swing arm.

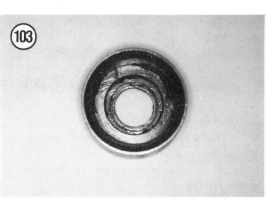

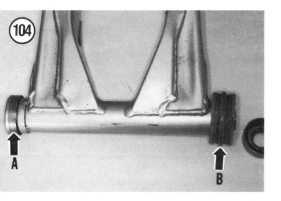

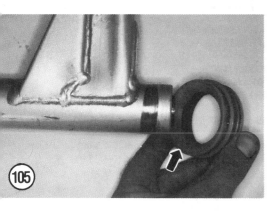

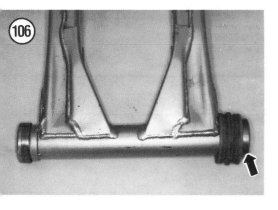

15. Install a plate washer (B, **Figure 101**) and oil seal (C, **Figure 101**) in its dust cover (A, **Figure 101**). See **Figure 103**. Repeat for the other side.

16. Install the right-hand dust cover assembly onto the swing arm; see A, **Figure 104**.

17. Install the chain guide–tapered bore facing inside (**Figure 105**)–onto the swing arm. See B, **Figure 104**.

18. Install the left-hand dust cover assembly onto the swing arm; see **Figure 106**.

19. Install the swing arm as described in this chapter.

Swing Arm
Needle Bearing Replacement

The swing arm needle bearings (**Figure 100**) should not be removed unless replace is required. When replacing the bearings, refer to **Figure 95**.

Replace both needle bearings at the same time.

1. Remove the collar (8, **Figure 95**) from the swing arm.

2. Support the swing arm and press out the old bearing.

3. Clean the bearing bore in solvent and dry thoroughly. Remove all corrosion from the bore as required.

4. Pack the bearings with a waterproof bearing grease prior to installation.

5. Wipe the outside of the bearing with grease prior to installation.

6. To install the needle bearings:
   a. Install bearings with their manufacturer's name and size code facing out.
   b. Press in the bearing until it bottoms in the bearing bore.

7. Apply grease onto the collar and slide it into the swing arm.

Installation

1. Assemble the swing arm collar and dust cover assemblies as described in the previous section.

2. Lubricate the pivot bolt with waterproof grease.

3. Position the swing arm between the frame and engine. Then install the pivot shaft from the left-hand side.

4. Install the swing arm washer and nut. Torque the pivot shaft nut to the specifications in **Table 3**.

11

5. Perform the *Swing Arm Bearing Inspection* check in this chapter.

6. Install the hub cover (**Figure 97**) onto the swing arm. Then install and tighten the hub cover mounting bolts securely.

7. Install the relay arm and connecting rod onto the swing arm as described under *Suspension Linkage* in this chapter.

8. Install the rear shock absorber lower end onto the relay arm as described under *Suspension Linkage* in this chapter.

9. Install the rear axle housing onto the rear swing arm as described in this chapter.

10. Reconnect the drive chain as described in this chapter.

11. Adjust the drive chain as described in Chapter Three.

12. Install the drive sprocket cover onto the engine.

13. Install the rear brake hose onto the rear swing arm as shown in **Figure 98**.

14. Install the rear brake caliper as described in Chapter Twelve.

Table 1 REAR SUSPENSION GENERAL SPECIFICATIONS

Rear suspension	Swing arm
Rear wheel travel	200 mm (7.9 in.)
Rear shock absorber	
Type	Coil spring, gas/oil damper type
Stroke	
1987	92 mm (3.62 in.)
1988-on	88 mm (3.46 in.)
Enclosed nitrogen pressure	
Standard	1,176 kPa (170 psi)
Minimum	784 kPa (114 psi)
Maximum	1,569 kPa (227 psi)
Rear shock absorber spring	
Free length	240.5 mm (9.47 in.)
Spring rate/stroke	
1987	5.5 kg/mm (308 lb.-in.)/0-112 mm (0-4.4 in.)
1988-on	5.5 kg/mm (308 lb.-in.)/0-108 mm (0-4.25 in.)
Installed spring length	
1987-1989	
Standard	228.5 mm (9.0 in.)
Minimum	220.5 mm (8.67 in.)
Maximum	235.5 mm (9.27 in.)
1990-on	
Standard	227.5 mm (8.96 in.)
Minimum	220.5 mm (8.67 in.)
Maximum	235.5 mm (9.27 in.)

Table 2 DRIVE CHAIN SPECIFICATIONS

Size	520
Number of links	
1987-1989	100
1990-on	98
Chain free play	30-40 mm (1.18-1.57 in.)

Table 3 TIGHTENING TORQUES

	N•m	ft.-lb.
Swing arm pivot shaft nut	85	61
Rear shock absorber bolts	32	23
Relay arm		
@ frame bolt/nut	48	35
@ connecting rod bolt/nut	32	23
Connecting rod @ swing arm	48	35
Footpeg @ frame bolt	55	40
Rear axle housing		
Upper bolts		
1987	100	72
1988-on	120	85
Lower bolts		
1987	50	36
1988-on	60	43
Rear bumper bolt	23	17
Rear wheel nuts	45	32
Rear axle @hub nut	120	85
Rear brake caliper mounting bolts	23	17

Table 4 REAR SHOCK REBOUND DAMPING ADJUSTMENT

	Clicks
1987-1989	
Standard	15 clicks out
Minimum	20 clicks out
Maximum	0 clicks out
1990-on	
Standard	12 clicks out
Minimum	20 clicks out
Maximum	0 clicks out

11

CHAPTER TWELVE

BRAKES

This chapter describes service procedures for the front and rear disc brakes.

Brake specifications are listed in **Tables 1-3** at the end of this chapter.

DISC BRAKE

The front and rear disc brakes are actuated by hydraulic fluid and controlled by a hand or foot lever on the master cylinder. As the brake pads wear, the brake fluid level drops in the reservoir and automatically adjusts for wear.

When working on hydraulic brake systems, it is necessary that the work area and all tools be absolutely clean. Any tiny particles of foreign matter and grit in the caliper assembly or master cylinder can damage the components.

Consider the following when servicing the disc brakes.

1. Use only DOT 4 brake fluid from a sealed container.

2. Do not allow disc brake fluid to contact any plastic parts or painted surfaces as damage will result.

3. Always keep the master cylinder reservoir and spare cans of brake fluid closed to prevent dust or moisture from entering. This would result in brake fluid contamination and brake problems.

4. Use only disc brake fluid (DOT 4) to wash rubber parts. Never clean these components with solvent or any other petroleum base cleaners.

5. Whenever *any* component has been removed from the brake system the system is considered "opened" and must be bled to remove air bubbles. Also, if the brake feels "spongy," this usually means there are air bubbles in the system and it must be bled. For safe brake operation, refer to *Brake Bleeding* in this chapter for complete details.

CAUTION
Disc brake components rarely require disassembly, so do not disassemble unless absolutely necessary. Do not use solvents of any kind on the brake system's internal components. Solvents will cause the seals to swell and distort. When disassembling and cleaning brake components (except brake pads) use new DOT 4 brake fluid.

CAUTION
Never reuse brake fluid. Contaminated brake fluid can cause brake failure. Dispose of brake fluid according to local EPA regulations.

FRONT BRAKE CALIPER
(1987-1988)

Refer to **Figure 1** when replacing the front brake pads or servicing the front brake caliper.

Front Brake Pad Replacement

There is no recommended time interval for changing the friction pads in the front brakes. Pad wear depends greatly on riding habits and conditions.

To maintain an even brake pressure on the disc always replace both pads in both calipers at the same time.

1. Read the information listed under *Disc Brake* in this chapter.

2. Remove the front wheel as described in Chapter Ten.

3. Remove the brake caliper mounting bolt (**Figure 2**) and pivot the caliper housing off of the brake pads (**Figure 3**). Slide the caliper off of its pivot bolt and secure it with a bungee cord.

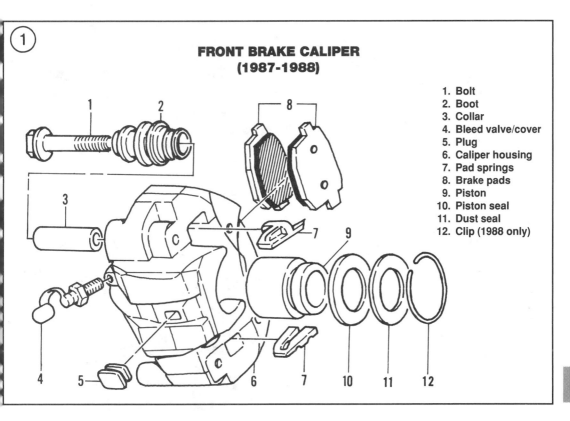

FRONT BRAKE CALIPER
(1987-1988)

1. Bolt
2. Boot
3. Collar
4. Bleed valve/cover
5. Plug
6. Caliper housing
7. Pad springs
8. Brake pads
9. Piston
10. Piston seal
11. Dust seal
12. Clip (1988 only)

12

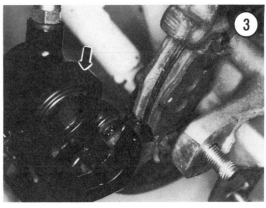

NOTE
If the pads are to be reused, handle them carefully to prevent grease contamination.

4. Slide each brake pad (**Figure 4**) outward and remove them from the caliper.

5. Check the upper and lower pad springs (**Figure 5**), mounted on the caliper arm, for damage. Replace the pad springs, if necessary.

6. Measure the thickness of each brake pad (**Figure 6**). Replace the brake pads if the thickness of any one pad meets or is less than the service limit in **Table 1**. Replace both brake pads as a set.

7. Inspect the brake pads for uneven wear, damage or grease contamination. Replace the pads as a set, if necessary.

8. Check the piston and seals as follows:
   a. Check the dust seal (**Figure 3**) for severe wear or damage.
   b. Check the end of the piston for fluid leakage. If the dust seal is damaged and/or if there is fluid leakage, overhaul the brake caliper as described in this chapter.

9. Check the brake disc for wear as described in this chapter.

10. To make room for the new pads, the piston (**Figure 3**) must be pushed back into the caliper. This will force brake fluid to backup through the hose and fill the master cylinder reservoir. To prevent the reservoir from overflowing, remove some of the brake fluid as follows:
   a. Clean the top of the master cylinder of all dirt.
   b. Remove the cap and diaphragm from the master cylinder.
   c. Temporarily install the inside brake pad into the caliper and slowly push the piston back into the caliper.
   d. Constantly check the reservoir to make sure brake fluid does not overflow. Siphon fluid, if necessary, before it overflows.

WARNING
Brake fluid is poisonous. Do not siphon with your mouth.

   e. The caliper piston should move freely. If not, the caliper should be removed and overhauled as described in this chapter.
   f. Push the caliper piston in all the way to allow room for the new pads.

g. Remove the inside pad.

11. Install the upper and lower pad springs (**Figure 5**) onto the caliper bracket.

12. Install the brake pads as follows:
   a. Install both brake pads with their round side (**Figure 7**) facing *forward*.
   b. Align the brake pads with the caliper bracket slots and push the pads into place (**Figure 4**).
   c. Check that the pads seat against the pad springs as shown in **Figure 8**.

13. Slide the caliper onto the pivot bolt (**Figure 3**), then pivot the caliper over the brake pads.

14. Install the caliper mounting bolt (**Figure 2**) and tighten to the torque specification in **Table 3**.

15. Repeat for the other brake caliper.

WARNING
Use new brake fluid clearly marked DOT 4 from a sealed container.

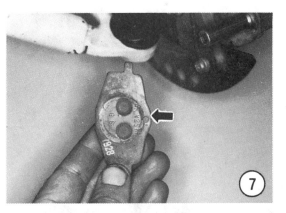

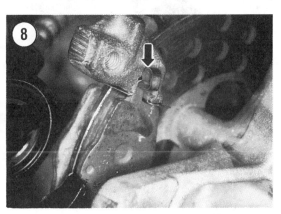

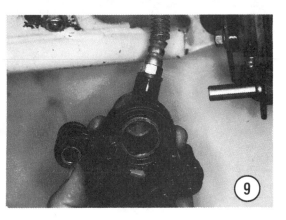

16. Pull and release the brake lever a few times to seat the pads against each disc, then recheck the brake fluid level in the reservoir. If necessary, add fresh DOT 4 brake fluid.

17. Install the master cylinder reservoir diaphragm and top cover. Tighten the cover screws securely.

18. Install the front wheels as described in Chapter Ten.

WARNING
Do not ride the vehicle until you are sure that both front brakes are operating correctly with full hydraulic advantage. If necessary, bleed the front brakes as described in this chapter.

**Removal/Installation
(Caliper Will Not Be Disassembled)**

If the brake caliper is to be removed without disassembling it, perform this procedure. If the caliper is to be disassembled, refer to *Caliper Removal/Piston Removal* in this section.

1. Remove the front wheel(s) as described in this chapter.

2A. If the caliper is to be completely removed from the vehicle, perform the following:

  a. Loosen the brake hose at the caliper.

  b. Remove the brake caliper mounting bolt (**Figure 2**) and pivot the caliper housing off of the brake pads (**Figure 3**). Slide the caliper off of its pivot bolt and secure it with a bungee cord.

  c. Hold the brake hose and turn the caliper to remove it from the brake hose (**Figure 9**). Remove the washer (**Figure 9**).

  d. Place the end of the brake hose in a container to prevent brake fluid from dripping onto the vehicle.

  e. Place the caliper in a plastic bag and tie the bag closed. Position the caliper so that brake fluid cannot run down the side of the caliper and contaminate the pads.

2B. If the caliper is only being partially removed and it is not necessary to disconnect the brake line at the caliper, perform the following:

  a. Remove the brake caliper mounting bolt (**Figure 2**) and pivot the caliper housing off of the brake pads (**Figure 3**). Slide the caliper off of its pivot bolt and secure it with a bungee cord.

12

b. Insert a wooden or plastic spacer block in the caliper between the brake pads.

NOTE
The spacer block prevents the piston from being forced out of the caliper if the brake lever is squeezed while the caliper is removed from the brake disc. If the brake lever is squeezed, the piston will be forced out. If this happens, the caliper will have to be disassembled and then reassembled to properly reseat the piston. Bleeding the system will also be required.

c. Support the caliper with a bungee cord or a wire hook. Do not allow the caliper to hang by its hose.

3. Install the caliper by reversing these steps, while noting the following.

4A. If the caliper was removed from the vehicle:
  a. Remove the caliper from the bag and check that the brake pads were not contaminated with brake fluid.
  b. Install the washer (**Figure 10**) onto the brake hose. Then hold the brake hose and thread the caliper onto it. Tighten the caliper hand-tight.
  c. Slide the caliper onto the pivot bolt (**Figure 3**), then pivot the caliper over the brake pads.
  d. Install the caliper mounting bolt (**Figure 2**) and tighten to the torque specification in **Table 3**.
  e. Tighten the brake hose securely.
  f. Refill the master cylinder and bleed both front brakes as described in this chapter.

4B. If the caliper was only partially removed from the vehicle:
  a. Remove the spacer block from between the brake pads.
  b. Disconnect the caliper from its hanger.
  c. Slide the caliper onto the pivot bolt (**Figure 3**), then pivot the caliper over the brake pads.
  d. Install the caliper mounting bolt (**Figure 2**) and tighten to the torque specification in **Table 3**.
  e. Operate the brake lever a few times to seat the pads against the brake disc.

WARNING
Do not ride the vehicle until you are sure that both front brakes are operating correctly with full hydraulic advantage. If necessary, bleed the front brakes as described in this chapter.

Caliper Removal/Piston Removal
(Caliper Will Be Disassembled)

If the caliper is to be completely disassembled, force will be required to remove the piston from the caliper. Force can be supplied by hydraulic pressure in the brake system itself, or compressed air. If you

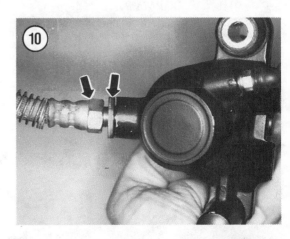

are going to use hydraulic pressure, you must do so before disconnecting the brake hose from the caliper. This procedure describes how to remove the piston while the caliper is still mounted on the vehicle.

1. Remove the brake pads as described in this chapter.
2. On 1988 models, remove clip (12, **Figure 1**).
3. Operate the front brake lever to force the piston out of the caliper bore (**Figure 11**).

NOTE
*If the piston will not come out, you will have to use compressed air. Refer to **Disassembly** in this chapter.*

4. Support the caliper and loosen the caliper brake hose. Then hold the hose and turn the caliper to remove it and the washer from the brake hose. Place the end of the brake hose in a container to prevent brake fluid from dripping onto the vehicle.
5. Take the caliper to a workbench for further disassembly.

Disassembly

1. Remove the caliper as described in this chapter.

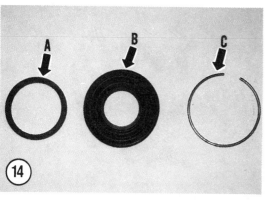

2. On 1988 models, remove clip (12, **Figure 1**).

NOTE
If you have removed the piston, proceed to Step 4.

WARNING
The piston will be forced out of the caliper with considerable force. Do not try to cushion the piston with your fingers, as injury could result.

3. Cushion the piston with a shop rag. Do not place your hand or fingers in the piston area. Then apply compressed air through the brake line port to force the piston out.
4. Remove the dust seal.
5. Remove the piston seal from the caliper bore. Do not damage the bore.
6. Remove the bleed valve from the caliper.
7. Remove the caliper friction and dust boots.

Inspection

1. Clean the caliper housing in solvent and dry thoroughly. Clean the dust and piston seal grooves with a soft-faced tool to avoid damaging the bore.
2. Discard the piston and dust seals. Discard the clip on 1988 models. Yamaha specifies to replace these parts whenever the caliper is disassembled.
3. Clean the piston in clean DOT 4 brake fluid.
4. Inspect the piston and the caliper piston bore (**Figure 12**) for deep scratches or other wear marks. Do not hone the piston bore. Replace if questionable.
5. Clean the bleed valve with compressed air. Check the valve threads for damage. Replace the dust cap if missing or damaged.
6. Replace the brake hose washer if cracked or otherwise damaged.
7. Replace missing or damaged caliper boots (**Figure 13**).
8. Measure the thickness of each brake pad with a vernier caliper or ruler and compare to the specification listed in **Table 1**. If the pad thickness is equal to or less than the wear limit, replace all 4 brake pads at the same time.

Assembly

Install a new caliper seal kit (**Figure 14**) during reassembly:

12

a. Piston seal (A).

b. Dust seal (B).

c. Clip (C) (used on 1988 models only).

NOTE
Use new, unused DOT 4 brake fluid
when brake fluid is called for in the
following steps.

1. Soak the piston seal (A, **Figure 14**) in brake fluid for approximately 5 minutes.

2. Lightly coat the caliper bore with brake fluid.

3. Install the new piston seal into the caliper bore groove as shown in **Figure 15**.

4. Remove the new dust seal from its package and note the shoulder on one side of the seal (**Figure 16**). Then install the dust seal into the piston groove so that the shoulder on the seal faces away from the piston body as shown in **Figure 17**.

5. Lightly wipe the piston O.D. with brake fluid.

6. Insert the piston partway into the caliper bore (**Figure 18**).

7. Pull the dust seal back and seat it in the caliper bore groove (**Figure 19**).

8. On 1988 models, install the clip into the caliper bore groove (**Figure 20**).

9. Push the piston all the way into the bore. Check that the dust seal seats squarely around the caliper bore (**Figure 21**).

10. Install and tighten the bleed screw.

11. Install the brake pads as described in this chapter.

Caliper Bracket
Removal/Inspection/Installation

1. Remove the brake caliper as described in this chapter.

2. Remove the caliper bracket mounting bolts (**Figure 22**) and remove the caliper bracket.

3. Inspect the bracket (**Figure 23**) for cracks or other damage.

4. Install by reversing these steps. Tighten the caliper bracket mounting bolts (**Figure 22**) securely.

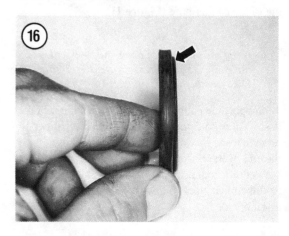

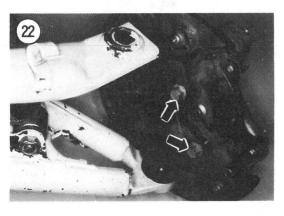

FRONT CALIPER
(1989-ON)

Refer to **Figure 24** when replacing the front brake pads or servicing the front brake caliper.

Brake Pad Inspection

You can measure brake pad wear with the brake caliper installed on the vehicle as follows.

1. Remove the front wheels as described in Chapter Ten.

2. Measure the distance from the disc surface to the back of the pad's friction material with a small ruler as shown in **Figure 25**. The brake pads should be replaced when the friction material thickness is equal to or less than the service limit specification in **Table 1**.

3. Install the front wheels as described in Chapter Ten, or replace the brake pads as described in the following section.

Front Brake Pad Replacement

There is no recommended time interval for changing the friction pads in the front brakes. Pad wear depends greatly on riding habits and conditions.

To maintain an even brake pressure on the disc always replace both pads in both calipers at the same time.

1. Read the information listed under *Disc Brake* in this chapter.

2. Remove the front wheel as described in Chapter Ten.

12

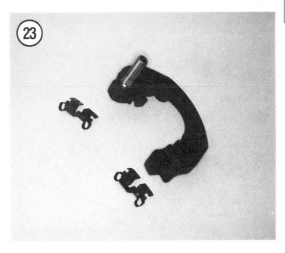

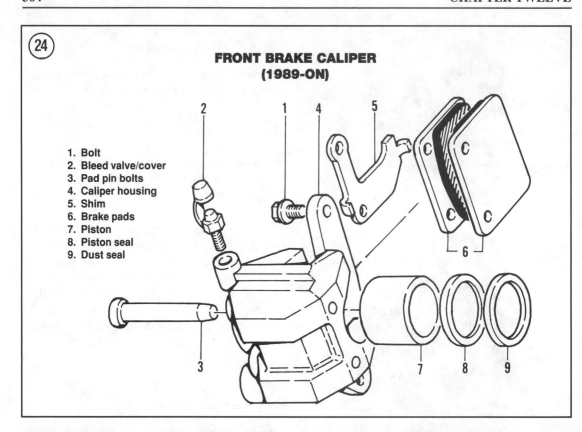

(24)

**FRONT BRAKE CALIPER
(1989-ON)**

1. Bolt
2. Bleed valve/cover
3. Pad pin bolts
4. Caliper housing
5. Shim
6. Brake pads
7. Piston
8. Piston seal
9. Dust seal

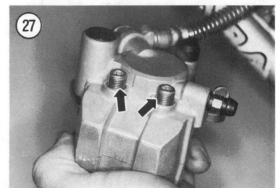

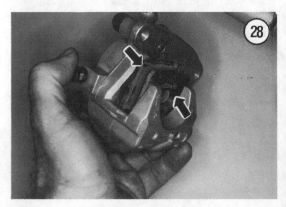

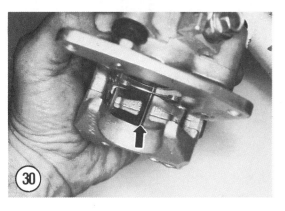

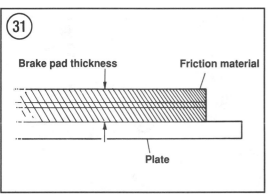

Brake pad thickness   **Friction material**

Plate

3. Loosen, but do not remove, the 2 pad pin bolts (A, **Figure 26**) that hold the brake pads to the caliper.

4. Remove the 2 bolts (B, **Figure 26**) that hold the brake caliper to the steering knuckle. Then slide the brake caliper off of the brake disc.

5. Remove the 2 brake pad pin bolts (**Figure 27**).

6. Lift the brake pads out of the caliper as shown in **Figure 28**.

7. Support the brake caliper with a bungee cord or heavy wire hook.

NOTE
*If the pads are to be reused, mark each pad so that they can be reinstalled in their original mounting positions. Note that an L-shaped shim is installed on the inside brake pad (**Figure 29**).*

8. Check the pad spring (**Figure 30**) in the caliper.

NOTE
*Currently, Yamaha does not sell the pad spring (**Figure 30**) as a replacement item. Handle the pad spring carefully so that you do not damage it.*

9. Measure the thickness of each brake pad (**Figure 31**). Replace the brake pads if the thickness of any one pad is equal to or is less than the service limit in **Table 1**. Replace all 4 brake pads as a set.

10. Inspect the brake pads (**Figure 32**) for uneven wear, damage or grease contamination. Replace all 4 brake pads as a set.

11. Check the end of the piston for fluid leakage. If the dust seal is damaged and/or if there is fluid leaking from the caliper, overhaul the brake caliper as described in this chapter.

12. Check the pad pin bolts for corrosion, bending or other damage.

13. Check the brake disc for wear as described in this chapter.

14. To make room for the new pads, the piston must be pushed back into the caliper. This will force brake fluid to backup through the hose and fill the master cylinder reservoir. To prevent the reservoir from overflowing, remove some of the brake fluid as follows:

    a. Clean the top of the master cylinder of all dirt.

    b. Remove the cap and diaphragm from the master cylinder.

12

c. Temporarily install the inside brake pad into the caliper and slowly push the piston back into the caliper.

d. Constantly check the reservoir to make sure brake fluid does not overflow. Siphon fluid, if necessary, before it overflows.

WARNING
Brake fluid is poisonous. Do not siphon
with your mouth.

e. The caliper piston should move freely. If not, the caliper should be removed and overhauled as described in this chapter.

f. Push the caliper piston in all the way to allow room for the new pads.

g. Remove the inside pad.

15. Install the brake pads as follows:

a. If you are installing new brake pads, hook the pad shim onto one of the brake pads as shown in **Figure 33**. This pad is now the inside pad.

WARNING
Do not use grease on the pad shim to
hold it in place. Heat produced during
braking will melt the grease and cause
it to run onto the brake pads and con-
taminate them and the brake disc.

b. Install the inside brake pad (with pad shim) into the caliper so that the pad shim faces against the caliper piston; see **Figure 29** and **Figure 34**.

c. Install the outside brake pad (**Figure 35**) into the caliper. The friction material on both brake pads must face toward each other.

16. Press both brake pads down and install the 2 pad pin bolts (**Figure 27**) through the brake pads. Using an Allen wrench, tighten the pad pin bolts hand-tight.

17. Slide the brake caliper over the brake disc. Then install the brake caliper mounting bolts (B, **Figure 26**) and torque to the specification in **Table 3**.

18. Torque the brake pad pin bolts (A, **Figure 26**) to the specification in **Table 3**.

19. Repeat for the other brake caliper.

WARNING
Use new brake fluid clearly marked
DOT 4 from a sealed container.

20. Pull and release the brake lever a few times to seat the pads against each disc, then recheck the brake fluid level in the reservoir. If necessary, add fresh DOT 4 brake fluid.

21. Install the master cylinder reservoir diaphragm and top cover. Tighten the cover screws securely.

22. Install the front wheels as described in Chapter Ten.

WARNING
Do not ride the vehicle until you are sure
that both front brakes are operating
correctly with full hydraulic advantage.

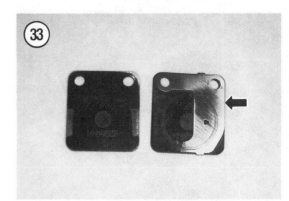

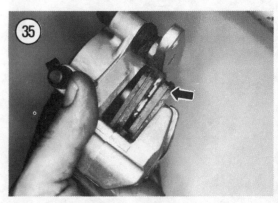

If necessary, bleed the front brakes as described in this chapter.

Removal/Installation
(Caliper Will Not Be Disassembled)

If the brake caliper is to be removed without disassembling it, perform this procedure. If the caliper is to be disassembled, refer to *Caliper Removal/Piston Removal* in this chapter.

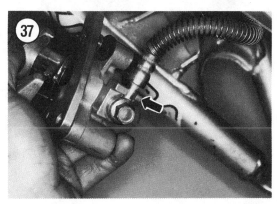

1. Remove the front wheel(s) as described in Chapter Ten.

2A. If the caliper is to be completely removed from the vehicle, perform the following:
   a. Loosen the brake hose banjo bolt (A, **Figure 36**) at the caliper.
   b. Remove the bolts (B, **Figure 36**) that hold the brake caliper to the steering knuckle. Then lift the caliper off the brake disc.
   c. Remove the banjo bolt and the 2 washers, then remove the brake caliper. Seal the hose so that brake fluid does not drip out.

2B. If the caliper is only being partially removed and it is not necessary to disconnect the brake line at the caliper, perform the following:
   a. Remove the bolts (B, **Figure 36**) that hold the brake caliper to the steering knuckle. Then lift the caliper off the brake disc.
   b. Insert a wooden or plastic spacer block in the caliper between the brake pads.

NOTE
The spacer block prevents the piston from being forced out of the caliper if the brake lever is squeezed while the caliper is removed from the brake disc. If the brake lever is squeezed, the piston will be forced out. If this happens, the caliper will have to be disassembled and then reassembled to properly reseat the piston. Bleeding the system will also be required.

   c. Support the caliper with a bungee cord or a wire hook. Do not allow the caliper to hang by its hose.

3. Install the caliper by reversing these steps, while noting the following.

4A. If the caliper was completely removed from the vehicle:
   a. Check that the brake pads were not contaminated with brake fluid. Wipe the caliper housing off with a clean rag.
   b. Route the brake hose through the 2 raised tabs on the brake caliper as shown in **Figure 37**.
   c. Place a washer on each side of the brake hose. Then install the bolt into the caliper (**Figure 38**). Tighten the banjo bolt finger-tight at this time.
   d. Carefully install the caliper assembly over the brake disc. Be careful not to damage the leading edge of the pads during installation.

12

e. Install the 2 bolts that hold the brake caliper to the steering knuckle. Then torque the bolts to the specification in **Table 3**.

f. Torque the brake hose banjo bolt to the specification in **Table 3**.

g. Refill the master cylinder and bleed the front brake as described in this chapter.

4B. If the caliper was only partially removed from the vehicle:

a. Remove the spacer block from between the brake pads.

b. Disconnect the caliper from its hanger and carefully install the caliper over the brake disc. Be careful not to damage the leading edge of the pads during installation.

c. Install the 2 bolts that hold the brake caliper to the steering knuckle. Then torque the bolts to the specification in **Table 3**.

d. Operate the brake lever a few times to seat the pads against the brake disc.

WARNING
Do not ride the vehicle until you are sure that both front brakes are operating correctly with full hydraulic advantage. If necessary, bleed the front brakes as described in this chapter.

Caliper Removal/Piston Removal
(Caliper Will Be Disassembled)

If the caliper is to be completely disassembled, force will be required to remove the piston from the caliper. Force can be supplied by hydraulic pressure in the brake system itself, or compressed air. If you are going to use hydraulic pressure, you must do so before the brake hose is disconnected from the caliper. This procedure describes how to remove the piston while the caliper is still mounted on the vehicle.

1. Remove the brake pads as described in this chapter.

2. Slide the support bracket out of the caliper.

3. Wrap a large cloth around the brake caliper.

4. Hold the caliper so that your hand and fingers are placed away from the piston and brake pad areas.

5. Operate the front brake lever to force the piston out of the caliper cylinder. Remove the piston.

NOTE
*If the piston will not come out, you will have to use compressed air to remove it. Refer to **Disassembly** in this chapter.*

6. Support the caliper. Then loosen the caliper banjo bolt (**Figure 37**) and remove the bolt and its 2 washers (**Figure 38**) from the caliper. Seal the brake hose to prevent brake fluid from dripping out.

7. Take the caliper to a workbench for further disassembly.

Disassembly

1. Remove the caliper as described in this chapter.

WARNING
The piston will be forced out of the caliper with considerable force. Do not try to cushion the piston with your fingers, as injury could result.

2. Cushion the caliper piston with a shop rag, making sure to keep your fingers and hand away from

the piston area. Then apply compressed air through the brake line port (**Figure 39**) to remove the piston.

3. Remove the dust seal (A, **Figure 40**) and piston seal (B, **Figure 40**) from the inside of the cylinder.

> *NOTE*
> *Replacement friction boots (A, **Figure 41**) and dust covers are not available from Yamaha. Handle the caliper carefully so that you do not damage them in the following steps.*

4. If necessary, remove the support bracket (B, **Figure 41**) from the caliper.

5. If necessary, remove the friction boot and dust cover from the caliper body.

6. Remove the bleed valve and its cover from the caliper.

7. If necessary, remove the pad spring (**Figure 30**) from the caliper.

Inspection

1. Clean the caliper housing in solvent. Remove stubborn dirt with a soft brush, but do not brush the

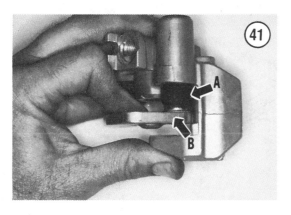

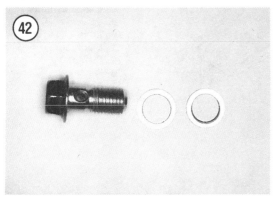

cylinder bores as this may damage them. Clean the dust and piston seal grooves with a plastic tipped tool so that you do not damage them or the cylinder bore. Then clean the caliper in hot soapy water and rinse in clear, cold water. Dry with compressed air.

2. Clean the piston in clean DOT 4 brake fluid.

3. Check the piston and cylinder bore for deep scratches or other obvious wear marks. Do not hone the cylinder. If the piston or cylinder is damaged, replace the caliper assembly.

4. Clean the bleed valve with compressed air. Check the valve threads for damage. Replace the dust cap if missing or damaged.

5. Clean the banjo bolt (**Figure 42**) with compressed air. Check the threads for damage. Replace worn or damaged washers.

6. Check the friction boot and dust cover. If swollen, cracked or severely worn, the entire brake caliper will have to be replaced.

7. Check the support bracket shafts for severe wear, damage or uneven wear (steps). The shafts must be in good condition for the caliper to slide back and forth. Remove all grease residue from the bracket. If the support bracket is damaged, the entire brake caliper will have to be replaced.

8. Measure the thickness of each brake pad with a vernier caliper or ruler and compare to the specification listed in **Table 1**. If the pad thickness is equal to or less than the wear limit, replace the pads.

9. Inspect the brake pads (**Figure 32**) for uneven wear, damage or grease contamination. Replace the pads as a set, if necessary.

10. Replace the piston seal and dust seal as a set.

> *NOTE*
> *Yamaha states that the piston seal and dust seal must be replaced whenever the caliper is disassembled.*

Assembly

> *NOTE*
> *Use new, unused DOT 4 brake fluid when brake fluid is called for in the following steps.*

1. Soak the piston seal and dust seal in brake fluid for approximately 5 minutes.

2. Lightly coat the piston and cylinder bore with brake fluid.

12

3. Install a new piston seal (B, **Figure 40**) into the second groove in the cylinder bore.

4. Install a new dust seal (A, **Figure 40**) into the front groove in the cylinder bore.

NOTE
Check that both seals fit squarely into their respective cylinder bore grooves. If a seal is not installed properly, the caliper assembly will leak and braking performance will be reduced.

5. Install the piston—closed end first—into the cylinder bore. See **Figure 43**.

6. If the support bracket was removed, perform the following:

   a. Apply a thin coat of PBC (Poly Butyl Cuprysil) grease (or equivalent) to the caliper bracket shafts.

CAUTION
PBC grease (or equivalent) is a special high temperature, water-resistant

grease that can be used in braking systems. Do not use any other kind of lubricant as it may thin out and contaminate the brake pads.

   b. Slide the support bracket shafts into the caliper (B, **Figure 41**). Slide the bracket back and forth, without removing it, to distribute the grease and to check the shafts for binding. The bracket

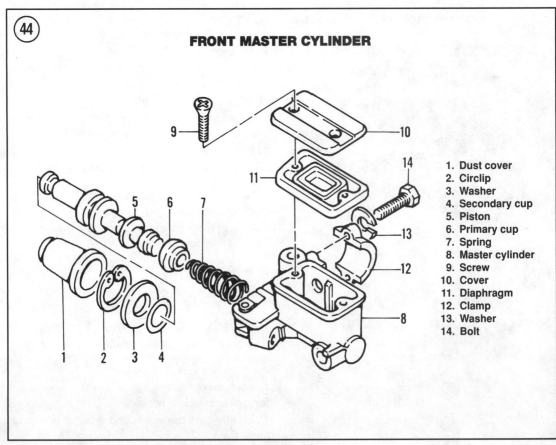

FRONT MASTER CYLINDER

1. Dust cover
2. Circlip
3. Washer
4. Secondary cup
5. Piston
6. Primary cup
7. Spring
8. Master cylinder
9. Screw
10. Cover
11. Diaphragm
12. Clamp
13. Washer
14. Bolt

must move smoothly; if any binding is noted, remove the bracket and inspect the shafts for damage. Wipe off any excess grease from the outside of the caliper or bracket.

7. If necessary, install the bleed screw and its dust cover. Tighten securely.

8. If necessary, install the pad spring (**Figure 30**) into the brake caliper.

9. Install the brake caliper assembly and brake pads as described in this chapter.

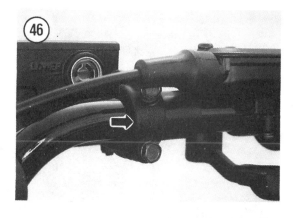

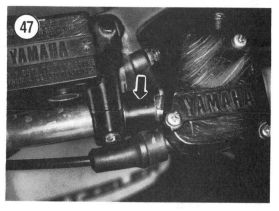

FRONT MASTER CYLINDER

The front master cylinder is bolted to the handlebar with 2 bolts and a removable clamp. A spacer positions the master cylinder a specified distance away from the throttle housing assembly.

Figure 44 is an exploded view of the front master cylinder. Refer to it when servicing the master cylinder in the following sections.

Read the information listed under *Disc Brake* in this chapter before servicing the front master cylinder.

Removal/Installation

1. Park the vehicle on level ground and set the parking brake.

2. Cover the area under the master cylinder to prevent brake fluid from damaging any component that it might contact.

> *CAUTION*
> *If brake fluid should contact any surface, wash the area immediately with soapy water and rinse completely. Brake fluid will damage plastic, painted and plated surfaces.*

3. To remove brake fluid from the reservoir:
   a. Remove the master cylinder cap and diaphragm.
   b. Use a clean syringe and remove the brake fluid from the reservoir. Discard the brake fluid.

4. Pull the rubber cover away from the brake hose at the master cylinder.

5. Remove the banjo bolt (**Figure 45**) and the washers securing the brake hose to the master cylinder. Seal the brake hose to prevent brake fluid from dripping out.

6. Remove the 2 bolts and the clamp holding (**Figure 46**) the master cylinder to the handlebar, then remove the master cylinder.

7. If necessary, service the master cylinder as described in this chapter.

8. Clean the handlebar, master cylinder and clamp mating surfaces.

9. Position the master cylinder onto the handlebar. Install its clamp—arrow mark facing up—and install the 2 mounting bolts (**Figure 46**). Then position the spacer so that the notch in the spacer fits into the alignment tab on the throttle housing as shown in **Figure 47**. Slide the master cylinder over so that it

12

contacts the spacer. Position the master cylinder brake lever to best suit your riding position and tighten the master cylinder mounting bolts securely.

10. Install the brake hose onto the master cylinder, using the banjo bolt (**Figure 45**) and the 2 washers. One washer should be installed on each side of the hose. Tighten the banjo bolt to the torque specification listed in **Table 3**.

11. Refill the master cylinder with DOT 4 brake fluid and bleed the brake as described in this chapter.

> *WARNING*
> *Do not ride the vehicle until the front brakes are working properly. Make sure the that the brake lever travel is not excessive and that the lever does not feel spongy—both indicate that the bleeding operation needs to be repeated.*

Disassembly

1. Remove the master cylinder as described in this chapter.

2. Remove the brake lever pivot bolt and nut from the master cylinder.

3. Remove the brake lever and spring (**Figure 48**) from the master cylinder.

4. Remove the master cylinder cap screws and remove the cap and diaphragm from the caliper.

5. Carefully remove the dust cover (**Figure 49**) from the groove in the end of the piston. See **Figure 50**.

> *NOTE*
> *If there is brake fluid leaking at the front of the piston bore, the piston cups are worn or damaged. Replace the piston assembly during reassembly.*

6. Compress the piston and remove the circlip (**Figure 51**) from the groove in the master cylinder.

7. Remove the circlip, washer and piston assembly (**Figure 52**) from the inside of the cylinder.

Inspection

Worn or damaged master cylinder components (**Figure 53**) will prevent proper brake fluid pressure from building in the brake line. Reduced pressure will cause the brake to feel weak and it will not hold properly.

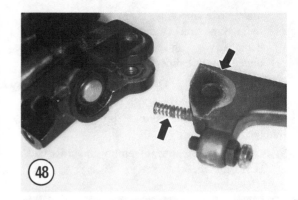

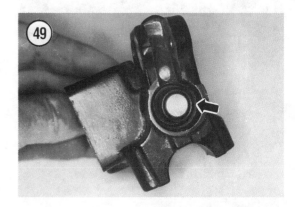

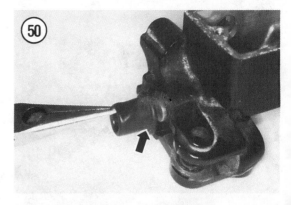

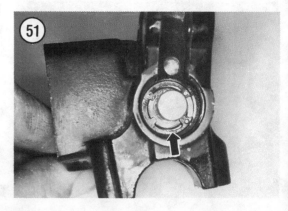

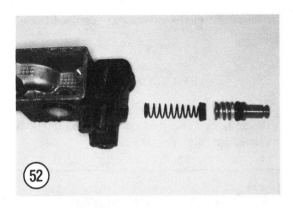

(52)

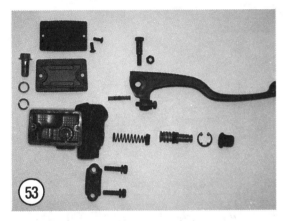

(53)

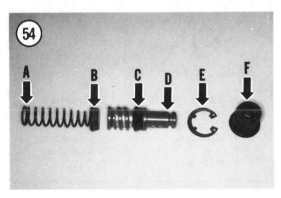

(54)

1. Wash the piston and cylinder with clean DOT 4 brake fluid.
2. The piston assembly is identified in **Figure 54**:
   a. Spring.
   b. Primary cup.
   c. Secondary cup.
   d. Piston.
   e. Circlip.
   f. Dust cover.

> *CAUTION*
> *Do not attempt to remove the secondary cup (C, **Figure 54**) from the piston. Removal will damage the cup, requiring replacement of the piston assembly.*

3. Check the piston assembly (**Figure 54**) for the following defects:
   a. Broken, distorted or collapsed piston return spring (A, **Figure 54**).
   b. Worn, cracked, damaged or swollen primary (B, **Figure 54**) and secondary cups (C, **Figure 54**).
   c. Scratched, scored or damaged piston (D, **Figure 54**).
   d. Corroded, weak or damaged circlip (E, **Figure 54**).
   e. Worn or damaged dust cover (F, **Figure 54**).

   If any of these parts are worn or damaged, replace the piston assembly.
4. Inspect the master cylinder bore (**Figure 55**). If the bore is corroded, scored or damaged in any way, replace the master cylinder assembly. Do not hone the master cylinder bore to remove scratches or other damage.
5. Check for plugged supply and relief ports in the master cylinder. Clean with compressed air.

> *NOTE*
> *A plugged relief port will cause the pads to drag on the disc.*

12

(55)

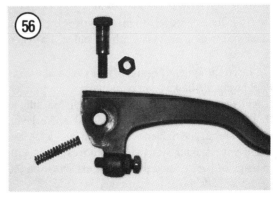

(56)

6. Check the brake lever, pivot bolt and spring (**Figure 56**) for severely worn or damaged parts.

7. Check the reservoir cap and diaphragm for damage. Check the diaphragm for cracks or deterioration. Replace damaged parts as required.

8. Check all of the threaded holes in the master cylinder. Clean with compressed air. The small Phillips screws used to secure the reservoir cap strip easily; check the screw heads and threads for damage and replace or repair if necessary.

Assembly

Use new, unused DOT 4 brake fluid when brake fluid is called for in the following steps.

1. If you are installing a piston repair kit, note the following:

    a. Check the repair kit to make sure that it contains all of the necessary new parts.

    b. Wash the new parts in new brake fluid.

2. Lightly coat the piston assembly and cylinder bore with brake fluid.

3. Assemble the piston assembly as shown in **Figure 54**. The primary cup fits onto the return spring.

> *CAUTION*
> *When installing the piston assembly in Step 4, make sure the primary and secondary cups do not tear or turn inside out; both cups are slightly larger than the bore.*

4. Insert the piston assembly into the master cylinder bore in the direction shown in **Figure 52**.

5. Compress the piston assembly and install the washer (if used) and circlip. Make sure the circlip seats in the master cylinder groove completely (**Figure 51**). Push and release the piston a few times to make sure it moves smoothly in the cylinder bore.

6. Slide the dust cover (**Figure 50**) over the piston. Seat the cover in the cylinder bore and in the piston groove.

7. Insert the spring (**Figure 48**) into the brake lever and install the brake lever onto the master cylinder. Lightly grease the pivot bolt shoulder and install the bolt through the master cylinder and brake lever. Install the nut and tighten securely. Then, operate the hand lever, making sure the lever moves freely with no sign of binding and that the adjust screw on the lever contacts the piston correctly.

8. Install the master cylinder as described in this chapter.

REAR CALIPER

The rear brake caliper is mounted onto the rear axle housing. The parking brake assembly is mounted onto the rear brake caliper.

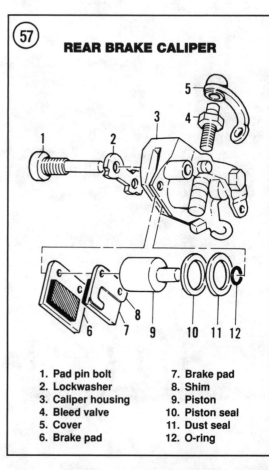

REAR BRAKE CALIPER

1. Pad pin bolt
2. Lockwasher
3. Caliper housing
4. Bleed valve
5. Cover
6. Brake pad
7. Brake pad
8. Shim
9. Piston
10. Piston seal
11. Dust seal
12. O-ring

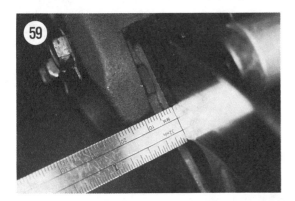

The only factory replacement components available for the rear brake caliper are those parts shown in **Figure 57**. The rear parking brake assembly (**Figure 58**) and the brake caliper dust boot and friction boot assemblies are not available separately. If these items are damaged, the entire rear brake caliper assembly will have to be replaced. When servicing the rear caliper in the following sections, handle these items carefully so that you do not damage them.

Refer to **Figure 57** when replacing the rear brake pads or servicing the rear brake caliper and parking brake assembly.

Brake Pad Inspection

You can measure brake pad wear with the brake caliper installed on the vehicle as follows.

1. Measure the distance from the disc surface to the back of the pad's friction material with a small ruler as shown in **Figure 59**. The brake pads should be replaced when the friction material thickness is equal to or less than the service limit specification in **Table 2**.

2. If necessary, replace the brake pads as described in the following section.

Rear Brake Pad Replacement

There is no recommended time interval for changing the friction pads in the front brakes. Pad wear depends greatly on riding habits and conditions.

To maintain an even brake pressure on the disc always replace both pads in the caliper at the same time.

1. Read the information listed under *Disc Brake* in this chapter.

2. Support the vehicle with all 4 wheels on the ground. Block the front wheels to prevent the vehicle from rolling forwards or backwards.

3. Release the parking brake.

4. Pry back the lockwasher tabs from the 2 brake pad pin bolts (**Figure 60**). Then loosen, but do not remove, the 2 brake pad pin bolts.

5. Remove the 2 bolts (**Figure 61**) that hold the brake caliper to the axle housing. Then slide the brake caliper off of the brake disc.

6. Remove the 2 brake pad pin bolts (**Figure 62**) and lockwasher.

12

7. Remove the brake pads from the caliper as shown in **Figure 63**.

8. Support the brake caliper with a bungee cord or heavy wire hook.

> *NOTE*
> *If the pads are to be reused, mark each pad so that they can be reinstalled in their original mounting positions. Note that an L-shaped shim is installed on the inside brake pad (**Figure 64**).*

9. Check the pad spring (**Figure 65**) in the caliper.

> *NOTE*
> *Currently, Yamaha does not sell the pad spring (**Figure 65**) as a replacement item. Handle the pad spring carefully so that you do not damage it.*

10. Measure the thickness of each brake pad (**Figure 66**). Replace the brake pads if the thickness of any one pad is equal to or is less than the service limit in **Table 2**. Replace both brake pads as a set.

11. Inspect the brake pads (**Figure 67**) for uneven wear, damage or grease contamination. Replace the pads as a set.

12. Check the end of the piston (**Figure 68**) for fluid leakage. If the dust seal is damaged and/or if there is fluid leaking from the caliper, overhaul the brake caliper as described in this chapter.

13. Check the pad pin bolts (**Figure 67**) for corrosion, bending or other damage.

14. Replace the lockwasher (**Figure 67**) if damaged.

15. Check the brake disc for wear as described in this chapter.

16. To make room for the new pads, the piston (**Figure 68**) must be pushed back into the caliper. This will force brake fluid to backup through the hose and fill the master cylinder reservoir. To prevent the reservoir from overflowing, remove some of the brake fluid as follows:

  a. Clean the top of the master cylinder of all dirt.

  b. Remove the cap and diaphragm from the master cylinder.

  c. Temporarily install the inside brake pad into the caliper and slowly push the piston back into the caliper.

  d. Constantly check the reservoir to make sure brake fluid does not overflow. Siphon fluid, if necessary, before it overflows.

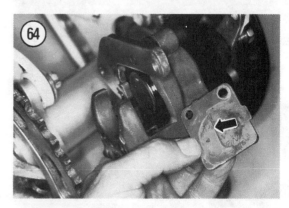

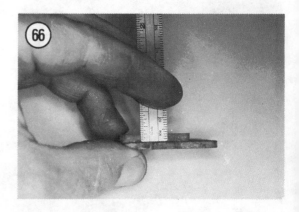

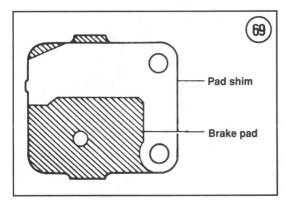

Pad shim

Brake pad

WARNING
Brake fluid is poisonous. Do not siphon with your mouth.

e. The caliper piston should move freely. If not, the caliper should be removed and overhauled as described in this chapter.

f. Push the caliper piston in all the way to allow room for the new pads.

g. Remove the inside pad.

17. Install the brake pads as follows:

a. If you are installing new brake pads, hook the pad shim onto one of the brake pads as shown in **Figure 69**. This is now the inside brake pad.

WARNING
Do not use grease on the pad shim to hold it in place. Heat produced during braking will melt the grease and cause it to run onto the brake pads and contaminate them and the brake disc.

b. Install the inside brake pad (with pad shim) into the caliper so that the pad shim faces toward the caliper piston; see **Figure 69** and **Figure 70**.

c. Install the outside brake pad into the caliper. The friction material on both brake pads must face toward each other.

18. Press both brake pads down and install the lockwasher and the 2 pad pin bolts (**Figure 62**) through the brake pads. Tighten the bolts finger-tight at this time.

19. Slide the brake caliper over the brake disc. Then install the bolts that hold the brake caliper to the axle housing (**Figure 61**) and torque to the specification in **Table 3**.

20. Torque the brake pad pin bolts (**Figure 60**) to the specification in **Table 3**. Bend the lockwasher tabs against the brake pad pin bolts.

WARNING
Use new brake fluid clearly marked DOT 4 from a sealed container.

21. Press and release the rear brake lever a few times to seat the pads against the disc, then recheck the brake fluid level in the reservoir. If necessary, add fresh DOT 4 brake fluid.

22. Install the master cylinder reservoir diaphragm and top cover. Tighten the cover screws securely.

12

WARNING
Do not ride the vehicle until you are sure that the rear brake is operating correctly with full hydraulic advantage. If necessary, bleed the rear brake as described in this chapter.

Brake Caliper
Removal/Installation
(Caliper Will Not Be Disassembled)

If the brake caliper is to be removed without disassembling it, perform this procedure. If the caliper is to be disassembled, refer to *Caliper Removal/Piston Removal* in this chapter.

1. Support the vehicle with all 4 wheels on the ground. Block the front wheels to prevent the vehicle from rolling forwards or backwards.

2. Release the parking brake. Then pull back the rubber cover and loosen the parking brake cable (**Figure 71**) at the handlebar cable adjuster. Disconnect the parking brake cable at the rear brake caliper.

3A. If the caliper is to be completely removed from the vehicle, perform the following:

   a. Loosen the brake hose banjo bolt (A, **Figure 72**) at the caliper.

   b. Remove the bolts (B, **Figure 72**) that hold the brake caliper to the axle housing. Then lift the caliper off the brake disc.

   c. Remove the banjo bolt and the 2 washers, then remove the brake caliper. Seal the hose so that brake fluid does not drip out.

3B. If the caliper is only being partially removed and it is not necessary to disconnect the brake line at the caliper, perform the following:

   a. Remove the bolts (B, **Figure 72**) that hold the brake caliper to the axle housing. Then lift the caliper off the brake disc.

   b. Insert a wooden or plastic spacer block in the caliper between the brake pads.

NOTE
The spacer block prevents the piston from being forced out of the caliper if the brake lever is pressed while the caliper is removed from the brake disc. If the brake lever is pressed, the piston will be forced out. If this happens, the caliper will have to be disassembled and then reassembled to properly reseat the piston. Bleeding the system will also be required.

   c. Support the caliper with a bungee cord or a wire hook. Do not allow the caliper to hang by its hose.

4. Install the caliper by reversing these steps, while noting the following.

5A. If the caliper was completely removed from the vehicle:

   a. Check that the brake pads were not contaminated with brake fluid. Wipe the caliper housing off with a clean rag.

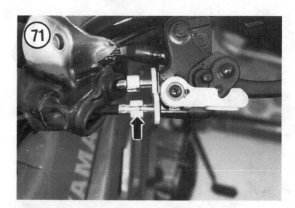

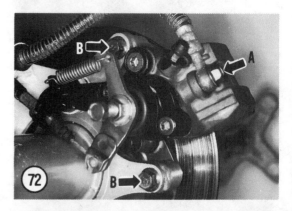

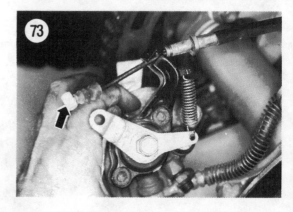

b. Route the brake hose across the top of the caliper as shown in **Figure 72**.

c. Place a washer on each side of the brake hose. Then install the bolt into the caliper (A, **Figure 72**). Tighten the banjo bolt finger-tight at this time.

d. Carefully install the caliper assembly over the brake disc. Be careful not to damage the leading edge of the pads during installation.

e. Install the 2 bolts that hold the brake caliper to the axle housing. Then torque the bolts to the specification in **Table 3**.

f. Torque the brake hose banjo bolt to the specification in **Table 3**.

g. Refill the master cylinder and bleed the rear brake as described in this chapter.

5B. If the caliper was only partially removed from the vehicle:

a. Remove the spacer block from between the brake pads.

b. Disconnect the caliper from its hanger and carefully install the caliper over the brake disc. Be careful not to damage the leading edge of the pads during installation.

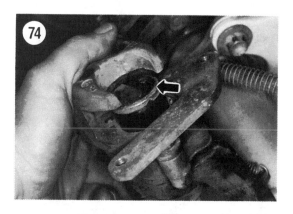

c. Install the 2 bolts that hold the brake caliper to the axle housing. Then torque the bolts to the specification in **Table 3**.

d. Press the brake lever a few times to seat the pads against the brake disc.

> *WARNING*
> *Do not ride the vehicle until you are sure that the rear brake is operating correctly with full hydraulic advantage. If necessary, bleed the rear brake as described in this chapter.*

6. Reconnect the parking brake cable. Then adjust the parking brake as described in Chapter Three.

Caliper Removal/Piston Removal (Caliper Will Be Disassembled)

If the caliper is to be completely disassembled, force will be required to remove the piston from the caliper. Force can be supplied by hydraulic pressure in the brake system itself, or compressed air. If you are going to use hydraulic pressure, you must do so before the brake hose is disconnected from the caliper. This procedure describes how to remove the piston while the caliper is still mounted on the vehicle.

1. Release the parking brake. Then pull back the rubber cover and loosen the parking brake cable (**Figure 71**) at the handlebar cable adjuster.

2. Remove the brake pads as described in this chapter.

3. Disconnect the parking brake cable at the lever mounted on the rear brake caliper (**Figure 73**).

4. Hold the caliper so that your hand and fingers are placed away from the piston.

5. Operate the rear brake lever to force the piston (**Figure 74**) out of the caliper cylinder. Remove the piston.

> *NOTE*
> *If the piston will not come out, you will have to use compressed air to remove it. Refer to **Disassembly** in this chapter.*

6. Support the caliper. Then loosen the caliper banjo bolt (**Figure 75**) and remove the bolt and its 2 washers from the caliper. Seal the brake hose to prevent brake fluid from dripping out.

7. Take the caliper to a workbench for further disassembly.

12

Disassembly

1. Remove the caliper as described in this chapter.

> *WARNING*
> *The piston will be forced out of the cali-*
> *per with considerable force. Do not try*
> *to cushion the piston with your fingers,*
> *as injury could result.*

2. Cushion the caliper piston with a shop rag, making sure to keep your fingers and hand away from
the piston area. Then apply compressed air through
the brake line port (**Figure 76**) to remove the piston.
See **Figure 77**.

3. Using a wooden or plastic rod with a flat, narrow
tip, remove the dust seal (A, **Figure 78**) and piston
seal (B, **Figure 78**) from the inside of the cylinder.

4. Remove the small O-ring (C, **Figure 78**) from the
inside of the parking brake housing.

5. To remove the rear parking brake assembly, perform the following:

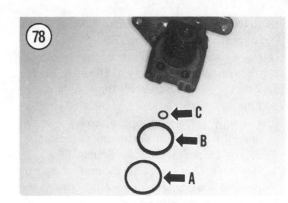

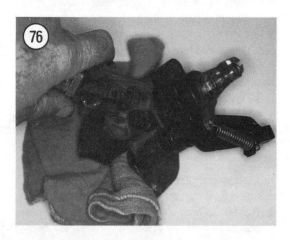

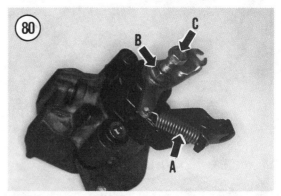

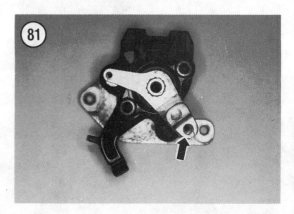

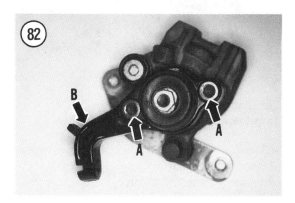

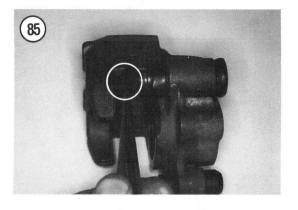

a. Measure the length of the exposed threads on the parking brake adjust bolt as shown in **Figure 79**. Record the measurement for reassembly.

b. Remove the return spring (A, **Figure 80**).

c. Loosen the locknut (B, **Figure 80**) and remove the adjust bolt (C, **Figure 80**).

d. Remove the parking brake lever (**Figure 81**).

NOTE
Remove the parking brake housing carefully in the following step to avoid damaging the gasket installed between the housing and brake caliper. Factory replacement gaskets are not available. If the gasket is damaged, you will have to make a new one.

e. Remove the 2 bolts (A, **Figure 82**) that hold the parking brake housing to the rear brake caliper. Then lift off and remove the parking brake housing (B, **Figure 82**).

f. Remove the gasket (**Figure 83**).

6. Loosen the bolt (A, **Figure 84**) that holds the support bracket to the rear brake caliper. Then pull the support bracket (B, **Figure 84**) out of the brake caliper. Remove the washer (**Figure 85**) from the bolt threads.

NOTE
Factory replacement friction boots and dust covers are not available from Yamaha. Handle the caliper carefully so that you do not damage them in the following steps.

7. If necessary, remove the friction boot (**Figure 86**) from the brake caliper.

12

8. If necessary, remove the caliper bracket bolt (A, **Figure 87**) and both dust covers (B, **Figure 87**) from the brake caliper.

9. Remove the bleed valve and its cover from the caliper.

10. If necessary, remove the pad spring from the caliper.

Brake Caliper
Inspection

1. Clean the caliper housing in solvent. Remove stubborn dirt with a soft brush, but do not brush the cylinder bores as this may damage them. Clean the dust and piston seal grooves with a plastic tipped tool so that you do not damage them or the cylinder bore. Then clean the caliper in hot soapy water and rinse in clear, cold water. Dry with compressed air.

2. Clean the piston in clean DOT 4 brake fluid.

3. Check the piston and cylinder bore (**Figure 88**) for deep scratches or other obvious wear marks. Do not hone the cylinder. If the piston or cylinder is damaged, replace the caliper assembly.

4. Clean the bleed valve with compressed air. Check the valve threads for damage. Replace the dust cap if missing or damaged.

5. Clean the banjo bolt (**Figure 89**) with compressed air. Check the threads for damage. Replace worn or damaged washers.

6. Check the caliper friction boot and dust covers (**Figure 90**). If swollen, cracked or severely worn, the entire brake caliper will have to be replaced.

7. Check the support bracket shafts and bolt (**Figure 90**) for severe wear, damage or uneven wear (steps). The shafts must be in good condition for the caliper to slide back and forth. Remove all grease residue from the bracket. If the support bracket is damaged, the entire brake caliper will have to be replaced.

8. Measure the thickness of each brake pad (**Figure 66**) with a vernier caliper or ruler and compare to the specification in **Table 2**. If the pad thickness is equal to or less than the wear limit, replace the pads as a set.

9. Inspect the brake pads for uneven wear, damage or grease contamination. Replace the pads as a set, if necessary.

10. Replace the piston seal, dust seal and parking brake O-ring as a set.

NOTE
Yamaha states that the piston seal and dust seal must be replaced whenever the caliper is disassembled.

Parking Brake Housing
Inspection

The rear parking brake assembly components (**Figure 91**) are not available separately. If these items are damaged, the entire rear brake caliper

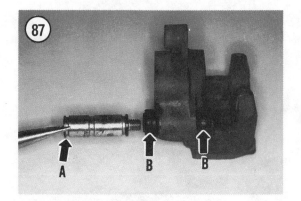

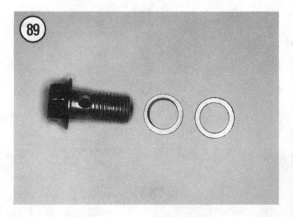

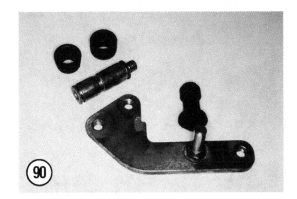

assembly will have to be replaced. When servicing the rear caliper in the following sections, handle these items carefully so that you do not damage them.

Refer to **Figure 91** when servicing the parking brake assembly.

> *NOTE*
> *Do not wash the parking brake housing (**Figure 92**) in solvent as this will wash the grease out of the housing.*

1. Inspect the spring in the parking brake housing. If the spring is damaged, replace the entire brake caliper assembly.

2. If the parking brake housing gasket (**Figure 91**) is damaged, cut out a new gasket, using gasket material.

3. Clean the parking brake lever, adjust bolt and nut, small return spring and the 2 Allen bolts in solvent. Dry with compressed air.

Assembly

> *NOTE*
> *Use new, unused DOT 4 brake fluid when brake fluid is called for in the following steps.*

1. If removed, install the 2 dust covers and caliper bracket bolt as shown in **Figure 87**.

2. If removed, install the friction boot through the caliper as shown in **Figure 86**.

3. Install the washer onto the caliper bracket bolt installed in Step 1. See **Figure 85**. Lubricate the support bracket shafts with a thin coat of PBC (Poly Butyl Cuprysil) grease (or equivalent). Then slide the support bracket into the brake caliper as shown in **Figure 93**. Torque the caliper bracket bolt (A, **Figure 84**) to the specification in **Table 3**.

> *CAUTION*
> *PBC grease (or equivalent) is a special high temperature, water-resistant grease that can be used in braking systems. Do not use any other kind of lubricant as it may thin out and contaminate the brake pads.*

4. If removed, install the parking brake housing assembly as follows:

12

a. Install the gasket (**Figure 83**) onto the brake caliper.

b. Place the parking brake housing (B, **Figure 82**) onto the brake caliper, aligning the mounting holes and gasket.

c. Apply Loctite 242 (blue) onto the parking brake housing mounting bolts prior to installation. Then install the bolts (A, **Figure 82**) and torque to the specification in **Table 3**.

d. Align the 2 dot marks (**Figure 94**) and install the parking brake lever onto the parking brake shaft.

e. Install the adjust bolt (C, **Figure 80**). Then set the bolt so that the original length of the threads, as recorded during disassembly (**Figure 79**), are exposed. Tighten the locknut (B, **Figure 80**).

f. Hook the spring between the parking brake lever and parking brake housing as shown in A, **Figure 80**.

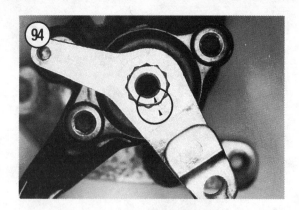

5. Soak the dust seal, piston seal and parking brake housing O-ring (**Figure 95**) in brake fluid for approximately 5 minutes.

6. Install the new parking brake O-ring (A, **Figure 95**) into the groove in the back of the parking brake housing. See **Figure 96**.

7. Lightly coat the piston and cylinder bore with brake fluid.

8. Install a new piston seal (B, **Figure 95**) into the second groove in the cylinder bore.

9. Install a new dust seal (C, **Figure 95**) into the front groove in the cylinder bore.

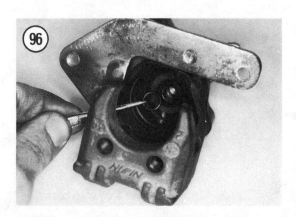

NOTE
Check that both seals fit squarely into their respective cylinder bore grooves. If a seal is not installed properly, the caliper assembly will leak and braking performance will be reduced.

10. Install the piston—shoulder end first—into the cylinder bore. See **Figure 97**.

11. If necessary, install the bleed screw and its dust cover. Tighten securely.

12. If removed, install the pad spring into the brake caliper.

13. Install the brake caliper assembly and brake pads as described in this chapter.

REAR MASTER CYLINDER

Refer to **Figure 98** when servicing the rear master cylinder in this section.

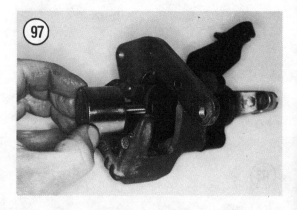

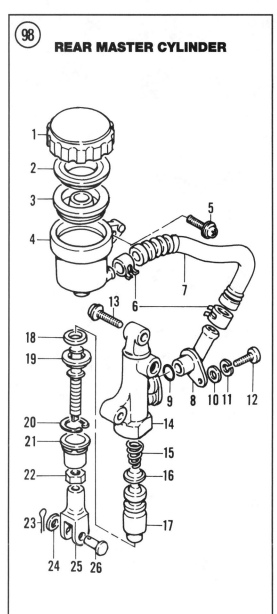

REAR MASTER CYLINDER

1. Cap
2. Diaphragm bushing
3. Diaphragm
4. Reservoir
5. Screw
6. Hose clamp
7. Hose
8. Hose nozzle
9. O-ring
10. Washer
11. Lockwasher
12. Screw
13. Screw
14. Master cylinder
15. Spring
16. Primary cup
17. Piston
18. Secondary cup
19. Pushrod/washer assembly
20. Circlip
21. Boot
22. Nut
23. Cotter pin
24. Washer
25. Connector
26. Clevis pin

Read the information listed under *Disc Brake* in this chapter before servicing the master cylinder.

Removal/Installation

1. Park the vehicle on level ground. Block the front wheels so that the vehicle cannot roll in either direction.

2A. To remove brake fluid from the reservoir:

   a. Remove the master cylinder cap and diaphragm. See A, **Figure 99**.

   b. Use a clean syringe and remove the brake fluid from the reservoir. Discard the brake fluid.

2B. To drain the reservoir and brake hose:

   a. Insert a tube onto the rear brake caliper bleed valve (**Figure 100**). Insert the other end of the tube into a clean container.

   b. Open the bleed valve and operate the rear brake lever to drain the master cylinder and brake hose of all brake fluid.

   c. Close the bleed valve and remove the tube.

   d. Discard the brake fluid.

3. Disconnect the brake pedal at the master cylinder pushrod. Remove the cotter pin (A, **Figure 101**) that locks the clevis pin between the pushrod and brake lever. Then remove the washer and pull out the clevis pin. Discard the cotter pin.

12

4. Loosen the master cylinder banjo bolt (**Figure 102**) and remove the bolt and its washers. Seal the brake hose to prevent brake fluid from dripping out.

5. Remove the brake fluid reservoir mounting screw (B, **Figure 99**).

6. Remove the master cylinder mounting screws (B, **Figure 101**), then remove the master cylinder and reservoir (C, **Figure 101**) from the frame.

7. If necessary, service the master cylinder as described in this chapter.

8. Mount the master cylinder housing onto the frame. Install and torque the screws (C, **Figure 101**) to the specification in **Table 3**.

9. Mount the brake fluid reservoir hose onto the frame and secure with its mounting screw. See B, **Figure 99**, typical.

CAUTION
The brake hose should be routed between the master cylinder bosses as shown in Figure 102.

10. Install the brake hose onto the master cylinder (**Figure 102**), using the banjo bolt and the 2 washers; a washer should be installed on each side of the hose. Tighten the banjo bolt to the torque specification in **Table 3**.

11. Connect the brake lever to the master cylinder pushrod with the clevis pin, washer and a new cotter pin (A, **Figure 101**). Bend the cotter pin arms over to lock it.

12. Refill the master cylinder with DOT 4 brake fluid and bleed the brake as described in this chapter.

13. Adjust the brake pedal height as described in Chapter Three.

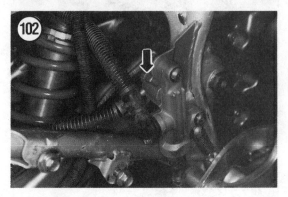

WARNING
Do not ride the vehicle until the rear brake is working properly. Make sure the that the lever travel is not excessive and that the lever does not feel spongy—both indicate that the bleeding operation needs to be repeated.

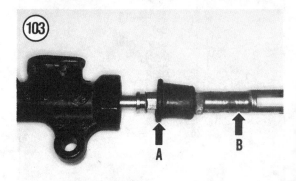

Disassembly

1. Remove the master cylinder as described in this chapter.

2. Remove the screw and washers that secure the reservoir hose joint to the master cylinder; see 12, **Figure 98**. Then remove the hose joint (8, **Figure 98**) and the O-ring (9, **Figure 98**).

3. Remove the master cylinder cap screws and remove the cap and diaphragm from the caliper.

4. Carefully pull the dust cover (A, **Figure 103**) out of the piston bore.

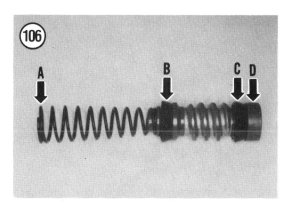

5. Compress the piston and remove the circlip (**Figure 104**) from the groove in the master cylinder.

6. Remove the pushrod assembly along with the washer and circlip (B, **Figure 103**) from the cylinder.

7. Remove the piston assembly (**Figure 105**) from the cylinder.

Inspection

Worn or damaged master cylinder components will prevent proper brake fluid pressure from building in the brake line. Reduced pressure will cause the brake to feel weak and it will not hold properly.

1. Wash the piston and cylinder with clean DOT 4 brake fluid.

2. The piston assembly is identified in **Figure 106**:
   a. Spring.
   b. Primary cup.
   c. Secondary cup.
   d. Piston.

> *CAUTION*
> *Do not attempt to remove the secondary and primary cups (**Figure 106**) from the piston. Removal will damage the cups, requiring replacement of the piston assembly.*

3. Check the piston assembly (**Figure 106**) for the following defects:
   a. Broken, distorted or collapsed piston return spring (A, **Figure 106**).
   b. Worn, cracked, damaged or swollen primary (B, **Figure 106**) and secondary cups (C, **Figure 106**).
   c. Scratched, scored or damaged piston (D, **Figure 106**).

If any of these parts are worn or damaged, replace the piston assembly.

4. Check the master cylinder bore (**Figure 107**) for severe wear, scratches or other damage.

5. Check the pushrod assembly (**Figure 108**) for the following defects:
   a. Cracked or damaged bracket. Stripped or damaged bracket nut.
   b. Severely worn or damaged pushrod.
   c. Worn, cracked or swollen dust boot.
   d. Bent or damaged circlip.
   e. Bent or damaged washer.

12

If any of these parts are worn or damaged, replace the pushrod assembly. The circlip can be purchased separately.

6. Check for plugged supply and relief ports in the master cylinder (**Figure 109**). Clean with compressed air.

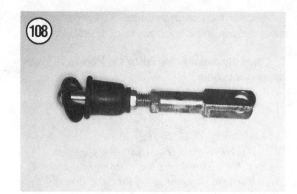

> *NOTE*
> *A plugged relief port will cause the pads to drag on the disc.*

7. Check the reservoir cap and diaphragm for damage. Check the diaphragm for cracks or deterioration. Replace damaged parts as required.

8. Check all of the threaded holes in the master cylinder. Clean with compressed air.

9. Clean and blow dry the reservoir and hose assembly. Replace the O-ring if worn, cracked or damaged.

Assembly

Use new, unused DOT 4 brake fluid when brake fluid is called for in the following steps.

1. If you are installing a piston repair kit, note the following:

   a. Check the repair kit to make sure that it contains all of the necessary new parts. Compare to the exploded view in **Figure 98**.

   b. Wash the new parts in new brake fluid.

2. Lightly coat the piston assembly and cylinder bore with brake fluid.

3. Assemble the piston assembly as shown in **Figure 106**. The return spring is tapered; fit the smaller end onto the piston as shown in **Figure 106**.

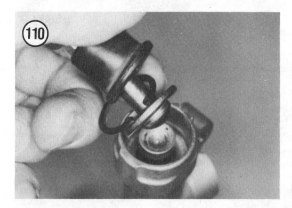

> *CAUTION*
> *When installing the piston assembly in Step 4, make sure the primary and secondary cups do not tear or turn inside out; both cups are slightly larger than the bore.*

4. Insert the piston assembly into the master cylinder bore, spring end first, as shown in **Figure 105**.

5. Install the pushrod ball into the end of the piston (**Figure 110**) and compress the piston slightly. Slide the washer down the pushrod so that it rests below the circlip groove in the cylinder. Install the circlip (**Figure 104**), making sure it seats in the cylinder groove completely. Push and release the piston a few times to make sure it moves smoothly in the cylinder bore.

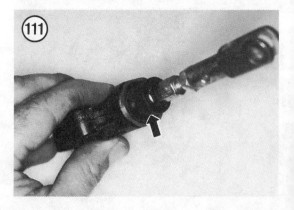

6. Pull the dust cover down the pushrod and fit it into the cylinder bore as shown in **Figure 111**.

7. Install the brake hose O-ring (9, **Figure 98**) into the master cylinder.

8. Insert the hose joint (8, **Figure 98**) into the master cylinder and secure it with the screw, lockwasher and flat washer.

9. Install the master cylinder as described in this chapter.

BRAKE HOSE REPLACEMENT

The brake hoses should be replaced when they show signs of wear or damage. The front brake hoses and their fittings are shown in **Figures 112-114**.

1. Place a container under the brake line at the caliper. Remove the banjo bolt and sealing washers at the caliper or master cylinder.

2. On compression fittings, hold the brake hose with a wrench and loosen the bolt. Separate the hose from the bolt.

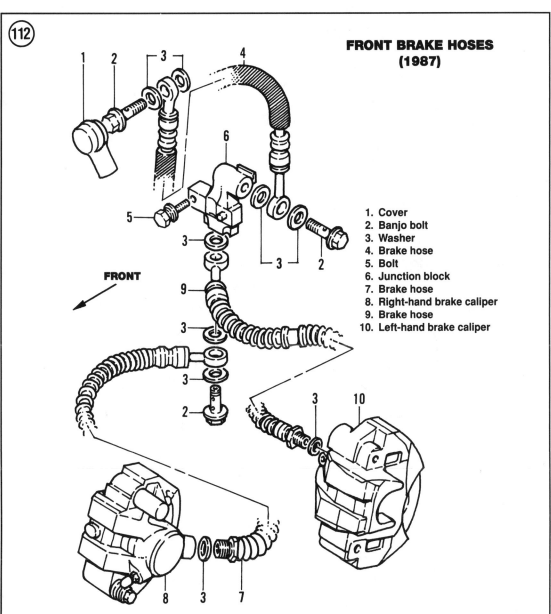

(112)

FRONT BRAKE HOSES
(1987)

FRONT

1. Cover
2. Banjo bolt
3. Washer
4. Brake hose
5. Bolt
6. Junction block
7. Brake hose
8. Right-hand brake caliper
9. Brake hose
10. Left-hand brake caliper

12

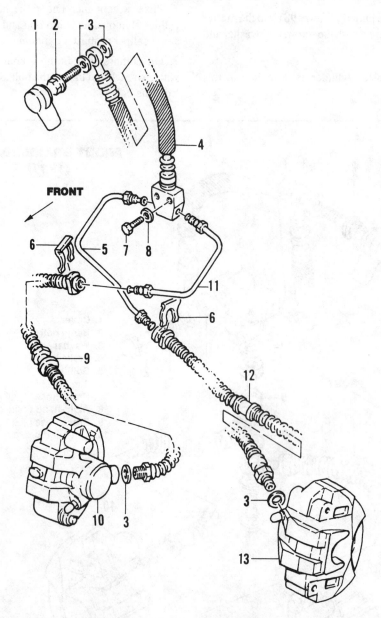

**FRONT BRAKE HOSES
(1988)**

FRONT

1. Cover
2. Banjo bolt
3. Washer
4. Brake hose
5. Brake tube
6. Clip
7. Bolt
8. Washer
9. Brake hose
10. Right-hand brake caliper
11. Brake tube
12. Brake hose
13. Left-hand brake caliper

(114)

**FRONT BRAKE HOSES
(1989-ON)**

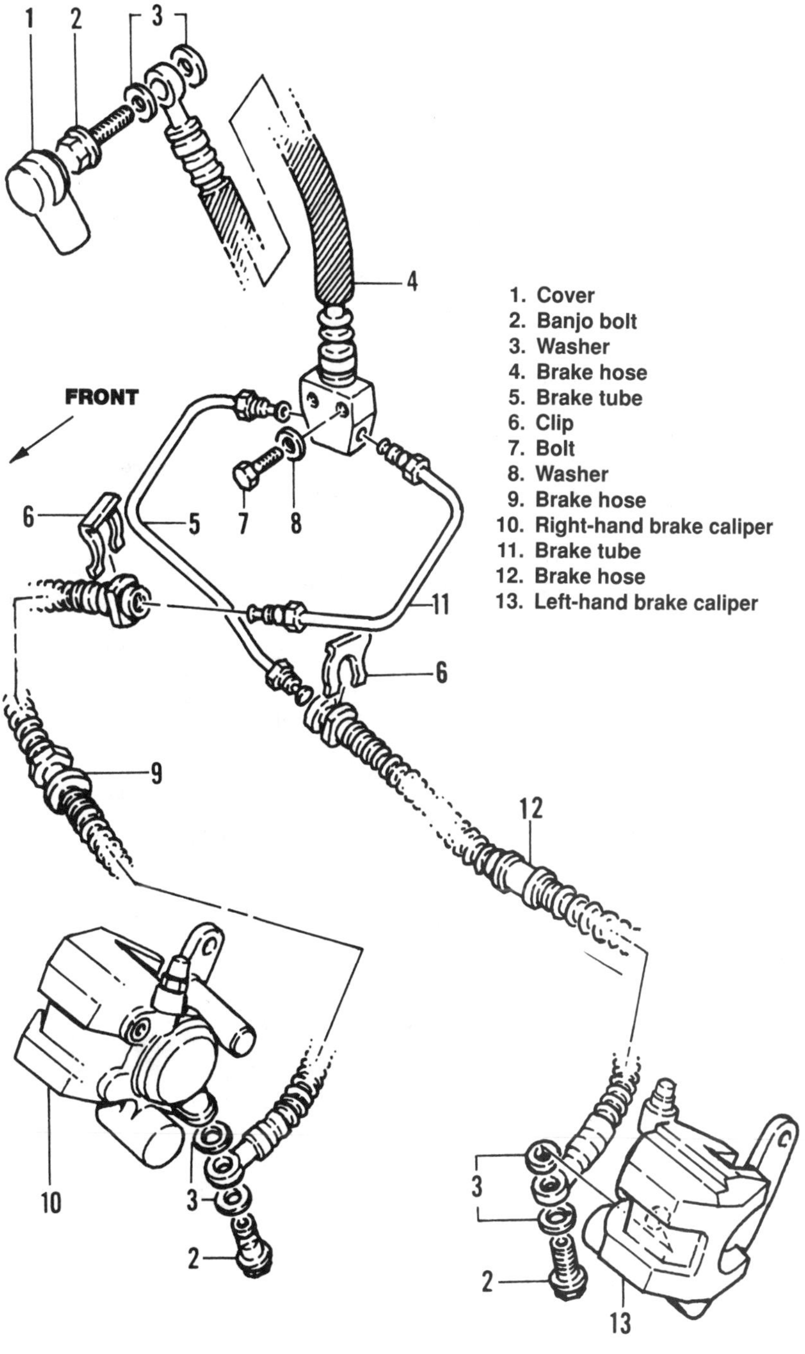

FRONT

1. Cover
2. Banjo bolt
3. Washer
4. Brake hose
5. Brake tube
6. Clip
7. Bolt
8. Washer
9. Brake hose
10. Right-hand brake caliper
11. Brake tube
12. Brake hose
13. Left-hand brake caliper

12

3. Place the end of the brake hose in a clean container. Operate the front brake lever to drain the master cylinder and brake hose of all brake fluid. Dispose of this brake fluid—never reuse brake fluid.

4. Install a new brake hose in the reverse order of removal. Install new sealing washers and banjo bolts (**Figure 115**) if necessary.

5. Tighten the banjo bolts to the torque specification in **Table 3**.

6. On compression fittings, thread the bolt onto the brake hose. Tighten the compression fitting securely.

7. Refill the master cylinder with fresh brake fluid clearly marked DOT 4. Bleed the brake as described in this chapter.

> *WARNING*
> *Do not ride the vehicle until you are sure that the brakes are operating properly.*

BRAKE DISC

The front brake discs (**Figure 116**) are mounted onto the front hubs. The rear brake disc (**Figure 117**) is mounted onto a splined hub that is installed onto the rear axle.

Inspection

It is not necessary to remove the disc to inspect it. Small marks on the disc are not important, but radial scratches deep enough to snag a fingernail reduce braking effectiveness and increase brake pad wear. If these grooves are evident, and the brake pads are wearing rapidly, the disc should be replaced.

Table 1 and **Table 2** list brake disc specifications. When servicing the brake discs, do not have the discs reconditioned (ground) to compensate for warpage. The discs are thin and grinding will only reduce their thickness, causing them to warp quite rapidly. If a disc is warped, the brake pads may be dragging on the disc, causing the disc to overheat. Overheating can be caused when there is unequal brake pad pressure on both sides of the disc. Four main causes of unequal pad pressure are: (1) the floating caliper is binding on the caliper bracket shafts, thus preventing the caliper from floating (side-to-side) on the disc; (2) the brake caliper piston seal is worn or damaged; (3) the small master cylinder relief port is plugged;

and (4) the primary cup on the master cylinder piston is worn or damaged.

1. Support the vehicle with all 4 wheels off the ground.

2. Remove the front wheels as described in Chapter Ten.

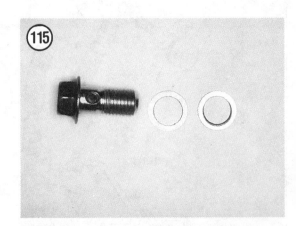

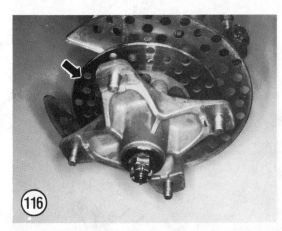

3. Measure the thickness around the disc at several locations with a micrometer (**Figure 118**). The disc must be replaced if the thicknesses at any point is less than the thickness specified in **Table 1** or **Table 2**.

4. Make sure the disc bolts are tight prior to performing this check. Using a magnetic stand, install the dial indicator and position its stem against the brake disc as shown in **Figure 119**. Then zero the dial gauge. Slowly turn the axle or hub to measure runout. If the runout exceeds 0.15 mm (0.006 in.), the disc must be replaced.

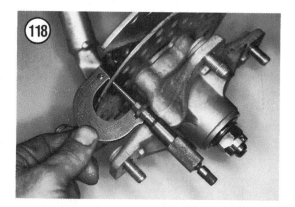

5. Clean the disc of any rust or corrosion and wipe clean with lacquer thinner. Never use an oil based solvent that may leave an oil residue on the disc.

Removal/Installation

1A. To remove the front brake disc:
  a. Remove the front hub(s) as described in Chapter Ten.
  b. Remove the screws securing the disc to the wheel and remove the disc (**Figure 120**).
1B. To remove the rear brake disc:
  a. Set the parking brake to lock the rear axle.
  b. Loosen, but do not remove, the bolts securing the rear brake disc to the axle hub.
  c. Block the front wheels. Then support the vehicle with both rear wheels off the ground.
  d. Remove the right-hand rear wheel as described in Chapter Eleven.
  e. Remove the brake caliper as described in this chapter.
  f. Remove the brake disc screws and remove the brake disc (**Figure 119**).
2. Install by reversing these removal steps. Torque the disc brake screws to the specification in **Table 3**.

CAUTION
The disc brake screws are made out of a harder material than similar screws that are not used in the braking system. When replacing these screws, make sure to purchase the correct type.

BRAKE BLEEDING

This procedure is necessary only when the brakes feel spongy, there is a leak in the hydraulic system, a component has been replaced or the brake fluid has been replaced.

NOTE
During this procedure, all the hose junctions in the brake system will be bled of air. It is important to check the fluid level in the master cylinder frequently. If the reservoir runs dry, air will enter the system which will require starting over.

1. Flip the dust cap from the brake bleeder valve.
2. Connect a length of clear tubing to the bleeder valve on the caliper (**Figure 121**). Place the other end of the tube into a clean container. Fill the container with

enough fresh brake fluid to keep the end submerged. The tube should be long enough so that a loop can be made higher than the bleeder valve to prevent air from being drawn into the caliper during bleeding.

CAUTION
Cover all parts which could become contaminated by the accidental spilling of brake fluid. Wash any spilled brake fluid from any surface immediately, as it will destroy the finish. Use soapy water and rinse completely.

3. Clean the top of the front master cylinder or the rear reservoir cap of all dirt and foreign matter. Remove the cap and diaphragm. Fill the reservoir to about 10 mm (3/8 in.) from the top. Insert the diaphragm to prevent the entry of dirt and moisture.

WARNING
Use brake fluid clearly marked DOT 4 only. Others may vaporize and cause brake failure. Always use the same brand name; do not intermix the brake fluids, as many brands are not compatible.

NOTE
During this procedure, it is important to check the reservoir fluid level periodically to make sure it does not run dry. If the reservoir should run dry, air will enter the system and you'll have to start over.

4. Hold the brake lever or pedal in the applied position and open the bleeder valve (**Figure 122**) about 1/2 turn—do not release the brake lever or pedal while the bleeder valve is open. When you open the bleeder valve, you will feel the lever loosen a bit as it moves to the limit of its travel. At this point, tighten the bleeder screw, then release the brake lever or pedal.

NOTE
As the brake fluid enters the system, the level will drop in the master cylinder reservoir. Maintain the level at about 10 mm (3/8 in.) from the top of the reservoir to prevent air from being drawn into the system.

5. Repeat Step 4 until the system is bled. If you are replacing the fluid, continue until the fluid emerging from the hose is clean.

NOTE
If bleeding is difficult, it may be necessary to allow the fluid to stabilize for a

few hours. Repeat the bleeding procedure when the tiny bubbles in the system settle out.

6. Hold the lever in the applied position and tighten the bleeder valve. Remove the bleeder tube and install the bleeder valve dust cap.

7. If necessary, add fluid to correct the level in the master cylinder reservoir. It must be above the level line.

8. Install the cap and tighten the screws (front master cylinder).

9. Test the feel of the brake lever. It should feel firm and should offer the same resistance each time it's operated. If it feels spongy, it is likely that air is still in the system and it must be bled again. When all air has been bled from the system and the brake fluid level is correct in the reservoir, double-check for leaks and tighten all fittings and connections.

WARNING
Before riding the vehicle, make certain that the brake is working correctly by operating the lever or pedal several times. Then make the test ride a slow one at first to make sure the brake is working correctly.

Table 1 FRONT DISC BRAKE SERVICE SPECIFICATIONS

	Standard mm (in.)	Service limit mm (in.)
Disc		
Outer diameter	161	—
	(6.34)	—
Thickness	3.5	—
	(0.138)	—
Brake pad thickness		
1987-1988	6.0	0.8
	(0.236)	(0.031)
1989-on	4.5	1.0
	(0.18)	(0.04)

Table 2 REAR DISC BRAKE SERVICE SPECIFICATIONS

	Standard mm (in.)	Service limit mm (in.)
Disc		
Outer diameter		
1987	203	—
	(7.99)	—
1988-1989	220	—
	(8.66)	—
1990-on	245	—
	(9.65)	—
Thickness		
1987	4.0	3.5
	(0.16)	(0.13)
1988	3.6	3.1
	(0.14)	(0.12)
1989	4.0	3.5
	(0.16)	(0.13)
1990-on	3.5	3.0
	(0.14)	(0.12)
Brake pad thickness	4.5	1.0
	(0.177)	(0.040)

Table 3 BRAKE TIGHTENING TORQUES

	N·m	ft.-lb.
Front brake		
Caliper mounting bolts	28	20
Brake pad pin bolts (1988-on)	18	13
Rear brake		
Brake caliper @ axle housing	23	17
Rear master cylinder @ frame screws	20	14
Brake pad pin bolts	18	13
Parking brake housing mounting bolts	28	20
Caliper bracket bolt	23	17
Disc brake mounting screws		
Front	28	20
Rear	23	17
Banjo bolts		
Front and rear	27	19

12

CHAPTER THIRTEEN

BODY

This chapter contains removal and installation for body panels and seat.

It is suggested that as soon as the part is removed from the vehicle, all mounting hardware (i.e. small brackets, bolts, nuts, washers, etc.) be reinstalled onto the removed part.

SEAT

Removal/Installation

1. Lift the seat latch (**Figure 1**) and remove the seat.
2. To install the seat, engage the front seat bracket with the frame, then push the rear of the seat down to lock it in place.
3. Lift up on the seat and make sure it is properly secured at the front and rear.

FUEL TANK COVER

Refer to **Figure 2**.

Removal/Installation

1. Remove the seat as described in this chapter.

3. Remove the front and rear bolts (**Figure 3**) that hold the fuel tank cover to the frame.

4. Remove the fuel cap (**Figure 4**) and remove the fuel tank cover. Reinstall the fuel cap.

5. Remove the fuel tank cover.

6. Install by reversing these steps.

FRONT PANEL

Refer to **Figure 2**.

②

FRONT PANEL/FUEL TANK COVER

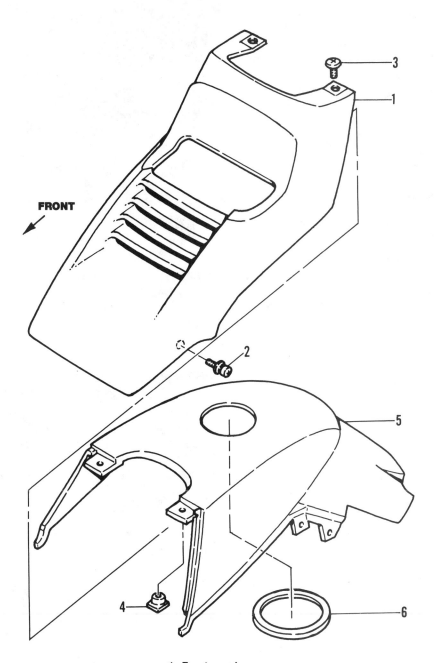

FRONT

1. Front panel
2. Screw and washer
3. Screw
4. Nut
5. Fuel tank cover
6. Damper

13

Removal/Installation

1. Remove the fuel tank cover as described in this chapter.
2. Remove the key from the main switch. Then remove large nut that holds the main switch (**Figure 5**) to the front panel.
3. Remove the bolts that hold the front panel to the frame and remove the front panel (**Figure 6**).
4. Install by reversing these removal steps.

FRONT FENDER

Refer to **Figure 7**.

Removal/Installation

1. Remove the fuel tank cover and front panel as described in this chapter.
2. Remove the bolts and washers securing the front fender to the frame.
3. Carefully pull the front fender (**Figure 8**) away from the frame. Then move the front fender up and toward the front. Spread the rear portion of the front fender out and pull it from the frame.
4. Install by reversing these removal steps, noting the following.
5. Do not overtighten the bolts as the plastic fender may fracture.

REAR FENDER

Refer to **Figure 9** (1987-1989) or **Figure 10** (1990-on).

Removal/Installation

1. Remove the battery (A, **Figure 11**) as described in Chapter Three.
2. Remove the bolt(s) securing the rear fender to the fender bracket (**Figure 12**). .
3. On 1990-on models, remove the bolts securing the rear fender to the footpeg assemblies (**Figure 13**).

NOTE
*Make a note of the battery cables and vent tube (**Figure 14**) prior to removing the rear fender.*

4. Lift the rear fender up slightly and pull the battery cables and vent tube through the fender openings (**Figure 14**). Then remove the rear fender (B, **Figure 11**).

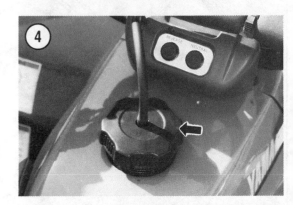

⑦ **FRONT FENDER**

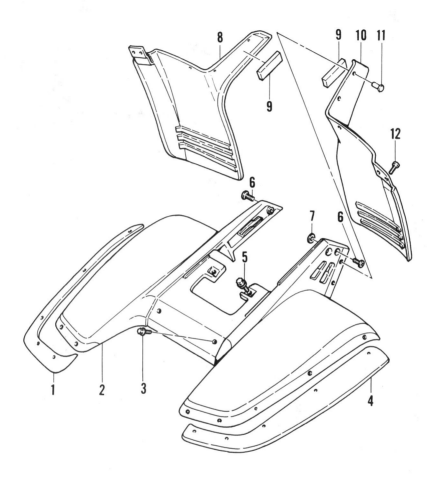

1. Outer cover
2. Front fender
3. Bolt
4. Outer cover
5. Bolt
6. Bolt
7. Washer
8. Flap
9. Damper
10. Flap
11. Blind rivet
12. Screw

13

5. Install by reversing these steps, noting the following.

6. Make sure to route the battery cables and battery vent tube through the rear fender openings, following their original path.

FOOTPEGS

Removal/Installation

Refer to **Figure 15** or **Figure 16** when removing and installing the footpeg assemblies. When installing the shift pedal, align the index mark on the shift

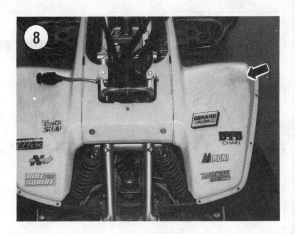

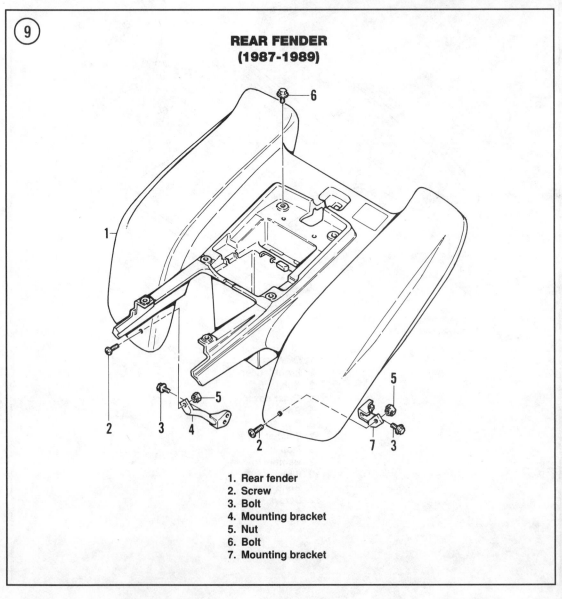

**REAR FENDER
(1987-1989)**

1. Rear fender
2. Screw
3. Bolt
4. Mounting bracket
5. Nut
6. Bolt
7. Mounting bracket

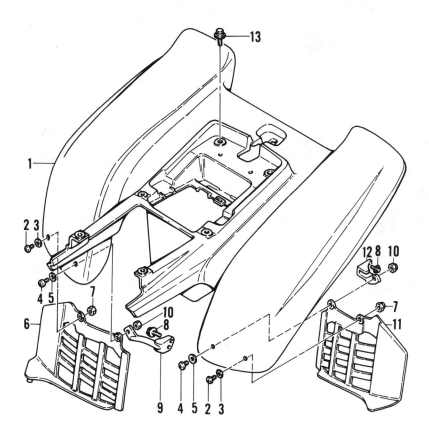

⑩

**REAR FENDER
(1990-ON)**

1. Rear fender
2. Bolt
3. Washer
4. Bolt
5. Washer
6. Flap
7. Nut
8. Bolt
9. Mounting bracket
10. Nut
11. Flap
12. Mounting bracket

13

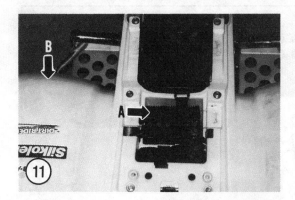

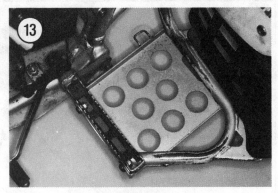

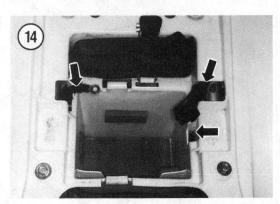

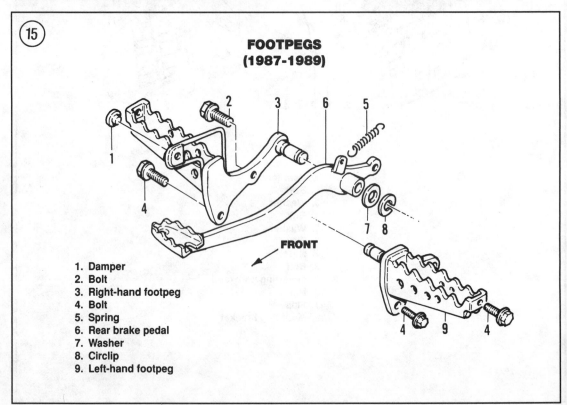

FOOTPEGS
(1987-1989)

FRONT

1. Damper
2. Bolt
3. Right-hand footpeg
4. Bolt
5. Spring
6. Rear brake pedal
7. Washer
8. Circlip
9. Left-hand footpeg

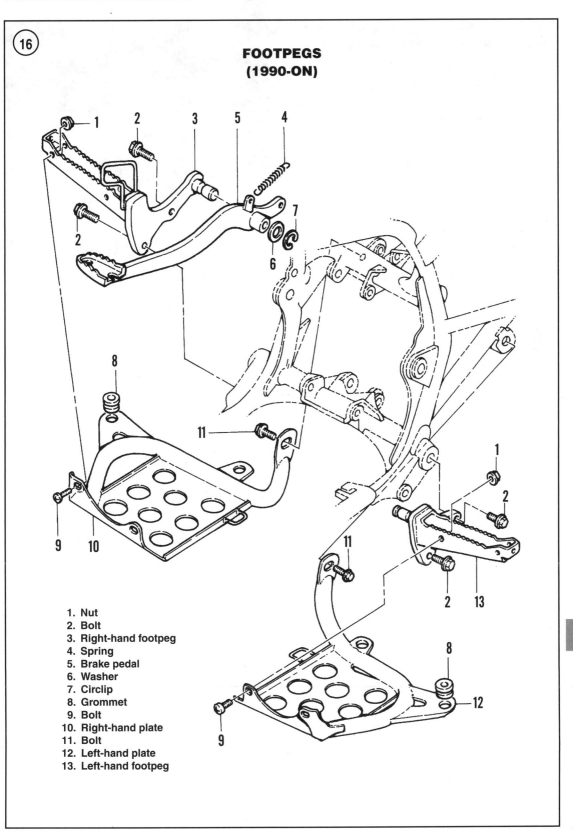

⑯ **FOOTPEGS (1990-ON)**

1. Nut
2. Bolt
3. Right-hand footpeg
4. Spring
5. Brake pedal
6. Washer
7. Circlip
8. Grommet
9. Bolt
10. Right-hand plate
11. Bolt
12. Left-hand plate
13. Left-hand footpeg

13

shaft with the boss slit (**Figure 17**). Tighten the footpeg-to-frame mounting bolts to 55 N·m (40 ft.-lb.).

FRONT BUMPER

Removal/Installation

The front bumper is secured to the frame with 4 mounting bolts. Tighten the bolts to 23 N·m (17 ft.-lb.).

REAR BUMPER

Removal/installation

The rear bumper is secured to the frame with 4 mounting bolts. Tighten the bolts to 23 N·m (17 ft.-lb.).

INDEX

14

14

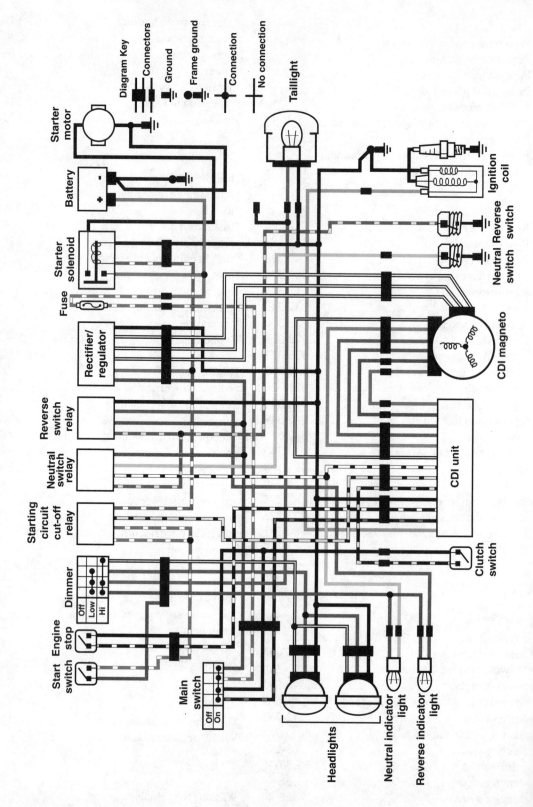

YMF350XT (1987)

YFN350XU (1988)

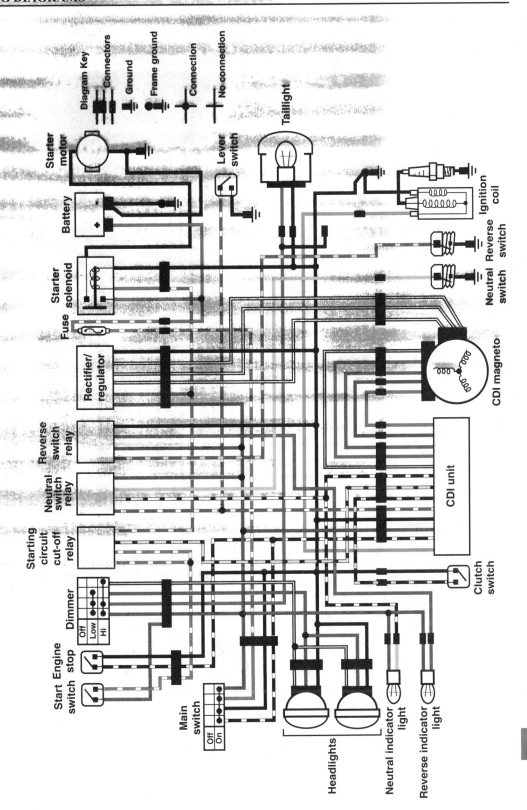

15

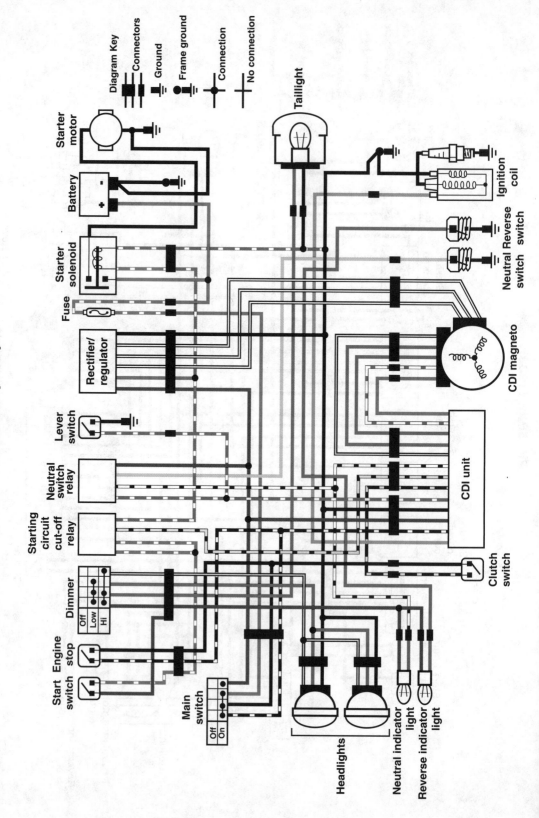

YFM350XW (1989)

YFM350XA (1990-1996)

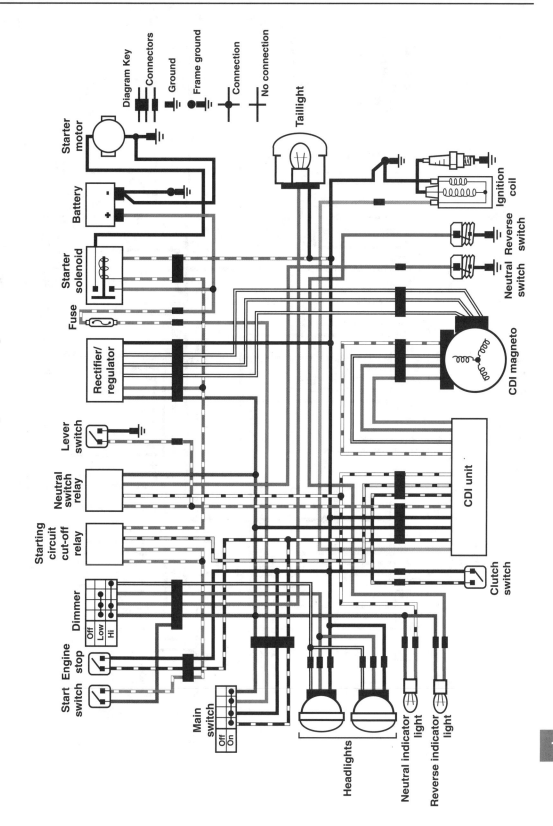

15

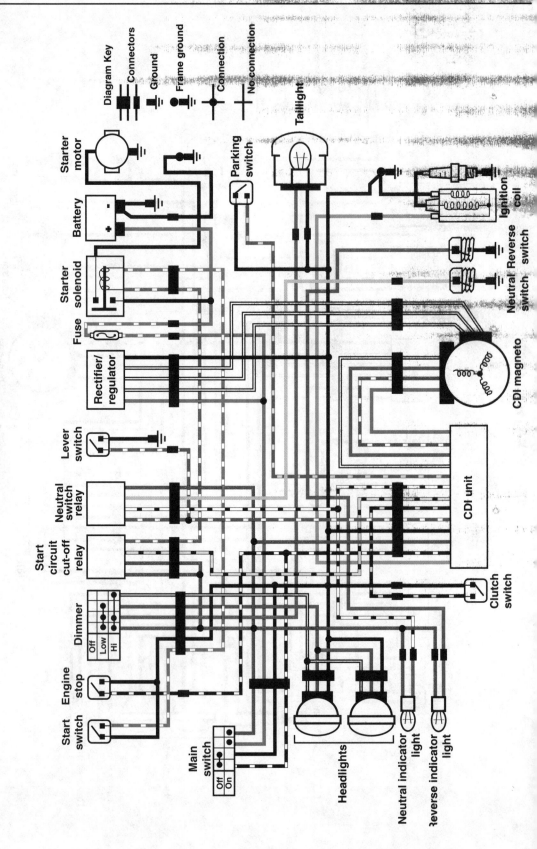

YFM350X (1997-2001)

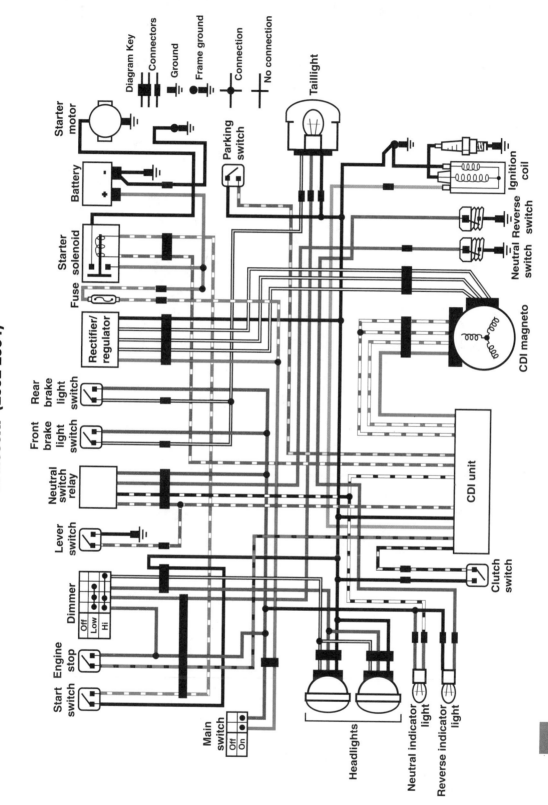

YFM350XP (2002-2004)

15

NOTES

NOTES

NOTES

MAINTENANCE LOG

Date	Hours	Type of Service

BMW

M308	500 & 600 CC Twins, 55-69
M309	F650, 1994-2000
M500-3	BMW K-Series, 85-97
M501	K1200RS, GT & LT, 98-05
M502-3	BMW R50/5-R100 GSPD, 70-96
M503-3	R850, R1100, R1150 and R1200C, 93-05

HARLEY-DAVIDSON

M419	Sportsters, 59-85
M428	Sportster Evolution, 86-90
M429-4	XL/XLH Sportster, 91-03
M427-1	Sportster, 04-06
M418	Panheads, 48-65
M420	Shovelheads, 66-84
M421-3	FLS/FXS Evolution, 84-99
M423-2	FLS/FXS Twin Cam, 00-05
M422-3	FLH/FLT/FXR Evolution, 84-99
M430-4	FLH/FLT Twin Cam, 99-05
M424-2	FXD Evolution, 91-98
M425-3	FXD Twin Cam, 99-05

HONDA

ATVs

M316	Odyssey FL250, 77-84
M311	ATC, TRX & Fourtrax 70-125, 70-87
M433	Fourtrax 90 ATV, 93-00
M326	ATC185 & 200, 80-86
M347	ATC200X & Fourtrax 200SX, 86-88
M455	ATC250 & Fourtrax 200/250, 84-87
M342	ATC250R, 81-84
M348	TRX250R/Fourtrax 250R & ATC250R, 85-89
M456-3	TRX250X 87-92; TRX300EX 93-04
M215	TRX250EX, 01-05
M446-2	TRX250 Recon & ES, 97-04
M346-3	TRX300/Fourtrax 300 & TRX300FW/Fourtrax 4x4, 88-00
M200-2	TRX350 Rancher, 00-06
M459-3	TRX400 Foreman 95-03
M454-3	TRX400EX 99-05
M205	TRX450 Foreman, 98-04
M210	TRX500 Rubicon, 98-04

Singles

M310-13	50-110cc OHC Singles, 65-99
M319-2	XR50R, CRF50F, XR70R & CRF70F, 97-05
M315	100-350cc OHC, 69-82
M317	Elsinore, 125-250cc, 73-80
M442	CR60-125R Pro-Link, 81-88
M431-2	CR80R, 89-95, CR125R, 89-91
M435	CR80, 96-02
M457-2	CR125R & CR250R, 92-97
M464	CR125R, 1998-2002
M443	CR250R-500R Pro-Link, 81-87
M432-3	CR250R, 88-91 & CR500R, 88-01
M437	CR250R, 97-01
M352	CRF250, CRF250X & CRF450R, CRF450X, 02-05
M312-13	XL/XR75-100, 75-03
M318-4	XL/XR/TLR 125-200, 79-03
M328-4	XL/XR250, 78-00; XL/XR350R 83-85; XR200R, 84-85; XR250L, 91-96
M320-2	XR400R, 96-04
M339-7	XL/XR 500-650, 79-03

Twins

M321	125-200cc, 65-78
M322	250-350cc, 64-74
M323	250-360cc Twins, 74-77
M324-5	Twinstar, Rebel 250 & Nighthawk 250, 78-03
M334	400-450cc, 78-87
M333	450 & 500cc, 65-76
M335	CX & GL500/650 Twins, 78-83
M344	VT500, 83-88
M313	VT700 & 750, 83-87
M314-2	VT750 Shadow (chain drive), 98-05
M440	VT1100C Shadow , 85-96
M460-3	VT1100C Series, 95-04

Fours

M332	CB350-550cc, SOHC, 71-78
M345	CB550 & 650, 83-85
M336	CB650, 79-82
M341	CB750 SOHC, 69-78
M337	CB750 DOHC, 79-82
M436	CB750 Nighthawk, 91-93 & 95-99
M325	CB900, 1000 & 1100, 80-83
M439	Hurricane 600, 87-90
M441-2	CBR600F2 & F3, 91-98
M445-2	CBR600F4, 99-06
M434-2	CBR900RR Fireblade, 93-99
M329	500cc V-Fours, 84-86
M438	Honda VFR800, 98-00
M349	700-1000 Interceptor, 83-85
M458-2	VFR700F-750F, 86-97
M327	700-1100cc V-Fours, 82-88
M340	GL1000 & 1100, 75-83
M504	GL1200, 84-87
M508	ST1100/PAN European, 90-02

Sixes

M505	GL1500 Gold Wing, 88-92
M506-2	GL1500 Gold Wing, 93-00
M507-2	GL1800 Gold Wing, 01-05
M462-2	GL1500C Valkyrie, 97-03

KAWASAKI

ATVs

M465-2	KLF220 & KLF250 Bayou, 88-03
M466-4	KLF300 Bayou, 86-04
M467	KLF400 Bayou, 93-99
M470	KEF300 Lakota, 95-99
M385	KSF250 Mojave, 87-00

Singles

M350-9	Rotary Valve 80-350cc, 66-01
M444-2	KX60, 83-02; KX80 83-90
M448	KX80/85/100, 89-03
M351	KDX200, 83-88
M447-3	KX125 & KX250, 82-91 KX500, 83-04
M472-2	KX125, 92-00
M473-2	KX250, 92-00
M474-2	KLR650, 87-06

Twins

M355	KZ400, KZ/Z440, EN450 & EN500, 74-95
M360-3	EX500, GPZ500S, Ninja R, 87-02
M356-4	Vulcan 700 & 750, 85-04
M354-2	Vulcan 800 & Vulcan 800 Classic, 95-04
M357-2	Vulcan 1500, 87-99
M471-2	Vulcan Classic 1500, 96-04

Fours

M449	KZ500/550 & ZX550, 79-85
M450	KZ, Z & ZX750, 80-85
M358	KZ650, 77-83
M359-3	900-1000cc Fours, 73-81
M451-3	1000 &1100cc Fours, 81-02
M452-3	ZX500 & 600 Ninja, 85-97
M453-3	Ninja ZX900-1100 84-01
M468-2	Ninja ZX-6, 90-04
M469	ZX7 Ninja, 91-98
M453-3	Ninja ZX900, ZX1000 & ZX1100, 84-01
M409	Concours, 86-04

POLARIS

ATVs

M496	Polaris ATV, 85-95
M362	Polaris Magnum ATV, 96-98
M363	Scrambler 500, 4X4 97-00
M365-2	Sportsman/Xplorer, 96-03

SUZUKI

ATVs

M381	ALT/LT 125 & 185, 83-87
M475	LT230 & LT250, 85-90
M380-2	LT250R Quad Racer, 85-92
M343	LTF500F Quadrunner, 98-00
M483-2	Suzuki King Quad/ Quad Runner 250, 87-98

Singles

M371	RM50-400 Twin Shock, 75-81
M369	125-400cc 64-81
M379	RM125-500 Single Shock, 81-88
M476	DR250-350, 90-94
M384-3	LS650 Savage, 86-04
M386	RM80-250, 89-95
M400	RM125, 96-00
M401	RM250, 96-02

Twins

M372	GS400-450 Twins, 77-87
M481-4	VS700-800 Intruder, 85-04
M482-2	VS1400 Intruder, 87-01
M484-3	GS500E Twins, 89-02
M361	SV650, 1999-2002

Triple

M368	380-750cc, 72-77

Fours

M373	GS550, 77-86
M364	GS650, 81-83
M370	GS750 Fours, 77-82
M376	GS850-1100 Shaft Drive, 79-84
M378	GS1100 Chain Drive, 80-81
M383-3	Katana 600, 88-96 GSX-R750-1100, 86-87
M331	GSX-R600, 97-00
M478-2	GSX-R750, 88-92 GSX750F Katana, 89-96
M485	GSX-R750, 96-99
M377	GSX-R1000, 01-04
M338	GSF600 Bandit, 95-00
M353	GSF1200 Bandit, 96-03

YAMAHA

ATVs

M499	YFM80 Badger, 85-01
M394	YTM/YFM200 & 225, 83-86
M488-5	Blaster, 88-05
M489-2	Timberwolf, 89-00
M487-5	Warrior, 87-04
M486-5	Banshee, 87-04
M490-3	Moto-4 & Big Bear, 87-04
M493	YFM400FW Kodiak, 93-98
M280-2	Raptor 660R, 01-05

Singles

M492-2	PW50 & PW80, BW80 Big Wheel 80, 81-02
M410	80-175 Piston Port, 68-76
M415	250-400cc Piston Port, 68-76
M412	DT & MX 100-400, 77-83
M414	IT125-490, 76-86
M393	YZ50-80 Monoshock, 78-90
M413	YZ100-490 Monoshock, 76-84
M390	YZ125-250, 85-87 YZ490, 85-90
M391	YZ125-250, 88-93 WR250Z, 91-93
M497-2	YZ125, 94-01
M498	YZ250, 94-98 and WR250Z, 94-97
M406	YZ250F & WR250F, 01-03
M491-2	YZ400F, YZ426F, WR400F WR426F, 98-02
M417	XT125-250, 80-84
M480-3	XT/TT 350, 85-00
M405	XT500 & TT500, 76-81
M416	XT/TT 600, 83-89

Twins

M403	650cc, 70-82
M395-10	XV535-1100 Virago, 81-03
M495-4	V-Star 650, 98-05
M281-2	V-Star 1100, 99-05
M282	Road Star, 99-05

Triple

M404	XS750 & 850, 77-81

Fours

M387	XJ550, XJ600 & FJ600, 81-92
M494	XJ600 Seca II, 92-98
M388	YX600 Radian & FZ600, 86-90
M396	FZ600, 89-93
M392	FZ700-750 & Fazer, 85-87
M411	XS1100 Fours, 78-81
M397	FJ1100 & 1200, 84-93
M375	V-Max, 85-03
M374	Royal Star, 96-03
M461	YZF-R6, 99-04
M398	YZF-R1, 98-03
M399	FZ1, 01-05

VINTAGE MOTORCYCLES

Clymer® Collection Series

M330	Vintage British Street Bikes, BSA, 500–650cc Unit Twins; Norton, 750 & 850cc Commandos; Triumph, 500-750cc Twins
M300	Vintage Dirt Bikes, V. 1 Bultaco, 125-370cc Singles; Montesa, 123-360cc Singles; Ossa, 125-250cc Singles
M301	Vintage Dirt Bikes, V. 2 CZ, 125-400cc Singles; Husqvarna, 125-450cc Singles; Maico, 250-501cc Singles; Hodaka, 90-125cc Singles
M305	Vintage Japanese Street Bikes Honda, 250 & 305cc Twins; Kawasaki, 250-750cc Triples; Kawasaki, 900 & 1000cc Fours